Shakespeare on Film

Also by Maurice Hindle

Mary Shelley's Frankenstein: Or, the Modern Prometheus, Penguin Critical Study (Penguin, 1994)

Singing His Heart and Speaking His Mind: The Songworld of John Lennon (in progress)

Edited Works

Shakespearean London Theatres, Peter Sillitoe (ShaLT, 2013)

The History and Remarkable Life of the Truly Honourable Col. Jacque (1723), Daniel Defoe, *The Novels of Daniel Defoe*, Vol. 8. Gen. Eds. W.R. Owens and P.N. Furbank (Pickering & Chatto, 2009)

Caleb Williams, William Godwin (Penguin Classic, 2005)

Frankenstein: Or, the Modern Prometheus, Mary Shelley (Penguin Classic, 2003)

Dracula, Bram Stoker (Penguin Classic, 2003)

Deloraine (1834), William Godwin, *Collected Novels and Memoirs of William Godwin*, Vol. 8. Gen. Ed. Mark Philp (Pickering & Chatto, 1992)

Cloudesley (1830), William Godwin, *Collected Novels and Memoirs of William Godwin*, Vol. 7. Gen. Ed. Mark Philp (Pickering & Chatto, 1992)

Shakespeare on Film

Second edition

MAURICE HINDLE

First edition published 2007
This edition published 2015 by
PALGRAVE

Palgrave in the UK is an imprint of Macmillan Publishers Limited, registered in England, company number 785998, of 4 Crinan Street, London N1 9XW.

Palgrave Macmillan in the US is a division of St Martin's Press LLC, 175 Fifth Avenue, New York, NY 10010.

Palgrave is a global imprint of the above companies and is represented throughout the world.

Palgrave® and Macmillan® are registered trademarks in the United States, the United Kingdom, Europe and other countries.

ISBN: 978–1–137–28685–7 hardback
ISBN: 978–1–137–28684–0 paperback

This book is printed on paper suitable for recycling and made from fully managed and sustained forest sources. Logging, pulping and manufacturing processes are expected to conform to the environmental regulations of the country of origin.

A catalogue record for this book is available from the British Library.

Library of Congress Cataloging-in-Publication Data
Hindle, Maurice.
　　Shakespeare on film / Maurice Hindle. — Second edition.
　　　pages cm
　　Includes bibliographical references and index.
　　ISBN 978–1–137–28684–0 (paperback)
　　1. Shakespeare, William, 1564–1616 – Film adaptations. 2. English drama – Film adaptations. 3. Film adaptations – History and criticism. I. Title.
PR3093.H56 2015
791.43′6—dc23   2015018161

Printed in China

In memory of
Barry Cole
poet and friend

... nowadays we see before we hear

Sir Richard Eyre
Shakespeare stage and screen director

Contents

Contents ix

List of Illustrations

Acknowledgements

I must first of all declare an enormous debt of gratitude to those writers from whom I have learned and borrowed much in my Shakespeare on film research, but especially the work of Roger Manvell, Jack J. Jorgens, Kenneth S. Rothwell, Anthony Davies and Samuel Crowl. At a more personal level, I am grateful to have received encouragement and advice from various quarters when writing the first edition, most especially from Owen Gunnell, whose immense knowledge of Shakespeare in performance in Britain since the sixties was such a boon to me. In the latter stages I was extremely appreciative of the detailed feedback given by Open University colleague Anita Pacheco, and for the comments of David Johnson, then chair of the Open University *AA306 Shakespeare: Text and Performance* course team, of which I was a part. The encouragement, suggestions and moral support of Luke McKernan, Robert Shaughnessy, Tony Howard and Peter Holland were also welcome at this time.

Second Edition

The support of Sir Richard Eyre is much appreciated. For their involvement as interviewees contributing valuable expertise and insights about filming Shakespeare, I heartily thank John Wyver and Ian Russell. Thanks are also due to Chui-Ye Cheung at Shakespeare's Globe, to Professor David Bordwell at the University of Wisconsin-Madison, and, closer to home, to the BFI library staff for all their kind help. I am grateful for the continuing support and friendship of Andrew Gurr, who (to use a phrase of his own) has given more help perhaps than he knew. I have also been very glad of the interest and moral support shown by Peter Barham, and especially by Gabrielle Brown. Finally, at Palgrave thanks are due to Rachel Bridgewater, who in the later stages inherited editorial responsibility for the book from Sonya Barker, initiator of the second edition.

Abbreviations/Acronyms

BAFTA   British Academy of Film and Television Arts Awards
BBC   British Broadcasting Company
BFI   British Film Institute
CBC   Canadian Broadcasting Company
F   Folio, first collected edition of Shakespeare's plays (1623)
LWT   London Weekend Television
PBS   Public Broadcasting Service
Q1, Q2   Quarto, individual edition of Shakespeare play, many of which were published in the author's lifetime
RADA   Royal Academy of Dramatic Art
RNT   Royal National Theatre
RSC   Royal Shakespeare Company
RTC   Renaissance Theatre Company

Preface to the Second Edition

Since this book first emerged in 2007 a good deal has happened in the world of Shakespeare on film, much of it occasioned by radical advances in digital film and sound technology and by a massive expansion of internet use by people accessing visual content on a wide variety and sizes of screens. Most cinema screens now use digital projection to show movies shot predominantly on digital cameras and using digital sound technology. If megapixels have displaced physical film, the resulting improvements in image and sound quality have produced a kind of convergence of big and small screen that makes access to Shakespeare movie adaptations much easier. No doubt there is some 'dumbing down' in the celebrity-obsessed domain of movies, especially where film as 'studio product' holds sway. But for a world audience whose critical values are better informed and tuned in to the delights of a well-adapted Shakespeare movie, creative filmmakers with a keen ear for Shakespearean text but unhampered by past reverential prejudices can and no doubt will continue to bring us even more life-enhancing adaptations. The additions, changes and updates for this edition I hope reflect this assessment. One can only be heartened by the fact that it was a single creatively enquiring mind that wrote the highest-grossing Hollywood movie of 2012, *The Avengers*, and in the same year brought us the low-budget but brilliantly inventive movie of *Much Ado About Nothing*. For Joss Whedon, who put together and directed both, Shakespeare and Marvel superhero worlds have much in common: 'big themes, big emotions, heroes, betrayals, low comedy, social criticism, and passionate implausible romances'. I understand that he wants to film *Hamlet* next. Please do – I look forward to it!

Maurice Hindle, London, 2015

Introduction

Shakespeare has always had an audience. Up to the beginning of the twentieth century, that audience, whether elite or popular, experienced Shakespeare exclusively in a theatrical space, and was relatively small. The invention of moving pictures changed all that. Not so noticeably in the silent era or the 1930s perhaps, but certainly from the success of Laurence Olivier's wartime production of *Henry V* in 1944 one can confidently speak of a film adaptation having found favour with a mass moviegoing audience for the first time. Olivier's achievement and popular success also went beyond issues of patriotism and propaganda, with at least two of the finest adapters of the Shakespeare play to the big screen becoming inspired by Olivier's filmic example to eventually produce their own Shakespeare movies: Franco Zeffirelli and Ian McKellen. Enthused by Olivier's *Henry V*, Zeffirelli went on to take Shakespeare to 1960s mainstream movie audiences with his Burton/Taylor vehicle *The Taming of the Shrew* (1966) before bringing a new young audience to the hugely popular *Romeo and Juliet* (1968). This success was partly repeated with his Mel Gibson/Glenn Close *Hamlet* (1990). For McKellen it was a viewing of Olivier's *Richard III* (1955) at the Bolton Odeon which inspired: 'A spell was cast as I watched the shadows of great actors and had confirmed my juvenile sense that Shakespeare was for everybody' (1995, 37). The experience of feeling that Shakespeare 'is for everybody' also drove Kenneth Branagh to produce a *Henry V* to rival in popularity Olivier's 1944 production, a move that in 1989 reinvigorated the Shakespeare film adaptation genre. It was the prolific and committed Branagh whose output dominated the continuing post-1989 era of Shakespeare movies up to 2006. But I would like to focus here a little on Ian McKellen and Richard Loncraine's fine adaptation of *Richard III* (1995).

I do this not because their *Richard III* broke any box-office records – far from it – but because its realization reveals an imaginative understanding at work of what matters in the tricky business of translating Shakespeare to the big screen for a modern audience. I deliberately use the word 'translating' because, as Jack Jorgens has observed, 'in a sense *all* Shakespeare films are translations', creative attempts 'to recast and reimage a work conceived in a different language and for a different culture' (1991, 14). Well aware that 'Translation is an inexact art, carrying responsibilities to respect the author's ends, even as you wilfully tamper with the means', McKellen's strategy of extracting a screenplay from Shakespeare's *Richard III* play text was governed by the decision 'to shorten it but without losing any of the detailed development of plot or character'. As a great Shakespearean actor also familiar with the language of cinema, McKellen offers a useful insight into how Shakespeare's own changing language use, developing as it did in sophistication over time, can have implications for the way big-screen adaptations are to be approached:

> Some reduction of the play's verbal impact was inevitable but much less damaging than in, say, *Macbeth*, where every poetical line is interdependent on the rest. The verse and language of *Richard III*, a much earlier play, are less dense than in the great tragedies. Although the young Shakespeare was writing almost entirely in verse, he frequently captured a conversational tone ... It is a tone that is ideal for cinema. (1995, 17)

Based – significantly so – on a theatrical production which had already 'updated' the play by relocating it to a 1930s Britain where a dictatorship like Richard's might plausibly have assumed power, *Richard III* was shaped and directed by Richard Loncraine to create a convincingly authentic 'period look'. However, far from being an end in itself, the film is 'just borrowing the period' (as McKellen says): 'We weren't pretending that Shakespeare had anticipated modern tyranny, but just saying that he would have understood it ... When you are playing it, it doesn't seem like an updating. You're just doing Shakespeare, and Shakespeare is up to date' (1998, 47). What I have called the 'periodizing' approach of reimaging and translating has the movie using its casting, costumes, locations and incidents such that throughout (in Peter Holland's words), 'authenticity is subordinate to argument'. One good example of how the movie avoids what Holland calls the 'cheap paraphernalia of filmic naturalism' (Holland, 1996, 19) is by having the characters who smoke (everyone smoked in 1930s Britain) do so in ways that signify and enhance character: Richard's own chain-smoking suggests the anxieties of the restless, haggard killer, ever on the watch; Buckingham's fat cigars stress the greasy grandee on the make; the Duchess of York and Queen Elizabeth convey English upper-class female elegance by using cigarette holders; military subordinates like Ratcliffe and Tyrell smoke furtively while waiting upon or serving Richard, their master. Many more features of this film dramatization of *Richard III* are considered in Part III and the essay in Part IV.

The principal aim of this book is to help readers interested in Shakespeare on film gain a critical perspective on the genre by offering exploration, discussion and analysis of how film adaptations of the plays communicate *as film texts*, rather than as plays on the page or the stage. These explorations are begun in Part I by comparing the different ways that stage and film convey the performance of Shakespeare's plays to their audiences. Part II provides a history of Shakespeare on film. This is partly to demonstrate how the products of this genre become conditioned by interlinked though shifting developments over time in film technology, directing, acting and shooting styles, but also by changing ideas and attitudes in social, cultural and political experience. The history also allows me to give a critical account of the latest significant adaptations. Part III explores the various modes, styles, genres and conventions which have been used to communicate Shakespeare on film over the years. Part IV offers a series of 'exemplary' essays on various film adaptations of Shakespeare comedies, histories and tragedies – wherever possible by comparing different adaptations of the same play – that develops out of the discussions of Parts I–III. To conclude, Part V examines how Shakespeare plays have been adapted for TV and small-screen audiences, discussing many examples. All five parts are concerned to draw attention to the distinctive means by which film's visual language and grammar are used to communicate dramatic meanings and effects to those who watch. To aid in this process, I have throughout **emboldened** many of the technical and critical terms used in creating filmed drama, explanations of these being given in the Glossary.

In Parts II and V, respectively, I have added for this edition analytic discussion of post-2004 large- and small-screen adaptations. In Part V this includes giving significant attention to a 2013 DVD release of the ground-breaking (for its time) BBC TV series *An Age of Kings*, originally broadcast *live* to UK viewers in 1960. This remarkable series dramatized all eight of Shakespeare's English history plays from *Richard II* to *Richard III*, regrouping them in the order of historical reign. This series preceded by nearly 20 years the 'complete canon' of 37 Shakespeare plays dramatized and broadcast by the BBC both in the UK and the USA between 1978 and 1985. I have also woven in new discussion where appropriate of Shakespeare on film developments that took place from 2006 onwards. These include 'live to cinema' global presentations of Shakespeare influenced by *The Met Live in HD* initiatives in New York. In Britain this resulted in the *NT Live* stage-to-cinema Shakespeare productions that began to appear on big screens around the world from 2008 onwards, and from about the same time *Globe on Screen* films of live productions mounted at Shakespeare's Globe on London's Bankside began. *Globe on Screen* films of these live stage productions are discussed under *Live Stage Productions of Shakespeare on Film in the Twenty-first Century*, in *The Theatrical Mode* (Part III.1). This section also includes discussion of live-to-cinema transmissions that the Royal Shakespeare Company (RSC) began to broadcast from its Stratford-upon-Avon stage in 2013, starting with *Richard II*.

The High Definition (**HD**) revolution occasioned by advances in digital technology that have improved the quality of image and sound to a level unimaginable ten years ago has resulted in a remarkable convergence in the way we now access films on both big and small screens. Much of Part V and some of Part III have been rewritten and updated to reflect these shifts. In recent years interest has grown in the *process* whereby film drama is created. Directors, though undoubtedly a kind of keystone in that creative process, need to be seen as contributing that essential part among many other essential parts. I have where possible begun to reflect the creation of Shakespeare on film as a collaborative process, especially in the new Appendix, comprising an interview with the British filmmaker John Wyver. This aims to reveal from an independent producer's point of view what is entailed in adapting successful RSC and other stage productions of Shakespeare to film for the small screen. Since the process of filmmaking is now similar, whether for big or small screens – budget being the main variable – I hope readers will find this practitioner's account informative and useful.

I should say something about my assumptions in writing and presenting what follows. It is beyond the scope of the book to introduce readers to Shakespeare's plays, so in writing I have had to assume some familiarity with them. Quotations from or allusions to Shakespeare's plays follow *The Norton Shakespeare* (1997), based on the Oxford edition. With the special exceptions of silent films and Kurosawa's *Kumonosu-Jô* (his version of *Macbeth*), I have throughout confined my discussions to filmed adaptations of Shakespeare's plays that use only the words of Shakespeare's play text, however truncated. I have tended to overlook tiny, unobtrusive textual changes that do not alter Shakespeare's meaning (McKellen's *Richard III* screenplay, for example, eschews 'thee', 'thou' and 'aye' in favour of equivalents fitting the film's 1930s periodization effectively). *It feels necessary to emphasize here that this book focuses on film adaptations using*

Shakespeare's own text. To repeat McKellen's informed observation: 'Shakespeare is up to date.'

There are many other adaptations I should like to have discussed, such as Derek Jarman's *The Tempest* and Celestino Coronado's *Hamlet* (both 1979), or Jean-Luc Godard's *King Lear* (1987) – to mention only three. But space forbids me from discussing these and other productions, such as Peter Greenaway's *Prospero's Books* (1991) or Al Pacino's *Looking for Richard* (1996). Shakespeare's plays have provided plots, characters and ideas for many films, such as Ernst Lubitsch's *To Be or Not to Be* (1942), Fred Wilcox's *Forbidden Planet* (1956) or Jocelyn Moorehouse's *A Thousand Acres* (1997). These 'Shakespearean cinematic offshoots' have been intelligently and entertainingly discussed by Tony Howard (Jackson ed., 2014). I also need to state that all of the Part IV essays and many of the discussions on more recent adaptations in Parts II and V are about films which at the time of writing are available on DVD or can be accessed in whole or part by searching the Web by film title. It would seem futile for me to write about film texts not fairly easy of access.

Finally, it is appropriate to say a word about what might be called the critical self-positioning of the discussions that follow. Like other areas of critical study in literature and drama over the last 40 years, Shakespeare film studies as a discipline has become a contested domain, a site for debate, some of it wide-ranging and polemical. I am acutely aware that any performative representation or discussion of Shakespeare's drama may trigger questions concerning race, class and gender, and where possible I explore these in context, as well as other of my concerns. But this book is practical rather than polemical, the scope for debating the ideological contexts of Shakespeare on film being limited. Those seeking a broader grasp of the range and reach of the discipline as a whole I would encourage to look at publications in 'Suggested Further Reading' and for supplementary information and discussion in 'Some Useful Websites'. Enjoy!

Maurice Hindle
London, 2015
www.mauricehindle.com

Part I

Shakespeare and the Language of Film

1

Filming and Staging Shakespeare: Some Contrasts

It seems obvious to state that the conditions of performance and reception of a Shakespeare play produced for film on the one hand, and stage on the other, are going to be different. However, exploring some of these differences will provide us with a useful way into learning about Shakespeare on film. To start with a very broad contrast between the two forms of production, it has been said that 'in the theatre we accept theatricality; in the cinema we demand actuality' (Manvell, 1979, 266). This requirement for an impression of actuality, or reality, is directly linked to the fact that film is a *recorded* medium of performance, a completed 'product' that is played back to cinema/DVD/Blu-ray/internet audiences watching in a space and time entirely remote from the original performance. Very obviously, a film audience can play no part in affecting the performance they are watching. By contrast, in the theatre where the performance is continuous and live, there is always some kind of interaction between the stage and the live audience. Consequently, if a **narrative film** (as most Shakespeare film adaptations are) is to communicate accessibly and coherently with the film audience, it needs to be made as realistically involving as possible, for an audience that will always be 'virtual'. As we all know, a continuous film performance is made from many smaller bits of filmed performance, edited together. The very different *conventions* of performance and reception operating in theatre and film also mean that movie actors need to use rather different performance *techniques* if they are to communicate with us effectively. The sound amplification technology, enabling a cinema audience to hear what is being said from anywhere in the screening auditorium, means that the actors are not required to 'project' their voices in the way stage actors do. Instead, they need to speak more at the level used in the interactions of everyday life that we all experience.

Without a live audience to cater for, film actors instead perform more exclusively to/with one another, such that the 'eye of the camera' is satisfied, the ultimate decision in this regard normally remaining with the film's *director*. The director usually has final say over whether their visualization of the script the movie is following has been successfully realized into filmed performance. This decision-making process points to another of the vital differences between the playing conditions of film and theatre. In a theatrical production, the cast frequently rehearses a play for weeks before it opens to the public, hopefully to ensure a high level of artistic performance. For a film, without a live audience, a scene can be repeated again and again until played and filmed to the satisfaction of the director (budget permitting), mishaps being eliminated and the best shots or shot sequences (**takes**) chosen for the 'final cut' of the movie. Once shot and edited into the connected sequences of the finished product, a filmed performance is 'fixed' forever, in and of its time of making. It provides a record of what all who have been involved in the production no doubt hope is the best that can be dramatically achieved, a complete recording 'secured' for all subsequent viewers of the film, who may eventually watch in thousands of locations around the world, wherever cinemas, DVD playback facilities or internet access are available.

2

The Audience: Individual and Collective Experience

Most new theatres these days are replacing the 'two-room' division of spaces produced by the old-style **proscenium arch** with more prominent stages that bring actor and audience closer together, in 'one room'. The main house of England's Royal Shakespeare Company (RSC) theatre at Stratford-upon-Avon has used this type of 'bold **thrust stage**, inspired by the Renaissance courtyard' since 2010. The aim is 'to articulate what's distinctive about theatre through the intimacy of the relationship between actor and the audience, and the audience with one another'. In England this kind of dramatic intimacy can best be experienced at the rebuilt Shakespeare's Globe on Bankside in London. Contained in the Renaissance outdoor-style amphitheatre playhouse, the audience inhabits the open yard and galleries ranged closely around the stage on three sides, their close proximity to the actors in 'same-light' performance conditions encouraging a frequently stimulating interactivity of experience between performer and spectator.

The kind of intimacy experienced by a cinema audience is very different from that achievable in even the most informal of playing spaces. However emotionally involved they may become in the recorded screen events, since they are physically remote from what has been filmed and edited in another time and place, moviegoers will relate differently to what they see on screen compared to the experience of the theatregoer (the 'hybrid' case of live stage to cinema productions are discussed in Part III). How film audiences receive, decode and engage with movies is therefore of prime importance to the people who create the drama projected on screen. Although they will never meet the audience for whom the movies they create are made, producers, directors and actors all want to attract and hold the attention of audiences who have paid to watch their cinematic work. This is why audience **test screening**s are used so much for big film projects. In an era when commercial film production is very costly, producers, directors and distributors seek an assurance that film audience members will understand, like, and be held by a film if their enterprise is to make large profits, or to gain slimmer returns in the case of **arthouse** movies.

Filmgoers are therefore most likely to be appealed to as 'self-contained' perceiving *individuals*, successive screen images and sounds being geared to producing in them emotionally and psychologically engaging *private* experiences. This audience requirement is quite unlike that made on a live theatre spectator. In the live theatre, although each individual's response to stage events will ultimately be their own, meanings and effects are generated in the context of a public, *collectively* interactive experience. A feature of this collective experience is that it is 'pluralistic' and relatively unpredictable, the theatrical spectator choosing which aspects of the performance to look at and focus on. The cinema or small-screen audience's focus, on the other hand, will be dictated by what the *camera* 'sees', and *only* by what the camera sees. Consequently, the film viewer's perception of the actions and images of the filmed story is mostly governed by what the film director, principally, chooses to show. Quite literally, it is the producer, the director and the editor who in the end 'call the shots' to be transmitted on film.

To the extent that the audience's viewpoint can therefore be directed by the sequence of images and actions put up on the screen, there is great scope for the audience's viewpoint and feelings to be *shaped* or manipulated in certain ways. (Once alerted to the fact, followers of Kenneth Branagh's Shakespeare films will notice how much the music soundtracks are used to stir up and shape their emotions.) On the other hand, the act of watching a **narrative film** can be and often is a complex process. The manipulation of cinematic techniques of **montage** and **mise-en-scène** by filmmakers in telling a story always makes demands on the perceptual capacities of the viewer, their ability to 'construct', from the sequence of images shown, an understanding of what is being conveyed to them. In a stage performance, our impressions are overwhelmingly defined by the strong presence of actors communicating with us through the mutually accepted pretence of *stage conventions*, mostly conveyed by their live dialogue. The impressions we experience from a narrative film are created instead by what Christian Metz calls our 'constant impulse to invest' those 'ghostly creatures moving on the screen' with 'the "reality" of fiction'. This 'reality of fiction', he says, 'comes only from within us, from the **projections** and **identification**s that are mixed in with our perception of the film' (Metz, 1974, 10, emphases added). Constituting the total world of the story that some film theorists call a film's **diegesis** (Greek for 'narrative'), this comprises everything we assume to exist in the world the film depicts – characters, objects, settings, and so forth. Besides the explicitly presented events we all see and watch in common, as mesmerized viewers we will also be subjectively adding unseen elements into the fictional mix. Such elements will include presumed and *inferred* events, objects and places that are not shown, as well as our feelings, fantasies and valuations about the characters depicted – the projections and identifications Metz speaks of. We construct and internalize a story that will make some kind of personal sense to each of us.

Whatever the 'impression of reality' we negotiate for ourselves in the transaction between the images on the screen and our own perceptions of them, it should not be forgotten that what is seen will also be dependent on an economic process and reality, lying behind the process of production. The range of cinematic techniques available to be used at any one time by a director will vary, partly depending on the production budget available, and partly depending on the connected question of the kind of cinema audience being targeted. A small but apt example linking Shakespeare adaptation and budgetary issues concerns a view expressed by film director Roman Polanski. In 2000 he said that were he to remake a film of *Macbeth*, he would use the **digital imaging** or **CGI** techniques available to modern filmmakers to create the outdoor castle sequences. To get the results he wanted in 1971, he was forced to use the unpredictable, time-consuming and expensive methods of outdoor location shooting.

The way economics relate to the respective targeting of **arthouse** or popular film audiences can be conveyed briefly and broadly by contrasting the approaches taken to filming Shakespeare by Orson Welles and Baz Luhrmann. In each of his three adaptations (*Macbeth* [1948], *Othello* [1952] and *Chimes at Midnight* [1965]), Welles's highly individualistic cinematic style makes no concession to the requirements or perceptual capacities of a worldwide popular movie audience. This meant his having to work within severely constrained production budgets for each film. In turn, this also ensured the audiences for his films would only ever be **arthouse**, i.e. commercially speaking very small, and attending a limited number of global cinematic venues. In the case of Baz Luhrmann, for his *Romeo + Juliet* (1996) he aimed from the start to communicate with an MTV-influenced youth audience. His stylistic approach and casting were designed for large-scale internationally popular appeal, an approach that attracted ample funding from Hollywood both for making and (a long lead-time of) publicizing the film. As a result, backed by highly successful **test screenings**, it was almost guaranteed that on release the movie would **open wide** (i.e. simultaneously across over 1000 cinema screens in the USA), massive audiences and profits being the result.

3

The Space of the Movie Screen

Unlike the Shakespeare *stage* play, the Shakespeare *screenplay* is liberated from the confines of the theatre's acting space by cinema's film technology. This offers the potential of virtually unlimited playing spaces, the number and range of interior or exterior locations only being constrained by time and cost. Before Laurence Olivier's film of *Henry V* was released in 1944, the battle of Agincourt in Act 4 had only ever been conveyed in stage productions by characters' reports or spoken interactions between characters involved in the battle. In both Olivier's film and then in Branagh's 1989 *Henry V* movie, the battle was realized in outside locations in more or less convincing ways. We are not therefore wholly reliant on what the characters *tell* us through the play dialogue to experience the impact of the battle scenes on both sides: we actually *see* the English and French battling it out. Film can also move us about instantaneously from one location to another, ensuring that we experience a sense of time passing, but without the effects of discontinuity which the conventions of live playing forces on us in the theatre (e.g. actors entering and leaving the stage).

However, because actors on screen are only ever 'discovered' by the watching audience as *already* being within the film frame space we are focused on (i.e. in the *mise-en-scène*), the dramatic events on screen are experienced as happening more *realistically* than can be the case on stage. It is as if we are being given a 'window' on to a realistic world of events which, with the connivance of our fantasies and imaginations, actually seem to be happening. In a theatre setting, by contrast, before they can start performing, the actors must physically enter and leave the playing space, and are perceived by the audience to be doing so. Nowadays, **scenography** – the sophisticated manipulation of lighting, sound and scenery, revealing the huge influence of film techniques on stage practice – makes this less problematic. Such choreographic and design considerations are eliminated entirely in filmed drama, where the well-edited movie creates such a seamless continuity of storytelling that the viewer, once engrossed in the screen images, need never have the illusion of screened reality broken. The spatial possibilities offered by location shooting are frequently exploited by movie-makers to model the visual realities of the 'external' world on to film in a very convincing way. And the more they do so, the more our capacity for absorbing such images of visual mimesis increases. We know that our human visualizing processes are already conditioned to register the actually moving world around us through our focused projecting of coherent images on to our retinas like a kind of internal screen, a phenomenon that involves us in perceptually experiencing the environment around us. In cinematic motion, two psychological processes are involved: **critical flicker vision** and **apparent motion**. Movie cameras and projectors use these processes to delude us into thinking the succeeding film images we watch on film are *moving* when in fact they are not. They are similarly effective in making us think that what we see on screen in the well-edited film is also 'real' (Bordwell and Thompson, 2013, 9).

Location filming for Shakespeare adaptations was only occasionally done from early days to the mid-twentieth century, more frequently in the post-war period, and then almost every time for the larger budget drama films of the 1990s onward. The effect has almost always been beneficial. This is especially the case where the numerous dramatic themes and turns created in Shakespeare's play scripts can be made more emphatic by using carefully chosen settings: Mogador for Welles's *Othello*, Tuscany for Branagh's *Much Ado About Nothing*, Mexico City for Luhrmann's *Romeo + Juliet*.

Just as scene locations may be multiplied for film, so can the number and range of actors used be greater than are employed for stage productions. Shakespeare on stage invariably requires a cast of trained actors practised in verse speaking to perform much of the play text, if the play's dramatic content is to be communicated successfully to a theatre audience. It is of course quite difficult to disentangle the relative importance of the words and the gestures used by stage actors to bring a Shakespeare play alive for a live audience. (Although the author did hint at the right approach in Hamlet's advice to the players:

'Suit the action to the word, the word to the action' (*Hamlet*, 3.2.16–17).)
One thing cannot be doubted: a theatre audience will rely heavily on
the *words* they hear as their primary means of understanding and
enjoying what is being dramatically communicated from the stage. As
the audience for film adaptations enlarged to embrace a 'non-tradi-
tional' Shakespeare audience becoming younger and younger from
the 1960s onwards, the use of the pared-down, image-led screenplay
text now expected for filmed Shakespeare has enabled actors less
experienced in Shakespearean performance to be cast for many of the
screen roles. Good examples are Zeffirelli's and Luhrmann's film versions of *Romeo and Juliet* (respectively, 1968 and 1996), where neither
male leads had ever acted in a Shakespeare play before, on stage or in
film. And what is true for lead roles is also true for smaller parts:
whereas success for the Shakespearean stage hinges crucially on an
actor's skills in manipulating theatrical conventions, on film it is possible to hire actors to perform Shakespeare with little or no experience
in playing classical theatre.

This last circumstance hints at another of the 'advantages' of film's
performance conditions. Since the main dramatic resource of the narrative movie is the **reaction shot**, where the camera cuts from the
actions or speech of one character to show another character's reactions, film often requires an actor to perform only for a short time in
front of the camera, in brief **takes**. Consequently, unless a long take is
undertaken for the sake of preserving a stagelike continuity of performance or effect (as with some of the long scenes in Welles's *Macbeth*
or Branagh's *Hamlet*), the use of short takes means an actor is not
required to learn long speeches. Actors can therefore be hired who are
unaccustomed to performing long continuous scenes, or have little
experience in remembering lots of lines, as stage actors must do; that
is to say, they can employ movie actors or stars. As short takes become
the order of the day, Shakespearean film actors may not always need
to be available for any sustained period in front of the camera. Stage
actors, on the other hand, must always be *present* in 'real time' to play
their ensemble part in a live theatrical performance of the complete
play, an event uniquely achieved each and every time.

4

Imagery: Verbal and Visual

The greatest single difference between the communicative methods of stage and cinema is that theatre is essentially a *verbal* medium foregrounding the spoken word, while film primarily communicates using *visual* techniques. Shakespeare has become the acknowledged leading playwright of English drama because his dramatic language, endowed as it so frequently is with imaginative verbal imagery, metaphor, and rhythmic word patterns, contributes powerfully to the creation and interaction of characters whose identities are often complex and rarely one-dimensional. Many people can enjoy reading a Shakespeare play for its literary qualities alone, just as one may gain pleasure from reading a novel or a poem. We now call those who write for the theatre 'playwrights', but in Shakespeare's time, they were called 'poets'.

No one is likely to accord such high literary value to a film script or screenplay. The reason for this lies in the principally visual bias of film, where *speech is but one part* of the dramatic totality being communicated to us from the screen. Setting aside for a moment the fact that all modern theatre audiences for a Shakespeare play need to accustom themselves to the archaisms of a 400-year-old vocabulary, it is vital to recognize the following: *The dialogue of any play performed from the stage must **in its own right** command the attention and interest of an audience.* In other words, the dialogue of the play performed from the stage must have the capacity to be 'pitched up' by the actors beyond the requirements of normal speech, such that it has the dramatic power to convey emotional tension, psychological involvement, wit or humour, to the live audience. At every point, the words performed need to create and underline the kind of character being portrayed, and to convey clearly the dramatic issues being explored. To that extent, successful stage actors need to have a high degree of *rhetorical* verbal skill, an ability to *persuade* an audience that what they are putting across feels *true* (whether it is morally 'correct' or not).

The performance of screen actors must also be convincingly expressive. But the *scale* of their verbal projection will be much less, bodily gesture or facial expression often being as important, or even *more* important as a mode of communication, than verbal expression. What is shown and seen can also take precedence over what is heard on the stage too, especially in a period when the potent visual images common in film, TV, advertising and mass culture persuade stage directors to use more and more *scenographic* visual effects to create dramatic impact. Yet because film accentuates the intimacy of every detail of acting through the **close-up**s afforded by the camera and the sounds amplified by microphones, dialogue on the screen usually needs little more projection than is required for the close proximities of situations we all encounter in our everyday lives. In film, dialogue is not only spoken at everyday levels, but altogether *less* of it is usually necessary than on stage. In fact, the emotional intensities or reactions of a character filmed in **close-up** are often revealed without recourse to verbal expression, a visual image of their actions and expressions being sufficient to show us what they are feeling inside. A good example of this occurs in Ralph Fiennes's film of *Coriolanus*, where the expression on the face of the eponymous hero (played by Fiennes) typically conveys more than words ever could the overwrought emotions going on inside this character.

Such visual revelation is sometimes elaborated on using **voice-over** technique, as when the central figures of Olivier's *Hamlet* or Polanski's *Macbeth* perform soliloquies revealing their private thoughts. Film terminology calls this **internal diegetic sound**. These are sounds having their source in the film's story world (the **diegesis**), here, inside the minds of Hamlet and Macbeth – not in the 'real' space of the scene played. Not only is the effort to externalize emotion required less for a screen performance than it is for the stage, but *showing* such effort can be damaging, as actor Micheál MacLiammóir reveals in a diary note recording his playing of Iago in Orson Welles's *Othello* movie:

Find out what I have long suspected: (a) that one's first job is to forget every single lesson one ever learned on the stage: all projection of the personality, build-up of a speech, and sustaining for more than a few seconds of an emotion are not only unnecessary but superfluous, and (b) that the ability to

express oneself just *below* the rate of normal behaviour is a primal neces-
sity ... One single sudden move of eyebrows, mouth or nostrils and all is
registered as a grotesque exaggeration. (MacLiammóir, 1994, 96)

The implications of this shift in perceptual emphasis for the successful
adaptation of Shakespeare plays to the screen are profound, and may
be troubling for some. For if it is as *viewers* rather than as 'hearers' that
cinema audiences are required to 'decode' the screen images and
sounds created for them, there is bound to be a *cutting* of the
Shakespeare text. Even in the theatre it is very common for the text of
Shakespeare plays to be cut, since in today's time-starved post-
industrial societies only the most dedicated of Shakespeare lovers will
want to attend live performances of up to three hours. The 'two-hours'
traffic of our stage' mentioned in the Prologue of *Romeo and Juliet*
relates to an early period when the stage language and vocabulary
heard by most of the orally orientated audiences would be compre-
hensible to most. Furthermore, this dramatic language was delivered
from the stage more rapidly than it is nowadays, when modern audiences often require more time to absorb and understand the earlier
forms of verbal and syntactical structures if they are to fully enjoy the
theatrical experience.

5

Bringing It All Together

To summarize. Modern film drama audiences are accustomed to watching a succession of 'action-driven' visual images accompanied by a relatively undemanding level of spoken dialogue. Such audiences 'read' a film largely by following the *visual imagery* of actors supplying the dramatic input we are *looking* to experience from the screen; we gain this experience from their *showing* us what they are thinking or feeling, rather than by using the kinds of dense *verbal imagery* so plentifully supplied in the texts of Shakespeare's plays. In order for a film audience to follow a screen narrative primarily transmitted through successive visual images, these images – camera shots, in effect – must be made to flow coherently and connectedly. The process of creating a seamless flow of images an audience can follow without effort involves skilful **continuity editing**. The principles of such editing have always dominated mainstream cinema around the world, but from the 1960s onwards the pace of **cutting (editing)** from shot to shot became more rapid. Fast-paced TV commercials and French New Wave cinema seem to have influenced this change, and certainly since computer-based editing made the fast-cutting of shots even easier, this style has come to govern filmmaking, not only for action films, but also in dramas, comedies – and many Shakespeare adaptations.

Most successful films on general release will eventually be seen on **DVD, Blu-ray Disc**, or via **VOD,** and many film directors have felt that fast-cutting can help to hold a small-screen viewer's attention more effectively, so they shoot their films accordingly. For those directors making Shakespeare adaptations, films that are likely to attain their largest audience over time on the small screen via DVD or **streaming**, an even more important change has taken place. Since **long shots** on TV have less visual impact, directors typically frame their shots of actors more tightly, so that we now find many more **close shots** or ultra-close shots on the screen than in the older days of cinema. The **medium-shots** in more traditional filmmaking certainly showed the actor's face, posture and gestures, but the newer, *intensified* type of continuity editing concentrates its efforts on faces, and in particular, on the actor's eyes. From the 1970s at least, when filmmakers 'realized that the movies they were making for theaters would find their ultimate audience on the home screen ... many directors have "shot for the box"'. On small screens, 'closer views look better than long shots, which tend to lose detail', so, since screen formats have now become not only wider and sharper on the big screen but on home TVs, laptops, tablets and even smart phones, 'we may find two or more facial close-ups filling the screen' (Bordwell and Thompson, 2013, 249).

So we see how the needs of the small-screen viewer are being catered for, even at the earliest stage, when a film is being shot. In the Shakespeare film drama adaptation, the close interest for audiences will be on the screen performances of the actors and how their characters interact with one another, so directors will tend to provide shots giving a single 'centre of interest', something to grab the visual attention of the screen audience. Even in Shakespeare films, where long takes are still sometimes used to give actors an opportunity to produce a 'theatricality' of effect, or to highlight a performance sequence, the tendency is nevertheless towards closer and shorter shots.

Finally, across the whole cinematic assemblage, there is an inclination to avoid complex patterns of staging. The movements of the actors tend to be kept fairly simple, with the camera moving around them in different ways, creating the kind of kinetic energy that provides small-screen viewers with the visual interest and variety that secure their attention. Such mobile camera movements can be achieved in a number of ways. They include the camera slowly **tracking** in towards each character in a **shot/reverse shot** exchange; the camera perhaps tracking in a circular pattern *around* a group of characters; or a complex series of moving camera shots, created with the use of a **Steadicam**. The latter two techniques are very evident in Branagh's Shakespeare adaptations, the circling camera movement being used most effectively in *Hamlet* (1996), especially at that point (in 3.1) where Rosencrantz and Guildenstern are reporting their findings on Hamlet's 'crafty madness' to Claudius and Gertrude. The Steadicam is also used to great effect in the unbroken two-minute climactic sequence concluding Branagh's *Much Ado About Nothing* (1993).

Whatever techniques are employed, serious makers of film drama today all shoot and edit using the **intensified continuity** approach. This is clearly beneficial for the Shakespeare adaptation. That is because, however much of the original text has been excised to make its visual translation work best for the screen audience's understanding of the play, viewers will not be served well unless the developing relations between the characters embedded in Shakespeare's original work can be followed easily on screen by them. Although the advanced acting and moviemaking skills and filming technology available to moviemakers today should make this 'bringing it all together' process more accessible for the screen audience, the challenge is daunting – just as it has always been. In the following history and exploration of what has been involved in creating Shakespeare for film audiences, I try to show that directorial imagination and inspiration as well as effective, hard teamwork have always been at the heart of successful Shakespearean film adaptations.

Part II

The History of Shakespeare on Film 1899–2014

1

Silent Shakespeare

The story of Shakespeare on film starts at the very end of the nine-teenth century in the context of a theatrical performance. On 20 September 1899, a production of *King John* opened at Her Majesty's Theatre in London, with the theatre's owner and actor-manager, Sir Herbert Beerbohm Tree, playing the title role. The same night a short film re-creating scenes from the play had its premiere at the Palace Theatre, London, and at other theatres in Britain, Europe and America. Four scenes from the play had been filmed earlier in September at the British Mutoscope and Biograph Company's open-air studio on the Embankment of the River Thames, each scene lasting about a minute.

The only fragment that survives of the first ever Shakespearean film, **Sir Herbert Beerbohm Tree's *King John* (1899)**, re-creates the final scene of the play, part of Act 5, Scene 7. This shows Beerbohm Tree as King John in a long white gown, poisoned and writhing in his death throes on a chair in front of a backcloth palely depicting classi-cal columns and a flowering bush. (In the play, John insisted on being brought outside into an orchard so that his scorching, poisoned 'soul hath elbow-room' to 'out' (5.7.28–29).) Tree is flanked by Dora Senior as Prince Henry his youthful son and the Earl of Pembroke (James Fisher) on one side, with Lord Robert Bigot (F. M. Paget) on the other: all sporting medieval period costumes. A hint that this is a Shakespearean 'first' on film is suggested by the fact that just before these attendants turn to gaze concernedly upon their king in his death agonies, we see them all glancing towards the camera before moving

21

'into character'; evidently they have waited with some amusement for the 'Action!' signal to come from film company director and photographer William Kennedy-Laurie Dickson.

As a film, *King John* is clearly limited, its primary purpose being to promote Beerbohm Tree's stage play. Surviving publicity material for the Palace Theatre film exhibition calls it 'A SCENE – "KING JOHN, NOW PLAYING AT HER MAJESTY'S THEATRE"', while a 1902 catalogue of the American Mutoscope and Biograph Company advertises it as 'BEERBOHM TREE, THE GREAT ENGLISH ACTOR, With leading members of his company in the death scene of "King John". Taken with all the scenery and effects of the original production' (McKernan and Terris, 1994, 81–2). Exaggeration prevailed in advertising then, as now: it is unlikely that the scenery and effects of the theatre production could have been used for Biograph's historic Thames-side open-air studio shoot. Nevertheless, there is something to be learned from viewing this earliest of Shakespeare films. Beyond the fact that the whole action consists of a single shot from a fixed camera, and that it was made to entice the public into a Shakespearean theatre production, we are bound to be struck by the way Beerbohm Tree performs as if playing to a stage audience. The film is silent, yet he speaks his lines and moves his body about using the exaggerated gestures we associate with late Victorian theatre. As a record of the acting style he and other actor-managers of the late nineteenth century (like his rival Sir Henry Irving) had practised, the movie is a valuable celluloid document of theatre history.

Important though it is as the first Shakespeare on film, Tree's brief attempt must be seen as a device that simply *photographs* actors in moving pictures for promotional purposes. At the dawn of the film era it is unfair to judge it as a Shakespeare-on-film adaptation as such. But as there were about 500 silent Shakespeare films of different kinds released before talkies were made, and since not one word of Shakespeare's play scripts could ever be heard in these movies, we may be entitled to ask, why did silent filmmakers even attempt to turn Shakespeare into film in the first place? Those who now enjoy Shakespeare's plays in the theatre are likely to say that their appeal lies in hearing the author's magical language being brought to life, in words that *need* to be heard to be felt, understood, and enjoyed. How can we take pleasure in what Stephen Greenblatt calls Shakespeare's 'infinite delight in language' (1997, 1) when we cannot hear the silent film actors speaking their lines on screen? Actually, posing the question in this way takes no account of how 'pictorial' theatrical Shakespeare had become by the end of the nineteenth century, as indicated by the *Era* reviewer of Beerbohm Tree's theatre production of *King John* in September 1899, who states that the play presented itself as

> without central purpose, but very eventful; and Mr Beerbohm Tree has done the best thing possible in the circumstances by cutting away the super-fluous matter, arranging the piece in three acts, and by a succession of splen-did tableaux, giving us a grand idea of the pomp and circumstance of war and politics in the thirteenth century.   (Quoted in Ball, 1968, 22)

The omission of any reference to the play's verbal text, much of which was no doubt considered 'superfluous matter', is very significant. The emphasis on creating pictorial stage realism begun by Garrick's mid-eighteenth-century withdrawal of the playing space into the **proscenium-arch** picture frame had by 1899 been taken by Irving and Beerbohm Tree as far as it could go. The projection of Shakespeare in their theatrical productions had all but replaced the nuances of verbal interpretation with what the audience now wanted – visual spectacle.

The birth of film as the twentieth century dawned introduced a visual communicative technology of artistic and commercial potential, so Shakespeare, already a staple of theatrical spectacle, was bound to be taken up and adapted for the screen in some earnest. American critic Kenneth Rothwell sets the scene rather well of what was now to come:

> The history of Shakespeare in the movies has [been] the search for the best available means to replace the verbal with the visual imagination, an inevi-table development deplored by some but interpreted by others as not so much a limitation on, as an extension of Shakespeare's genius into uncharted seas.   (Rothwell, 5)

All kinds of attempts to bring Shakespeare to the screen would be made during the twentieth century by enterprising directors commit-ted to taking Shakespeare on film into 'uncharted seas'. Yet it is impor-tant to see that this 'inevitability' of Shakespeare being translated to film was also triggered by specifically commercial motives. The popu-larity of silent cinema grew rapidly, as did the silent film trade's search for source material they could turn into filmed stories. Inevitably, texts by a variety of established literary and dramatic authors would be sought out for adaptation. Shakespeare was known as a great story-teller as well as a brilliant poet and dramatist – a tried and tested 'property' in the language of film commerce. His plays were bound to be exploited, especially since copyright presented no problem.

There was another compelling reason for filmmakers to bring Shakespeare to the cinema screen. Almost from the outset, the film trade was sensitive to its lowly reputation as a supplier of popular entertainment, a 'low-life' status akin to that enjoyed by the music hall – vaudeville. Of course, such entertainment had no pretensions to provide 'high culture' – far from it. Consequently, Shakespeare the cultural icon could be drawn on to 'elevate' the status of the film. This process would not only help to make films seem more 'respectable' by linking them to the world of the theatre (cinemas were already beginning to be designed like theatres), but also enlarge the existing (working-class) film audience by drawing in the middle class as well.

Conveying filmed Shakespeare in silence

Of the many films produced, it is well worth exploring some examples. I shall say a little about some of the short films transferred on the BFI DVD *Silent Shakespeare* (2004) and two other longer silent movies, James Keane's *Richard III* (the first American feature film) and Svend Gade's *Hamlet* (the so-called female Hamlet).

The **British Clarendon Film Company's** *The Tempest* **(1908)** is a charming example of how a Shakespeare play can be 're-imagined to suit the means available' (McKernan, in McKernan and Terris, 3). Running at about 12 minutes, the film shows 11 scenes retelling the story in the simplest of terms, intertitle cards explaining each scene depicted. The first scene shown (the opening titles are missing) is not part of the play's action at all, but fills in **backstory** for narrative purposes by depicting Prospero arriving on the island with his little daughter Miranda. The crude **flats** stepped through by Prospero are the kind of scenery we associate with the stage, but the film is conceived mostly as a piece of cinema in its own right, **stop-motion** shooting used to create magic scenes being one example of this. Its most ostentatious cinematic sequence occurs when the camera places us near to Prospero and Miranda as they gaze out at the sinking ship through a kind of **proscenium arch**. Scratches on the print are used here to suggest lightning, while layered effects of superimposition to depict near and distant actions simultaneously are made by rewinding the film into the camera and reshooting over the same strip of film.

The **Vitagraph Company of America** was the largest of the pre-Hollywood studios (bought by Warner Brothers in 1924), specializing in so-called quality films, movies based on historical, biblical and literary subjects. One contemporary review of a Vitagraph movie shows how the company's effect on a growing mass audience was designed and perceived to be 'in the nature of an educational service which is deserving of the heartiest support of all who are working for the improvement of humanity' (Pearson and Uricchio, in McKernan and Terris, 202). With extensive production facilities in Brooklyn, New York, Vitagraph made 14 Shakespearean adaptations between 1908 and 1912, the largest number of Shakespeare films ever made by one company. *Macbeth* was the first of seven movies released in **1908**, eliciting admiration from the *Kinematograph and Lantern Weekly* (London):

> This firm are to be congratulated on the masterly way in which they have staged Shakespeare's tragedy. The famous play contains many situations which lend themselves admirably to effective treatment in picture form, and the company have made the most of them. Thus in the first scene, when the three 'Weird Sisters' prophesy that Macbeth shall be King we are shown him as in a vision, in the King's robes and crown...Then in order are pictured the other famous scenes of the play, culminating in Macbeth's death.
> (Quoted in Ball, 42)

But there were anxieties. Though clearly an admirer of Shakespeare, the Chicago police lieutenant who acted as the city's film censor was worried by the graphic representation of Duncan's murder on screen:

> The stabbing scene in the play is not predominant. But in the picture show it is the feature. In the play the stabbing is forgotten in the other exciting and artful and artistic creations that divert the imagination. On the canvas [i.e., film screen] you see the dagger enter and come out and see the blood flow and the wound that's left.   (Ball, 42)

In saying this, the city's moral guardian unwittingly reveals two of film's key features compared with the stage: (1) its capacity to show scenes that Shakespeare chooses merely to report, and (2) how scenes conveying realistic images can impact viscerally on the viewer's imagination and feelings. Sixty years later, Roman Polanski would be accused of making his *Macbeth* movie too realistically bloody.

A Midsummer Night's Dream became Vitagraph's hit film of the year in **1909**, trick photography being part of its charm. However, a key feature of the movie was its attempt at filmic realism. Trade papers sang its praises for effective location shooting, the woodland scenes being shot in summertime near Vitagraph's south Brooklyn studios. This outdoor location allows the actors to create interesting performances as they move through or hide behind the trees, light and shade adding realism and mystery to the setting. The film was marketed imaginatively too, for although this *Dream* was filmed in summertime, release was delayed until Christmas Day 1909, a seasonally festive moment for a festive comedy.

Other silent adaptations doing more than merely 'entertain' also sought to make artistically informed and inventive use of film's possibilities to communicate effectively with the audience. **James Keane's** ***The Life and Death of Richard III* (1912)**, starring American veteran stage actor Frederick Warde, may have been America's first feature movie, but much of Warde's over-stagey performance is mercilessly exposed by the camera. Nevertheless, Keane's use of (what later became known as) *mise-en-scène* cinematography, altering the relationships within the film frame to convey visual meaning, cumulatively creates a series of silent images that tells the story with dramatic use of film language. Outstanding for combining clever camerawork and lighting to create a dramatic *mise-en-scène* is a scene of Keane's own invention – 'Death of Lady Anne'. As James Loehlin puts it, the action here 'occurs in three distinct planes, all held simultaneously in focus'. While Anne is seen lying prone in bed, well-lit in the foreground, an attendant half in silhouette behind prepares to give her wine, whereupon Richard appears from a passageway, **backlit**, which puts most of his face in shadow. He urges the attendant to add poison to the drink, which is done, and as the wine produces Anne's collapse, Richard slinks away. As Loehlin says, such filmic techniques look forward to the scary Expressionist effects to be created by Murnau's *Nosferatu* (1922), as well as the **deep-focus** camerawork of Orson Welles's films (Loehlin, in Burt and Boose, 2003, 184).

An even more sophisticated approach to rendering Shakespeare on silent film comes with **Svend Gade's *Hamlet: The Drama of Vengeance* (1920)**, starring Danish film actress Asta Nielsen, a film that Rothwell claims 'struck a great blow in liberating the Shakespeare movie from theatrical and textual dependency and moving toward the filmic' (Rothwell, 21). This filmic advance is marked in a number of significant ways. Running at 134 minutes in its original German release, it was a full-length feature made primarily as a vehicle for Nielsen, Germany's most popular film actress and an international movie icon of the period. Scripted from Edward Vining's eccentric 1881 theory that Hamlet is a woman who must for reasons of state conceal her true sex and appear as a man, she nevertheless loves Horatio, who in turn loves Ophelia. Despite this bizarre refashioning of Shakespeare's text,

Nielsen's performance of Hamlet produces an intriguing effect, her androgynous appearance and sexual ambivalence creating a suspenseful interest that is compelling. Perhaps surprisingly, it is not so much Nielsen's cross-dressed Hamlet but the movie's strategy of appropriating 'familiar and popular film codes rather than stage performance codes for the cinematic transformation of Shakespeare's material' that really counted (Guntner, in Drexler and Guntner, 1995, 54). As Lawrence Guntner persuasively argues, despite receiving a mixed critical response, what made *Hamlet: The Drama of Vengeance* the popular box-office success of 1921 was primarily two factors: its nuanced display of Nielsen's identity as a popular film icon, and its use of German Expressionist film techniques, designations Guntner calls *film codes*, discussed at length in Part III.5 as *film genre conventions*.

Just as the film audience would later be drawn to see Zeffirelli's 1990 film because for them it meant 'Mel Gibson's Hamlet', so was it 'Asta Nielsen's Hamlet' they wanted to see in 1921 – the first time a movie icon had been used to 'sell' a Shakespeare film adaptation. Nielsen's enchanted fans would already be drawn by her low-key but naturalistic acting style, more geared to the needs of the camera rather than the stage. Many **close** and **medium-shot**s of her frequently also display the pallid beauty of her face and large, glowing, dark eyes, besides a figure well known for showing off trendsetting fashions. Her ability to convey a character caught between inner female and outer male personas is cleverly supported by the techniques of film expressionism, most pervasively in the use of shadows and shadowy **chiaroscuro** lighting effects that create a sense of unease, mystery or even evil. Most of these elements feature in other Expressionist classics of this historical moment in film, like Robert Wiene's *The Cabinet of Dr Caligari* (1920), Paul Wegener's *The Golem* (1920) or Friedrich Murnau's *Nosferatu* (1922).

2

The Thirties: Hollywood
Shakespeare

We have seen that in the silent era, some filmmakers were finding (using Rothwell's general formula) 'the best available means to replace the verbal with the visual imagination'. When Hollywood sound films became established by the early 1930s, the visual certainly became a preoccupation, though often through a compulsion to create lavish visual *spectacle*. The 'verbal' was not so much getting transformed imaginatively into film imagery; rather, it was being uneasily adapted for a film audience not accustomed to listening attentively to Shakespearean dramatic dialogue (continuing the tradition of late Victorian/Edwardian spectacular theatre). Since Hollywood cinema was in transition from silent to sound film, the filmmakers were primarily focused on two tasks: 'establishing the first principles of matching sight and sound, while at the same time rebuilding an impregnable star system after the silent era in order to sustain the very costly medium which the sound films had become' (Manvell, 1971, 35).

Sam Taylor's *The Taming of the Shrew* **(1929)** illustrates the challenges of the transition well. Initially released as a silent film (not all cinemas were equipped with sound in 1929), dialogue was shortly after dubbed in and a sound version released, making it the first-ever feature-length Shakespeare talkie to be made. As Manvell observes, the text of this very early Shakespeare comedy 'is not normally treated with much respect in the theatre; the spoken word is often severely cut, while the stage business between Katherine and Petruccio is stretched out to win more laughs. This is precisely what Sam Taylor's production did; the struggle was developed into a farcical battle between Douglas

Fairbanks and Mary Pickford' (Manvell, 1971, 23–4). In the silent version, the resulting slapstick comedy style was no doubt perfectly acceptable to a silent-cinema audience. But in the sound version the verbal delivery was problematic, as Laurence Irving the film's designer reports: 'Whenever dialogue that could not be cut tended to lag or was reckoned incomprehensible to the ninepennies ... two gagmen ... with an inexhaustible fund of practical comicalities in the Mack Sennett tradition ... were called upon for a diversion. And here and there Sam [Taylor], who was a secret dramatist, interpolated a line or two in the vernacular' (Manvell, 1971, 24). Mary Pickford spoke Shakespeare's and Taylor's lines effectively, Irving finding her Katherine 'engagingly shrewish', but he thought Fairbanks's voice 'too thin to match his robust action'. Perhaps his frequent screen braggadocio posturing and Taylor's modern 'vernacular' with a reliance on knockabout gags shows this earliest Shakespeare sound movie to be more Hollywood entertainment than 'Shakespeare'. Yet Rothwell is also surely right that the Hollywood filmmakers were so highly skilled in film art that the storyline survived through their 'clever exploitation of visual **metonymy**'. A good example of this is when 'Multiple analytical **close-up**s and **reaction shot**s spliced in from several different camera set-ups clinically document the Minola family's dysfunctionality' (Rothwell, 31).

Many critics have admired **Reinhardt and Dieterle's *A Midsummer Night's Dream* (1935)**, Kenneth Rothwell regarding it as 'the best Hollywood Shakespeare movie'. Although it failed at the box office, it was a spectacular dramatization of screen Shakespeare, the spectacle achieved by ambitiously lavish and highly effective use of choreography, costumes and special effects, all shot on a massive sound stage of over 38,000 square feet. Much of its critical success comes from Max Reinhardt's long-standing interest in and experience of staging the play. He began with a 1905 Berlin production, followed over the years by productions in Salzburg and Oxford, then finally a fabulous version at the Hollywood Bowl in 1934. This was so impressive that the Warner Brothers invested $1.5 million for an extravagant Hollywood movie adaptation. The large cast of gossamer-winged fairies is expertly choreographed to emerge from a mysterious forest set in a swirling mist, and seeming to spiral up into the sky upon music based on Mendelssohn's thrilling *Overture to a Midsummer Night's Dream*, all of this echoing the atmosphere of a romantic nineteenth-century stage production. The remarkable artiness of the gothic lighting effects is balanced by the studio casting famous Hollywood actors in the main parts in the hope that a mass audience would bring in hefty financial returns – a ploy since used repeatedly in casting Shakespeare films. A brilliant 11-year-old Mickey Rooney as Puck mimics the calling voices of Hermia (voluptuous Olivia de Havilland) and Lysander (chirpy Dick Powell) as they lose their way in the forest, while in the mechanicals' rehearsal of *Pyramus and Thisbe* (3.1), James Cagney brings his own special brand of swagger to the playing of Bottom. Until, that is, Puck comes along to make an ass of him. But this is a play with a dark side, too. Victor Jory's gruff, black-costumed Oberon produces a certain Dracula-like malevolence, his costume reminiscent of that used by Henry Irving in his late Victorian stage performances of Mephistopheles.

Like Reinhardt and Dieterle's *A Midsummer Night's Dream*, **George Cukor and Irving Thalberg's *Romeo and Juliet* (1936)** was a Hollywood extravaganza, this film costing $2 million and aiming, like its predecessor, to provide romantic grandeur, spectacle and sparkle – despite the fact that in genre terms the play was a tragedy. MGM's choice of *Romeo and Juliet* to follow up the Warner Brothers' critical success was well calculated since their themes bounce off each other. The inset *Pyramus and Thisbe* play performed bumblingly before their Athenian masters by the 'rude mechanicals' not only self-referentially spoofs the antics of the four lovers of the frame play, but is also a kind of parody of the tragic climax of *Romeo and Juliet*, in which Romeo, thinking that his lover Juliet is dead, commits suicide, whereupon Juliet stabs herself; just as Thisbe despairingly does when she finds Pyramus dead.

The MGM *Romeo and Juliet* failed for a number of reasons. First, it did not emerge from any previous stage production. In the history of Shakespeare on film it often happens that a prior stage production helps to supply the artistic vision and vitality necessary to make a film *dramatically* successful. Rather, the business-orientated yet over-reverential MGM producer Irving Thalberg still cherished the earlier silent-movie ambition to make movies with 'class' for 'classier audiences'. In a coinage worthy of George W. Bush, he regarded what he called the 'picturization' of a Shakespeare play 'as the fulfilment of a long-cherished dream', viewing the English playwright as a writer whose 'dramatic form is practically that of a scenario'. An insight of sorts, this – but his casting went awry. Aiming for what he considered some kind of English 'authenticity', the deadly decision was made to use established, middle-aged expatriate British actors for the main roles. There was a long stage tradition of mature actors playing Romeo and Juliet, but casting 43-year-old Leslie Howard as Romeo and 35-year-old American Norma Shearer (Thalberg's wife) as Juliet were surely disastrous decisions. When Juliet's Nurse comes looking for Romeo in 2.3, encounters Mercutio, Benvolio and Romeo, and enquires, 'Gentlemen, can any of you tell me where I may find the young Romeo?', there is a pause until the mature and confident Howard as Romeo steps forward in response; the viewer is bound to feel nonplussed, if not cheated.

3

The Forties: Olivier and Welles

A fourth major Shakespeare film of the 1930s made in Britain was **Paul Czinner's** *As You Like It* **(1936)**, made for $1 million by Twentieth Century Fox. Like the previous three Hollywood sound films, this production was (as Manvell says) 'again a victim of the star system'. Czinner conceived the film as a vehicle for the talents of his wife Elizabeth Bergner, who in the event was unsuitable for Rosalind, the central character of both play and film. The charm of her screen character, according to Manvell, was in depicting 'an ageless, kittenish quality, a kind of self-destructive femininity', but a characterization foreign to that of Shakespeare's Rosalind, who was written as 'a forthright woman, capable, provocative and determined beneath her surface diffidence and charm' (Manvell, 1971, 30, 31). Co-starring with Bergner as Orlando was 28-year-old Laurence Olivier. This was Olivier's first role in a Shakespeare film, having turned down an offer to play Romeo in Cukor's *Romeo and Juliet* on the grounds that 'Shakespeare could not be filmed' (Manvell, 36, n.3).

By the early 1940s Olivier's prejudice was a distant memory, his filming experience bringing a vital insight concerning the difference between Shakespeare for the stage and Shakespeare on film: 'audiences in the theatre swallow dialogue and acting conventions that on screen would draw howls of derisive laughter'. **Laurence Olivier's** *Henry V* **(1944)** was filmically innovative in many ways, and only the first of a three-movie cycle where we 'see the first imaginative adaptations of the plays to the screen' (Manvell, 35). In meeting the challenge of film adaptation, he discovered how to structure the play as a movie and also found ways to explore the questions about theatrical style and conventions that so interested him. (Olivier's grasp of the differing *conventions* required for stage and film productions cannot be stressed enough for the breakthrough he made. I explore this element in the films in more depth in Part IV.) An inspired decision was to frame the film within an 'authentic' reconstructed Elizabethan performance of the play, using a live audience. This 'framing' approach to filming *Henry V* permitted Olivier to '"play" with style in a Shakespearean way, to shift and blend styles scene by scene, matching Shakespeare's **metadrama** with **metacinema**' (Jorgens, 1991, 133).

With the success of *Henry V*, work soon began on **Olivier's *Hamlet* (1948)**, another British Shakespeare film that this time would gain four Academy Awards: Best Picture, Best Actor, Best Art Direction and Set Decoration, and Best Costume Design – a record for this genre yet to be surpassed. As with *Henry V*, Olivier made many textual cuts, ruthlessly so here, *Hamlet* being Shakespeare's longest play. The film was attacked by some critics on this score at the time, but it is important to remember that any *popular* film adaptation of Shakespeare will always be contingent on various factors, the primary one being that the movie should appeal to cinema audiences accustomed to two-hour entertainment films.

Olivier's film was again innovative in that it drew heavily on the styles and techniques of 1940s Hollywood **film noir** as well as earlier German Expressionist cinema. Developed at a time when totalitarian regimes and technology-led mass markets were creating societies of individuals feeling increasingly anxious and powerless, the film-noir style typically created darkly oppressive settings inhabited by characters struggling heroically against forces seemingly beyond their control. Classic examples of the genre are Billy Wilder's *Double Indemnity* (1944) and Howard Hawks's *The Big Sleep* (1946).

Although Olivier's *Hamlet* was the more skilfully finished artistic production, winning all the honours, the film artistry used for **Orson Welles's *Macbeth* (1948)** pares back fidelity to the Shakespeare text even more than Olivier does, in order that fidelity to Welles's *own* vision, sometimes extravagant, can be brought forward and expressed. Like Olivier, Welles was an actor-director familiar with the acting and production conventions of both stage and film, and was willing and able to mix these together effectively in his Shakespeare films. Yet Welles's facility for finding visually symbolic equivalents for Shakespeare's meanings (**metonymy**) brings him closer to the visionary Shakespeare adaptations of Kurosawa and Kozintsev.

4

The Fifties: Post-war Diversity

Just as the material economies of America and Europe grew with the pursuit of wealth and consumerism from the late 1940s into the 1950s following a half-century of world wars, so did the cultural economies expand too, and this expansion included an increase in the number and kind of Shakespeare film adaptations. (The growth in domestic TV ownership and audience programming on both sides of the Atlantic spawned an ever-increasing production of small-screen Shakespeare, discussed in Part V.) Interestingly, as Shakespeare increasingly became an international theatrical phenomenon in the post-war years through faster communications making the world a smaller and smaller place, so were the film adaptations produced emerging from a more diverse range of cultures and countries, beyond Britain and the USA. This is evident when we take note of the most significant films of the Fifties: Welles's *Othello* (Morocco/Italy, 1952), Joseph Mankiewicz's *Julius Caesar* (USA, 1953), Renato Castellani's *Romeo and Juliet* (UK/Italy, 1954), Olivier's *Richard III* (UK, 1955), Yutkevitch's *Othello* (Russia, 1955) and Kurosawa's *Kumonosu-Jô* (Japan, 1957).

Orson Welles's *Othello* (1952) takes the essential elements of a Shakespeare play and (as with his *Macbeth*) fashions a creation embodying Welles's own special cinematic vision and style. The film opens with a version of the play's ending, as had Olivier's *Hamlet*, so we see the bodies of Othello and Desdemona being carried along in a funeral cortège on the ramparts of the 'Cyprus' fort (actually Mogador, Morocco). As well as sombrely evoking a tragic atmosphere with the dirge-like sounds of a pounding percussive piano and a wailing choir in the four-minute pre-titles opening sequence, Welles creates a striking ensemble of visual and aural effects that capture several of the play's key themes, especially entrapment. After being bustled along on a rope like a captured wild animal, Iago is hoisted up in a cage against high walls, displayed to all as the deadly conspirator and enemy to the Venetian state that he is. As with Welles's *Macbeth*, images of Christian good (the cross) and demonic evil (the animalistic) are strikingly set one against another. In announcing this *Othello* as 'A Motion Picture **Adaptation** of the play by **William Shakespeare**', Welles's emboldening of the words 'Adaptation' and 'William Shakespeare' in the titling somehow suggests that the movie will embody as much of his own authorial persona as that of the originating writer. In fact, his approach to adapting this particular play for the big screen is spelt out in his view that

> *Othello*, whether successful or not, is about as close to Shakespeare's play as was Verdi's opera [i.e. *Otello*, 1887]. I think Verdi and Boito were perfectly entitled to change Shakespeare in adapting him to another art form; and, assuming that the film is an art form, I took the line that you can adapt a classic freely and vigorously for the cinema.   (Manvell, 1971, 61)

In many ways this statement may be thought to serve as a kind of credo for many of the 'filmic' adaptations of Shakespeare to come.

Joseph Mankiewicz's *Julius Caesar* (1953). It would not be difficult to characterize *Macbeth, Hamlet* and *Richard III* as plays revolving around the theme of murderous political usurpation. In 1948 the politically conscious Welles was producing *Macbeth* at a time when the regicide and Macbeth's ultimate defeat could easily be read in the context of the rise and defeat of a Hitler whose fanatical ambitions had been focused on absolute (German) political supremacy, to the exclusion of all else. *Julius Caesar* is also a play in which the successful efforts of Cassius, Brutus and their supporters to assassinate the vainglorious Caesar, only for him to be replaced later by another dictator in the shape of Caesar's nephew Octavius, can be interpreted as demonstrating the tendency for demagogues to triumph over easily led populations. With the return of Hollywood to Shakespeare in the shape of Mankiewicz's film we know that such an 'anti-fascist' interpretation of the play was what the producer John Houseman had in mind, since he discloses that

> While never deliberately exploiting the historic parallels, there are certain emotional patterns arising from political events of the immediate past that we were prepared to invoke ... Hitler at Nuremburg and Compiègne, and

later in the Berlin rubble; Mussolini on his balcony with that same docile mob massed below which later watched him hanging by his feet, dead.
(Jorgens, 1991, 96)

Much of the film's impact stems from the fine playing of well-cast actors being allowed to speak their parts with what are, for a Hollywood film, surprisingly few textual cuts. Yet, given this is an overtly 'political' play posing questions about how a *polis* might best be governed, certain cuts made do seem significant in the context of the politics of the period from which Mankiewicz's production emerged. Including the senseless mob murder of Cinna the poet would seem perfect to invoke the 'anti-fascist' perspective on the play that the filmmakers wanted. And indeed, this scene was scripted and filmed, but finally cut from the released movie. It may be that the climactic scene preceding Cinna's murder, where Antony stirs up the Roman plebeians to mutiny, was thought to provide a sufficient indictment of the mob's gullibility when addressed by a clever orator. Movie newcomer Marlon Brando, deploying his brilliant acting skills as Antony – supplemented by tips provided by his on-set acting coach John Gielgud – certainly portrays a powerful manipulator of the crowd's emotions.

Yet it is also worth noting that in January 1953, the year in which this *Julius Caesar* was released, Senator Joseph McCarthy became chairman of the 'Un-American activities' Permanent Subcommittee on Investigations in the USA, instituting a kind of official political inquisition in which the careers of many artists and writers working in Hollywood were destroyed by the innuendo-laden anti-communist charges made against them. It is therefore possible that the depiction of Cinna the Poet being murdered by a mob mindlessly mistaking him for Cinna the conspiring politician was excised because the filmmakers were fearful of including a scene that could be read as an innocent (Hollywood) artist being attacked by forces stirred up to hate those who would dare to challenge the political status quo.

Renato Castellani's *Romeo and Juliet* (1954) has been widely viewed as a critical failure, through its poor casting and because of the director's approach of **editing** the connected rhythms of Shakespeare's poetic language and story into 'realistic' (prosaic) speech patterns designed to supplement the audience's visual enjoyment of this *cinema vérité*-influenced film. The costumes, settings and locations were lovingly created and photographed (by Robert Krasker, cinematographer on Olivier's *Henry V*) to make viewers feel they were gazing into everyday scenes of old Italy. Castellani certainly brought a new dimension to the Shakespeare adaptation by shooting on location in medieval Italian towns like Verona, Siena, Venice and Florence, newer, portable filmmaking equipment having liberated filmmakers from Hollywood-style sound stages. He also innovated by casting young actors for the roles of Juliet and Romeo. But whereas Zeffirelli would later use young actors to play naturally and convincingly, English actor Laurence Harvey delivered a highly mannered Romeo whose fruity diction seems laughable to twenty-first-century ears. In turn, Susan Shentall, untrained and in her first acting role, played the notoriously difficult part of Juliet in an equally stilted fashion. Castellani's casting here was emblematic of the priority Castellani gave to the 'Renaissance look' he wanted for his film. Resembling one of the young female Italian figures seen in the famous Renaissance paintings he drew on for many of the film's costumes, properties and camera set-ups, Shentall embodied that look perfectly – no matter that her acting skills were woefully lacking. Of the numerous visual elements modelled on Italian artistic sources, Juliet's dress for the Capulet Ball came from Botticelli's *Wedding of Nostagio degli Onesti,* while Capulet in his study follows Raphael's portrait of the Pope. Consequently, Castellani can be credited with initiating 'the vogue for "authentic" Renaissance settings in Shakespeare movies and teleplays' (Rothwell, 125), an approach Jonathan Miller rediscovered 25 years later, using it to style the adaptations he produced or influenced in the BBC-TV Shakespeare series.

Olivier's *Richard III* (1955) can be read as another post-war commentary on the fearful dynamics of political dictatorship which had been deranging the world for so long by the mid-1950s. Welles's *Macbeth* and Mankiewicz's *Julius Caesar* had self-consciously addressed the issue of usurpation in contemporary power politics, and the ultra-usurping figure of Shakespeare's Richard III can be read in the context of obsessive tyrants like Hitler or Stalin. But Olivier's use of Technicolor for his third Shakespearean film adaptation shows he is primarily interested in returning to a display of mediaeval visual pageantry. Whereas Welles's *Othello* gained impact from being shot on location in Morocco, Olivier was content in his third Shakespeare movie to maintain the careful balance of theatrical and filmic techniques that had worked for him in *Henry V* and *Hamlet. Richard III* presents as a history play, but Olivier can satisfy his theatrical inclinations and Hollywood film requirements by making a movie that (like *Hamlet*) focuses on the progress of a single character who, for audiences, is always the main attraction. Furthermore, with the opportunity to make some 18 direct addresses to the audience playing Richard, Olivier deploys the 'intrusive' camera (used so effectively in *Hamlet*) to make the nastily cynical point of view of his treacherous hero unnervingly ours for the first half of the film.

Sergei Yutkevich's *Othello* **(1955)**, like Castellani's film, reveals a desire to utilize exterior settings, the director claiming he had 'broadened the frame of the tragedy by introducing a new element: nature, which can play a much bigger role on the screen than in theatre' (see Davies and Wells, 202). Natural settings and textures are therefore used throughout the movie to register the play's changing dramatic intensities. One example is the low **mid-shot** of Desdemona's hands being grasped by Othello on the citadel steps against a bright blue sky on his arrival in Cyprus, helping to signal the joy and optimism of reunited lovers – though an ominous immobile presence stands above them in the shape of Iago. Then there is the film's solemnly spiritual closing shot showing the ship that carries their dead bodies towards a cloud-darkened sunset over a vast sea, conveying the film's tragic denouement. Yutkevich's romanticism also emphases the personality of characters in their own right, the Moor's 'pure' nobility being sharply contrasted with the treacherous duplicity of Iago. For in Russia, as Jan Kott observed, 'The tragedy of jealousy there became a tragedy of betrayed confidence, in which Othello fell victim not only to Iago's intrigues but to the envy of the Doge and the entire Venetian senate' (Kott, 102). Some may feel that having a seemingly innocent and noble Othello being brought down solely by the betrayal of Iago without the Moor's own weaknesses being part of the tragic equation is a simplification. But the visual 'expansiveness' of Yutkevich's film does not either help it to capture the essentially claustrophobic nature of the character relationships and spatial confinements of Shakespeare's play, something that Welles's more visually experimental production certainly does achieve.

Following Yutkevich's Russian *Othello*, a number of Shakespeare adaptations appeared by moviemakers in other non-Anglophone countries. Apart from Kozintsev's Russian films of *Hamlet* and *King Lear*, none has received wider acclaim than the Japanese version of *Macbeth* by **Akira Kurosawa,** *Kumonosu-Jô* **(*The Castle of the Spider's Web*, 1957)**, distributed in the West as *Throne of Blood*. It has been argued that Kurosawa's film is 'a transmutation, a distillation of the *Macbeth* theme, not an adaptation' (Manvell, 1971, 107). But as my analysis of the film in Part III shows, despite little or nothing of Shakespeare's text being drawn on verbally, a film drama is produced as dramatically nuanced and humanly complex – as Shakespearean, we might just as well say – as the Jacobean play. This is no doubt why Shakespearean director Peter Hall said in 1969 that Kurosawa's was 'perhaps the most successful Shakespeare film ever made', even though it 'had hardly any words, and none of them by Shakespeare' (Manvell, 1971, 113, n.5). Kurosawa's film stands alone as the only powerful sound-film adaptation of a Shakespeare play not to use actors speaking his text, relying instead almost wholly on cinematic means to convey the drama.

5

The Sixties and Seventies: Cultural Revolution, Filmic Innovation

In 1960 Kurosawa released *The Bad Sleep Well*, a study of corruption and revenge set in the corporate business world of modern Japan and conveyed as a **film-noir** thriller, while also loosely drawing on a complex of themes from *Hamlet*. The setting of his 1985 film *Ran* returns to the Japanese medieval civil-war epoch, its power conflicts again being mediated by the samurai warrior codes so effectively deployed for *Kumonosu-Jô*. Kurosawa stated that Shakespeare was not the inspiration for *Ran*, yet many echoes of *King Lear*, especially its dramatically bitter rivalries, are to be found in it. The film is about what happens when three sons turn on the great warlord father who has decided to divide his kingdom among them in order to seek a peaceful retirement: a kind of Japanese medieval hell on earth ensues. Both films are fine artistic achievements, and are certainly worthy of further discussion and analysis. But neither are Shakespeare adaptations within the terms of this book (or in Kurosawa's own terms either), so are beyond its scope.

If some critics have seen fit to pronounce Kurosawa's *Kumonosu-Jô* a 'masterpiece', many also regard **Grigori Kozintsev's *Hamlet* (1964)** an artistic triumph of film Shakespeare. This was the first major Shakespeare movie of the 1960s, and like Olivier's 1948 film version (from which it partly borrows), it was shot in black and white. 'In *Don Quixote* I used colour because I wanted to capture the quality, the ambience of the warm South,' says Kozintsev, 'for *Hamlet* I want the cool greys of the North' (Manvell, 1971, 80). The influence of Olivier's *Hamlet* is mainly revealed in the oppressively prison-like Elsinore setting, full of stony halls and mysterious staircases, and also in symbolically linking the dangerous life of the castle under the usurper Claudius to a tumultuous sea far below. This Hamlet (played by Innokenti Smoktounovski) is Nordically blond-headed, as Olivier's hero was, and as Branagh's would be in his marathon 1996 version.

But there the similarities between Kozintsev's film and Olivier's end, since the 'entrapping' forces that drive along the Russian Dane are dominantly political, as opposed to the psychological obsessions affecting Olivier's neurotic prince. Kozintsev reinstates Rosencrantz and Guildenstern, and also young Fortinbras, the son of Norway whose mettle, like that of the son of Denmark, is being tested. Kozintsev's political sensibilities had been shaped in the murderous Stalin era, his film deriving from a 1954 stage production at the Pushkin Academic Theatre of Drama in Leningrad, the moment Stalin had died and the Soviet state soon began its slow political 'thaw' under Khrushchev. Yet there is no evidence of a thaw in Kozintsev's film. Stating that Hamlet was 'a man of our time', he evidently regarded the one-party state of Russia in the same way Hamlet regards Denmark – as 'a prison' (2.2.239). This is metaphorically indicated in the opening sequence when Hamlet, arriving at Elsinore, gallops through the gates of the castle, the drawbridge laboriously rising up and the shark-like teeth of a portcullis descending behind him, terrifying images of entrapment.

This visual **metonymic** is merely one example of Kozintsev's imaginative approach to adaptation. His primary intention for *Hamlet* was to 'emphasize man's essential dignity in a world representing his indignity, and his desire to "make visible" the poetic atmosphere of the play' (Manvell, 1991, 78). This is captured well in the way he represents Hamlet's and Ophelia's relationship to the royal court around them. Since Hamlet regards Denmark as a 'prison', it could be tempting to convey his sense of entrapment by showing him in a physically constraining setting. But as Kozintsev argues, 'court life is comfortable' in reality, so that 'for a person of ideas and feelings' like Hamlet the stifling conventions embodied in this can themselves 'constitute a *prison*'. The film therefore shows Hamlet being treated 'royally' and respectfully by courtiers, many of his acid insights being spoken in **voice-over** while he struts sternly around the castle among his bowing and scraping inferiors. Just as he wanted to get away from the long-established practice of 'Hamletism' – presenting an enfeebled intellectual unable to act – Kozintsev also wanted to avoid the melodramatic style of showing Ophelia in Act IV as a jilted and demented headcase vacantly gathering flowers – pretty much how she appeared in Olivier's version.

Instead, she is shown as the 'single happy person' walking about 'a palace that is paralyzed by alarm', her pathetic madness being conveyed so much more emphatically by allowing us to understand that 'To be out of one's mind here is to be happy' (Kozintsev, 1972, 191).

Kozintsev's thoughtful approach to visualizing *Hamlet* for the screen was applied just as effectively when he came to film *King Lear* **(1970)**. The starting point was again the 'here and now' of his country's one-party state. He was anxious to convey the essential meanings of the play in the context of his perception of Russian social struggles while working within a distinctly 'Russian' cultural and artistic tradition. Using a translation by Boris Pasternak, as he had for *Hamlet*, and again a powerful musical score specially written by the brilliant Dmitri Shostakovich, Kozintsev creates for his *King Lear* a range of visual **motifs** and an **image system** aiming to show 'certain aspects' of the play 'which the theatre cannot manage'. To 'read Shakespeare in the light of the present day' in the late 1960s was for him to emphasize the suffering of the world's dispossessed, those socially disenfranchised by the force and meanness of overbearing political regimes. In Shakespeare's play, the man who possesses most at the beginning – Lear – is by the end deprived of most, having lost all his property and his favourite daughter, with his country collapsed into the strife of war and division. But before Cordelia is killed and he himself dies, there is reconciliation between them even as they stand surrounded by Edmund's heavily armed forces. This is shown in an image Kozintsev describes as 'goodness encircled by iron, weapons of murder – people gripped by a mania for destruction, by hatred'. It is through the power of such images and by the sight and sound of Lear's ragged 'Fool-musician' playing on his hand-made wooden pipe, the plaintive sound of which opens and closes the film, that in Kozintsev's words, 'the voice of human suffering is accorded more significance than the roar of thunder' (1972, 198).

Another Shakespeare film of this moment that carved an artistic triumph out of a tragic conception was **Orson Welles's** *Chimes at Midnight* **(1966)** – *Campanadas a medianoche* in Spanish, for it was filmed on locations in Spain – and eventually emerged as a Spanish/Swiss production (known as *Falstaff* in the USA). Leaving behind the virtuoso cinematic productions of *Macbeth* and *Othello*, Welles's relatively orthodox conception here grew out of his conviction that 'Falstaff is the best role that Shakespeare ever wrote.' Manvell expresses his aims as being to 'isolate the story of Falstaff's friendship with Prince Hal – their strange friendship in the taverns and streets of London and the tragedy of Hal's final rejection of the old man once he had become king'. Welles regarded the outcome as a 'lament for Merrie England', a comedy 'viewed all in dark colour' (Manvell, 1971, 64).

By focusing on a kind of triangular relationship in which Hal is caught between his love for Falstaff and the low-life freedoms he represents, and his need to be mindful of the day he will become king, Welles manages to achieve a remarkable balance of contrary energies in the film. An enormous amount was inevitably cut from each of the plays he draws on (*Richard II*, *1* and *2 Henry IV*, *The Merry Wives of Windsor*, *Henry V*), so that key characters and scenes could be focused on. Yet he not only manages to 'render powerfully the personal, political and mythical dimensions of the original plays', but also succeeds 'as few interpreter-adapters have in preserving Shakespeare's double perspective, the tensions, contrasts, and discontinuities which give the drama life' (Jorgens, 1991, 109).

The film starts in winter with a **close-up** of the gigantic Falstaff (played by an immensely fat Welles) as he sits in reminiscent mood by the fire, good-humouredly enduring the piping chatter of his senile friend Justice Shallow, whose guest he is in Gloucestershire, and to whom he utters the words from which the movie's title comes: 'We have heard the chimes at midnight, Master Shallow' (*2 Henry IV*, 3.2.197–8). The film's action then alternates between the high intrigues and happenings of the court of Henry IV (played by John Gielgud), typically shot in the grand and sober loftiness of Córdoba cathedral, and the comic bawdiness of the Boar's Head tavern and whorehouse. Here the king's son Prince Hal both partakes in and studies the antics of the characters comprising a lowlife 'court' presided over by the witty, cunning and benignly dissolute Sir John Falstaff. The **low-angle** shot, Welles's cinematic signature, is used a great deal, often to contrast the power struggle that the austere and aloof figure of the king on his high throne is engaged in, with the discontented nobility. Shafts and pools of bright light from high windows are also frequently used (an idea Welles perhaps borrowed from Kozintsev's *Hamlet*) to pick out favoured individuals like the king, and Prince Hal when he inherits the throne. But **tilted-up shot**s are also used to lend dignity to Falstaff's bulky influence – over Hal in particular.

A hilarious and brilliantly executed sequence of burlesque is achieved in the Boar's Head tavern (shot in the basement of a block of Madrid workers' apartments) when Falstaff and Hal take turns at imitating Henry IV on a makeshift 'throne' set on a tavern table. The Eastcheap audience of customers and Mistress Quickly's whores roar

with justified laughter at the performance. But, for the knowing spectator of Shakespeare's drama it also turns into a poignant spectacle,
when Hal, with a cooking pot for a crown, chides Falstaff (as Hal) for
associating with 'a devil ... in the likeness of a fat old man', the camera
for once **down-tilted** on the man whom we know one day will necessarily be rejected by the successor to Henry IV. The film also has very
serious elements, such as its widely admired ten-minute battle sequence.
This is shot with a gruesome realism in which the *sounds* of the battle
– constantly clashing metal, death-dealing thuds from heavy clubs, the
shrieks and groans of the wounded whom we see squirming in mud –
pain our ears mercilessly. At times speeded up to convey the high
energy of opposing first encounters between combatants, and slowed
down to emphasize their sheer physical exhaustion later, the sequence
has been compared by filmmaker Peter Bogdanovich to 'the war paintings of Goya' (as against the charming 'pageantry' of Olivier's *Henry
V* Agincourt sequence). If, as Leonardo da Vinci said, it is the job of
an artist 'to breathe life into a two-dimensional plane', then *Chimes
at Midnight* breathes life into the two-dimensional form of film art
with an authority and a faithfulness to Shakespeare's subtle and all-
embracing artistic vision rarely equalled on screen.

If in 1966 Welles had created a near-masterpiece as the culmination
of a series of films now dubbed 'Shakespeare for the art houses', then
this moment was also when Shakespeare for the mass cinema audience was being born in earnest, by way of **Franco Zeffirelli**'s adaptations of ***The Taming of the Shrew* (1966)** and ***Romeo and Juliet* (1968)**.
Although television at this time was providing a serious alternative to
the hitherto unchallenged supremacy of the big screen, the glamour of
film was still a crowd-puller, few stars of the period being more glamorous than the 'reigning king and queen of the movies', Richard Burton
and Elizabeth Taylor. Alert to the fact that film audiences were increasingly 'gender aware', Zeffirelli sidestepped possible controversy by
turning the play into an opera-like carnivalesque farce, a form then
more often than not impervious to questions of inequality and other
such social issues. Manipulating and radically cutting Shakespeare's
text to create a boisterous vehicle for the notoriously stormy pairing
of Burton and Taylor, Zeffirelli excised a good deal of the Bianca and
Lucentio love-plot and much else to foreground Petruccio's spirited
pursuit and conquest of the explosive Katherine.

The focus is on colourful display and knockabout humour. The pre-
wedding sequence, and the wedding scene itself – only reported by
Gremio in the play but played out here for over ten minutes – both

reveal Zeffirelli's preference for 'display' over fidelity to Shakespeare's text. Sourly noting how the movie is 'loaded with pleasant but syrupy melodies in the best Hollywood tradition', Jack Jorgens nevertheless persuasively argues (following C. L. Barber's perceptive analyses of Shakespeare's 'festive comedies' (1972)) that Zeffirelli cleverly replaces Shakespeare's frame story of Christopher Sly with his own frame story of Saturnalian revels, Petruccio and Kate functioning as a Lord and Lady of Misrule offering a 'good-natured but thorough assault ... on Padua and Paduan values' (1991, 72).

Zeffirelli's *Romeo and Juliet* (1968) is one of the most popular and commercially successful Shakespeare films of all time: originally funded by Paramount with only $800,000, the movie would eventually gross $48 million at the box office. The reasons for its success were many, and I will touch on only a few here. A factor not be underestimated (especially by 'purists' regarding him as a butcher of Shakespeare's verse) is the extent to which Zeffirelli had by 1968 developed immense skills for both staging and filming Shakespeare. He had produced the wildly successful *The Taming of the Shrew*, and now planned to follow up his energetic and highly praised 1960 live staging of *Romeo and Juliet* at London's Old Vic with a film based on that production. But he had also learned much from studying previous Shakespeare films, especially Olivier's *Henry V*. Not only is the panoramic opening shot of *Romeo and Juliet* a tribute to the opening of Olivier's film, but he has Olivier himself reading Prologue and Epilogue in **voice-over**, providing the dubbed voice of Lord Montague as well as voicing smaller parts and crowd noises. For his last Shakespeare movie, Zeffirelli would also closely follow Olivier's 1948 *Hamlet* interpretation.

The Royal Shakespeare Company Influence: Hall and Brook

Zeffirelli's films were visually lush, engagingly vivacious and hugely popular at the box office, success achieved by ruthless cutting and a tendency to underplay Shakespeare's verse in favour of spectacle and sentimental song. Yet there were new and brilliant British theatre directors also working in the Sixties who not only gave primacy to Shakespeare's language, but were eager to translate their thoroughly researched and rehearsed theatrical successes into films, often in experimental ways. Furthermore, excepting Olivier's movies, by far the greater number of Anglophone Shakespeare film adaptations to appear by the early 1960s had tended to star actors from cinema rather than the stage. By the late Sixties this changed. Along with the new breed of Shakespearean directors came a cadre of energetic, highly skilled and articulate Shakespearean actors. Most of these had passed through the rigorous training ground of the Royal Shakespeare Company (RSC) founded by John Barton and Trevor Nunn at Stratford-upon-Avon, where the art of verse-speaking was a mandatory skill. They then often went on to the new National Theatre, run at first by Olivier himself, until Peter Hall took over in the mid-Seventies. The two most prominent examples of films benefiting from these new talents were Peter Hall's *A Midsummer Night's Dream* (1969) and Peter Brook's *King Lear* (1970).

Peter Hall's *A Midsummer Night's Dream* (1969). This was filmed on location in a country-house park near Stratford-upon-Avon in the autumn, Hall deploying the young and talented RSC-coached actors 'to bend the medium of film to reveal the full quality of the text'. Most of the movie was filmed **close-up** in one, **two-** or **three-shot**s because this approach seemed to him 'the only way to scrutinize coolly the marked ambiguity of the text', which he thought the cinema could do 'better than the theatre'. The result completely vindicated his approach, the superb cast revealing the nuances of Shakespeare's multi-levelled text brilliantly. Hall also managed to preserve what he calls the 'lightness and precision' of the actors' spoken performance by using **ADR** (automated dialogue replacement). This technique enables us not only to hear clearly every word spoken by the likes of Ian Richardson (Oberon), Judi Dench (Titania), Diana Rigg (Helena) and David Warner (Lysander), but also helps to deliver the anti-realistic dreaminess of a play Hall thinks of as 'artificial', and 'not a natural one requiring natural sound'. As with the 1909 Vitagraph silent, Hall deploys trick camerawork to make Puck (Ian Holm) and all the other characters of the fairy world magically appear and disappear at various points. But this is the nearest the production gets to any earlier versions of the *Dream*, Hall once again relying on the text of the play in order to deliver an approach diametrically opposed to the kind of glittering and sentimentally romantic spectacle found in Reinhardt and Dieterle's film. Drawing on the full text of the play allows Hall to show how the contriving magical powers of Oberon and Puck are a key dynamic of it, and how the quarrelling king and queen of the fairies 'have upset the balance of nature'. As Hall says, 'This is what the play is all about. It is not a pretty, balletic affair, but erotic, physical, down to earth.' So his decision to film in a wet out-of-doors Warwickshire autumn setting derives from the play text, where Titania (in 2.1) makes clear we are in 'an English summer in which the seasons have gone wrong'. The relationships between the lovers have 'gone wrong' too, until 'sweet peace' is finally brought to them by the magical interventions of Oberon and Puck. The film also shows that the play is much 'darker' than in the prettifying versions people had expected until now. But as well as the magical and human malevolence on display in the drama, Hall points out how there is also 'great charm and humour as well' (all quotes from Manvell, 1971, 126, 121, 122, 123). This charm and humour is so successfully brought to the screen by Hall that it offers an object lesson in how, with the help of a uniquely talented cast of actors, to use Shakespeare's whole play text to skilfully communicate the fullest range of meanings it suggests; always providing the viewing audience is prepared to engage with the Shakespearean English being used to do that.

Peter Brook's *King Lear* **(1970)**. We have already noted how Kozintsev brought a particular kind of cinematic quality to his versions of *Hamlet* and *King Lear*. Through expressive landscape settings and scenes that build towards big dramatic moments frequently driven by Shostakovich's orchestral score, effects are created that may be thought of as romantically epic. Brook's *Lear* could not be more different. Employing no music whatever, and shot in the freezing north Danish wastes of Jutland in deep winter, he pares back the text of the play to its essentials, focusing closely on characters either perpetrating or suffering cruelty in a hostile nature and hopeless world where death feels inevitable. Jack Jorgens aptly contrasts these two *Lear*s by describing Kozintsev's as 'a Christian-Marxist story of redemption and social renewal', while Brook's is 'a bleak existential tale of meaningless violence in a cold, empty universe' (Jorgens, 1991, 237, 236). The reasons for this remarkable variance in approach and effect lie in the strikingly different cultural experiences shaping the directorial vision of each filmmaker. As has already been mentioned, Kozintsev worked in the political context of a totalitarian dictatorship. By contrast, in Brook's dehistoricized adaptation, few 'positives' are allowed to enter the film's bleak vision.

The reason for excluding all notions of redemption seems to be because Brook's 'take' on *King Lear* is very much in the 'existential' mould rendered by Jan Kott's pessimistic interpretation of the play in his influential book *Shakespeare our Contemporary* (1964). The little humour Brook introduces is very much of the 'absurd' kind, a dark wit playing with or even relishing the prospect of scrutinizing, dissecting and imaging a world where human meaning and value have all but vanished. We often find such worlds conveyed in the Fifties and Sixties drama of playwrights like Eugene Ionesco and Antonin Artaud in France, and in England by the plays of Harold Pinter and Samuel Beckett. There is a definite cultural logic to Brook's reading of *King Lear* in this 'Beckettian' fashion in late Sixties Britain, where traditional notions of history, nature, politics and culture were all under challenge. In Shakespeare's England, 'divine-right' monarchy was certainly an institution under threat from an increasingly secularized society, *King Lear* offering prime evidence that the thoughts and actions of 'Machiavellian monsters' are chillingly in evidence. Writing and working in the wake of monumentally destructive world wars undertaken by power-fixated political regimes that in 1940s Germany had led to the obscenity of the Holocaust, and in the Fifties and Sixties to the Vietnam War, it may not be surprising to find many artists and intellectuals by the 1960s feeling that human value had drained out of the world, and that it was time for decades of rigid cultural conformity to be exposed and countered.

Brook counters such conformity by imaging for us a comfortless tragicomedy in which power is thoughtlessly ceded to ruthless machiavels who destroy themselves as well as others by their own nasty deficiencies of insight. This comfortless imaging is managed by foregrounding the play's great and central metaphor, sight itself. Lear himself begins by issuing the dark commands that will lead to disintegration and death, wilfully brushing aside Kent's injunction to 'See better, Lear' (1.1.157). Stripped of power and its delusions, he meets his final end in the brutally blinding light of Brook's Dover beach, where he is shown slowly and literally falling away into death through the bottom of the film frame. In between, seeing and not-seeing are ideas constantly played with, most innovatively by Brook's camera lens often blurring or going to black, to show the distorted or limited point of view of characters who – like Lear himself – cannot see too well when their minds are disturbed. Perhaps Brook's cleverest exploration of the sight metaphor – in which he also toys with the viewer's own perceptions – is in the famous 'fall' of blind Gloucester. We as well as Gloucester are persuaded by the darkly comic machinations of his son Edgar, in **close-up shot**s of them both, that the despairing father is about to tumble to his death from a cliff. In the middle of the climactic moment of tumbling, we cut from a **medium-close shot** of Gloucester to a high **crane shot** that reveals him taking what Jorgens calls a 'silent pratfall on a barren stretch of sand'. Soon after, Lear will say to him, 'You see how this world goes', to which Gloucester replies, 'I see it feelingly.' Curiously, despite the relentless withdrawal of sentiment and feeling in Brook's film, this is how we too are finally encouraged to reflect on what he has shown us.

Tony Richardson's *Hamlet* **(1969)** was staged and filmed at the Roundhouse in London because the space allowed the director to shoot in **close** and **medium-close shot**s. Nicol Williamson's angry Hamlet emerges as a product of his time, the video publicity blurb's report that he is 'not the conventional poet and scholar', but rather 'the anti-establishment drop-out, rough, sensual, impulsive', being essentially correct. The late Sixties ethos of rebelliousness and sensuality in the film does not end with Hamlet either. Before his departure from Elsinore, the warning that Laertes (Michael Pennington) gives to his sister Ophelia (Marianne Faithfull) to stay away from Hamlet seems curiously at odds with her smiling willingness to receive deep and repeated kisses on the mouth from him that suggest an incestuous relationship. This suggestiveness is all of a piece with Sixties' flouting of social convention, as are the flaunted sensual displays towards each other of Claudius (Anthony Hopkins) and Gertrude (Judy Parfitt), who choose to receive Polonius (Mark Dignam) while they sup, drink and cavort in the royal bed of Denmark.

Two of the three remaining films to be mentioned in this prolific era of screen Shakespeare adaptations were productions in which the American actor Charlton Heston figured large. **Stuart Burge's** *Julius Caesar* **(1970)** had an Anglo-American cast including Heston as Mark Antony and Jason Robards, Jr as Brutus, while English actors John Gielgud played Caesar, Diana Rigg, Portia and Richard Johnson, Cassius. The film was not without credit, with Johnson's brilliant portrayal of Cassius certainly realizing the 'lean and hungry look' and resentful personality of that character. What did damage the unevenly cast production was the flat, lustreless and utterly uninflected performance of Robards as Brutus, one critic commenting that he appeared 'to be receiving his lines by concealed radio transmitter, and delivering them as part of the responsive reading in a Sunday sermon' (Quoted by Rothwell, 161). In **Charlton Heston's** *Antony and Cleopatra* **(1972)**, Heston again plays Antony, with South African actress Hildegard Neil cast as the Egyptian Queen. By no means an inexperienced Shakespearean actor, Heston was nevertheless held back by a modern equivalent of the over-respectful Thirties method, approaching Shakespeare 'deferentially, taking the high road, without a jot of Brook's or Polanski's bitter irony' (Rothwell, 163). This brings us to the last major Shakespeare film of this period, Roman Polanski's accomplished *Macbeth* (1971).

If the adaptations of Hall and Brook had been dyed in Kott's tincture of existential darkness to one degree or another, purist critics feeling these directors had profaned their Bard, **Roman Polanski's Macbeth (1971)** created even more shock. Polanski's film is realistic, but his method of making *Macbeth* 'quite realistic' (his words) is by tapping into the cynicism, political assassinations and terrors abroad at a time of violent political upheaval across the world. The assassinations of politically progressive leaders (John F. Kennedy, Martin Luther King), America's deadly anti-communist war in Vietnam, and the brutal invasion of a liberalizing Czechoslovakia by the Soviet Union – to name only three globally significant phenomena – had produced a wholly justified cynicism about international power politics. Polanski and his co-screenplay writer the distinguished Shakespeare critic and National Theatre dramaturge Kenneth Tynan were both of this critical and highly articulate generation. Such articulation emerges in the consummate filmic techniques and effects deployed by Polanski to expose the violent and bloody process of political usurpation, and how its outcome diseases and engulfs almost the whole fabric of society as well as its obsessive instigators.

6

The Nineties: Branagh's Renaissance and the Shakespeare on Film Revival

On its release, much critical attention was given to Polanski's *Macbeth*, which is still taught in schools and universities as a comparison text with Welles's movie and regarded by many as among the best Shakespeare films ever made. Yet it did badly at the cinema box office, its commercial failure prompting some to feel this could be a factor in the virtual disappearance of Shakespeare cinema adaptations over the next two decades, until Kenneth Branagh's *Henry V* revived the genre in 1989. However, other factors contributed to this decline. The explosive cultural energies released in Western Europe and the USA by the 1960s had created numerous lines of fresh cultural enterprise, especially in Britain. In the area of British Shakespeare performance, once the challenge of exploring how plays could be creatively translated into the film medium had been met by innovative directors like Peter Hall and Peter Brook, they moved on to other drama projects: for them Shakespeare on film had been one cultural project to pursue among others. Then there was the competition from television, which for a time seduced filmgoers away from the cinema. As domestic television audiences across the increasingly prosperous 'First World' enlarged dramatically, so did interest in making Shakespeare available to big audiences via the small screen. When the BBC-TV project of dramatizing, recording and broadcasting all 37 of Shakespeare's plays began in the late 1970s, the initiative channelled a good deal of British Shakespearean theatrical energies into these small-screen productions, a process that continued well into 1985.

But by 1985 two other key transformations had taken place, one being that in the USA multiplex cinemas had taken off in a big way, multi-screen cinemas boosting movie production, which in turn provided a greater choice of movies to tempt bored TV channel-hoppers out into public viewing spaces again. This phenomenon soon came to Britain too, intimately linked as the UK has been to the consumption of US popular culture trends since the 1950s. By the mid-1980s the other key transformation – Thatcherite popular capitalism – was also well established and picking up on that part of the Sixties' British cultural revolution which old-style socialism could not comprehend or exploit. Popular cultural enterprise had been moving on apace in Britain too. Shakespeare and his company at the Theatre, the Globe and the Blackfriars in their time had always relied on a paying audience to keep their popular dramatic enterprise going. Nearly 400 years later, in the mid-1980s, the mass-movie audience, its collective visual expectations shaped by the inventiveness of filmmakers like Coppola, Scorsese and Spielberg to want more and more sophisticated film 'product', were primed and ready to pay to see artistically challenging movies – always assuming that these would also be accessible and entertaining.

Branagh's Renaissance, its approach and influence

The young actor Kenneth Branagh was both a beneficiary of, and shaped by, these shifts towards a new entrepreneurially minded British cultural climate and market place. Although trained at the prestigious Royal Academy of Dramatic Art (RADA) in London, his personality and values were indelibly influenced by being raised in a large, lively and character-filled working-class Belfast family, his cultural imagination moulded by TV and popular film rather than by the theatre. In fact, he performed as many of his earliest professional acting roles in front of TV and film cameras as he did in the live theatre. Having played the title role of *Henry V* for the entire time he worked in the Royal Shakespeare Company at Stratford and London (1984–85), this was to be the play he felt compelled to adapt and star in on film for his independent Renaissance Films plc. Stifled by the increasingly bureaucratic repertory system of the RSC, he yearned to offer productions of Shakespeare's plays to the public directed by seasoned actors eager to make them accessible to a popular audience, as they had been in Shakespeare's own day. So in 1987, along with his friend David Parfitt, he founded the distinctly un-bureaucratic Renaissance Theatre Company (RTC) for just such a purpose, to promote a drama of (as he puts it) 'life-enhancing populism'. By mid-1988, with a company of like-minded actor-directors that included Derek Jacobi, Judi Dench and Geraldine McEwan, the RTC had been achieving just this kind of success with sold-out productions throughout the UK of *Hamlet, Much Ado About Nothing* and *As You Like It*. His gamble of having seasoned actors to direct Shakespeare for smallish theatre audiences (Jacobi/*Hamlet*; Dench/*Much Ado About Nothing*; McEwan/*As You Like It*) was thus vindicated.

So far, so good. But Branagh's next question was, 'How is intimate acting in Shakespeare shared by lots of people?' Answer: 'By making a film of *Henry V*.' By the time everything was ready and in place for him to direct and star in this film – independently funded by City finance in London – he was persuaded that he had 'the gritty realistic approach that was necessary to make it the truly popular film I had in mind' (Branagh, 1991, 205, 220). His gamble paid off. Within a few months of release, he and his Renaissance team not only had a popular film success on their hands, but *Henry V* went on to gain Academy and other awards. As Rothwell has observed, 'by a shrewd merger of art and commerce' Branagh had also 'magically resuscitated the Shakespeare movie just when everyone was announcing its death at the hands of television' (Rothwell, 246).

What lay behind the success of Branagh's first Shakespeare film? Three key aspects of his approach not only brought a market-place hit, but were also to give his films that followed a distinctive signature and identity. First, he was determined to make the performance of Shakespeare's text as clear as possible for the audience, summed up in his credo that 'Words and thoughts and actions must always be linked to provide the correct clarity and tone of sound' (Branagh, 1991, 140). More particularly, he sought for 'an absolute clarity that would enable a modern audience to respond to Shakespeare on film, in the same way that they would respond to any other movie' (Branagh, 1993, viii). This aim was ambitious and has involved Branagh in embracing a range of techniques and requirements in the attempt to make his films internationally popular. In all of his movies to date, he has for the most part created screen characters whom the audience cares about, by casting talented actors able to convey strong characters whom we become acquainted with through the sustained use of **close-up** shots. We come to know and care about most of the characters in Branagh's *Henry V* because the camera repeatedly brings us in close to them. The same cannot really be said of Olivier's film, where most of the characters are kept at a distance. A second and crucial move by Branagh has been to provide accessible screen worlds for his audience by drawing on influential movie genre conventions to create the world of each Shakespeare film story. All of his post-*Henry V* Shakespeare films to date have been invested with visual settings, references and ambiences appropriated from an established Hollywood genre. A third and continuing feature of Branagh's Shakespeare films from *Much Ado* onwards has been to use a cultural mix of actors, including famous Hollywood faces previously unknown for playing Shakespeare.

In many ways Branagh's populist approach can be seen to have benefited from the examples provided by **Franco Zeffirelli**. The latter's Shakespeare films had already demonstrated that using the conventions of narrative realism and naturalistic acting were the way to attract a mass audience to a genre the film financiers usually preferred to avoid. In approaching his *Much Ado* Branagh seems also to have taken a tip from **Zeffirelli's *Hamlet* (1990)** and used a mix of American and English actors. But there the similarities end, naturalistic as the acting may be in both films. For whereas Zeffirelli has often been content in the interests of effortless audience comprehension to drastically cut and paste the Shakespearean text in the registers and rhythms of ordinary speech, Branagh has always encouraged his actors to 'speak the speech' in the poetic rhythms embedded in Shakespeare's own dramatic scripts. Furthermore, whereas Branagh generally deploys film genre conventions to help his Shakespeare play text 'more available' to a popular audience, Zeffirelli's decision to make *Hamlet* as an action movie was dictated by his choice of a particular actor to play Hamlet – Mel Gibson. In 1990 Gibson was known by film audiences for his roles in the *Mad Max* and *Lethal Weapon* action films. In a further bid to draw large audiences, Zeffirelli cast Glenn Close, fresh from prominent Hollywood performances in *Fatal Attraction* (1987) and *Dangerous Liaisons* (1988), to play Hamlet's mother, Gertrude. Since Zeffirelli was determined to adopt Olivier's 'oedipal' interpretation of Hamlet, it was almost inevitable that foregrounding such sexually charismatic and volatile actors as Gibson and Close would produce a film where 'lethal weapon meets fatal attraction in what turns out to be a dangerous liaison' – as one critic has quipped. The explosive mix of this family melodrama comes close to detonating in the film's pivotally central closet scene. Here, Hamlet only seems prevented from having sex with Gertrude as they writhe together on the royal bed of Denmark through being interrupted by Old Hamlet's ghost (his only appearance, the

Ghost having been excised completely from the opening scenes of the film). For Gibson's Hamlet, the scene is clearly cathartic. From here on in he assumes the action-hero persona denied to previous Hamlets, routinely condemned as they had been to playing the inconveniently complicating textual elements inducing the Prince's melancholy irresolution, most of which Zeffirelli removes so that action may prevail.

Christine Edzard had worked with Zeffirelli on his 1968 hit movie *Romeo and Juliet*. But the low-budget adaptation of *As You Like It* **(1992)** she made from her small studios at Rotherhithe, in the then run-down docklands riverside district of east London, had little hope of attracting a popular audience. Edzard had been best known for her award-winning dramatization of *Little Dorrit* (1988), Dickens's novelistic exploration of the impoverishment by raw capitalist greed visited upon mid-Victorian London lives, both high and low. She now bravely sought to deliver a comparable illustration of the social effects of 1980s Thatcherite 'greed is good' economics, using Shakespeare's comedy as a vehicle. For the most part, the substitution of an urban for a wooded pastoral sits neither comfortably nor convincingly with this Shakespearean woodland comedy. Edzard had perhaps hoped we would 'see her Arden as a spatial metaphor – a symbolic landscape of the imagination, not some slice of the Warwickshire countryside' (Crowl, 2003, 160). But the conventions of narrative cinema in the realist mode dictate that what we see on film will be read 'as if' it is 'real': cinema audiences do not understand the settings of stories they see on screen as 'symbolic' landscapes, but rather as real ones (see my discussion of Edzard's as the first 'periodizing' Shakespeare adaptation in Part III).

By contrast, **Kenneth Branagh's *Much Ado About Nothing* (1993)** is such a well-wrought Shakespeare film comedy that it has become famous for the 'feel-good' effects it invariably produces in its viewers. Branagh had sought for 'a certain fairy-tale quality to emerge' in his adaptation, and he secured it by filming in the kind of pastoral setting so wanting in Edzard's film. By shooting his movie at a hilltop villa in the golden summer warmth of Italy's Tuscany amid 'a magical landscape of vines and olives ...untouched by much of modern life', Branagh provided a setting to project a festive atmosphere for a comic drama having much witty wordplay. All the elements for assembling one of the most popular and entertaining Shakespeare films ever to have emerged came together for this *Much Ado About Nothing*, triggering in earnest the Nineties boom in this genre: only Luhrmann's *Romeo and Juliet* surpassed its box-office success in that decade. In a post-feminist world, the spirited playing of Emma Thompson's Beatrice, who speaks her mind intelligently while addressing men in a defiant manner, proved very attractive, the resulting 'war' between her and Benedick evidently appealing to a new generation whose entertainment needs were of a particular kind. This was the kind of witty comic banter soon to be exchanged between sophisticated young men and women in the US hit TV-sitcom series launched the following year – *Friends*. It seems exceedingly unlikely that the six major Shakespeare film adaptations that appeared in the years 1995–96 would have made it to the screen without the prior success of Branagh's comedy.

Indeed, **Trevor Nunn's *Twelfth Night* (1996)** could not have emerged without the prior commercial success of Branagh's *Henry V* and *Much Ado*, according to its director. This Renaissance Films production was one of the four films of 1996 – the others being Branagh's *Hamlet*, Luhrmann's *Romeo and Juliet* and Adrian Noble's *A Midsummer Night's Dream* – that together made that year the *annus mirabilis* for modern Shakespeare movie adaptations. The imaginative quality of Nunn's film derives from his long experience of directing Shakespeare in the theatre, but his approach also benefited from having produced popular musicals like *Cats, Starlight Express* and *Les Misérables* in London's West End. Its music has often been seen as important to achieving a certain tone for *Twelfth Night* in performance, and of the various interlocking elements of this brilliantly crafted play that Nunn realizes for the screen so effectively, perhaps none of these is drawn on so cleverly as the play's songs. Branagh had used the song 'Sigh no more' to give 'a strong sense of the interpretive line' of *Much Ado*, and here Nunn deploys both 'O Mistress Mine' and 'The Wind and the Rain' to invest his version of *Twelfth Night* with the bitter-sweet quality that is so defining of this melancholy 'comedy'. His film has appropriately been called Chekhovian, both for its thoughtful tone and for its setting in the Edwardian period. It also has a visual style and atmosphere benefiting from being shot on location on St Michael's Mount at the geographical extremity of West Cornwall, near Land's End, where the natural light which gives a certain quality to the objects it illuminates for Nunn's exteriors makes it every bit as special as that of Tuscany.

The other Shakespeare comedy released on film that year, **Adrian Noble's *A Midsummer Night's Dream* (1996)**, does not make location setting a feature in the way that Branagh's and Nunn's films do. In fact, limited finance dictated that the film be shot in five weeks on a sound stage at Bray, near London. But Noble's vividly colourful adaptation uses the new device of a dreaming child to convey this most **metatheatrically** magical of Shakespeare's plays. We are shown the young boy dreaming, waking, and silently observing, while sometimes participating in the *Dream* being filmed in a kind of *Alice in Wonderland* fashion. While these elements work effectively for the most part – including a bicycle-across-the-moon shot referencing Spielberg's *ET* 'childhood fiction' – at certain points the low budget forced Noble into adopting devices from his stage production that did not entirely work on film.

Despite money being in plentiful supply for the Hollywood-financed and widely released *A Midsummer Night's Dream* by **Michael Hoffman (1999),** all the forest scenes were shot on what have been called 'unconvincing sets' in a 'disappointingly cramped and sanitized studio woodland'. But it is Hoffman's decision to have Bottom as the centrepiece of his film that makes this *Dream* so different from previous adaptations. Kevin Kline is a brilliant actor, and the performance that turns this *Dream* into 'Bottom's Dream' is accomplished and often very moving. Yet in the same way that Crowl notices how the brilliantly moving acting achieved by Sam Rockwell as Flute's Thisbe nevertheless 'runs against the grain of the comedy' in the play-within-the-play sequence, so does the idea of extending the character of Bottom from a hempen homespun fond of declaiming to a dandyish and extrovert, though pensive, dreamer.

Drawing productively on earlier film versions of the play, **Oliver Parker's *Othello* (1995)** also benefited from having Kenneth Branagh's input: by playing the scheming Iago, and by bringing his regular designer Tim Harvey to design this movie. Beyond this, Parker's clever adaptation seems uniquely his own, going well beyond his expressed aim of adapting the play as 'an erotic thriller'. The movie is in no way pornographic, but Hollywood star Laurence Fishburne certainly supplies a physically powerful and erotic presence as Othello. The theme of sexual jealousy is also effectively portrayed by interpolated 'mind's-eye' sequences in which Othello fantasizes the sexual coupling of Cassio and Desdemona put into his head by Iago's psychological manipulation. However, it is the way Parker uses film language to convey such manipulation that counts so much here. Deriving from an Iago whose own sexual jealousy of 'the Moor' – 'it is thought abroad that twixt my sheets / He has done my office' (1.3.369–70) – this feels as powerful in its fiendish racism as the hatred he feels for his master. Parker's filmic strategies come into their own when the action shifts to Cyprus. Both the 'monstrous birth' (1.3.386) of Iago's plan to destroy Othello and a device to visualize his strategy on film is 'engendered' when Parker has Iago observe Cassio and Desdemona whispering together in the reflected image of his knife blade as he cuts into a fruit on the ramparts of the citadel in Cyprus, just before Othello's triumphant arrival. This device is borrowed from the moment in Yutkevitch's *Othello* (1955) when Iago watches in reflection the same innocent exchange in the bright hilt of his sword.

But Parker takes the idea of what the blurred image could *seem* to suggest – a guilty rather than innocent dalliance of friends – much further by having Iago resolved to implant this blurred 'image' of a torrid affair between Cassio and Desdemona as a reality in Othello's mind. Until the moment that Iago's devilish manoeuvrings are finally discovered, Parker not only makes Iago the shaper of Othello's perceptions, as he is in the play, but also, as Judith Buchanan has argued, he displays and 'identifies him as the film's internal cinematographer' (Buchanan, in Burnett and Wray, 2000, 186). Besides manipulating Othello into seeing only what he wants him to see, Iago is also constantly telling us where to look, Parker often 'allowing' him to produce images through the camera lens that reveal his mastery over Cassio, Othello, Roderigo, Desdemona and others. In stage performances of *Othello*, audiences are frequently made complicit with Iago's scheming by way of his soliloquy at the end of 1.3 and other asides, when he shares his evil designs with us. By seeming to give Branagh's Iago 'virtual use' of the camera to convey his demonic powers (a partial echo of Olivier's techniques in *Richard III*), Parker finds a subtle filmic device to extend this engrossing but uncomfortable relationship to a screen context.

If Parker brought a subtle expertise to his camerawork in creating a cinematically sophisticated *Othello*, then the collaboration of **Ian McKellen and Richard Loncraine** that produced *Richard III* (1995) was in conception and effects nothing short of stunning. It is the *visual context* in which McKellen's clever ability to make the crookback Richard 'humanely' charming and witty as he schemes and murders his way to the English throne that makes the film so audaciously effective. The London theatre production had reset the play's action from a 1480s to a 1930s Britain where Richard gains the throne using murderous totalitarian techniques, and this setting was now to be translated into cinema. Faced by the familiar problem of how to make a complex Shakespeare play with many characters attractive to a popular film audience, McKellen turned to award-winning film director Loncraine, responsible for making hundreds of successful film commercials as well as feature films. Loncraine 'knew how to appeal to wide segments of an audience in record time', so that within the first ten minutes of the film, using a predominantly visual storytelling mode, they were able 'to draw in fans of action films, period drama, musicals, and even, with the entrance of Robert Downey Jr., light comedy' (Freedman, in Jackson ed., 2000, 66). If there is a test case for the issue of whether Shakespeare's text or cinematic images should take primacy in film adaptations of the plays, *Richard III* probably provides this.

Where the McKellen/Loncraine film ends with a sensational image of manic anti-hero Richard being engulfed in the inferno of war, the opening sequence of **Baz Luhrmann's *Romeo + Juliet* (1996)**, packed with references to John Woo and Clint Eastwood action movies, climaxes with a gas station exploding into flames after a gun battle between youths of the feuding 'Latino' Capulet and 'Anglo' Montague family clans. Aiming to make his movie 'rambunctious, sexy, violent and entertaining the way that Shakespeare might have if he had been a filmmaker', Luhrmann wanted to attract the widest possible audience for his film. This meant appealing to American and other youth audiences around the world whose grasp of their own music, fashion and visually orientated pop culture was so sophisticated that it would require a good deal more edge and irony than a film about young idealistic lovers caught in a painful 'generation-gap' situation. Breaking all box-office records to date when *William Shakespeare's Romeo + Juliet* 'opened wide' at 1276 screens across the USA in early November 1996, the film evidently found its audience very quickly. Analysis shows that it achieved this by exploiting and exploring what cultural theory has come to call the 'hyperreal' – a world in which 'the real' has in many ways been displaced by fantastic media images. In the process Luhrmann produced a complex Shakespeare adaptation which, among all the later adaptations making media history and media transition a part of their message, could be the most 'postmodern' of them all.

Although lavish funds supported the production of **Julie Taymor's *Titus* (1999)**, as with Hoffman's *A Midsummer's Night's Dream*, poor box-office returns brought commercial failure. Hoffman's version of Shakespeare's comedy probably failed because of the director's wayward decision to make Bottom the film's hero. Taymor's adaptation of *Titus Andronicus* did not find a big audience, perhaps because it was difficult for viewers to connect with the characters of the movie, or with the seriously ideological purposes she embedded in it. The decision to cast Anthony Hopkins as Titus Andronicus was shrewd, in a story that culminates with fallen Roman military hero Titus as a chef overseeing the 'cannibal' Hannibal Lector-like consumption of

Tamora's two sons Demetrius and Chiron in steaming, crusty pies. And the many inspired cinematic moments and sequences that successfully translate Shakespeare's play text into filmic imagery clearly derive from the major talent for creating visual spectacle that made Taymor's staging of Disney's *The Lion King* such a worldwide hit. Furthermore, as Stephen Buhler has said, the words of the play text were spoken in 'a variety of accents' but delivered 'with a sure sense of metrical power and range', Stratford's voice coach Cicely Berry having provided guidance on the production. So there is nothing amiss either with the film's cinematic visions or with the acting.

Rather, the problem seems to lie in Taymor's attempt to make her film accomplish more than this early revenge tragedy is capable of delivering. She casts Osheen Jones, the young actor used by Adrian Noble as the 'framing dreamer' of his *Midsummer Night's Dream*, this time as young Lucius, a 'framing witness' to the unfolding violent events of *Titus*. This is done to indict the violently masculinist military machine that not only makes possible the ancient Rome of the play, but which was also integral to fascist rule in 1930s Italy, brought out in the film by representing Saturninus, to whom Titus has disastrously ceded the imperial crown, as a petulant, fascist playboy. As Taymor has said, 'The development of the child from innocence through knowledge to compassion is, to me, the essentially most important theme [of the film]' (quoted by Crowl, 2003, 206). The crowning moment of this 'development' comes in the final frames when Aaron's black baby son is carried cradled in the arms of young Lucius out of the Roman 'arena where cruelty, racial difference, piety and entertainment had merged' (Buhler, 2002, 192). Following young Lucius through a Roman archway, the camera moves him and us towards the dawning of a new day, the scene effectively shot in **slow motion** while hypnotically repeated waves of orchestral sound engulf us. This superadded feature was to suggest the possibility that a new generation may learn from the mistakes of the old, putting the ways of violence aside. This is fine counterpoint to a stunning visual effect at the opening of the film, where young Lucius witnesses Titus's victorious mud-caked troops mechanically marching into the arena, their loud, exaggeratedly choreographed clanking movements making them seem like terrifyingly lethal toy soldiers.

The film's problem here is that compared to another epic Roman melodrama launched at the turn of the millennium, Ridley Scott's outstandingly successful *Gladiator* (2000), the ultimately ideological argument about violence Taymor embeds in *Titus* probably makes it uncongenial to the cinema audience of this moment. Scott's Roman revenge drama tracks the struggle of Maximus along the lines of a Western-style revenge drama, a structure that Hollywood audiences find easy to follow. The cinema audience's taste for following ideologically charged arguments at a time when the global struggle between capitalism and communism had evaporated was perhaps limited. In the early twenty-first century, it has been suggested that 'horror movies have overtaken tragedy'. But though it has horrors aplenty in it, *Titus* is no horror movie. Rather, by creating her own sophisticated visualization of this early revenge tragedy, Taymor's most vital achievement has not been to connect with a mass culture audience, but with the 'arthouse' viewer.

7

Shakespeare on Film in the Twenty-first Century

It was primarily an **arthouse** audience that saw **Michael Almereyda's Hamlet (2000)**, 'the surprise Shakespeare film success of 2000, outgrossing both Taymor's *Titus* and Branagh's *Love's Labour's Lost*' (Crowl, 2003, 245, n.15). It was a surprise indeed, since the inspiration for this *Hamlet* had been Orson Welles's *Macbeth*, a commercial failure in its own time. Nevertheless, the *Macbeth* Welles dubbed a 'rough charcoal sketch' of the play convinced Almereyda that 'you don't need lavish production values to make a Shakespeare movie that's accessible and alive' (Almereyda, 2000, vii). The film certainly is that, and for a small-budget movie it also manages to achieve a kind of lavish look by making the expensive steel and glass commercial landscape of Manhattan a vital character in the film. Partly taking his cue from Luhrmann's hip-modern *Romeo + Juliet*, Almereyda reasoned that because 'global corporate power is as smoothly treacherous and absolute as anything going on in a well-oiled feudal kingdom...an omnipresent Denmark Corp.' would provide 'an easy vehicle for Claudius's smiling villainy'. Hamlet tells Rosencrantz and Guildenstern that 'Denmark is a prison' early on, and this film, in contrast to Luhrmann's, conveys how contemporary consumer culture may entrap rather than liberate its young protagonists, as Almereyda says, the 'bars of the cage' being defined 'by advertising, by all the hectic distractions, brand names, announcements and ads that crowd our waking hours'. When we see Ethan Hawke's Hamlet angrily muttering his 'To be or not to be' soliloquy while pacing up and down the 'Action Film' aisles of a Blockbuster Video store, or Sam Shepard's chillingly real Ghost dissolving into a Pepsi machine, Almereyda is using these visual constructions to create 'something more than casual irony. It's another way to touch the core of Hamlet's anguish, to recognize the frailty of spiritual value in a material world, and to get a whiff of something rotten in Denmark on the threshold of our self-congratulatory new century' (Almereyda, 2000, xi).

Kenneth Branagh's *Love's Labour's Lost* **(2000)** was the director's fourth Shakespeare film, an ambitious attempt to deliver this infrequently performed early comedy in the form of a Hollywood musical. The movie is ambitious because of Branagh's idea of replacing most of the play's competitive verbal quipping, obscene punning and rhetorical complexity with song and dance sequences modelled on 1930s Hollywood film musicals. But this trading of Shakespeare's verbal wit (in a play where the dramatist was clearly at pains to display it) for the lyrics of Broadway 'standards' by Gershwin, Porter, Berlin and Kern is done without sufficient attention being paid to whether the paying cinema audience might like it or not. Low box-office returns in the USA and UK reveal that not many cinemagoers did like it.

Conveying a plot even slighter than *Much Ado*, the enthusiastic cast of *Love's Labour's Lost* sing and dance themselves out on a small number of studio sets – library, quadrangle, riverside, garden – offering the kinds of 'stage frame' indispensable for the effective performance of comedies and musicals (see the Introductory note to Comedies, Part IV). Branagh certainly captures the luminous 'look' of the classic Technicolor film musical, and part of the production's charm undoubtedly comes from what a *New York Times* critic called its 'gee-whiz amateurism'. The difficulty is that the impact of the singing and dancing becomes compromised by this amateurism – that, and because the film communicates itself in too many generic registers to attract a favourable audience response. Reacting to negative **test screening**s in which audiences failed to 'read' the film (are we engaging with a Shakespeare play adaptation, or watching a Hollywood-style musical? – can it really be both?), Branagh's insertion of black-and-white Pathé-like period newsreel sequences using a 'cheeky-chappy' English male **voice-over** to help support the plot only makes matters worse. The reasons are various. One is that we are required to deal with radically different shifts of communicative register, moving between sequences of Shakespearean dialogue, song and dance, and comedy routines. Another is the Second World War perspective (via the Movietone news sequences) evoking a nostalgically British tone of 'togetherness in adversity' – something that is in utter contrast to the all-American tone of the Hollywood film musical so emphatically at the core of the movie's semiotic system. *Love's Labour's Lost* is an interesting hybrid experiment, but one that failed to find an audience enthusiastic enough to enjoy Shakespeare filtered through a Hollywood musical in the same way as Branagh and his cast evidently did.

Christine Edzard's *The Children's Midsummer Night's Dream* (2001) is also an experiment of sorts, but if it was a risky move for Branagh to foreground the efforts of amateur singers and dancers for his movie, then offering a film of 'William Shakespeare's play performed by children' between 8 and 12 years old, with no dramatic experience whatever, is bound to be even more fraught with risk. Samuel Crowl is right that Edzard's film is 'cleverly structured, handsomely costumed, sweetly scored, and often a delight to hear'. But he is even more right to say that Edzard is less interested in popularizing Shakespeare for the world of mass entertainment 'than using his art to make, or make a statement about, community'. As an attempt at community theatre, the film is thoroughly worthy, and one can understand the impulse to offer a range of young schoolchildren local to Edzard's Rotherhithe Sands Studios the chance to perform a complete Shakespeare play, given the energy, enthusiasm and natural acting ability so often evident in children of primary-school age. These elements are present in this production to some extent, with plenty of delightful moments in the woodland scenes – such as when the fairies giggle with delight at Bottom's appetite for hay and dried peas. There is also an interesting conclusion when the schoolchild audience, engrossed in the performance of *Pyramus and Thisbe* before them, irritatingly quieten the interrupting stage aristocrats (marionettes of Theseus, Hippolyta and Philostrate voiced by Derek Jacobi, Samantha Bond and Richard Clifford), their applause frequently drowning out the voices of the Shakespearean professionals. (It is hard to avoid the community 'political' point being made that the child audience prefer to listen to local 'hempen homespun' performers from their own community than to professional actors speaking 'received pronunciation' – as the adult actors rather exaggeratedly do.) Some of the performances also stand out: Oberon performs sturdily and has real screen presence, and Bottom is energetic and entertaining, while both Hermia and Helena can be very engaging when agitated and annoyed. But the charm and novelty of watching so many young children concentratedly repeating their lines in flat and toneless voices soon wears thin. Despite a clever filmic structure of having a child audience who watch a puppet version of the play enter it and take it over to become the characters themselves, and carrying this through in ways that the cinematography sometimes makes magical, the child performers are not capable of conveying with any depth the richness of Shakespeare's characters and language. The experience and nuanced judgments of adult actors is needed to make the most of these: *A Midsummer Night's Dream* may be a play in which some characters become enchantingly infantilized by magical means, but the delight and comedy of the resulting drama lie in the fact that they are *adult* characters becoming so muddled, and adult characters so reduced need the skills of adult actors to entertainingly persuade us of it all.

Michael Radford's *The Merchant of Venice* **(2004)** is the first cinematic adaptation of this play since the silent era, and by its attractive use of subdued painterly textures and Venetian location shooting shares some similarities with the beautifully tinted *Il mercante di Venezia* made by Film d'Arte Italiana in 1910 (BFI *Silent Shakespeare* DVD). Filmmakers must always have found difficulty in finding ways of delivering a drama that so provokingly presents conflicting issues of race, religion, commerce and justice, and which has the additional challenge of interleaving these with the love and comic elements of a Shakespearean comedy. In Shakespeare's time, Shylock may have been viewed as a scapegoat figure of fun whose intransigence over the defaulted bond with Antonio was a device to dramatically expose the hypocrisy of Christian commercial society's hostility to the usury it nonetheless required to function effectively. For a post-Holocaust world, Shylock is more of a tragic figure whose persecution as a Jew can be read as representative of the treatment of any ethnic group, alienated, viciously attacked or 'ethnically cleansed' by others asserting racial, religious or ethnic superiority over them. Perhaps by 2004, in a post-Cold War world in which race, class and gender were firmly and widely established as serious issues both in educational practice and social policies, it had become slightly easier to tackle on film a play like *The Merchant of Venice*. Yet given the attempt to posthumously collaborate with a playwright whose poetic facility with words is such that his text constantly and mischievously bristles with possibilities, and which cannot resist a paradox, a joke or a pun, what is the twenty-first-century adapter to do with Shylock's challenge to Antonio: 'I say, / To buy his favour I extend this friendship. / If he will take it, so. If not, adieu' (1.3.163–5), in which the last word spoken can easily be heard as punning jokily about 'a Jew'?

Attention is deflected away from the punning joke in Radford's film when Al Pacino's Shylock chooses to pronounce the word 'ado', perhaps part of a strategy to speak his lines with a Yiddish-inflected accent the gutturally staccato style of which is only occasionally broken in on by his native New Yorkishness. (As the film progresses, Pacino occasionally lets his 'mafia-style' anger get the better of him, cutting across the more contained character design he perhaps started out with.) Cuts there are aplenty of course to meet the needs of a cinema audience (it runs for 131 minutes). But whereas the supposedly comic Gobbo scenes add little value to the movie and could have been excised, Portia's lines are cut when she rejoices at her black Moroccan suitor's failure to choose the correct casket (as does Nunn's 2000 TV adaptation) – 'Let all of his complexion choose me so' (2.7.79). However liberal the world has become, it would still perhaps be too shocking to admit that the charming, wily, but (in this movie) ravishingly beautiful princess-like figure is also a racist, something deeply unpalatable to modern film audiences, who like an attractive, strong and independent heroine to prevail.

According to Benoît Delhomme, the film's cinematographer, Radford and he resolve the problem of 'tone' presented by the play's substantially conflicting elements by structuring their movie as a thriller. The film is set and costumed in the year commonly thought to be the one in which Shakespeare wrote the play, 1596, and it is framed by visual devices indicating that although Venice was the most liberal city state in Europe, allowing Jews to practise their religion openly (which they were not in Britain) and to trade as moneylenders and pawnbrokers, they were nevertheless socially separated from the Gentile community, confined to an island called 'the ghetto' (not so evident either in the play or the film, however), and compelled to wear distinctive garb. The predominant image emerging in Radford's scene-setting written preamble and opening is of *exclusion* – a bolt being shut on the door of the Jewish community, separating them from city life. At the end, too, we see the door of the synagogue being bolted against Shylock, now forced, by Antonio and the Duke's decree following his failure to exact the pound of flesh demanded in his 'merry bond', to become a Christian. Within this structure, an accumulating series of thriller-like episodes are built, the frequent shifting of locations in the play affording Radford the opportunity of some slick and stylish **cross-cutting** between Venice and Belmont, Shylock's painful and strained world, and the gentlemanly Gentile world of commerce and pleasure.

From early on, an operative and equivocal theme of 'flesh' and Christian hypocrisy is established: the **montage** of early shots that evoke the jostling commercial life of the Venetian Rialto includes naked-breasted prostitutes flaunting their wares. In a series of **two-shot**s where Bassanio and Shylock debate Antonio's credit-worthiness, the flesh of a freshly killed goat is being weighed on the scales for Shylock; and as Bassanio follows him through bustling crowds his wayward eyes are drawn by the bare breasts of a touting whore. In this frank depiction of a society where sex is a trade like any other, Radford is also bold enough to weave a strong thread of homoeroticism – both male and female – into the film. Quite apart from the frolics of courtesans and the cross-dressing of Portia and Nerissa, there is no attempt to disguise the eroticism of Antonio's and Bassanio's relationship. The kiss and stroke of the cheek that Bassanio (Joseph Fiennes) gives to Antonio (Jeremy Irons) signals a homoerotic bond that no heterosexual marriage is likely to alter. Bassanio makes this explicit in the court scene by swearing he will sacrifice his own life and that of his wife to Shylock if Antonio's could be saved (4.1.276–82).

The movie was bound to be primarily perceived, evaluated and marketed as a star vehicle for Pacino. But strong ensemble playing also has the effect of foregrounding many of the play's ethical complexities, the stylishly shot and edited **medium-close** and **close shot**s of the principals drawing us into the tangled web of the story's suspenseful plotting. At the same time, while Delhomme states that 'We don't have many landscapes in the film, partly because we didn't have time; the faces are our landscapes', achieving a filmically stylish 'look' seems to have been a major concern for Radford. This look and the soundtrack's counter-tenor voice help create a melancholy atmospheric smoothing-away of some of the text's prickly conflicts. Yet visual style also creates meanings and effects that resonate with us. For example, the impressive **shot/reverse shot** hand-held camera sequence in which Shylock delivers his 'Hath not a Jew eyes?' speech against a cool, early morning blue light also produces a coolly dramatic atmosphere. When the spare sombreness of colour and mood soon give way to the richer and more finely textured colours of Belmont isle, we are encouraged to feel that fairytale solutions seem possible, such upbeat oversimplification cleverly signalled by the fairy-tale-like **digitally composited images** of Belmont so often used to introduce us to it.

One has to say 'seem possible', for although Portia mischievously carries the day in the trial scene, then leads a meek Bassanio off to her marriage bed, the film's final frames return us to the melancholy blue tones enveloping Shylock's lament over his lost ducats and his eloped daughter, Jessica. It is Jessica's sadness that fills the final frames, which show her gazing towards archers spearing fish in the lagoon with their arrows, a reminder of that part of Bassanio's early speech to Antonio concerning the 'hazard' and 'adventuring' (not heard in the film) of arrows (investments). Her pain leaves us with an aptly melancholy question mark over what has really been won and lost in the preceding adventures. Most Shakespearean comedies where court or city alternate with a 'green world' of mystery and promise usually end with marriages in one of those settings. By not returning us to Venice here, Shakespeare is perhaps hinting that the real, mixed-up world of commerce and desire is more intractable to negotiate than a charmed fictional world, raising difficult questions of a kind he will return to in the later so-called 'problem' comedies. Radford offers us a courageous, if muted attempt at raising the profile of one of Shakespeare's more controversial plays in the world of popular film.

Kenneth Branagh's *As You Like It* (2006) was his fifth Shakespeare movie, and the third film adaptation of Shakespeare's challenging pastoral comedy to appear on screen. It is a great advance on the 1936 Czinner and 1992 Edzard productions, using a fine multicultural cast of actors whose performances are captured by Branagh's regular cinematographer Roger Lanser in the sumptuous colours and velvety blacks of the 35mm Fujicolor Super film stock that makes (especially the first part of) the movie look so good. Branagh's *Much Ado* demonstrated a brilliant capacity for delivering Shakespearean comedy to the big screen. Unfortunately this film is held back by the kind of conceptual errors that spoilt *Love's Labour's Lost*, which I earlier described as 'an interesting hybrid experiment ... that failed to find an audience'. *As You Like It* initially failed to obtain a distributor, but then found a kind of audience when HBO (Home Box Office) agreed to bring it to American TV audiences in the summer of 2007, after which it had a narrow and brief cinematic exposure in the UK before going to DVD. So what went wrong, and what went right?

Whatever went right with this film undoubtedly owes a lot to Branagh's skills in directing, in cutting and rearranging the Shakespeare text, and by his familiar strategy of providing a high-quality Anglo-American cast, smaller parts being played by actors of 'Asiatic' appearance to perform the screenplay adaptation he wrote. But Stephen Buhler's conclusion that 'the problematic figure of Kenneth Branagh' has produced a 'muddled but fascinating attempt at a multiracial, multicultural *As You Like It*' (Buhler, 2008) only hints at the problems with this adaptation. To a degree, Branagh's take on the play is fascinating. It seems to explore the implications of the classical court/city versus community/country pastoral contrasts that underpin Shakespeare's play, by making the 'communitarian' forest ethos more socially, politically and culturally inclusive. But forcing the play into a late nineteenth-century Japanese mould is misconceived. It may seem appropriate that Branagh's opening focuses on the inciting incidents in the play's first act, whereby men turn aggressively on their brothers, Duke Frederick banishing his older brother Duke Senior to assert his own power in the court, while Oliver de Boys schemes to rid himself of his younger brother Orlando to retain his power as older brother for personal gain. Branagh's Ninja warrior attack by Duke Frederick on Duke Senior and his court while they are watching a peaceful Kabuki dance performance may also provide a violent and bold cinematic 'action-movie' opening that speeds us on to the Forest of Arden story. Yet this structure threatens to alienate an audience familiar with the play, and who look to be entertained by a witty comedy with two delightful characters at its centre, Rosalind and Celia – rather than a Zhang Yimou martial-arts picture.

This approach derives from Branagh's somewhat simplistic view that 'there are two central themes in the play – one is romantic love, the other is getting away from the rat race'. Inspired by a visit to Kyoto in 1990, he felt his Japanese setting could characterize 'the clash between what's peaceful and natural – reflected in gardens – and the neon-lit world of most Japanese cities' (Falk, 2006). The movie's opening frames do possess a certain charm, showing pale green and brown silk hangings, upon which are gradually superimposed words that encapsulate Branagh's version of the play: 'A dream of Japan – Love and nature in disguise – All the world's a stage.' But the statement only goes to reveal how the impressionistic cinematic vision of Branagh's conception also extends to the seemingly limited grasp he shows of Shakespeare's textual concerns – not merely a plot, but questions (however playfully treated) that can take us deeper into that text. These are primarily concerned with using the critical capacities of the pastoral literary tradition to explore the problems of injustice, of 'loving well' and to probe the (remarkably) complex question of what is natural in questions of love and desire.

Once the court of Duke Senior (Brian Blessed) has been quickly usurped by the Ninja-clad warriors of Frederick (also Brian Blessed), Senior and his followers retreating to the safety of Arden (where most of the remaining action takes place), he and we may have been removed from the embattled social and political divisions of high society to the forest's bucolic freedoms, but the significance of this removal is somewhat hard to fathom, taking a long time to sink in. The forest scenes are certainly played and shot very effectively, though with occasional errors of judgement. For example, when the **Steadicam** tracks the most famous speech of the play by Jaques (Kevin Kline) beginning 'All the world's a stage' (2.7.138–65) it does so from a distance, only beginning to capture his thoughtfully edgy performance towards its end, in **mid-shot**. To allow the audience to grasp the true significance of the speech, this needed to be the shooting distance used throughout it. What happened? But perhaps the film's principal misreading and loss concerns the extent to which its foregrounding of Duke Frederick's usurpation of Duke Senior (only reported in the text) and bringing forward the Oliver/Orlando plot all tend to skew it towards 'masculine' concerns. This is at the expense of showing the central position that Jean E. Howard calls the 'mobile, loquacious and bossy' figure of Rosalind occupies in the play, that, and the importance of her 'coupled and inseparable' (1.3.70) relationship with Celia (Howard, 1997, 1595). Despite having to work within the narrowed scope of Branagh's ensemble design, Bryce Dallas Howard (Rosalind) and Romola Garai (Celia) still manage to give us studied, natural and delightfully accomplished performances.

Branagh's seeming obsession with the 'ensemble', both in front of and behind the camera, leave the film with two shortcomings. He mimics the visually delightful denouement of his own *Much Ado About Nothing* in such a faithfully predictable way that the dancing and swirling about captured by the camera feel empty: an attempt at what Kierkegaard would have called a 'bad repetition'. He also chooses to bypass any exploration of Shakespeare's clearly persistent intentions of playing freely – if comically – with the erotic possibilities between the sexes, especially as embodied in the cross-dressing liberties taken by Rosalind. This drama plays freely with various erotic options because people of the early modern period were not assumed – as they often can be today – to have fixed sexual identities. This is why it was a mistake to have Bryce Dallas Howard stepping forward, half in and half out of character, to speak the Epilogue. This is the only Shakespeare play in which a 'female' character does this. When the original Globe audience heard and watched the young male actor playing Rosalind dressed in Ganymede's male attire, a good part of their enjoyment relied on the fact that the he/she before them was playing provocatively with gender relations. We still await the *As You Like It* movie that dares to do justice to Shakespeare's exploration of these seriously playful concerns.

Julie Taymor's *The Tempest* **(2010)** also has an ending presenting problems in the way this play's more famous epilogue is handled on film. *The Tempest* was Shakespeare's last single-authored play, with Prospero's Epilogue to the audience often taken to imply his 'farewell' to the theatre. There is no historical authority for this idea, best accounted for as part of an ill-informed 'bardolatry' tradition seeking to elevate this most gifted of writers into a godlike figure for a godless modern world. Rather, in the twenty lines of the Epilogue, Prospero employs various witty conceits on his character's magical powers from the foregoing action of the play, now given up, and conventionally enjoins the theatre audience to put their hands together as a show of approval for the performance, so that he may leave the stage ('As you from crimes would pardoned be, / Let your indulgence set me free', Epilogue, 19–20). Taymor saw the Epilogue being spoken to the movie audience as unappealing, so decided to have the words set to music (*Raising the Tempest*, *The Tempest* DVD). The results are sung over the movie's final credits for seven minutes in a kind of repeated gloomy plaint, the pleading female voice seeming to take its cue from a literal interpretation of the words, 'my ending is despair / Unless I be relieved by prayer' (15–16).

Although off-putting, luckily the gloom is only cast over the final credits, spoiling though not necessarily marring what is undoubtedly a cinematic *tour-de-force* of imaginative power, technical brilliance and superb performances by all the actors. This evaluation also stands despite the fact that Taymor changes the gender of the play's lead character to a female sorceress, Prospera, played by Helen Mirren. Interestingly, we learn that 'the idea of Mirren as Prospera was not the result of any feminist superimposition on the text, but a natural out-growth of two consummate artists wanting to collaborate on an ambitious project' (Magnus, 2010). Mirren herself says that she met Julie Taymor at a time when she was thinking about casting the film, and Mirren explained to her how she felt Prospero 'could be played by a woman quite easily, and you wouldn't have to change very much in the play' (*Raising the Tempest*). RSC-trained Mirren had played many parts on stage and film in her life to great acclaim, including both Elizabeth I and II (gaining an Oscar for the latter, *The Queen*), and had evidently reached the stage in her career where playing a magus-like Prospero held no terrors, assured admirer and performer of Shakespeare's work that she was. Significantly perhaps for the challenge of playing this commanding and strangely nuanced Shakespearean role, she once said that she has 'no maternal instinct whatsoever', while one participant in *Raising the Tempest* states that he didn't 'see any fear in her, just a lot of power'. The casting of Mirren for this film was therefore a major key to its achievement. But the other actors were also cast with inspiration, their strong playing bringing a range of fine dramatic responses to the extraordinary location setting in which they both lost and found themselves.

The film echoes in many ways the visionary and visceral elements that Taymor had injected into the setting for a minimalist 1986 off-Broadway New York small-scale stage production of *The Tempest*, her first attempt at Shakespeare. Starting from her concept of Prospero's island as being essentially 'sand in isolation', much of the performance then took place – challengingly for the actors – on an 'acting platform that appeared as a steeply raked bank of black sand' (Quarmby, 388). When, around 15 years later, Taymor visited the Hawaiian island of Lāna'i, so stunned was she by its volcanic black and red rock landscape, awesome cliffs and unpredictably wild weather – all making it look 'as if some supernatural event happened there' – that she found this location to be perfect for a film of *The Tempest*. From the opening shot to its closing images, Taymor's acute understanding of the play's profound themes of nature versus nurture, the transformative powers of 'magic' versus its transgressive dangers, and the transcendent effects of forgiveness versus revenge, enable her to envisage visual metaphors, images and sequences of optical delight that not only frequently echo Shakespeare's text, but also provide links with the elemental and shifting landscape that is her primal inspiration.

The opening image of the film's first sequence (the storm) is among its most potent. We see in **close-up** against a background of land, sea and sky, the towers, turrets, staircases and battlements of a castle elaborately sculpted from black volcanic sand. As the shot widens, this structure, now rapidly dissolving in rain (as does the overlaid title, 'The Tempest'), is shown to be a miniature castle balanced in the palm of a hand – that of the preoccupied Miranda. Her attention is caught by a crack of thunder and lightning, then by the bellowing of distressed men on Alonso's storm-tossed ship, foundering in the bay below. This is a scene conjured by Prospera's magic, of course, and here created by **CGI**, the first of many conjurations of visual magic tricked up by Taymor's technical artistry. This literal 'dissolve' we see opening the film is so powerful because the metaphoric density with which it plays (mainly) references a famous passage of *The Tempest* spoken by Prospero, when he has had to abruptly end the staged betrothal masque he has conjured up to entertain and impress Ferdinand and Miranda:

> Our revels now are ended. These our actors,
> As I foretold you, were all spirits, and
> Are melted into air, into thin air:
> And like the baseless fabric of this vision,
> The cloud-capped towers, the gorgeous palaces,
> The solemn temples, the great globe itself,
> Yea, all which it inherit, shall dissolve:
> And, like this insubstantial pageant faded,
> Leave not a rack behind. We are such stuff
> As dreams are made on, and our little life
> Is rounded with a sleep. (4.1.148–58)

However penetrating its effects on us, stage art is only as substantial as its momentary creation allows for as we witness it, then it is lost to the elements of time, just as our individual lives on earth ultimately are. But movies allow us to record such creative dreams, and Taymor's film is full both of visual magic and moments of memorable acting.

The elements of visual magic begin in earnest in 2.1, a long **exposition** scene in which a quarter of Shakespeare's lines and 30 minutes of film time (of 138) introduce us to Prospera's own history, as she tells it to Miranda, and to the characters Ariel, Caliban and Ferdinand. Having put Miranda into a sleep, Prospera calls up her magical agent Ariel, who bursts forth from watery depths into her cavern. Ariel is the 'airy spirit' who will help her enact vengeance on the plotters who banished her from Milan – Alonso, Sebastian and her treacherous brother Antonio. Able to move at immense speeds and manipulate all manner of material situations and events – including the weather – Ben Wishaw as Ariel here gleefully describes and visually 'replays' for his master-magus the terrifyingly fiery storm that brought her enemies to the island. Here and in other key scenes and moments, special effects of shimmering visual power are used to convey Ariel as an ethereal being whose presence and voice are repeatedly conjured in a stunningly beautiful and apposite fashion as he swoops about the island magically carrying out the bidding of his master Prospera. Most stunning of all perhaps is the scene where as the 'Ariel like a Harpy' he enters to harangue Alonso, Sebastian and Antonio for their evil acts against Prospera and Miranda. Appearing as a gigantic cormorant-like black-winged and toothed 'minister of Fate', his look referencing the primeval black volcanic soil of the island, he informs them that he has made them mad, in a chillingly hollow synthesized voice that pre-echoes Alonso's later report of it as 'That deep and dreadful organ pipe' of thunder (3.3.98).

Requiring no more special effects than his supremely virtuosic acting skills and some complex make-up, Djimon Hounsou as Caliban draws on his native Benin culture to present a highly physicalized performance. Like that of Ariel, Caliban's formation is linked to the elements, but his decidedly un-spirit-like character, while fiercely bristling under the commanding pressure of a Prospera he acknowledges to be 'an artist of such power', he also has distinctive powers, materializing mainly in his lofty nobility of expression and physical movements. His self-choreographed ways of moving are sometimes angular and aggressive, yet they are always beautifully emphatic and dancelike. These features are all of a piece with that half of his body layered with lava, suggesting both his 'natural' origins in the belly of the island's volcanic soil as well as that of its original 'queen', his witch-mother Sycorax.

While all of the actors provide inspired performances under Taymor's direction, many of the standout acting moments belong to Helen Mirren, whose skills as a performer underpin the dramatic authority and weight of the production. Perhaps surprisingly, some of these moments reveal the benefits of having Prospero played by a female actor – or at least *this* female actor. Towards the beginning, for example, when a distressed Miranda (Felicity Jones) implores her wild-eyed mother to halt the storm she is conjuring, lest those on board Alonso's ship suffer, Mirren listens to her daughter's pleas, and becomes noticeably affected by them. A male actor's response to these pleas is frequently patronizing. When Ariel reports to Prospera that 'so strongly' have her charms worked to turn the wits of her enemies Alonso and the rest, reducing the 'good old lord Gonzalo' to tears, he suggests that, could she witness these woeful effects in person, her feelings 'would become tender' towards them. The response in Mirren's face, as she turns with her 'Dost thou think so, spirit?' is so full of genuine shocked surprise that when he diffidently answers, 'Mine would, master, were I human', she delivers the decisive 'And mine shall', this important decision clearly feeding into Prospera's later judgement that 'The rarer action is / In virtue than in vengeance' (5.1.12, 15–16, 17–20). There is much food for thought in the fact that this earlier change of mind was occasioned by Prospera's acting on the advice of her 'non-human' spirit-servant, who has educated her feelings such that the 'redemptive' dimension of the play's resolution becomes possible. Finally, when the moment arrives of Prospera's planned 'giving away' of her daughter in marriage to Ferdinand, Mirren, it seems (despite previous pronouncements), cannot help revealing a protective mother's look towards her daughter, her face revealing only a half-humorous regret at the loss.

One cannot end without mentioning how well the only romantically intimate and innocent exchanges of the film are achieved. These are between Miranda and Ferdinand, played by Reeve Carney, whose beautifully tender voice delivers 'O mistress mine' (from *Twelfth Night*) to his betrothed so exquisitely that this love scene bears comparison with some of the best moments of the balcony scene in Baz Lurhmann's 1996 *Romeo + Juliet*.

Ralph Fiennes's *Coriolanus* **(2011)** is in many ways a unique achievement. No big-screen version of Shakespeare's final tragedy was ever attempted before it. As a long, politically complex late play second only in length to *Hamlet*, it is infrequently performed, so less familiar than others. It therefore presents a significant challenge to anyone adapting it for the popular cinema. Ralph Fiennes was well prepared for the task, a major catalyst having been his experience of playing the lead role of Coriolanus in London's Almeida stage production of 2000. Over succeeding years he became increasingly convinced that the play on film 'could become a contemporary, urgent political thriller, with a Greek tragedy at its center, involving the mother and the son ... There's something in the spirit of Coriolanus, in the essence of his character, which spoke to me very strongly and wouldn't leave me.' Despite being its brainchild and director, he was unable 'to let go of re-playing the part' in the film. I think some part of me felt I hadn't quite fully achieved it onstage ....' Cinema could permit him to explore 'the interior life of Coriolanus', making the unsaid 'as meaningful as speech' (Logan, 2011, 115, 120). Fiennes's filmic instincts proved to be correct. The grim, disturbed look of haughty contempt he typically assumes when playing Coriolanus, along with other prideful grimaces and gestures imaging the dark interior matter animating this character, expose with scary accuracy the uncompromising and difficult nature of this strangest of Shakespeare's tragic heroes. 'I like characters that challenge an audience', says Fiennes, and with this play 'Shakespeare takes a really hard-ass man who despises the people and makes him the protagonist' (Logan, 115–16).

Fiennes explains how Shakespeare's play sets up three kinds of 'visceral dynamic of confrontation', supplying the 'strong narrative drive'

Illustration 1   **Ralph Fiennes's** *Coriolanus* **(2011):** Ralph Fiennes as
Coriolanus stares at us with menace and haughty contempt, here a charismatic leader for the cult following of Volscian soldiers who mimic his scalp-
shaved 'badass' look. Fiennes had found it difficult on stage to vocalize 'the
variation within the rage' of this character. But on film the 'interior life of
Coriolanus could be explored', making the unsaid 'as meaningful as speech'.

for a film that is both 'exciting and approachable' for audiences. These
confrontations begin with the rebellious citizens of Rome being out-
faced by Coriolanus, who enters by sneeringly telling the people 'to go
fuck themselves'. This contemptuousness not only stirs up antagonistic
feelings in the Roman plebeians, but in us as well. There then develops
'an intimacy of opposites between him and Aufidius, head of the
Volscians and his arch enemy'. Lastly, there is the 'extraordinary tension between Coriolanus and his mother Volumnia' (Logan, 115–16).
Fiennes and John Logan (screenplay writer) figured 'an organizing
principle' for the film's dramatic spine: 'keep the focus on the protagonist'. As Logan notes, 'Master dramatist that he is, Shakespeare wrote
a play about a ferocious warrior whose climax depicts not a battle, but
a son weeping in his mother's arms. It is a harrowing family drama as
much as anything' (Logan, ix).

The implications of focusing on Coriolanus's story in a long play
results in radically cutting many of the play's more public elements

concerning people, politics and military issues, making instead 'the "private" and psychological story central' (Logan, ix). While Fiennes and Logan were committed to using only Shakespeare's dialogue, since this was turning into a kind of political thriller and action film, Logan tells us he 'sought to play the active verbs more than the ruminations or poetry ... Short jabs, not long caresses' (Logan, ix). This action-orientated approach certainly meets the movie audience's need to feel **identification** with the antagonists and a small, tight dramatic ensemble. Fiennes also wanted a contemporary look, finding it in the visibly war-torn sites of Serbia and Montenegro, where the film was shot. This makes it a movie undoubtedly using the *periodizing mode*. (For more discussion see Part III.4, *The Periodizing Mode*.)

In some ways resembling the approach of Loncraine and McKellen's 1995 *Richard III*, the film opens in its first two minutes without dialogue, 'showing not telling' the visceral quality of hate in one of its protagonists. Tullus Aufidius (Gerard Butler) sharpens the blade of his combat knife in a dimly-lit room while glancing at a TV screen. As the camera follows Aufidius's limited activity, a **close-up** studies the bulging muscular movements of his tattooed shoulder and arm as he scrapes the knife blade on a whetstone, its coarse sound the only thing to be heard. His Volscian forces are portrayed throughout as a kind of insurgent tribal guerrilla army challenging Rome. As the TV **close-up** of Martius reveals the name on his battle tunic, a **non-diegetic** swell of music enters, the pounding of a kettledrum melding with Aufidius's sinister blade-sharpening as he becomes transfixed by the sight – this is his deadly enemy.

A succession of news headlines tells the story over a **montage** of short *vérité* screen sequences: 'Thousands wait for food'; 'Senate declares state of emergency'; ending, 'General Martius suspends Civil liberties.' As cars are overturned and jeering rioters confront police on burning streets, a **freeze-frame** proclaims: 'A place calling itself Rome.' But this is not Rome, Italy, for as Fiennes emphasizes, 'our Rome could be just about any city in the world' (Logan, 117). Aufidius and his old enemy Martius finally clash when Martius's army attacks the Volscian city of Corioles. The ensuing battle sequences, filmed on location by **DoP** Barry Ackroyd, provide some of the most enthralling and memorable elements of the film. Ackroyd's documentary skills using a **hand-held** camera enable him to grab **shot**s within continuous action that, when expertly **edited** together in a fast-cutting mode (12 minutes being a lot of screen time in such a mode), deliver a realistic sense to the audience of the deadly dangers of modern military combat.

On his return to Rome Martius is given the honorary sobriquet 'Coriolanus', to the delight of his ambitious widowed mother Volumnia (Vanessa Redgrave), for whom martial valour is not only the greatest virtue but was the central principle in rearing her illustrious son. He reluctantly agrees to seek the office of Consul, but almost immediately the political tide turns when scheming tribunes of 'the people', Sicinius and Brutus, whip up opposition in the 'fickle' plebeians to banish him from Rome as a haughty 'tyrant'. The scenes in the market and Senate where these matters are (almost literally) thrashed out are finely captured (again with **hand-held** camera), Fiennes flinging the oily tribune Sicinius (exquisitely played by James Nesbitt) down the Senate house steps. This key political twist now turns Coriolanus against what he considers an easily flattered Roman populace, dismissing *them* with his 'You common cry of curs...There is a world elsewhere' speech (3.3.124–39), and leaves. Shockingly, he now seeks out Aufidius, offering to assist the Volscians in their grim determination to defeat Rome, giving him the opportunity to avenge himself on those he considers unworthy of his patrician leadership. Shakespeare seems here to be performing a gratuitous dramatic reversal, but he is merely following the narrative account of his literary source, Plutarch. He seems to do this because it enables him to anatomize with dramatic boldness social and individual pathologies (only hinted at in *Julius Caesar*) in the Jacobean English state of 1608. James I and his sons Henry and Charles all admired the absolutism of imperial Rome and its 'military hero' figures. By contrast, their opponents in Parliament frequently invoked the Roman Republic.

Military hero that he is, Tullus soon overcomes his suspicions about his fellow warrior, and (literally) embraces Coriolanus, expressing in his 'homoerotic' speech how 'Know thou first, / I loved the maid I married...But that I see thee here, / Thou noble thing, more dances my rapt heart / Than when I first my wedded mistress saw / Bestride my threshold' (4.5.112–17). Aufidius, thus 'wedded' to his new warrior partner, decides to share the Volsci military command with Coriolanus, a filmic master stroke being achieved when he has his scalp shaved, this 'badass' look making Fiennes's scowl more menacing than ever. When a cult following of Volscians mimic the 'hardman' image, this threatens Aufidius's leadership, the latter's admiration turning to a deadly resentment that finally proves fatal to his overreaching rival.

Yet the film's most astounding dramatic reversal is to come. When the entreaties of Coriolanus's former political patron Menenius (Brian

Cox) to spare Rome fail, Volumnia enters the Volscian camp with Coriolanus's wife Virgilia and young son Martius to beg her vengeful son to think again. Is he really willing to tread 'on thy mother's womb / That brought thee to this world' (5.3.125–6)? Seeking to avoid Volumnia's emotional bullying, Coriolanus rises to go. He is halted in his tracks by the stonily persistent mother dragging herself and his family down to 'shame him with our knees', offering the icy farewell that a gaunt-faced Vanessa Redgrave plays to perfection: 'Yet give us our dispatch. / I am hushed until our city be afire, / And then I'll speak a little.' Coriolanus cracks, unable to resist the emotional working-over that the woman who raised him to be a heroic warrior has expertly wielded. So effective is this that her broken son tearfully utters the insightful response: 'O mother, mother! / What have you done? ... You have won a happy victory to Rome; / But for your son, believe it, O believe it, / Most dangerously you have with him prevailed, / If not most mortal to him. But let it come' (5.3.170, 181–4, 187–90). One of the most stunning scenes in all drama, this is convincingly played and filmed, justifying Fiennes's comment on Redgrave that 'It was extraordinary to play opposite her on that day' (Logan, 119). It shows.

Joss Whedon's *Much Ado About Nothing* (2012), shot on location in only 12 days at his own Santa Monica home, is a triumph of American filmed Shakespeare, engaging and delighting at many levels. Whedon had wanted to film this play for ten years, primarily as a vehicle for actors Amy Acker (Beatrice) and Alexis Denisof (Benedick), both well-known from his hit TV series *Angel*, and for him the ideal 'movie couple' for these roles. Many others in the cast had worked with him before, too, creating an ensemble that takes us effortlessly through a drama both tense and hilarious by turns. As it does so, the obstacles and knots men and women get into when struggling to engage with the significant other they love are artfully exposed.

Behind the uniformly excellent acting that brings Shakespeare's play so splendidly to life here, Whedon crafts what he calls a 'DIY aesthetic' to make this modern-dress adaptation connect effectively with us. There are three main elements to this: camera technique; the use made of his own house as location; and the **film-noir** 'look' and mood that help animate the 'darker' parts of the story. Although this was a low-budget movie, he reports using three RED Epic ultra **HD** cameras that ran for most of the shoot, enabling him to capture and **edit** between scenes from three different standpoints, so avoiding the need for distracting camera movements. This allows the audience to follow the dialogue and emotional interactions between characters more organically. The multi-levelled but compactly coherent architecture of Whedon's house provides a variety of rooms, stairways and other spaces for the characters to perform in, windows, interspace openings and mirrors enabling the actors to gaze at or spy on one another. The location thus facilitates the performance of intrigue, lying and snooping by the 'wealthy, powerful, important' and highly self-conscious American central characters. As their perceptions become warped by the 'fronts' they create for themselves, we are drawn into intriguing and often comic situations where all are 'playing' each other (Whedon, DVD Commentary).

Whedon's decision to film in black and white so as to bring elegance to the movie also led him to the discovery that his primary attraction to the play's combination of 'mean-mindedness and romance' made him think of **film-noir** movies by Billy Wilder and Preston Sturges, where criminal darkness and screwball comedy frequently coexist. The film therefore benefits in its darker scenes – frequently engineered by or involving the scheming Don John – from a highly effective use of **chiaroscuro** lighting. But it also transforms one of the play's most stunning moments into something that could well have come out of the noir classic, Wilder's *Double Indemnity*. After the wedding debacle, where Hero is falsely exposed as a 'wanton' following Don John's resentful manipulations, Benedick and Beatrice finally declare their love for each other, Benedick's joy leading him to say, 'Come, bid me do anything for thee.' To which she answers, their arms still wrapped around each other, 'Kill Claudio' (4.1.286–7). This is not the language of romantic comedy, but rather that of **film noir**, where the stakes are always high, as they are here. For the ultimate aim of this play is to bring Benedick and Beatrice, the hesitant, melancholy lovers, *together in love*.

If the dark plottings of Don John are effectively conveyed by evoking mixed-genre 'noirish' movies, the scenes concerning the malapropism-ridden Constable Dogberry and his incompetent deputy Verges, which intersect with them, are made hilarious by having them conduct their investigations in a clever parody of American TV detective shows. Nathan Fillion's pompous Dogberry is the serious but inept station captain, while Tom Lenk's moustachioed deadpan Verges could have stepped out of a 1970s American TV cop show. For the first time on film, these scenes are played with true comedy. But the greatest comic episodes come in the gulling scenes with Alex Denisof's Benedick and (especially) Amy Acker's Beatrice, at the pivotal heart of the play. Following his gulling by Leonato, Pedro and Claudio, Denisof indulges aloud in reflections on his feelings for Beatrice in the garden's tiny amphitheatre of stone slabs, and when Beatrice appears 'against her will' to invite him in for dinner, he starts doing physical jerks in front of her as a kind of mating display. The man in love can cut a ridiculous figure, and here his antics are ridiculously funny – as Shakespeare meant them to be. But 'Graceless in the way that only a supremely graceful performer can be', it is the beautiful Acker who 'gives the film's show-stopping performance'. Her physical comedy begins in earnest when, 'overhearing' Ursula ask Hero at the start of 3.1, 'Are you sure Benedick loves Beatrice so entirely?', Acker is shocked into tripping and falling out of sight down a stairway in a glorious pratfall designed to produce out-loud laughter in us – it does. As has been said of this consummate actor, Acker here unfolds 'her elegant lines with the same skill with which she folds herself under a kitchen counter to eavesdrop in awkward delight', and in doing so reveals 'the affective and embodied intelligence of the classic comedienne, a skill and style underappreciated to the point of absence in contemporary cinema' (Mayer, 2013). Joss Whedon has produced an adaptation of *Much Ado About Nothing* taking American Shakespeare and Shakespeare on film to a new level of excellence.

The Shakespeare on film boom that began in 1989 shows little sign of abating, some new adaptations being due for release in 2015 or beyond. Despite his live stage-to-cinema performance as Macbeth at the Manchester International Festival in summer 2013, Kenneth Branagh is not working on a movie version, though wanting to make a film of *The Winter's Tale* at some point. Branagh has held back from filming the Scottish play because a cinematic *Macbeth* directed by Justin Kurzel is due for release in 2015, Michael Fassbender playing Macbeth and Marion Cotillard Lady Macbeth. Kurzel's *Macbeth* has been shot on location in England and Scotland and is said 'to feature the original Shakespearean dialogue' – as if this were an optional extra. We are moving into a period where the appetites of the popular cinema audience are persuading filmmakers to adapt the *story* of a Shakespeare play for the big screen rather than using Shakespeare's own play text – however cut down.

This conjecture may or may not be confirmed by a forthcoming film version of *Macbeth* from director Vincent Regan, called *Enemy of Man*. Macbeth is played by Sean Bean, who has said, 'Vincent wants to present the audience with something that's not necessarily very word-heavy Shakespeare, a dark and completely new take on the play.' This worrying description seems confirmed by Regan's stated aim to 'strip back the dialogue and crank up the action and produce an atmospheric and blood-soaked chiller'. That he aims to change Shakespeare's drama into a revenge drama is suggested by Regan's 'take' on *Macbeth* as being 'the tragedy of a successful childless couple'(?) whose 'inner lives' he 'strongly believes' are tormented in the way he thinks Shakespeare's was by the death of his young son Hamnet in the 1590s. This fantasy of the origination of *Macbeth* is very much of the psychological 'what's my motivation?' kind, seeming to ignore the play's real complexities. It remains to be seen how much the action film *Enemy of Man* will suffer from the 'stripping-back' treatment: *remove Shakespeare's text and it will no longer be Shakespeare.*

Another Shakespeare movie adaptation for release in 2015 is Michael Almereyda's *Cymbeline*. Its trailer shows a fast-moving film severely cutting back its Shakespearean dialogue (as with many adaptations), yet in a way that feels as astutely achieved here as it was in Almereyda's 2000 *Hamlet*. Described as being 'in the vein of *Sons of Anarchy* [the US TV series about a California motorcycle club] and in the style of [Luhrmann's] *Romeo + Juliet*', it tells the 'gritty story of a take-no-prisoners war between dirty cops and a drug-dealing biker gang'. This description seems very remote from the first and only previous movie version, filmed sedately as a silent in 1913. But when we hear that 'extortion, betrayal and fiery passions threaten' the criminal empire of a 'drug kingpin' (Ed Harris), driving him 'to desperate measures', those who know Shakespeare's later Jacobean play will be reminded of what is at stake in his dark, complexly plotted and peculiarly passionate drama. Almereyda reworked *Hamlet* with great filmic invention to a succinct 106 minutes. It will be fascinating to see how effectively he has brought in his version of the even more involved *Cymbeline* (with Ethan Hawke as Giacomo) at 85 minutes.

All of the foregoing suggests a movie industry still wanting to bring Shakespeare's plays to the big screen. In many ways, Shakespeare as a classic 'property' of both popular and arthouse twenty-first-century film entertainment seems to have come of age over the last few years. Even if many of us will be viewing such films at home on video, or **streaming** them via the internet, it seems to remain true that

> A theatrical screening focuses public interest. Critics review the film, television and the press publicize it, and people talk about it. The theatrical run usually determines how successful a movie will be in ancillary markets. Theatrical hits may account for as much as 80 percent of subsequent rentals.
>
> (Bordwell and Thompson, 2013, 42)

Part III

Communicating Shakespeare on Film: Modes, Styles, Genres

Introductory note, Sections 1–4

In the first chapter of his book *Shakespeare on Film*, Jack Jorgens offered a helpful method of approaching the artistic and dramatic potential of film for communicating adaptations of Shakespeare's plays via the big screen, by analysing and discussing them in terms of three modes of representation: the *theatrical*, the *realistic* and the *filmic* (Jorgens, 1991, 7–12). Since this typology of Shakespearean film adaptation has yet to be bettered for surveying the range of adaptations produced, I rehearse below my understanding of Jorgens's categories, giving illustrative examples for study purposes (all referenced quotations from Jorgens's book, unless otherwise stated). However, I have thought to add a further mode to his typology, the *periodizing* mode. This additional category has enabled me to cite and discuss some film adaptations that dramatize and dress a play by transposing it to the culture and society of a distinct historical period.

1

The Theatrical Mode

For Jorgens the *theatrical* mode of filming Shakespeare has 'the look and feel of a performance worked out for a static theatrical space and a live audience' (7). Before the first decade of the twenty-first century, attempts to capture this stage performance 'look and feel' tended to use the film frame as if it were a theatrical **proscenium arch**. Captured in **medium** or **long shot** using lengthy **take**s stressing the durational quality of time, the mode's style came from the style of the performances, which were 'of a distinctly theatrical cast – more demonstrative, articulate and continuous than actors are usually permitted in films' (8).

The theatrical mode's chief potency should therefore be in giving maximum exposure to the performance of Shakespeare's text, bringing to life his full range of verbal and dramatic styles, 'from stark naturalism to **metatheatrical** playfulness' (8). The stylistic effects of this screen mode are bound to be influenced by the manner of staging, whatever the theatrical performance space used. Until relatively recently, the number of live stage performances filmed skilfully enough to hold the interest of a screen audience was tiny, one fascinating example being the *King Lear* recorded on camera for TV during summer 1974 as part of the New York Shakespeare Festival held in New York City's Central Park, directed by Edwin Sherin and produced by Joseph Papp. The evening performance was shot under arc lights and captured on four cameras in a lively range of single, **two-**, **three-** and **wide shot**s, with expertly managed **shot/reverse-shot** sequences catching some of the best dramatic exchanges. One argument for making such films is to record exceptional stage performances, and the King Lear given here by accomplished black American actor James Earl

Jones has many high points, although the **close shot**s of Jones's Lear frequently reveal a vitality of movement unconvincing for an 'old and reverend' man of 'four score and upward'. Other performances vary from the unremarkable – 'the women were disappointedly wooden', one critic accurately observes – to the scintillatingly witty and well-timed, exampled by Lear and his Fool (Tom Aldredge) in 1.4. The great virtue of the DVD is that it conveys the excitement and atmosphere *of a live* stage performance being enjoyed *by a live* audience, who sometimes even applaud the entrances and exits of actors.

Two 1960s films providing 'the look and feel of a performance worked out for a static theatrical space and a live audience', though filmed without an audience and played in very different theatrical settings, are **Stuart Burge's** *Othello* **(1965)**, starring Laurence Olivier, and **Tony Richardson's** *Hamlet* **(1969)**, starring Nicol Williamson. I shall spend a little time discussing these highly contrasting filmed theatrical pieces before moving on to more recent twenty-first-century productions.

Stuart Burge's *Othello* **(1965)**, originally directed by John Dexter for the new National Theatre of Great Britain in 1964, was captured on Technicolor film running in three Panavision cameras at Shepperton Studios. The stylized studio sets closely followed the designs used for the **proscenium** stage production, the aim being 'to recreate completely the atmosphere, effect and immediacy of the theatre performance'. Producer Anthony Havelock-Allan added that the film would enable 'millions of people throughout the world, who would not have had the remotest chance of seeing Sir Laurence on the stage, to share the experience' (Manvell, 1971, 117). Olivier's stage performance as Othello had been widely acclaimed, and the movie version undoubtedly accomplishes something that the 'director-ridden art of film seldom permits: an unfettered actor-generated performance' (194). Retaining the actors, design and **blocking** of Dexter's stage original, if we keep in mind that what we are seeing is a *record* of Olivier's highly demonstrative style of acting originally put on for a large theatre audience, it is certainly possible to become highly engrossed in the performance.

However, it is hard at times to ignore how the overpowering physicality of Olivier's performance filmed in **medium** and **close shot** feels over-intense and exaggerated. These are the same gestures and movements which had no doubt communicated Othello's pain and bewilderment to a theatre audience – sitting much further away from the stage than we are from the screen – but which feel too expansively melodramatic for a movie-viewer. This is especially noticeable when Olivier reaches crescendos in certain speeches, such as where the poisonous lies planted in Othello's susceptible mind by Iago become disturbingly apparent at 'Farewell the tranquil mind' (3.3.353–62), and again at 'Damn her, lewd minx!' (3.3.478–81). Interestingly, Frank Finlay's performance of Iago succeeds better in the film than it did in the stage production. Whereas the swelling speech climaxes of Olivier's Othello that so impressed in the theatre can feel overdone on film, the cool and calculating playing of Finlay's Iago, often thought too restrained on stage, matches perfectly the **medium-** and **close shot**s of film. Olivier knew well enough from making his own three Shakespeare films the importance of 'scaling down' his performance from the proximities of theatrical to film space, so as not to overwhelm the cinema audience. Perhaps the opportunity of capturing a 'heritage' movie record of Olivier's bravura style of Shakespearean acting proved too tempting, and took precedence over more filmic considerations.

Tony Richardson's *Hamlet* (1969) was the work of a new Sixties' British theatre and film director with a radically realistic 'edge', and this was bound to set him poles apart from Burge and Olivier's more 'stately' style of playing and production. In staging and filming *Hamlet*, Richardson's priority was for the actors to communicate with the audience more directly and closely than had been possible in traditional theatres. The location that enabled him to create this more intimate kind of connection as one of the leading London avant-garde venues of the time was a converted brick-built circular Victorian railway engineering shed called the Roundhouse, at Chalk Farm, north London. It was a setting which he felt would

> put the actors into immediate contact with the audience instead of being stuck behind the picture-frame of a proscenium. It does away with that terrible formality, and lets actors speak in a room instead of up on an artificial platform ... The most vital thing is space, and at the Roundhouse we have that.   (Quoted by Manvell, 1971, 127–8)

The closeness to the audience that Richardson achieved for these live theatrical performances became even more emphatic for his film of the same production. His concern to make this *Hamlet* 'a real film, not a photographed version of the stage production', urged him to use a mobile camera and microphones to catch every gesture and word of the performance. From the beginning, when Francisco brushes past the camera into shot *from behind it* to challenge Barnardo as the latter emerges from the shadows – the dank and dimly lit Roundhouse interior providing a convincing atmosphere for Elsinore castle's ramparts – we are brought very close to the performing actors. Consequently, the reactions on their faces and the speaking of their lines are caught clearly, despite an ambient background drone caused by exterior traffic noise – another reason perhaps to film the actors so close up. This **close-up** focus upon the faces of characters in single, **two-** and **three-shot**s is very apparent throughout the film. The first example occurs when the terror-struck faces of Horatio, Marcellus and Barnardo are lit by a blinding light representing the Ghost, whose arrival is accompanied by solemn, gong-like reverberations. The text is here severely cut back to emphasize the shocking impact on the observers this sudden appearance has had.

In contrast to a scene frequently played as a formal banquet and filmed in **medium** and **medium-close shot** (e.g. in the films of Olivier and Branagh), we see here the succeeding scenes of Claudius and Gertrude celebrating their marriage as a carefree party (1.2), played in **close shot**. A wine-swilling Claudius (Anthony Hopkins) is followed around by the camera as he pokes fun at 'impotent and bed-rid' old Fortinbras, much to the hilarity of the courtiers jostling carelessly together at his elbow. The party atmosphere caught here by this style of shooting has immediacy, registering the contemporary late Sixties' values of 'permissiveness' emerging in Britain and the USA at this time. Similarly, the close-seeing camera of the following scene when Williamson's Hamlet speaks his first soliloquy ('O that this too too sullied flesh would melt ...' 1.2.129) allows us to observe and absorb every nuance of his mood. The camera tracks him closely as he moves from directly addressing it (us), to giving a speech of pensive utterance obliquely focused on some point near it, visibly tormenting himself with an enraged knuckling of the brow at the thought of his mother's hurrying with 'such dexterity to incestuous sheets!' (1.2.167). Here, in Williamson's quick, intense and nasal delivery, and throughout the movie from all other speaking characters, we are given a level of naturalistic performance matched to the requirements of the screen, and not to the spacious acoustic of the traditional theatre.

What Richardson's *Hamlet* gains by adopting this more intimate style of performance is a form of production more accessible to a movie audience than the Dexter/Burge *Othello* is likely to be, since the latter can be too revealing of the self-consciously stylized 'artifice' used by Olivier to create performance effects designed for a large theatrical acoustic. In creating such a naturalistically intimate form of playing for the camera, Richardson also either consciously or inadvertently generated the kind of performance that works very well for a TV audience, suited as the small screen is for delivering dramatic material on a more 'domestic' scale. In many ways, the theatrical mode of presenting Shakespeare on screen has worked best when successful theatre productions are dramatized for television and/or DVD, many such productions of which are discussed and illustrated in Part V.

Live Stage Productions of Shakespeare on Film in the Twenty-first Century

The wide use of digital film and sound technology in the century's second decade has made the experience of watching high-quality Shakespeare on film productions clear and accessible for both movie-theatre and small-screen audiences. Combining these advanced visual and sound technologies with refined multi-camera filming techniques also means that some excellent live theatre productions of Shakespeare are now being captured on film and commercially distributed. Notable in this revolution are the plays filmed at Shakespeare's Globe Theatre in London, available to see in cinemas and on DVD. As an attempted reconstruction of the Bankside playhouse used by Shakespeare's company (from 1603, the King's Men), the rebuilt Globe has an open **thrust stage** that does away with the 'terrible formality' of the **proscenium arch** so disliked by Tony Richardson, linking the players more intimately with the audience on three sides around them. In another advance, following the initiative of New York Metropolitan Live Opera **HD** transmissions to movie theatres in the USA and around the world from 2006–7 (*The Met Live in HD*), London's National Theatre began 'NT Live' stage broadcasts of Shakespeare to cinemas in 2009, with a production of *All's Well That Ends Well* relayed to some 300 cinemas worldwide. In November 2013 the Royal Shakespeare Company launched their first live broadcast of a production to cinemas around the world from the Stratford **thrust stage** – *Richard II*, starring David Tennant as Richard. In the remainder of this section I shall discuss the RSC live production transmissions, as exemplified by *Richard II*, followed by an exploration of the 'Globe on Screen' initiative, focusing on their filmed production of *Twelfth Night*.

RSC Live Stage-to-Cinema Productions

RSC live screen producer John Wyver explained to me that 'doing a big live-to-cinema production is quite an operation, with precise processes working together immaculately. It's a difficult process to deal with six cameras across three hours of drama shooting eight or nine hundred shots, and to get every single shot right – to plan and to carry that out is bloody difficult. There's a great team doing it, but it ultimately depends upon Robin Lough, the very experienced screen director.' Despite the complexity of the filming skills needed, compared to making a Shakespeare TV film adaptation there are major advantages to creating live stage-to-cinema broadcasts, including lower costs and bypassing the need for a TV broadcaster. An RSC live-to-cinema performance can be made for around a fifth of the £1 million required to shoot a bespoke TV film, with the possibility of 'getting the outlay back from the market' in the form of cinema ticket and DVD sales.

The benefits to the audience are many. Using **HD** cameras 'and crucially, *really* good sound, it is possible to make broadcasts from a theatre at a very high creative level'. Although you are not 'coterminous, in spatial terms, with the people in the theatre, you are unquestionably in a communal, social context and experiencing something, *both* with the 200 people in the cinema around you, *and* in a virtual kind of way, with the 50–60,000 people watching it via satellite in many cinemas around the world – as well as the 1800 watching it in Stratford-upon-Avon'. For Wyver and the RSC, this process is all about 'extending the theatre event to other communal gatherings of people watching it in real time along with the people in the theatre at Stratford, to give a coherent and vivid sense of what it's like to be in the theatre watching the play. We combine **wide shot**s of the stage with **close-up**s and they complement broad images of the playing area with details.' His cameras are certainly determining which elements are in **wide shot**, **close-up** and **mid-shot**, as well as controlling the movement and duration of those shots. But the constant aim is to underscore the meaning and expressive impact of the play. The result – particularly through **wide shot**s – is that the viewer is allowed to explore a high-quality, finely detailed image in the same way as someone at the theatre spectacle itself might be doing, picking out the things that interest them. 'So it's not *completely directed*', says Wyver. What the viewer sees 'is certainly not *over-determined* by the shots, the **editing** and the visual presentation. It allows people to engage with the performance in many ways, with the same feeling of implicit jeopardy existing in the theatre. Live theatre is unpredictable, which makes for exciting live presentations that are far more vivid and interesting than the encores [recorded repeats] or seeing it on DVD. These broadcasts are inherently about the live experience.'

These more theatrically 'open' filming techniques were exemplified in the RSC *Richard II* stage production broadcast in November 2013. Cinema viewers were given **wide shot**s of the full stage space, including parts of the audience that appeared frequently throughout the performance, usually at the opening and end of each scene. Cinema audiences therefore become familiar with the layout and use of the stage before the camera moves them into the more closely framed shots typical of TV and film drama. For watcher Erin Sullivan, this RSC filming approach mixed camera angles and perspectives 'in a more varied, measured, and satisfying way' than any broadcast production she had ever seen. '**Wide** and **mid-shot**s of the stage and characters were sensitively mixed with tighter **close-up**s, creating a roving and fluid perspective that loosened its grip on the viewer's gaze', she observed, recognizing that 'there's more than one best seat in any theatrical house' (Sullivan, 2014). As well as facilitating such a range of viewpoints for the worldwide audience of this live relayed performance of *Richard II*, the production itself is exquisitely designed, performed and directed. It opens with an **overhead shot** of the Duchess of Gloucester (Jane Lapotaire) hanging over the Duke's coffin, the camera gradually pulling back and down to capture in **wide shot** other court characters entering, and audience members right and left. We also see three spotlit female choristers who sing a *Lacrimosa* from a high balcony, their melancholy voices blending with pale blue lighting to convey an atmosphere of religiosity. This blue tinges much of the production, lending emphasis to the figure of Richard II, who as the last medieval monarch strongly believed he was anointed by God in his inviolable rule. Productions often cut 1.2 for performance, but Doran includes this because the wrought exchanges between Gloucester's brother Gaunt (Michael Pennington) and his widow the Duchess serve to establish the complex political context of Richard's reign, both of them standing for a long and ancient royal line now abused by Richard's profligacy. 1.2 also reveals the **backstory** of Richard as the man behind Gloucester's death, the dispute having flared up between Bolingbroke and Mowbray in 1.1. Once Richard's power falls and Bolingbroke's rises at the mid-point of Shakespeare's highly symmetrical play, Richard takes on the persona of a self-pitying

Christian martyr-king, Tennant's idea for Richard to have very long 'Christ-like' hair becoming especially effective in the deposition scene.

One extraordinary feature of the production accessible only to live-broadcast and DVD viewers comes before this (in 3.3), when a long crane is used to move the camera deeply **upstage** to capture Richard (David Tennant) and his cousin Aumerle (Oliver Rix) in **close-up** together on a high gantry. This represents the scene where Shakespeare has Richard on the castle ramparts confronting a Bolingbroke who stands below on what Richard disdainfully calls the 'base court'. Wyver describes how 'in a continuous **developing single shot** the camera slowly moves in very close for Richard's long kiss with Aumerle that Greg [Doran] has put into the production'. What was the significance of creating and capturing this moment? 'I think the idea was to hold together the sense of Richard's exalted highness of office and the intimate vulnerability he feels at this point. In this single shot you move from the public spectacle to the private drama. The ability of the **crane shot** to capture that shift in a continuous sweep I think is powerfully expressive, and more so – I don't know quite why or how – than if you had a **wide shot** of Richard high up in the gantry, cutting to a **close shot** of him and Aumerle together.'

At the time of writing, the RSC has done three further live broadcasts of stage productions from Stratford: *1 Henry IV*, *2 Henry IV* and *The Two Gentlemen of Verona*. In 2015, they broadcast live *Love's Labour's Lost*, *Love's Labour's Won* (aka *Much Ado About Nothing*) *The Merchant of Venice*, *Othello* and *Henry V*, with a special live broadcast in the week of the 600th anniversary of the Battle of Agincourt.

Globe on Screen

Shakespeare's Globe Theatre on London's Bankside was designed as a replica of the outdoor style of English Renaissance playhouse built 'on the Roman plan'. That means it was and is a polygonal 'amphitheatre' structure using a **thrust stage** surrounded on three sides by three steeply raked levels of gallery for seated members of the audience and a yard for those standing – the **groundling**s. This compact design brings the large audience into close contact with the actors so they can hear and see the performers properly under 'same-light' conditions – there was no lighting for such theatres in Shakespeare's time, all performances being in daylight.

Expert screen producer and director Ian Russell, maker of some seven *Globe on Screen* productions – including *Twelfth Night* and *Titus Andronicus* – emphasized to me the significance of the Globe's intimate theatre space, compared to the ubiquitous and more 'remote' **proscenium arch** style: 'The live audience around the stage is very much part of the Globe experience. I understand some actors are terrified of playing there because they're confronted by an audience only three feet away – it's a sort of bear pit you're playing to. It's been said that at the Globe there's no such thing as a monologue, because even if you are the only person on the stage, there's another character – the audience. When you're filming, you can't avoid them. When you cut to a **wide shot**, the action on stage is continuing, but you are quite naturally including the audience, which is brilliant, because that's what you see when you're there. The fact that they're in every shot, listening, laughing, responding, is what makes the Globe experience different. Sometimes an actor will interact with a groundling or other member of the audience, and of course you'll see that as well. During some of the funnier moments of *Twelfth Night*, we decided to go one step further and show audiences *enjoying* the play. If there was a really big laugh and the actors had stopped for that, we'd cut to a shot of the audience really enjoying themselves. It just feels the right thing to do, to include the audience as part of the production, and having a ring of cameras around the stage enabled us to take audience shots you wouldn't normally be able to do.'

NT Live and the RSC film their theatre productions for live broadcast to cinemas, but *Globe on Screen* films, although shot from live productions for cinemas and DVD, do not use the live broadcast model. That is because the open Globe stage is vulnerable to the elements and noise from overhead aircraft. To avoid these external factors, which would distract and annoy viewers, Globe films are created from two movie shoots. According to Russell, there are also benefits to not broadcasting live. 'Directing anything live requires a little caution. You have to take your foot off the gas a bit: you are pushing the camera movements and changing shots trying to follow the stage action around, but because it's live, you don't want anything to go wrong. So you tend to slow down a bit, shooting a bit cautiously to avoid any errors in the **coverage**. But if you're *not* live, and you've recorded the output for the camera so that you may re-edit, you can *go* for it a bit more – you can try and get the shots that for shooting live you might like, but are wary of getting because it might have an adverse effect on the overall **coverage**. You can plan to be a bit more risky *and* back it up on tape, so if the risk doesn't come off, you know you've got the safety net – you can't do that if you're live.' There is another advantage to what Russell calls the 'two-recording approach': 'It gives us all an opportunity to tighten up or change our plans, if what we imagined doesn't work out as we'd hoped. With *Twelfth Night*, Act 3, Scene 1, if I've remembered correctly, there are six characters, and there is a lot of walking around the stage, speaking half-lines of dialogue quickly at each other and moving around the stage. That's technically very difficult to **cover**, and on the first recording I wasn't too happy with it. So on the second recording I re-camera scripted, changing the approach, and it worked much better: with one recording we wouldn't have had that opportunity.'

The number of cameras used for a *Globe on Screen* production varies, according to how a play is staged. 'If the action is **upstage-downstage**, using more of the theatre yard, you may need more cameras at the **upstage** end to capture **downstage** characters whose faces you wouldn't otherwise see. The planning process is firstly to watch the play to get to know the production, noting where cameras might be needed. It only takes one character looking one way to need another camera, so we can see their face. Then, you need to negotiate within budget for the cameras you need: directors always want more. In the Globe I'd say the minimum is six, going up to nine, which we had on *Twelfth Night* and *Titus Andronicus*, both very 'busy' productions. The Globe way of performing means that actors rarely stay still for long, turning left and right and up and down frequently to include the audience on three sides, the **groundling**s in the yard, and up in the three tiers of galleries.'

I told Ian Russell that one of my favourite places to watch a Globe performance is high up on the side from one of the Lords' Rooms, where I assumed he'd had cameras for shooting both *Twelfth Night* and *Titus*. 'We did!' he said. 'It's quite often difficult when you're cutting between cameras to get round to complete what might need to be a **shot/reverse shot** from that angle. That can be tricky. But it provided us with some fantastic shots. There were also times when characters were largely looking **upstage**, and the only cameras that could capture those shots were up in the Lords' Rooms. In fact, one of the main reasons for those side shots was that in the discussions we had about filming with the company, stage director Tim Carroll said that he, Mark Rylance (Olivia) and everyone involved were all concerned that there would be a "circle of cameras" covering the performance, since the Globe is a circular space. That firm point of view allowed us to get the shots we would otherwise not have had. *Titus Andronicus* and *Twelfth Night* were similar in that respect, but for different reasons, in needing that ring of cameras to capture the performance of each play. We also got some lovely **wide shot**s across the stage, with the audience as a backdrop, which is fantastic. I'm often tempted to elaborate and have a big crane, to make a big movie, to be more cinematic or filmic with the cameras. But I don't think the **coverage** should draw attention to itself. If you are watching in a cinema or on DVD, the filming should very quickly involve you in the live play performance. If you are made to feel you are watching a film, it's gone wrong. It must feel like what it is, a live performance.'

As Ian Russell says, filming Shakespeare in the theatre 'isn't to replace the stage performance – it couldn't anyway. It's to bring a wider audience to it, which I think is beneficial, for all sorts of obvious reasons. I think the job of the screen director is to be as invisible as possible. You don't want any tricksy, filmicky things going on – just to watch a stage performance going on, without too many flashy camera angles. You should just be drawn into what's happening on the screen as you would be in the cinema, to be enveloped by it, to forget where you are. Which is why I think at the end of a *NT Live*, or a *Globe on Screen*, or an opera from the opera house, or wherever, I've never been to one where the audience didn't applaud – they applaud the screen! That's because they feel they've been part of a shared experience – and that's whether it's live or recorded.'

2

The Realistic Mode

The *realistic* mode of conveying Shakespeare on film makes for 'the most popular kind of Shakespeare film,' according to Jorgens, 'not merely because filmmakers are most familiar with it and mass audiences enjoy the spectacle of historical recreations, but because everyone senses that at bottom Shakespeare is a realist'. He elaborates:

> If realism in film implies something more than a visual style or authentic costumes and settings, it seems to many that this playwright – who filled his Globe with duels, battles, shipwrecks, tortures, assassinations, storms, coronations, trials, suicides, feasts, and funerals, who juxtaposed the ugly with the sublime, the base with the noble, everyday with holiday, who ruthlessly explored both the need for and the dangers of centralized power, the conflicts of young and old, the rocking of order and tradition by frightening, invigorating forces of change – virtually demands screen realism. (8–9)

Shakespeare's play texts do produce a vast range of dramatic events, contrasts and situations. It is because these are conveyed by convincing characters whose speaking lines describe, suggest or imply a multitude of *recognizably human experiences in particular social settings or locations that feel 'just like life'* that film, with its capacity to 'realize' such settings, locations and situations on screen, can come into its own. If, as Hamlet states in his advice to the players, it is the purpose of theatrical playing 'to hold as 'twere the mirror up to nature' (3.2.20), then many film directors adapting Shakespeare to the big screen have seen fit to enhance this playing by positioning it in a variety of realistic 'local habitations' designed to enlarge the scope of the 'nature' being mirrored. However, the ways that such attempts at screen realism are communicated to us have been as diverse as the stylistic approaches brought to the task by each individual filmmaker, inevitably perhaps, since movies are by definition almost always 'director-led'.

Jorgens noted the approach of various directors using this mode. Zeffirelli's *The Taming of the Shrew* and *Romeo and Juliet* he regards as being of the 'decorative, spectacular, orchestrally accompanied variety ... a descendant of the elaborate productions of the nineteenth century'. Fine as this description probably is for his first two films, it does not really hold so well for the later *Hamlet*, although, as Crowl has observed, that movie does reveal Zeffirelli's 'romantic and grandly operatic' sensibility by projecting Glenn Close's Gertrude as a 'tragic diva' figure. Peter Brook's *King Lear* Jorgens regards as having a 'harsh documentary style'. Shot in black and white in an inhospitably cold northern European setting, it is certainly bleak and unadorned in its approach. Yet, as I argue in the next section, it has as many or more 'filmic' qualities in its screen rendering of the play as it has 'realist' elements. According to Jorgens, a 'mixed style' is used for Polanski's 'gory, twilight *Macbeth*', the 'fortress and tangled forest of Kurosawa's *Throne of Blood*', and for 'the silences and wintery empty spaces of Welles's *Chimes at Midnight*'. It could be argued that to do justice to any version of *Macbeth* – or *Hamlet* – ensuring that the supernatural element in each is communicated effectively, a 'mixed style' of cinematic delivery is required, the mix being composed of realist and non-realist techniques.

In the post-1989 era of Shakespeare on film, it was Kenneth Branagh who epitomized the use of the realistic mode, his *Henry V*, *Much Ado About Nothing* and *Hamlet* all employing realistic strategies of cinematic communication. *Love's Labour's Lost*, though realistic in its acting style, remains predominantly what the opening credits of that film announce it to be: a 'romantic musical'. Where Branagh from *Henry V* onward led, many filmmakers of the Nineties' Shakespeare film genre revival tended to follow, most shooting their films in the realistic mode. The reason for this was that it was Branagh's particular *style* of employing the realistic mode that set the pattern for others. One key feature of this style was his frequent and strategic referencing earlier Hollywood movies to help convey in a vivid way the *story* of the Shakespeare play he was working to adapt at any one time. Thus, our first glimpse of his *Henry V* film shows him in becloaked triangular silhouette closely resembling the sinister figure of Darth Vader (*Star Wars*); or near the opening of Branagh's hugely successful *Much Ado About Nothing* Don Pedro and his men are shown galloping towards Messina side by side, in (as he himself puts it) 'a nod to *The Magnificent*

Seven' (Branagh, 1993, viii). Another key element of his approach to gaining a larger, international audience for his Shakespeare films from *Much Ado* onwards was to add high-profile American movie stars to his core British cast: a key pattern for the Nineties' realistic Shakespeare adaptation had been established.

Whatever the kind of realism deployed by a filmmaker, we can see that film has the capacity to *show* an immense variety of images that may complement and enhance key elements of the text. But what about that text? Despite the strengths of the realistic mode to provide some version of verisimilitude to the realistic elements implied by a play text, there is a danger that if such realism is conceived too narrowly, focusing on lavish settings and a mass of 'authentic' detail (for instance) at the expense of conveying the essential meanings of the play text in an accessible way, the audience will not be engaged. Several examples spring to mind. Reinhardt and Dieterle's 1935 *A Midsummer Night's Dream* was in many ways a cinematically innovative film, a kind of culmination of Max Reinhardt's interest in using extravagant Expressionist styles to animate his dramas. The problem is that the expensive sets, **props** and costumes developed for this glittering Warner Brothers movie were so extravagant as often to be distracting, distorting the shape of the picture more towards its 'look' than its effect as a comedy. One does not expect a non-realist play like *Dream* to be conveyed as a realistic drama, yet by focusing his efforts on a clear, actor-led performance of the text, as well as employing some visual tricks to convey 'the magic', Peter Hall's 1968 film version of the play in many ways is dramatically more effective.

3

The Filmic Mode

Peter Brook has observed how the 'reality of the image gives to film its power and its limitation' (1987, 192), his suggestion being that the film's capacity to articulate images so very emphatically means there is a danger that only a *single level of meaning* might be conveyed to the viewer. Jorgens therefore argues that to be true to the effect of what is invariably a whole *play of meanings* carried by Shakespeare's verbal text, such realistic emphasis must be subordinated to an overall design in which 'the aural has been made visual'. This was a phrase coined by Grigori Kozintsev, whose approach to Shakespeare on film exemplifies for Jorgens the advantages of the *filmic* mode. He sees this approach as being that of the 'film poet', whose works 'bear the same relation to the surfaces of reality that poems do to ordinary conversation' (10).

Everyday language can be transformed in good poetry to convey in us powerful meanings, images, emotions and other effects. But for such poetry to be created, the various literary techniques available (rhythm, rhyme, 'voice', word-patterning, simile, metaphor, etc.) need to be used to effect such a transformation. In transforming a Shakespeare text often already saturated with poetic imagery and rhythms to the screen, the various techniques and approaches of film language (discussed in Part I) must therefore be embraced and creatively manipulated, if the characters, themes, situations and insights are to be communicated in a resonant way to the screen audience. As Peter Holland has said in discussing the filmic mode, 'filmic films' of this type 'accept the peculiar intensity of the visual over the aural, of sight over sound that is fundamental to the cinema' (Holland, 1994, 56). To get into focus the particular problem facing Shakespeare filmmakers, Holland, like

Jorgens and other writers on this vital translation issue, offers a much-quoted passage from Kozintsev's essay '*Hamlet* and *King Lear*: Stage and Film':

> The problem is not one of finding means to speak the verse in front of the camera, in realistic circumstances ranging from **long shot** to **close-up**. The aural has to be made visual. The poetic texture has itself to be transformed into a visual poetry, into the dynamic organisation of film imagery.
>
> (Kozintsev, 1972, 191)

In seeking to go beyond both theatrical and realistic modes Kozintsev would no doubt be as scornful of the crassly literal film image mentioned below as the critic who cites it, Peter Holland:

> There is a film of *Macbeth* in which, when Macbeth speaks of 'pity, like a new-born babe, / Striding the blast, or heaven's cherubim, horsed / Upon the sightless couriers of the air' [1.7.21–3], the film showed, through a window, a ghastly little cherub on a horse riding on the wind.   (Holland, 1994, 56)

If this sort of literalism is to be avoided and Kozintsev's problem answered productively, 'there must be an imaginative recreation of the language of the play into the terms of the film', as Holland says. Kozintsev achieves this imaginative re-creation in a variety of ways in his *Hamlet* and *King Lear* movies, as do other directors whose impulse is to use the language of film to translate the essential meanings and moods of the text of Shakespeare's play into a text of cinema. In the middle era of Shakespeare on film up to 1971, these directors were principally Laurence Olivier, Orson Welles, Akira Kurosawa, Kozintsev and Peter Brook; in 2000 and beyond it has been Michael Almereyda, Julie Taymor and Ralph Fiennes who create the most interesting attempts at 'making the aural visual'.

Most filmmakers will acknowledge the import of Peter Brook's statement that in the world of film, 'space and time are loose and meaningless terms'. But since the communicative currency of that world has (for understandable commercial reasons) favoured the realistic mode, few adapters of Shakespeare to the movie medium have been prepared to experiment very radically with it in their works of 'translation'. They well understand the British film director Alex Cox's observation that 'ambiguity is great, but in the cinema it's almost *verboten*'. Yet non- or anti-realist film techniques have been used from the earliest days to put across significant aspects of some Shakespeare films: trick photographic effects to make delightful magic in the silent

1908 *Tempest*, for instance; a darker magic evoked by the fantastic sets and romantic choreography of Reinhardt and Dieterle's *Dream*. Critics preoccupied with stressing the 'patriotic propagandist' elements of Olivier's *Henry V* are perhaps inclined to miss his use of cinematic devices and settings to accentuate this play's own exploration of drama as artifice; all of Olivier's films in fact subtly avoid using straightforwardly realistic forms of representation. Welles's approach to screening Shakespeare exemplifies the filmic mode at its most experimental – perhaps one would expect no less from the maker of *Citizen Kane*. *Othello* is the film where his manipulation of a range of film techniques is at its most pronounced, most 'Wellesian'. Skewed camera angles, **deep focus**, **dissolve**s, powerfully graphic compositions, long **tracking shot**s, surrealistic reflections – all serve to pictorialize the unstable and claustrophobic world of destructive emotions and behaviours set in motion by devilish Iago. Welles's enthusiasm for creating a multiplicity of stunningly lit architectural shots or adventurous **tilt-shot** portraits, when delivered in quick succession (as they often are), can sometimes fragment the **montage**, diluting the dramatic effect aimed at, by aesthetic excess. Yet his mastery of filmic techniques and effects also enables Welles to translate much of Shakespeare's poetic text on to film in memorably filmic ways: the early shot of Iago trapped in a cage swinging high up against the Cyprus fortress walls; an **image system** of iron bars or barred verticals that, together with repeated images of stony vaults or high walls, conveys with emphatic visual power the forces of entrapment that relentlessly develop in the play text.

The aims of Kurosawa, Kozintsev and Brook in their adaptations are also to 'make visible' the poetic atmosphere of each of the Shakespeare tragedies they film for the screen, investing what is photographed with *metaphoric*, rather than realistic value, thus multiplying meanings and effects. Kurosawa's *Kumonosu-Jô* makes no attempt to verbalize Shakespeare's original text of *Macbeth*, but instead shifts the essential structure, themes and characters of his play to a Japanese medieval setting, creating a highly filmic version of the play that is rich in visual metaphor. Its mysterious forest scenes, its fort settings, its use of wood as an elemental **motif**, its use of Noh drama methods for the ritually stylized performances, all contribute in conveying powerful dramatic meanings through cleverly wrought cinematic imageries. The elemental forces and textures of nature are self-consciously deployed by Kozintsev in his *Hamlet* and *King Lear* as metaphors for the various powerful forces, situations or qualities that condition and animate the characters of each play. For *Hamlet*, Kozintsev explains the visual codings:

Stone: the walls of Elsinore, the firmly built government prison

Iron: weapons, the inhuman forces of oppression, the ugly steel faces of war

Fire: anxiety, revolt, movement; raging fiery tongues

Sea: waves, crashing against the bastions, ceaseless movement, the change of the tides, the boiling of chaos ... the silent endless surface of glass

Earth: the world beyond Elsinore, amid stones – a bit of field tilled by a ploughman, the sand pouring out of Yorick's skull, and the handful of dust in the palm of the wanderer-heir to the throne of Denmark.

(Kozintsev, 1967, 266)

The stylistic and pictorial values of Brook's fine *King Lear* movie are also informed by a focus on nature, for as Brook sees it, 'One real element that emerges from the plot is the notion of nature as something hostile, against which man has to battle.' As he says, the play revolves around the storm, but since from a psychological point of view what counts is 'the contrast between the safe, enclosed spaces and the wild, unprotected places', this logically led to 'two denominators of security: fire and fur'. The movie was therefore shot in the appropriately inhospitable location of North Jutland, Denmark, in the winter, the brilliant playing of this adaptation's focus on the drama's essential themes of power and powerlessness being informed and shaped by the material conditions of life in a cold, primitive setting. Brook's manipulation of the ***mise-en-scène*** is metaphoric almost at every turn because of his focus on 'who has the fire and the fur, and who hasn't'. He takes his filmic approach even further when stressing the other key themes of the play – blindness and insight – manipulating the camera lens to give us Lear's blurred, black and sometimes blank subjective viewpoint in the turbulent scenes of his madness in the storm. This is a bleak film, bleakly executed in an attempt to evolve what Brook calls 'an impressionistic movie technique, cutting language and incident to the bone, so that the total effect of all things heard and seen could capture in different terms Shakespeare's rough, uneven, jagged and disconcerting vision' (Brook, 1987, 204, 206). This is a Shakespeare adaptation of great filmic power. Yet because its power derives from a densely concentrated use of the filmic mode, it may not be assimilated so easily by those accustomed to the less demanding methods of the realistic mode.

It is probably the onset of the more 'commercially populist' Shakespeare film genre revival of the 1990s so favouring a Hollywood-style realistic mode, which explains the reluctance of filmmakers to adopt the more 'poetic' approaches of the filmic mode, appealing as these traditionally have been to the less commercial and thus smaller **arthouse** audiences. Michael Almereyda's *Hamlet* is an exception in this trend, as his film, coming 30 years after Brook's *King Lear*, can easily be seen as employing 'an impressionistic movie technique, cutting language and incident to the bone'. The camerawork and frame imagery of Almereyda's movie uses surfaces in the ***mise-en-scène*** in a way that recalls the metaphoric imagery of Welles's adaptations, impressionistically 'showing' far more than 'telling' us about the dilemmas of a young, disenchanted Hamlet and a lonely Ophelia as they struggle to make sense of the slick, manipulative business world of AD 2000 Manhattan.

In the case of Julie Taymor's *Titus*, the movie is so eclectic as to be drawing on the 'widest mixture of film and acting styles' in the history of Shakespeare on film (according to Crowl). In doing so various elements of her movie frequently convey themselves with meanings and effects that communicate in an essentially filmic mode. As well as including the remarkable dream sequences she calls 'Penny Arcade Nightmares' in 'dreamlike and mythic' counterpoint to the realistic events of her film narrative, Taymor can also create what may be thought of as filmic epiphanies of great power. Such an epiphany comes with the pivotal crossroads scene (3.1) when the camera shows the Andronici family members, ruined and sunk to their lowest moral ebb, gazing together at their images in a puddle. As Titus (Anthony Hopkins) quietly enjoins them to 'Plot some device of further misery, / To make us wondered at in time to come', rain begins to fall, blurring the watery reflections we gaze upon; until, in an inspired visual transformation the image **dissolves** to that of the saintlike face of young Lucius, staring out at the rain from a window, the transformation somehow suggesting that a resurrection of the family fortunes may be possible. It is the 'somehow' of such effects which the filmic mode can use to captivate our imaginations, offering moments of poetic intensity that are as moving as the effects created in fine stage performances of Shakespeare's poetic drama.

4

The Periodizing Mode

The primary feature of the *periodizing* mode is that it takes the story and characters of a Shakespeare play and transports them wholesale into the cultural trappings and social dynamic of a distinctly recognizable historical period. An approach familiar in stage productions for many years, this mode only really took off in film adaptations as the Shakespeare film revival of the 1990s got under way. Directors of 'updating' theatre productions had long employed special costuming, sets, **props**, lighting and sound effects to 'periodize' them into evocative cultural or political settings aimed at making the drama more alive and relevant to a modern popular audience. Such productions frequently used these techniques to evoke and critically allude to the way people are manipulated and put under pressure in the cultures of modern political regimes or business empires; the modern analogues, as modern directors might see it, of the machiavellian structures of courtly and mercantile power prevailing in Shakespeare's time. In *Hamlet* the prince instructs Polonius to see that the visiting players 'be well used', warning him that 'After your / death, you were better have a bad epitaph than their ill / report while you live' (2.2.503–6). Many of us will take Hamlet's stern words to Polonius as suggestive of the cultural, social and political values that the public theatre had for Shakespeare himself. If these players (among whose number he would include himself) really 'are the abstracts and brief chronicles of the time' (2.2.504), might there not even be an *obligation* on those who present his dramas to the public to make them as *relevant* as possible to 'the time' in which we ourselves happen to be living?

The answer to this must of course be a resounding 'yes'. But the historical transposition used must communicate as effectively with the audience as Shakespeare's language should. Within the transposed settings of the periodizing mode for the big screen, there is scope for using both realistic and filmic modes, as can be seen in those Shakespeare adaptations embracing it thus far. Taymor's *Titus* is an interesting experiment in filming *Titus Andronicus* across a variety of period settings, dominantly those of ancient Rome and 1930s Italy. Here I consider five movies that stand out as attempts to convey Shakespeare plays wholesale through the cultural optic and social dynamic of a distinct historical period. These are Christine Edzard's *As You Like It* (1992), Richard Loncraine's *Richard III* (1995), Baz Luhrmann's *William Shakespeare's Romeo + Juliet* (1996), Michael Almereyda's *Hamlet* (2000) and Ralph Fiennes's *Coriolanus* (2011).

Periodized settings can create problems, as shown by **Christine Edzard's *As You Like It* (1992)**. The original comedy draws on the pastoral tradition to set up competing value systems of court and country, creating opportunities for the 'outlaw' forest exiles to satirize the world of corrupt courtly values. Edzard opens her film with one of these exiles, Jaques (Edward Fox), giving his 'Seven Ages of Man' speech ('All the world's a stage ...') as a way of quickly engaging the film audience, this being the one speech they may recognize. Familiar as it may be, the cynical and world-weary perspective of Jaques is not necessarily the most inviting or dramatic introduction to this subtle Shakespearean festive comedy. Yet it does ease us into Edzard's modern urban setting, where rebellious and disenchanted Orlando and banished Rosalind desert the grand edifice of a large London corporate enterprise ('the court') for a riverside wasteland where the already banished Duke Senior and his followers scratch a living like down-and-outs on the bleak and rubbish-strewn foreshore ('the forest'). It quickly becomes clear that this modern period setting is being used to show how capitalist economics creates a deprived underclass. But it is hard to see how those unfamiliar with the play could 'match the heightened speech of the text to the naturalistic décor', as Michael Hattaway puts it (2000, 95). All too often, the gap between Shakespeare's text and the created film setting is unbridgeable. This is especially noticeable when words or phrases are heard that make no sense in such a setting – witness references to killing venison, or Corin's claim that 'good pasture makes fat sheep' (a jumbo jet is heard passing close overhead as he speaks). Elsewhere, I have referred to the fact that most Shakespearean comedies thrive on the presence of a live theatrical audience (Introductory note to Comedies, Part IV). In this play too, there are many lines which ache for direct audience response to bring the comedy alive, as with Touchstone's semi-aside to Audrey during his 'wooing' of her: 'Sluttishness may come hereafter' (3.3.32–3), a line inevitably falling flat for a film audience who merely 'overhear' it.

If there is a mismatch in Edzard's adaptation between Shakespearean text and setting, the other four films fare better in integrating the language of their scripts into their periodized settings. *Hamlet, Romeo + Juliet, Richard III* and *Coriolanus* all have strongly defined, exciting plots, memorable leading characters and the suggestion of culturally convincing settings, these features together offering the potential for an engaging **identification** between character and viewer shot in a realistic situation. With **Michael Almereyda's** *Hamlet* **(2000)** the text of the play – much cut – has been integrated successfully into the periodized postmodern Manhattan location. It succeeds largely because of the strong congruence between the power structures of the Denmark Corporation represented and the machiavellian structures of courtly and mercantile power prevailing in Shakespeare's time. This is not to say that certain elements of the translation of the action from 1600 English Renaissance court to 2000 New York City business culture do not produce occasional oddities. The duel scene with rapiers between Hamlet and Laertes held on a balcony of Denmark Corp's headquarters in the Elsinore Hotel high up among the vertiginous heights of the Manhattan skyline might to some seem a little out of key with what has gone before.

Baz Luhrmann's *Romeo + Juliet* **(1996)** also targets a young movie audience. But instead of Almereyda's sophisticated camerawork and use of reflective surfaces to convey meaning, Luhrmann's phenomenal commercial success with a youth demographic emerges from a rather different approach. The periodized socio-cultural setting he constructs is designed so that the audience can be grippingly engaged by the many flashy, loud and sophisticated elements of popular culture used to convey the play's story. At the same time, the integration of its leading characters into this cultural texture enables them to **identify** with such characters. Partly shot on location in Mexico City, the film's constructed locations also suggest contemporary (mid-1990s) cityscapes of southern US states like Los Angeles or Miami. Brilliantly capturing the macho posturing of the feud at the heart of the play, the story of the trigger-happy rival 'Anglo' Montague and 'Latino' Capulet youth gangs offers a seductively exciting and violent context for the audience. Luhrmann's movie communicates with its sophisticated street-savvy Generation X audience best when it puts the tragic story (as opposed to text) of Shakespeare's play across using a brash MTV visual style and soundtrack. This is a dimension of 'periodizing' style that teenage audiences can empathize with. When the action is visually extended by dressing it with the types of designer clothes, cars, film references and witty allusions to the world of advertising they encounter in their everyday lives, this delivers a cinematically convincing and richly satisfying semiotic.

Richard Loncraine's *Richard III* (1995) is the only one of the periodizing films considered here to have been based on a (highly successful) stage production. Designed to convey the action of the play in a 1930s British political setting, Richard Eyre's production had already projected Richard, Duke of Gloucester (Ian McKellen) as a political opportunist who murders his way to the throne using the fearfully ruthless techniques of the totalitarian tyrant. His private army were seen (after 3.4) dressed in Blackshirt uniforms, the whole design of his dictatorship becoming increasingly tricked out with Nazi-like displays. Skilfully building on the 30 per cent of Shakespeare's lines that McKellen had retained for the draft screenplay, Loncraine's film takes the décor and design process much further, evoking the fascistic style of Richard's fear regime with far more elaborate visual detail than was evident in the stage production. Yet it is not only that almost every detail of the film's *mise-en-scène* makes the period setting realistic and believable. Compared with other periodizing adaptations, many of the elements that help re-create an 'authentic 1930s look' here have the deeper and more vital function of informing character identity and story development. McKellen has explained how important it is for a cinema audience to be able 'to recognize who is royalty, aristocrat, commoner and who is politician, civil servant, military', among such a multitude of characters. 'By their clothes', he states, 'you shall know them' (McKellen, 1996, 12). This repeats a formula applying not only to a re-creation of 1930s Britain, but which resonated even more for Shakespeare's period, when the lives of those playing and watching stage dramas in Elizabethan, Stuart and Caroline England were regulated by rigid social distinctions that included matters of dress. Comparing some of the changes made between stage and screen versions reveals the importance Loncraine and McKellen attached to the different ways a film needs to communicate with world cinema

Illustration 2   **Richard Loncraine's *Richard III* (1995)**: Ian McKellen as Richard III, ruthless military dictator, with his batman Sergeant Ratcliffe in attendance. Their black Nazi-like uniforms are but one part of the film's periodizing of the play to the 1930s, a decade of European tyrannies when a dictatorship like Richard III's might have overtaken Britain as it had Germany, Italy, Spain and the Soviet Union empire. Far from creating a '1930s look' for its own sake, the movie's meticulously periodized settings and décor inform character identity and clarify story development in remarkably persuasive ways.

audiences, as opposed to theatregoing audiences of Europe or the USA. Here it must suffice to focus on two changes.

In the stage version of what was turned into a banquet scene (1.3), not only were Elizabeth's sons Dorset and Gray and her brother Lord Rivers present, but so was old Queen Margaret, dominating the action so much that this took the focus off Richard for much of the time. (Generally speaking, as was discussed in Part II, it is important for film audiences to be able to focus on and identify with the progress of a single protagonist.) Not only this, but since Rivers and the others also partly *supported* Richard in expressing his animus against Margaret, there is little doubt that a cinema audience find difficulty in following the lines of dramatic action and interaction of this scene, among so many players. In the film, not only is Margaret omitted, but so are Dorset and Gray, leaving only Elizabeth and her brother Rivers to 'represent' the Woodville faction. Since Lady Anne, Richard's new 'conquest' from the Lancastrian regime he has defeated, is also introduced at his side, the opposition between Yorkist and Woodville factions now becomes very apparent to us. This factional opposition is made even more noticeably emphatic for a cinema audience by having Queen Elizabeth and Rivers played by American actors whose accents and social behaviour identify them as commoner 'arrivistes' in the court, as compared with the marked aristocratic drawl and distantly cool behaviour of Richard and his traditionally English Yorkist followers. A further notable change between stage and film relates to the character of Richard himself. When Richard rows with his mother the Duchess of York in the stage version (4.4), he reveals no sense of vulnerability to her insults and curses. In the film, Richard is visibly shaken by his mother's attack, providing evidence of a character coded differently for a film audience.

Ralph Fiennes's *Coriolanus* **(2011)** takes the periodizing approach to a new level of immediacy. Not only do the location settings and cultural paraphernalia of the period in which the adaptation is 'dressed' completely fit the dramatization, but Fiennes conveys the drama in a setting that realistically conveys the kinds of political, civil and military conflicts being endured in many war-torn regions of the world today. Like *Richard III*, it deals with political power and its manipulation. But *Coriolanus* is the first 'postmodern' Shakespeare play adaptation to the screen that dares to tangle with the relatively recent very violent political, ethnic and military struggles of south-east Central Europe in the 1990s to early 2000s. Serbia and Montenegro, political states newly independent of totalitarian communist regimes, and still working through the political turmoil of creating an equitable system of governance, offer an astonishingly vivid modern parallel to the period in which Shakespeare's play was set, at the very beginning of the Roman republic in the early fifth century BC. This was when Lucius Junius had driven out the corrupt monarchy of King Tarquin, replacing it with a new form of republican government led by a senate composed of patricians (aristocrats). For military and civic matters requiring executive authority, the senate appointed consuls for short terms. However, this system soon proved inadequate, with the large plebeian order (of workers) agitating for a say in the city's rule. This is the situation we are confronted with in the first scene of *Coriolanus*, where a rebellious populace complains to the authorities of hunger (a situation only too familiar to the English people of Shakespeare's time), led by the two manipulative tribunes, Junius Brutus and Sicinius.

   As he developed the film, Fiennes saw how well his political thriller uncannily paralleled the aftermath of the political and military conflicts which had devastated the post-communist states of south-east Central Europe throughout the 1990s. He tells how he would read 'the newspaper and constantly see variations of events that happen in the story that felt like they came from our film. That's one reason it was important that the film look like today's world, not some indeterminate time period. So, the suits, electronics, cars – they're what we see in our everyday lives. But our "Rome" is not Rome, Italy. Just as the events that happen in *Coriolanus* could happen anywhere, our Rome could be just about any city in the world' (Logan, 117). The need for a certain kind of contemporary look resulted in most of the filming being done on location in historically battle-scarred sites of Serbia and Montenegro. This made for a movie revealing itself as one that deploys the periodizing mode in the most immediately modern way possible.

   In political regimes suffering radical social division and conflict, military rule has frequently been employed to maintain social order, as was witnessed in the new state of Israel almost from the beginning, in Northern Ireland from the 1970s, and especially in the satellite states of the Soviet Union, following its collapse after 1989. Ralph Fiennes points out how, seeking strong political leaders, such states frequently turn towards prominent ex-military figures 'who are so unwavering and potent in their determination' that they 'can be very attractive to an electorate'. As player of the uncompromising Coriolanus, Fiennes mentions how he had in his 'image book' the ex-military general turned prime minister of Israel Ariel Sharon and the ex-KGB leader of Russia since 2000 Vladimir Putin, figures who have been both admired and feared. Such figures can 'also be extremely dangerous' says Fiennes: 'Coriolanus sits right at the nerve center of this ambivalence' (Logan, 118).

5

Film Genre: Conventions and Codes

How do we choose which movie to see in theatrical release at the cinema, by rental, online streaming, or on DVD/Blu-ray disc at home? With a worldwide movie industry fiercely competing for the attention and money of filmgoers requiring various kinds of entertainment, this is a question filmmakers have always had to consider from the outset. They need to provide films that entertain, but which also make money, moviemaking being an expensive business. From the first commercial cinema screenings, the process of choosing has been made easier for viewers through films being conceived, made, marketed and consumed according to type or *genre*. Some people may be dismissive of 'genre films' because the less imaginative products can seem formulaic and predictable. Yet the world of film cannot do without generic categories, since most of us have specific preferences: action pictures, romantic comedies, horror movies, musicals, gangster or sci-fi thrillers, 'European' or 'foreign' movies – or even maybe Shakespeare adaptations. Furthermore, as the fiction entertainment film grows in popularity, it can be increasingly difficult to make choices, since movies increasingly mix one genre with another. This makes film genres – such as the 'thriller' – harder and harder to contain or define in a single category. The thriller has changed in style a good deal over the years, and can embrace elements taken from horror, erotic, detective, political, gangster (or other) film genres, creating the need for more and more mixed-genre labels so that 'film product' can be identified and marketed successfully.

This situation is not new, as Shakespeare himself wittily illustrated around 1600, when he parodied the classifications of contemporary dramatic theorists by having Polonius in *Hamlet* refer to plays of 'tragedy, comedy, history, pastoral, pastoral-comical, historical-pasto-ral,tragical-historical,tragical-comical-historical-pastoral'(2.2.379–81). In fact, Shakespeare exemplifies the case of a dramatist who frequently wrote mixed-genre drama, creating and mingling together in the same play sophisticated and low-life characters, juxtaposing serious themes and episodes with comic ones. Numerous instances of such juxtaposi-tion exist in many of his plays, one of the most famous being the gravediggers' scene in *Hamlet*, where dark comedy sits cheek by jowl with tragedy. At times he troublingly embodies in one character the capacity for being humorous and violent, as with his earliest stage hero, Richard III. One very good reason why Shakespeare repeatedly produced plays in this generically mixed style was a commercial one. More money could be made at Theatre, Globe and Blackfriars play-houses (where he was resident playwright) if a play appealed to the widest possible paying audience, an audience ranging from university-trained wits and the professional orders, to tradespeople and labour-ers. Whoever they might be, it was also important for the audience to know what kind of play they could look forward to seeing, should they decide to attend a performance one afternoon: whether they could expect to laugh, to cry, or to reflect. This is why Shakespeare did not call his essentially serious and questioning play *Hamlet*, but rather *The Tragicall Historie of Hamlet, Prince of Denmarke* (1603), and why he provided titles like *Much adoe about Nothing* (1600) to let playgoers know this was to be a comedy.

Playbills pinned up giving suitable titles and descriptions that adver-tise the play would have set up a psychological and emotional expecta-tion – a *genre* expectation – that the audience then looked to have satisfied by the performance itself. This is what the jargon of market-ing nowadays calls 'positioning the audience'. It is a process commonly seen at work in the advertising and marketing campaigns on billboards, TV, internet and movie-theatre trailers for numerous large-budget Hollywood movies. What makes one film succeed more than another will of course depend on many factors, not the least of which are the ways in which the audience are persuaded to continue watching, entranced and entertained, for the two hours or so that they sit gazing at the large or small screen. Part of how they become engaged by the film may well be determined by the way their *genre expectations* are fulfilled, and the extent to which the demands behind what has been called 'the contract between filmmaker and audience, the promise of something new based on something familiar', are met (Bordwell and Thompson, 2013, 338). The elements that provide this 'something new based on something familiar' apply to most popular narrative fiction entertainment films that are written, marketed and watched around the world, and almost always sponsored by the major film distributors. These elements are usually called *genre conventions* – sometimes *film codes*. Surprising though it may seem, for most Shakespeare on film-makers who have wanted to attract and to connect with a larger movie audience, such genre conventions have also been woven into their adaptations.

6

Genre Conventions and the Shakespeare Film Adaptation

To see how all this may apply to Shakespeare adaptations on film, we first need to explore what genre conventions consist of, the areas where films resemble each other in certain ways, given that filmmakers, audiences and reviewers do share a kind of community of expectation concerning the distinct film genre identities that have developed and which prevail in the world of film. Film genre conventions may be considered under four main headings: ***Plot elements, Themes, Film techniques*** and ***Iconography***. By recognizing the conventions that give a film genre its identity, a viewer is provided with a pathway into that genre, an approximate guide to what to expect in approaching and 'reading' the film. Makers of the most popular, 'mainstream' Shakespeare film adaptations have certainly attended to the need to communicate effectively with a popular cinema audience, manipulating genre conventions in order to grab the attention of the viewer, and having engaged it, working to sustain that attention. After briefly exploring what the major genre conventions are, I illustrate below in each case how some Shakespeare adaptations have deployed these film codes.

Plot elements

We expect certain plot elements to shape films in the various genres. *Westerns* often embody a revenge plot, and frequently involve family conflicts/vendettas or the competition over land or livelihood. (As a 'pure' genre, the Western has now all but disappeared, yet was extraordinarily popular during most of the twentieth century up to the 1980s.) In a *detective* or *mystery* film, we expect some kind of systematic and progressive investigation to take place. *Gangster* film plots often focus on the rise and fall of a central gangster figure struggling against rival gangs and the law. *Musicals* will manipulate plot to provide situations allowing the actors to sing or dance. *War films* tend to focus on the fortunes of a heroic individual courageously facing the dangers of combat, and emerging a battered survivor who has lost one or more close friends or 'buddies' along the way. The plots of *action* films are like those of war films, but instead of a war between nations, the ingenious and usually strong hero is an 'outsider' or 'vigilante' figure pitting his wits against an evil gang or organization intent on some form of large-scale domination. The *epic film* is a movie in which the plot is often vast, meandering, and peopled by a large cast, many of whom may be famous actors playing 'cameo' parts: the issues at stake in the plot are usually large-scale, as are the settings, pacing and scope of the movie, often shot in a widescreen format.

Quite obviously, the plot elements contained in any Shakespeare play pre-exist in the play text coming down to us. Filmmakers adapting a play for the screen may choose to cut or restructure parts of that text to make the movie more accessible to the audience. But if the translation to film is to be a *Shakespearean* adaptation of the play and not something else, then the film must carry the plot elements that the lines of the original Shakespearean text invariably produce. This does not mean to say that such 'fixed' plot elements cannot be *conveyed* in ways that may draw on modern genre conventions to increase audience accessibility, appeal and involvement. As we have already seen in 'The Periodizing Mode', Loncraine's *Richard III* uses a 1930s British cultural setting to deliver Shakespeare's play on screen. Yet the manner in which that film's plot is conveyed is also indebted in many ways to those of the classic 1930s gangster movies, Richard's powermongering career drawing on the rise-and-fall pattern of the ruthless and bullying gangster-type. For Kenneth Branagh, the plot of *Love's Labour's Lost* seemed to fit so well with the style and mood of 1930s Hollywood musicals that his film of the play cuts much of Shakespeare's linguistic wit, substituting romantic love-song 'standards' instead, almost turning a Shakespeare film into a 1930s Hollywood musical movie.

So alert was Laurence Olivier to the importance of incorporating film codes into *Henry V* to communicate effectively with the popular film audience that he drew on Western and Robin Hood film conventions of the period. In doing so he created the first really successful Shakespeare play adaptation in English on film. The simplified characterization Olivier achieved by extensive cutting of the play text was further enhanced for a wartime audience primed for the consumption of patriotic sentiment, by his 'setting up' the invasion of France in the film along the lines of a Western 'revenge' plot. The Dauphin's gift of tennis balls to Henry is designed to come across to us (and his boisterously loyal 'ready-made' on-screen Globe audience) as an insult to 'Englishmen'. This must surely be avenged – we feel – and it will be. In the outdoor scenes involving horsemanship skills (Olivier mounts and rides like a cowboy) and in the battle of Agincourt, all the Western genre conventions come into play for a screen audience already 'trained' to read them through a regular diet of consuming Western movies at the cinema. A clear sense of the moral superiority of the English is thus solidly established, while the French are conveyed as the 'baddies' (rather than the usual 'Injuns'). The riders on horseback also echo the positive association between man and nature so well established in Westerns. In turn, **wide** and **long shot**s connected by **tracking shot**s and camera **pan**s, together with the parallel **montage** sequences of the approaching armies (in Westerns it is usually US Cavalry vs The Indians), all convey the atmosphere, setting and sense of limitless space of the Western.

Branagh's 1989 *Henry V* also incorporated tried and tested genre conventions, but this time the film codes he drew on were from 1980s Vietnam War movies. Where Olivier draws on the ethos of the Western hero and the frontier-range war for his audience, Branagh adapts Oliver Stone's and Stanley Kubrick's **subjective camera** techniques (from Vietnam movies *Platoon* (1986) and *Full Metal Jacket* (1987)) to convey the more personal and painful elements of war. The idealization of male bonding, the *aestheticization of violence*, immersing the viewer in the often complex emotions affecting individuals and their frequently strained relations with one another, are all expressed by way of long and detailed camera **close-up**s. Branagh even deploys Western genre conventions in adapting a Shakespearean comedy for the screen, the arrival of Don Pedro and his comrades on their return from the wars near the opening of his 1993 adaptation of *Much Ado About Nothing* being played with (as Branagh says) 'a nod to *The Magnificent Seven*', John Sturges's popular 1960 Western movie.

Branagh's 1996 *Hamlet* bears many of the features of the film epic. The text used is the fullest available, from the Folio edition, and this is supplemented by lines from the shorter Q2 *Hamlet*, so that the movie, shot on 'epic gauge' 70mm film, runs to four hours with an intermission. Like many of its predecessors with life and death themes, shot on a large canvas with exotic costumes (*Spartacus, Dr Zhivago, Lawrence of Arabia*, etc.), the film takes us through every detail of the play's large variety of incidents and scenes, creating a sweeping, epic arc of plot at a pace measured out by a score of symphonic dimensions, shot variously in the magnificent opulence of Blenheim Palace or on enormous sound stages. The end of the first part just before the intermission has Branagh's Hamlet speaking the 'How all occasions do inform against me' soliloquy as an isolated figure standing alone on a vast frozen plateau, just about to be taken to England. The large cast includes many 'cameo' appearances from famous American actors like Jack Lemmon, Charlton Heston (himself a veteran of film epics), Billy Crystal and Robin Williams, whose presence give the film scale, as does the massive commando-style invasion of Elsinore by Fortinbras, his forces toppling the great statue of Old Hamlet, bringing one cycle of Denmark's history to a close.

Themes

Some genre conventions can be *themes* that are produced repeatedly in films to convey broader meanings. Loyalty to one's comrades, often involving immense sacrifice, danger or death in the service of an ideal, is a recurring theme in *war films*. A common theme of *gangster films* is the price to be paid for criminal success, the gangster becoming self-obsessed and cruel in his rise to power, typically enjoyed only briefly before an aloof isolation and neurotic instability ensure his demise. What used to be called the 'battle of the sexes' can be a thematic staple of so-called *screwball* and *romantic comedies*. Here, the male and female leads are typically in conflict with each other – and also perhaps with a socially constraining milieu – for most of the movie, before a final reconciliation takes place. *Mystery* or *detective films*, especially those tending towards the '*noir*ish', may, with their meandering and labyrinthine plots, involve the theme of the hero-investigator's sanity or mental strength being tested in the face of those hostile to or unsympathetic with the aims of the investigation.

The status of 'theme' as a potential genre convention to be drawn on in the Shakespeare adaptation is similar to that of 'plot element', since the themes in a Shakespeare play are often those produced by the pre-existing play text. It is no surprise to learn that the plots of Shakespeare plays which tend to appeal most to audiences will also generate the themes of greatest audience appeal. Much of the success of Branagh's

Henry V was due to the way it delivered its themes of loyalty-testing among an army warring on foreign soil, and how a leader against all the odds could inspire his men to follow him in adversity and yet still succeed.

The ability of Loncraine and McKellen to manipulate the already resonant theme of ruthless Elizabethan machiavellianism in *Richard III* into a form that parallels almost exactly the rise-and-fall themes of the classic gangster film is an achievement of great filmic skill. One thematic convention of this genre is for the gangster anti-hero to feel excluded from society, his writhing resentment and humiliation often stemming from low or shameful birth. In two famous American gangster films, this feeling of being set apart is caused by a physical problem, Paul Muni being disfigured in *Scarface* (1932) and James Cagney suffering from a mental illness in *White Heat* (1949). Similarly, in Loncraine's movie, feeling socially excluded because of his crooked body, Richard is also obsessed by a mother who has rejected him from birth. This lack of maternal affection was the primary motivation for his resentment-driven ruthless climb to power, rather than any political, racial or military drive, despite the film's overt storyline of the rise and fall of a British fascist-like dictator. Coming from the world of TV ads and commercial films, Loncraine was quite at home drawing on a range of genres, from the slasher movie to the 'English heritage' film, and also in deploying the kind of fast **editing**, upbeat period music and visually stylish design that would appeal to a popular audience.

The 'battle of the sexes' theme, so beloved of screwball and romantic comedies, has been exploited in at least three Shakespeare film adaptations: Zeffirelli's *The Taming of the Shrew* (1966) and the *Much Ado About Nothing* movies by Branagh (1993) and by Joss Whedon (2013). Contemporary screen icons Richard Burton and Elizabeth Taylor (see **Iconography** later) were celebrated in real life for their love–hate marriage, and this fed easily into the play's theme of reluctant bride pursued by penniless gold-digger, Taylor's ferocious temper and Burton's swaggering nonchalance providing the kind of overblown romantic convention that popular audiences craved. The lively, real-life and highly public relationship of Kenneth Branagh and Emma Thompson in the 1990s was ready-made to animate the skirmishing antics of Beatrice and Benedick in Branagh's *Much Ado*. Amy Acker and Alexis Denisof were character actors so well known to TV viewers of Joss Whedon's hit TV series *Buffy the Vampire Slayer* and *Angel* that his casting of them as Beatrice and Benedick in this most recent adaptation of *Much Ado* was an inspired choice. The outcome brings to fans of screwball and 'rom-com' in its latest Shakespearean manifestation on film the most entertaining performances of this play to date.

Film techniques

Film techniques are sometimes associated with specific genre conventions. Lighting that creates sombreness and shadows is characteristic of mystery films – especially **film noir** – of thrillers and (most decidedly) of horror films. The increasingly powerful lighting technology of the 1940s that made **chiaroscuro** techniques and low-key illumination so helpful in creating the mysterious atmosphere of many melodramas of the 1940s and 1950s also made the cinematographer's technique of **deep focus** a major stylistic option throughout the same period. This technique (also facilitated by faster film and shorter-focal-length lenses) can create a number of effects from the watcher's point of view. By maintaining both near and distant figures and settings in sharp focus, the camera forces the observer to scan the whole of the frame, encouraging us to consider the *relationship* between a near and a more distant figure, rather than just one of them. On the other hand, this refusal to focus on the significance and actions of a single human figure or event can also have the effect of 'dehumanizing' the scene in front of us by 'objectifying' (making an object of) all that we see, an effect that is also potentially destabilizing and disturbing for the viewer. By seeming to shift the power for effective human agency away from any single protagonist, we can see how the **deep-focus** technique might appeal to filmmakers interested in creating a powerful non-human presence, of a threatening or mysteriously alien nature. This is perhaps why deep-focus photography was revived in Steven Spielberg's 1970s films, particularly *Jaws* and *Close Encounters of the Third Kind*.

The **chiaroscuro** lighting so characteristic of Expressionist-influenced *films noirs* and melodramatic thrillers of the 1940s was used extensively in Olivier's *Hamlet* and also by Welles in his *Macbeth*, both films being released in 1948. For the story of a man who 'could not make up his mind' (Olivier's view, expressed by him in **voice-over** at the film's beginning), the shadowy passageways of Elsinore created by chiaroscuro effects provided a sombre, haunted look entirely fitting for a Hamlet suffering mental torment and indecision. The guilty unease distinguishing the afflicted mind of Welles's usurping Macbeth is a characterization also given emphasis by this director's use of light and shadow. Just as Olivier's lighting of a labyrinthine Elsinore images the anxious workings of Hamlet's brain, so does the sinisterly lit setting that Welles creates for Macbeth's castle, its dim, dark and dripping cavernous passages functioning as a kind of visual **metonymy** for the 'scorpion-filled' intellect of Macbeth. **Deep-focus** photography is used extensively by Olivier in *Hamlet* to suggest both the alienation of the Prince in relation to others (especially to Ophelia) and the way all in Elsinore seem to be at the mercy of large, impersonal forces (the world of the Ghost). Similarly, in a number of the scenes shot for *Macbeth*, Welles uses deep-focus photography to indicate the controlling, mysterious supernatural forces of the witches.

The battle scenes of both Olivier's and Branagh's versions of *Henry V* use rapid **cutting** techniques in order to convey the atmosphere of violent excitement experienced in battle. The famously powerful ten-minute battle sequence of Welles's *Chimes at Midnight* (the battle at Shrewsbury) is often made more effective through the use of speeded-up shots. These capture in a grimly unsentimental way the suddenness of death in battle; while slowed-down shooting shows the weary ignominy of exhausted men flailing grimly at each other in a muddy waste of death.

Iconography

A film genre can often be identified by the repeated use of visual elements signifying or symbolizing meaning in a conventionally iconographic way. Settings, or the objects in them, can supply iconography for a genre. The setting of a battle-torn landscape, for instance, usually tells us that we are in some kind of war film, while a **long shot** of a stagecoach snaking its way across a wide-open prairie signals our being in an American Western. Machine-guns fired from a sleek, fast-moving black 1920s automobile should be enough to tell us we are watching a gangster movie. A large mansion in semi-darkness or a castle with a labyrinth of sombre, shadowy corridors is often the setting for gothic horror, and silver spaceships sliding through the dark vacuum of star-filled space signify that we are caught up in a science-fiction film. Even film stars can become iconographic: Arnold Schwarzenegger, Mel Gibson or Gerard Butler for the action-adventure film, John Wayne for the Western, Fred Astaire and Ginger Rogers for Hollywood song-and-dance musicals.

It would be difficult to claim that the Shakespeare film genre displays a specific iconography, except that the most traditional and conventional of film adaptations trying for an 'authentic historical look' have created a *mise-en-scène* imitating Elizabethan settings, dressing the actors in Elizabethan costume. Examples of such 'men-in-tights' adaptations are George Cukor's glittering Hollywood *Romeo and Juliet* of 1936, Olivier's *Hamlet* and *Richard III*, and the *Romeo and Juliet* movies of Castellani (1954) and Zeffirelli (1968). Perhaps the most iconographic element of any Shakespeare film adaptation is the frequently bold display of Shakespeare's name itself, given either in or near the main titles: after all, the name 'William Shakespeare' has for so long maintained 'classic' status, synonymous with 'genius', that no filmmaker at work in the 'designer label'-conscious market place is likely to resist attaching the peerless 'Shakespeare' brand to their movie. When it comes to iconographic film stars for the Shakespeare film, there are of course a good number: Laurence Olivier and Orson Welles for an older generation, Kenneth Branagh for a more recent one. All are actors who have made and starred in several of their own Shakespeare adaptations. Yet there are others who also crop up repeatedly in Shakespeare movies for the cinema or TV, and have become iconographic, particularly Judi Dench, Ian McKellen, Helen Mirren and Patrick Stewart. Many famous screen actors have played lead parts in Shakespeare films, but few have done this more than once.

7

A Cross-cultural Shakespeare Adaptation: Kurosawa's *Kumonosu-Jô*

I conclude this part of the book with an analysis of Kurosawa's version of *Macbeth* not only because many admire *Kumonosu-Jô* as a movie that stands brilliantly alone for adapting Shakespeare's play to film without using one word of the original text. As will be seen, it does this by utilizing the most creatively filmic of 'filmic' approaches, drawing on many of the elements of mode, style and genre convention previously discussed. In addition to being a tour de force of cinematic artistry, the film reworks Shakespeare's play so radically in its use of a non-Western society's culture and history that the result is unique in the Shakespeare film genre.

Kumonosu-Jô (The Castle of the Spider's Web) [*Throne of Blood*] (Japan, 1957)

Director: Akira Kurosawa

Adaptation: Akira Kurosawa, Hideo Ognuni, Shinobu Hashimoto, Ryuzo Kikushima

Editing: Akira Kurosawa

Design: Yoshiro Muraki

Production company: Toho

Medium: Black and white, 16mm, 110 minutes

Main actors: Toshiro Mifune (Taketoi Washizu/Macbeth); Isuzu Yamada (Asaji/Lady Macbeth); Minoru Chiaki (Yoshiaki Miki/Banquo); Akira Kobu

(Yoshiteru/Fleance); Takamaru Sasaki (Kuniharu Tsuzuki/Duncan); Yoichi Tachikawa (Kunimaru/Malcolm); Chieko Naniwa (Forest Witch)

Photography: Asaichi Nakai

Music: Masaru Sato

Akira Kurosawa's highly acclaimed Japanese samurai films *Seven Samurai* (1954) and *Yojimbo* (1961) became the basis of successful Westerns, the first being the model for *The Magnificent Seven*, while *A Fistful of Dollars*, Sergio Leone's first 'spaghetti Western', drew loosely on the second for its plot. The samurai film genre conventions of swordplay and revenge translate well in many ways to the Western genre, with its frontier-town stories of bad blood and shoot-outs. But Kurosawa discovered that the genre for which he had attained fame was also the ideal vehicle for dramatizing *The Tragedy of Macbeth* by Shakespeare, as he explains:

> During the period of civil wars in Japan, there are plenty of incidents like those portrayed in *Macbeth*. They are called *ge-koku-jo* [where a supposedly loyal retainer usurps power by murdering his lord]. Therefore the story of Macbeth appealed very much to me, and it was easy for me to adapt it.
>
> (Quoted in Manvell, 1971, 102)

As Thane of Glamis, Macbeth in effect fights as 'warrior retainer' under King Duncan at a time when (in medieval Scotland) warring rival kings and their clans battled for supremacy by force of arms in a social, political and military setting, which does obviously parallel the structure of the samurai warrior society of the Japanese medieval civil wars. So the parallels of history and social power structures are authentic and they resonate for us in Kurosawa's film. Another indispensable element from *Macbeth* that Kurosawa also embeds most effectively into the dramatic dynamic of *Kumonosu-Jô* is the supernaturally evil prophecy, which seizes the imaginations of both Macbeth and Washizu (Kurosawa's Macbeth figure) so obsessively. In the Japanese version no occasion ever occurs for Washizu to dismiss his belief in the witches' prophecies in the way that Macbeth does: 'be these juggling fiends no more believed / That palter [equivocate] with us in a double sense', says Macbeth, just before he and Macduff fight to the death (5.10.19–20). Nevertheless, the notion of each protagonist's belief in witches, who prophesy the succession to a supreme power ordained by what Banquo calls the 'instruments of darkness' (1.3.122), is one that underpins and animates the narrative flow of both tragic dramas.

The famous opening scene of *Macbeth* has three witches chanting magical rhymes, ritual formulae that signal the play themes to come of paradox and ambiguity. But these utterances also establish an important ritualistic framework for the play. As if to demonstrate to us how effective the power of the witchcraft over Macbeth already is, Shakespeare has Macbeth in his very first entrance tell Banquo as they return from battle that 'So foul and fair a day I have not seen' (1.3.36). This echoes the witches' collective chant, 'Fair is foul, and foul is fair, / Hover through the fog and filthy air' (1.1.10–11). In Kurosawa's film, ritualistic elements are introduced from the beginning too, the whole being shaped by various formal conventions and visual images that serve as important signifying functions in translating the play into a different culture and the film medium. The set design and acting style of the film are based on the highly formal Japanese Noh drama which developed over the period of the medieval warring samurai factions. Noh music is drawn on too, the otherworldly sounds of a piercing Noh pipe and hypnotically pounding sticks being played over the opening Japanese titles. The film itself is also formalistically 'framed' at beginning and end by a chorus of deep, droning male voices. As we are shown a bleak and misty landscape containing only a wooden monolith memorializing the site of the once 'mighty fortress' of 'Spiderweb Castle', the sternly chanting chorus tells us (in translation) that this is the story of a 'proud warrior murdered by ambition'. Yet his spirit is 'walking still', for 'what once was so, now still is true'. What could be construed as a ghost story at one level supplies a chilling moral conveyed in the style of a sung epic tale taking us back to earlier times.

As the obscuring mist clears to reveal a mighty fortress, we see a number of frantic messengers reporting to Tsuzuki (Duncan), Lord of Spiderweb Castle, and his council, on the progress of a rebel attack on their forts. The Noh style of playing is evident from the start as the ruling samurai council sit rigidly immobile on a raised platform before a horizontal war screen, all staring intently ahead, only occasionally consulting with each other in short, vehement, barked exchanges. This is the style of playing – where intense emotion and physical stillness coexist – that will characterize the performance of Mifune's Washizu. When Tsuzuki learns that Washizu and Miki (Banquo) have turned the tide of battle against the rebels, he beams, stating that they will be rewarded. The camera cuts to Washizu and Miki making their way towards Spiderweb Castle, only approachable through the Spiderweb Forest, described by one of Tsuzuki's generals as a 'natural labyrinth' that confuses enemies of the prevailing order.

The image of the Spiderweb which Kurosawa applies both to the Forest and to the Castle is the film's central visual metaphor. This is because the Forest is not so much a natural as a *supernatural* labyrinth, a site of mystery and potential threat familiar to anyone attentive to the universal folk-myth warning about the danger of venturing into wooded areas, and captured in the words of the song, 'if you go down to the woods today, you're sure of a big surprise'. Before Washizu and Miki encounter their big surprise in the shape of an evil, androgynous forest spirit, we see them at a bewildered stand on their horses in the Forest amidst a strange mixture of lightning, pouring rain and wide beams of sunlight streaming down through the high canopy of trees. 'What weather!' declares Washizu, 'I have never seen anything like it' – the equivalent of Macbeth's 'So fair and foul a day I have not seen.' The camera then gives us repeated glimpses of both samurai behind a screen of trees and thickets galloping along forest paths in repeated attempts to leave the Forest and reach Spiderweb Castle. Even when it is clear they are lost, they laugh this off by telling each other how Spiderweb Forest makes their enemies lose their way, while they are privileged to know every trail. It is only when Washizu's defiant action of firing an arrow high into the trees creates echoing shrieks of unearthly laughter throughout the Forest that he realizes 'an evil spirit is blocking our way'. Their curiously compulsive response is to charge off furiously along the selfsame trails, Washizu firing arrows wildly, while Miki fiercely brandishes his spear at nothing in particular. This pointless activity is finally halted when they (we, from their **POV**) glimpse ahead a white-stick hut behind a large tree trunk. What the astonished pair see behind the white wooden uprights of the hut after dismounting is a kneeling, white-haired, white-cloaked figure turning a spinning wheel. Its quavering, high–low voice produces a song, warning about the false beliefs that men's minds fabricate when deluded by pride, vanity and ambition. When Washizu finally snaps out of being entranced by the scene, tearing open the door of the fragile, cagelike hut, the witch calmly prophesies that after taking over the North Castle he will become Lord of Spiderweb Castle. We soon become aware that Washizu's ridiculing response masks his ambitions as a samurai warrior. It is only after the witch prophesies that Miki's son will eventually become Lord of Spiderweb Castle that she and her spinning wheel unaccountably fly up and vanish into thin air, proving that she is indeed an evil spirit, and not human.

The set made for shooting this scene and the camera and lighting techniques used in it not only produce the various kinds of image required to make such an otherworldly and magical encounter feel convincing, but they also seem to offer **metacinematic** comments on the nature of filmic perception and space. Jorgens suggests that, like the witch who sits 'like a spider at the centre of a web', spinning her wheel and toying with the vulnerable minds of Washizu and Miki, Kurosawa as filmmaker also 'enmeshes his characters in a formal pattern so rigid that it becomes an aesthetic equivalent of Fate'. The spinning wheels that Jorgens says resemble reels of film at an **editing** desk 'seem to inscribe the circles followed by Washizu and Miki as they ride in circles in the forest, and are caught up in the cycles of war, fear and ambition that give the illusion of movement in this futile form of feudalism' (Jorgens, 1983, 172). The 'illusions of movement' so evidently at the animated core of the cinematic process we typically view are certainly cleverly achieved in this scene, with its flickering light source, the demonstrated insubstantiality of the witch and the hut, made to disappear through trick photography, and the 'screening' effects, used here and elsewhere throughout the film (Donaldson, 1990, 60–91). These all offer perspective and depth, yet ultimately do so only through the flickering images created in front of our eyes by spinning reels of film.

In complete contrast to the spirit-controlled tangles and enmeshments of the Forest that Kurosawa **metonymically** deploys to convey the tangled emotions of Washizu (while also establishing the seeds of the 'inner' narrative), the Noh interiors inhabited by Washizu and Asaji (Lady Macbeth) we soon see at North Castle are neatly geometric. The worlds of the fortresses and castles throughout the film are in fact largely figured in horizontals and verticals, from the opening shots of the war council sitting in a horizontal line, to the last scenes showing Washizu's defeat as he moves ever downwards, floor by floor, in the Spiderweb Forest Castle to final death at the hands of his own men. An affinity with the spatial techniques used by Welles in *Citizen Kane* is shown by Kurosawa's stress on the horizontal, his designer Yoshiro Muraki observing that in order to 'emphasize the psychology of the hero, driven by compulsion, we made the interiors wide with low ceilings and squat pillars to create the effect of oppression' (Richie, 1970, 123). The verticals and horizontals of the man-made forts in effect represent the rigidly hierarchical Japanese feudal order. The contained decorum of this social order is made dramatically emphatic in turn by the Noh choreography and ritual used to play out the scenes when Asaji, using arguments of *Realpolitik*, finally convinces Washizu of the need to kill the Lord of Spiderweb Castle, a sequence concluding at the point where Asaji raises the alarm of 'intruder, murderer!' following the assassination of Tsuzuki.

In Shakespeare's *Macbeth*, Lady Macbeth's speeches in 1.5 align her with the malevolent supernatural realm of the witches. Kurosawa creates a similar alignment by providing strong visual identifications between the Forest Witch and Asaji, especially in the scene where Washizu is persuaded by Asaji to kill his lord, which starts with Washizu uneasily mocking her cynical attitude towards 'loyalty' in much the same way that he had earlier laughingly dismissed the Forest Witch's songs. Asaji's calmly seated posture, her position in the right of the frame, and the boldly lit harsh whiteface make-up aimed at re-creating the look of a Noh mask are all strongly reminiscent of the Forest Witch's presentation. 'I firmly believe in that prediction', says Asaji, commenting that 'the stage is set' for him to make it come true, an apt metaphor given the deployment of compelling Noh-choreographed movement that is to follow. The calling of the crows, which Asaji says is telling him 'the throne is yours', marks Asaji's move from stony immobility to initiative-taking, ritual Noh music accompanying her motions of standing up to literally lead Washizu by the hand into a new physical position, while she explains what must be done to bring about the fulfilment of the prophecy. It is at this point that Washizu becomes startled by the flickering lights of the servants seen passing along behind the *shoji* screen, the camera moving round to frame him and Asaji in front of it. This shot of them in front of an illuminated screen viewing the opaque flickering lights behind seems once again a **metacinematic** device, this time perhaps suggesting a link between the seductive illusions of the cinematic screen world and the mysteries of the supernatural realm. This link is reinforced when Kurosawa has Asaji eerily disappear through a doorway to fetch drugged wine for the guards by using a fade-to-black, fading in her image again on her return with the wine pitcher. This makes her seem like a spirit. She is made to 'disappear' once more when her image **dissolve**s to that of the unconscious guards, sprawled out, legs akimbo, their horizontal line of stability destroyed by the drugged drink. The only sound to be heard after this is that of her swishing kimono as she shuffles purposively along the wooden floors, to the accompaniment of a Noh pipe. In fact, from the moment that Asaji takes the initiative from Washizu, the only significant noise to be heard on the soundtrack is the unsettling Noh sound effect of her swishing kimono as she busily scurries about, performing her otherwise silent, single-minded and deadly business.

We are prepared for the deed to be committed by Washizu by further cinematic techniques of 'showing', rather than 'telling'. While Asaji is busy obtaining the murder weapon from one of the comatose guards, Washizu sits awaiting her return in the bloodstained room earlier 'purified' by his servants. Several times he glances apprehensively towards the bloodstained wall through a rack of vertically stacked arrows, and it is here, in the camera's precise imaging of Washizu against the stain's ugly, irregular outline 'so at variance with the quiet angles and lines of design', that 'prophecy and destiny become irrevocably knit' in this drama (Davies, 1988, 162). For the wood of the deadly arrows links this 'forbidden room' where the traitorous Fujimaki died, to the tempting prophecies of the Forest Witch (the magic Forest is made of wood), and also to Washizu's own vacillation about undertaking the same treasonous action on Tsuzuki. This vacillation lasts only until the swishing reappearance of Asaji, who plants the guard's spear at a diagonal angle into his hands. This diagonal line functions visually as a sign of disruption and treachery, confounding the horizontal lines of feudal power and defence shown in many other sequences of the film. The emotional agitation of Washizu seen before now intensifies as, preparing for murder, Toshiro Mifune performs a panting, animal-like grimace with bared teeth that mimics so well the Noh warrior mask Kurosawa had asked him to imitate. After his departure to kill Tsuzuki, Noh theatricality continues when Asaji, left alone, twice glances round at the arrows and the wall (just as Washizu had) before springing up and, to the accompaniment of hectic Noh syncopation, performs a small but ecstatically vigorous dance between the arrow rack and the wall, as if symbolically acting out the violence which her husband is committing on his Lord at that very moment. (Peter Donaldson may be right that this sequence creates perhaps 'the most remarkable of the many screening effects in the film'.) It then only remains for Asaji to purposefully remove the blood-soaked spear from the grip of a returned Washizu, who sits panting convulsively after the murder; to put it in the hands of a drugged guard; to ritually wash her hands of the blood; to raise the alarm – and this extraordinary sequence is at an end.

Of course, Asaji is only able to persuade Washizu to murder because, as with Macbeth in the source play, these warriors have a deep need to be 'winners', driven by ambition, albeit of a clumsily 'vaulting' variety (1.7.27). In Kurosawa's film the disturbed emotions fuelling Washizu's ambition are revealed in various ways, seen fairly openly in his vain encounter with the Forest Spirit, but conveyed more subtly in other episodes. Eschewing recourse to speech, Kurosawa finds clever visual means to image these powerful emotions as Washizu responds at North Castle to Asaji's first blunt attempts to persuade him to usurp Tsuzuki's power and position by killing him. We watch him pacing around in discomfort as she coolly proposes treason, while in the courtyard stockade just behind we also glimpse and hear a horse being galloped about wildly. This image of powerful instinctive forces under constraint is an exquisite visual **metonymic** of the true emotional ferment churning up inside Washizu, and which is at complete variance with the unconvincing, hissed remonstrations of loyalty he makes to the sphinx-like Asaji.

We see a similar visual metonymic of Washizu's tense emotional life following Asaji's startling announcement of her pregnancy, news that produces a terrible conflict of loyalty in him, since he has promised to make the son of his friend Miki his successor. This agitation is imaged in the careering uncontrollability of Miki's horse that we are now shown, and which Miki's son says (correctly) is an 'ill omen'. The horse episodes echo the exchange between Rosse and the Old Man in *Macbeth* where Rosse reports how Duncan's horses had 'Turned wild in nature, broke their stalls, flung out, / Contending 'gainst obedience' (2.4.14–19). The final eruption of animal energies to disturb the cool angularity of the fortress interiors is the one that Washizu mistakenly regards as a lucky omen, but which is once again a visual emblem of his hopelessly self-deceiving emotional impulses. This eruption occurs when Spiderweb Castle is invaded by birds which have lost their home in the forest, a location that Kunimaru (Malcolm), with Noriyasu and their invading army, have partly torn down to create their forest camouflage (as in Shakespeare's play). This is an action enabling them to defeat Washizu, fulfilling the Forest Witch's prophecy that the only battle he will lose is the one where the Spiderweb Forest begins to move and approach the Castle (when 'Birnam Wood / Do come toward Dunsinane' (5.5.42–3)).

The chopped-down wood of the enchanted forest that turns an illusion into reality for the incredulous Washizu also brings him face-to-face with the realities of retribution and death, a festoon of arrows mortally piercing his body. Yet before this happens, as, floor by floor. he staggers down the wooden steps of Forest Castle, we see him somehow seeming to be able to defy death. Mortally porcupined by the arrows of his own men, he yet confronts these soldiers who have turned on him, but who now back away as if terrified by a ghost or demon – as well they might. For the arrow transfixing his neck has arrested the typical warrior grimace into a demonic mask-like rigidity. Death does finally take him, but even in his final collapse he falls trying to draw his sword, a samurai warrior to the end. This final sequence has been described as 'the very keystone of the film's formal structure', since 'here at last that tense, horizontal alternation between scenes of decentred frenzy and dramatic but static scenes is resolved into a vertical orgasm of on-screen violence' (Burch, 1979, 317).

Kozintsev's comment that he thinks Kurosawa's film 'is the finest of Shakespearean movies' (1967, 29) is no doubt inspired by the fact that Kurosawa had been so successful in achieving Kozintsev's own ambition as a Shakespearean filmmaker, that of 'making the aural visual'. As we have already noted, to achieve this Kozintsev says that the 'poetic texture' of a Shakespeare script 'has itself to be transformed into a visual poetry, into the dynamic organization of film imagery'. Analyzing his film has shown us that the power of Kurosawa's 'visual poetry' derives from a design of delivering the story and inner life of Shakespeare's drama in a structure of images whose meaning and effects draw on a highly formalistic non-Western dramatic tradition (Noh theatre) and film genre (the samurai movie) that are arguably as rich in cultural signification and resonance as the verbal text of the Shakespearean original.

Part IV

Critical Essays

1. Comedies

INTRODUCTORY NOTE

Far fewer notable translations of Shakespearean comedies to film
have been achieved than is the case for the tragedies and histories. The
reason for this is succinctly expressed by Michael Hattaway:

> Shakespeare's comedies create relationships with their theatre audiences
> for which very few directors have managed to find cinematic equivalents.
> (Hattaway, in Jackson ed., 2000, 85; bracketed page-references in what fol-
> lows refer to his essay 'The Comedies on Film')

Another way of expressing this is to say that the *stage conventions* for
which the comedies were written and which assume the presence of a
live audience do not transfer well to film, which has to find ways of
involving *its* audience without requiring their active participation in
the same way (see Part I). The conventions of *film realism*, whereby an
identification between the actor and their role is created for an audience member, who in turn is drawn to *identify* with the characters on
screen, are more readily suited for the adaptation of Shakespearean
histories and tragedies to film, than are the comedies.

It is much more difficult to make the conventions of film realism
work for Shakespearean comedies, since the theatrical precondition
for creating comic effects relies *not* on an identification between actor
and role, but on what Hattaway calls an 'aesthetic estrangement or
alienation between actor and role' (90). In other words, there is in
comedy a 'distance' established between the role performed and the
actor performing it. This disjunctive factor is something readily perceived and enjoyed by the audience. Characters in theatrical comedies
tend towards being person *types* rather than individualized, fully
rounded personalities. They frequently perform within groups or
ensembles, with the actors relying on 'audience response in order to
conjure the folly of the play, to demonstrate and to exploit the difference between themselves and their roles' (91). Since the performance
of film comedy by definition is deprived of the benefits of a live audience, its effectiveness with the movie audience is therefore more reliant on how the screen characters function as an audience *for each
other*. Their dramatic responses to each other up on screen should
enable *us* to identify with them and with their comic situations or
dilemmas. Such film comedy will also work best set in a physical 'stage
frame' that functions for the audience as a continually visible 'sign of
those conventions for game and revelry that govern the action' (86).

In the three comedy adaptations discussed here, I hope you will be stimulated to think about the extent to which film directors have found ways of actively involving the screen audience in their productions. Kenneth Branagh's *Much Ado About Nothing* works the comedy-producing mechanisms outlined above with some skill. This is because much of the comic action takes place among the high hedges and numerous walkways of the film's Tuscan villa location, providing the kind of 'stage frame' needed for the episodes of deception, overhearing and spying that is at the heart of this play's comedy. Also at its heart are the characters of Benedick and Beatrice. Branagh not only makes the most of their virtuoso flourishes of witty verbal artistry, but also of their love interactions, unusually complex for a Shakespearean comedy and therefore very welcome for a Hollywood audience that thrives on 'true love'. The film is less successful in the scenes involving the exaggerated playing of Dogberry and Verges, for without a live audience to register the highly conventional response required for overblown farce, their grotesquerie falls flat.

Adrian Noble carried some of the devices he had used in his stage version of *A Midsummer Night's Dream* over to his film, but these are sometimes too 'abstract' to work well in the realistic settings needed for film. Nevertheless, his creation of the Boy who 'dreams the action' of the play works well as an imaginative equivalent to a 'stage frame', inside which the characters 'play' at love, and are also metatheatrically 'played with' by Noble to conjure up colourful images of dreamlike wonder and delight. All Shakespearean comedy revolves around love, 'but for Hollywood, "falling in love", the necessary prelude to bourgeois marriage, is too serious to be treated as a sport or crucial negotiation' (92).

Michael Hoffman's *Dream* does, however, take its love seriously in this sentimental fashion, and modifies the character of Bottom to satisfy the romantic fantasy needs of a Hollywood audience. Having little of the theatre about it other than elaborate sound stage sets that outdo its glittering 1935 Warner Brothers predecessor, Hoffman's 'frame' uses operatic song, ensemble comedy and Kevin Kline's skills as a superlative comic actor to create a 'Bottom's Dream' that in some ways has the feel of a sentimental opera rather than a film adaptation of a Shakespeare play.

Kenneth Branagh's *Much Ado About Nothing* (UK, 1993)

Medium: Technicolor, 35mm, *c*.104 minutes

Main actors: Kenneth Branagh (Benedick); Emma Thompson (Beatrice); Denzel Washington (Don Pedro); Keanu Reeves (Don John); Robert Sean Leonard (Claudio); Richard Briers (Leonato); Brian Blessed (Antonio); Michael Keaton (Dogberry); Ben Elton (Verges); Kate Beckinsale (Hero)

Director: Kenneth Branagh

Screenplay: Kenneth Branagh

Design: Tim Harvey

Producers: Stephen Evans, David Parfitt, Kenneth Branagh

Photography: Roger Lanser

Music: Patrick Doyle

Kenneth Branagh has been described as the 'flamboyant realist' of Shakespeare-on-film (Kael, 1992, 216), and this coining is nowhere more applicable than in the case of his most commercially popular success, *Much Ado About Nothing*. Branagh's basic approach continued that of his ground-breaking *Henry V*, to provide (in his own words) 'an absolute clarity that would enable a modern audience to respond to Shakespeare-on-film, in the same way that they would respond to any other movie'. The 'absolute clarity' required for a movie audience unfamiliar with the play would again be achieved through an 'utter reality of characterization', and since three-quarters of the play's dialogue is in prose this could help the (especially non-Shakespearean) actors provide an even more accessible conversational tone. Branagh is only too aware that in the absence of a strong plot line the dramatic life of the comedy relies heavily on well-timed use of dialogue, a necessarily ample amount of which (over 50 per cent) is retained for this production. His aim of providing a 'user-friendly' approach to Shakespeare's language right from the beginning includes having the words of Balthasar's song from the play 'Sigh no more, ladies, sigh no more' (2.3) appear on the screen in time to Emma Thompson's rhythmic performance of the lines as Beatrice. This was a 'determined attempt to show' how the words can be 'dramatic in themselves', allowing 'the audience to "tune in" to the new language they are about to experience' (Branagh, 1993, xiv).

In this second Shakespeare adaptation, much of the 'flamboyant' element enabling the film audience to respond as they would to 'any other movie' was to be influenced by a new factor – the example and practice of Franco Zeffirelli's Shakespeare moviemaking. Branagh's general approach to directing and performing Shakespeare in theatre and film already possessed the energy of Zeffirelli's work. But to present a Shakespearean comedy of Italian setting there could be no better cinematic models to follow than his vivid, colourful and sunny movies *The Taming of the Shrew* and *Romeo and Juliet*. Furthermore, since the ground-breaking release of what Branagh had called his 'quintessentially English project' *Henry V* in 1989 (Branagh, 1991, 217), Zeffirelli's 1990 *Hamlet* had shown how the casting of internationally famous stars in key roles could make a Shakespeare adaptation reliably bankable. Big box-office returns are evidently what Branagh now wanted, for at the moment that he was playing Hamlet for the second time at London's Barbican Theatre and also editing his *Much Ado*, he told Samuel Crowl in an interview: 'If I can't make Shakespeare live for a broad audience with all the Hollywood that got packed into the film, then I doubt I will be able to raise the financing for a *Hamlet* film' (Crowl, 2003, 231, n.8). He need not have worried, for the US teenage audience at which the film was targeted flooded into cinemas to see Keanu Reeves, Robert Sean Leonard, Michael Keaton and Denzel Washington deliver a *Much Ado About Nothing* that was to amply exceed the box-office take of Zeffirelli's *Hamlet*. The high-profile marriage of Branagh and Oscar-winning actress Thompson also encouraged the media to turn the couple they dubbed 'Ken and Em' into a Burton and Taylor for the 1990s – helping to further popularize the movie.

Yet there was more to Branagh's remark about 'all the Hollywood that got packed into the film' than the casting of money-making iconographic US movie stars. One aspect of the Hollywood mix he put together also drew on the Zeffirelli film said to have made more money over the years than any other Shakespeare adaptation, the 1968 *Romeo and Juliet*. In framing and suffusing the texture of his *Much Ado* with 'Sigh no more, ladies, sigh no more', Branagh echoes the pervasive use of the Nino Rota song 'What Is A Youth?' that gives Zeffirelli's film its attractively melancholy mood. Without doubt, the catchy tune of 'Sigh no more', which is spoken, sung or played at the beginning, middle and end of the film *and* over the credits, supplies an infectiously joyous atmosphere, uplifting the imagination and feelings of the audience as much as the heat of the Italian sun evidently warmed and energized the cast. It was an inspiration to set the movie in a Tuscan hilltop villa in high summer, rather than – bearing in mind the needs of a youthful cinema audience – in the potentially more subdued urban setting of Messina, Sicily. Other elements of the 'Hollywood mix' are also clearly aimed at engaging the screen audience, two in particular drawing on earlier film genre conventions. First, besides the use of accessible upbeat music already mentioned and the verdant, bucolic setting fore-grounded at the beginning, there is the exciting approach of Don Pedro and his men thundering ostentatiously towards Leonato's villa on horseback, with a lively **cutting** between 'the men's sexy arrival' in 'heat haze and dust' (Branagh, 1993, 8) and the women's frenzied excitement as they prepare themselves for the men's closer approaches. For despite being atypical among Shakespeare's earlier romantic com-edies in *not* having lover-pairs forced to overcome obstacles like parental disapproval or lack of fortune before they can marry, the ulti-mate conclusion of *Much Ado* will nevertheless be the conventional comedic one of the play's lovers ending up happily married.

A full nine minutes of screen time are taken up between the open-ing read performance of 'Sigh no more' and the confrontation of Don Pedro's male group with Leonato's predominantly female household, captured in an **overhead shot** where each group faces the other in V formation, the moment punctuated by the climax of Doyle's brassy, boisterous musical score. From the languid images of Leonato's 'fam-ily' responding to Beatrice's incitement to be 'blithe and bonny' in the face of 'men's deceptions', through the rapid **cross-cutting** between the bare flesh of male and female bodies as they bathe and frolic in splash-ing water, until the moment when both groups meet, these opening nine minutes prepare us for the picture's key dramatic themes: sexual attractions and tensions between men and women, their playful delights and intrigues. Even the music of the sequence provides a kind of miniature exposition of the emotional ups and downs to come – though throughout the movie as a whole the predominantly sentimen-tal musical style will be a vital component in manipulating and registering the emotions of the drama. The 'battle of the sexes' implied by the initial confrontation between male and female groups then gets played out in the drama of the film proper in the register of the Hollywood 'screwball comedy' (as noted by several critics, e.g. Jackson in Davies and Wells, 1994, 117; Crowl, 2003, 66ff).

This Hollywood film coding is discernible in the episodes of prickly banter between Beatrice and Benedick throughout the film – 'There is a kind of merry war betwixt Signor Benedick and her', says Leonato (1.1.49–50). But it is especially noticeable in their earliest encounter, where a subtle use of the camera gives Beatrice narrative control as the main **focalizer** of the scene. Her **POV** is prioritized in a number of ways by the camera (it had been through her eyes that we observed the approach of the galloping men in the title-credit sequence). When Benedick makes a witty remark about Hero's resemblance to her father, a **medium-close reaction shot** of Beatrice shows her observing him with a sceptical look. This is revealing, for despite her next comment to him that 'nobody marks you', we see her marking him very closely indeed. When they are framed together for the first time, the camera follows her brushing flirtatiously past him, she ending up much nearer the camera than he does, a position promoting her cause at this point. When their verbal skirmishing starts in earnest, this is captured in a series of **shot/reverse shot**s where she only ever looks at him, while he turns away twice to look at the others, as if to gain their support. This gives her narrative control, as does the fact that it is *she* who opens and closes the exchange of gazes. Furthermore, whereas at the end of their exchange in the play text, Beatrice's remark 'You always end with a jade's trick. I know you of old' (1.1.118) is regularly played as part of their barbed banter, here Thompson performs the line as a regretful aside, unheard by him, a dramatic manoeuvre suggesting she retains some deep hurt from a past failed relationship with Benedick; we are thus persuaded to sympathize with her.

Before long it will be Benedick's turn to gain the audience's sympathy, when in the villa garden he is gulled into believing Beatrice loves him. Before that there are the various inciting plot incidents to set up which produce the range of contrasting emotional registers and rhythms in the film's structure; key to these varying rhythms are the 'overhearing' scenes so beloved of comedy and farce. Don Pedro's agreement to intercede on Claudio's behalf to win Hero's hand is overheard by Borachio, whose disclosure of this to Don John marks the beginning of the latter's determination to ruin the marriage plans of Claudio and Hero. To make the second phase of his villainy more dramatically effective for the film, Branagh moves Don John's agreement to carry out Borachio's plan of 'showing' Hero's supposed sexual betrayal of Claudio at her window in 2.2 (a mere 'talking' with Borachio in the play text) back to a position after 3.3, following the antics of Dogberry, Verges and the Watch on duty. The consequent alternations of positive and negative emotional shifts achieved certainly help sustain dramatic suspense.

It is in the pivotal outdoor scenes at the heart of the movie, where both Benedick and Beatrice are gulled into believing each is passionately in love with the other, that it achieves its most engaging and comically brilliant moments. These scenes showcase Thompson and Branagh – especially the latter – displaying their natural talents for comic acting. Having heard Benedick confusedly debate with himself – somewhat flamboyantly – the selfsame issues Beatrice had broached at the mask festivities, we are encouraged to sympathize with his dilemmas when he is made to hear the Prince, Leonato and Claudio concocting the story of how Beatrice pines for him. Both gulling scenes are crucially dependent on the split-second timing of **inter-cut** camera shots capturing the faces of the scheming gullers and the shocked reactions of the gulled; the latter straining to hear themselves discussed while dodging back and forth for concealment behind the indispensable theatrical-like **props** of the ornamental high hedges. Of the several brilliantly timed comic moments during and after Benedick's gulling, perhaps none is so cleverly achieved as when, with a Cagney-like gesture (and Branagh knows his Cagney inside out), he beams, cackles, and, as he brings himself to a halt with an upflinging of his arms, declares with genuine puzzlement: 'Love me? ... *Why*? – It *must* be requited.' The key pause strategically inserted between the two questions cleverly manipulates the play text's blander 'Love me? Why, it must be requited' (2.3.199), creating an extraordinarily appropriate laugh at the expense of someone unable to comprehend why *any* woman should love him. When in his extended reverie Benedick spots a ferocious Beatrice marching forth under orders to invite him into dinner, *we* see someone bristling with the classic look of the scorned female lead of screwball comedy, while *he* spies 'some marks of love in her'. This leads him to strike a pose and a tone of voice sitting on the edge of the fountain (as the screenplay tells us) 'that reminds one of Tony Curtis as Cary Grant in *Some Like It Hot*' (another Hollywood coding). Once Beatrice is also 'limed' into believing Benedick loves her, the garden scenes end with a series of **intercut slow-motion dissolves** showing them ecstatically happy at feeling both in love and beloved. Benedick kicks up the water of the fountain (recalling another classic Hollywood image, Gene Kelly in *Singin' in the Rain*), while Beatrice 'beatifically swings' in a 'fairyish bower'. As Doyle's music swells to a triumphant crescendo, this is meant to be the film's most romantic moment; it actually becomes its 'cheesiest', simply because the **slow-motion** imagery has the clichéd quality of a TV chocolate or perfume ad.

It is only after the aborted wedding, where Claudio accuses Hero of being an 'approved wanton', that the feelings of Beatrice and Benedick are more fully explored. Beatrice's distress over the slandering of Hero provides the focus for Benedick to finally show emotional maturity and a commitment to the woman for whom he now declares his love. In the chapel scene, after a series of **close-up shot/reverse shot**s of Benedick and Beatrice in which Benedick makes a solemn emotional commitment by agreeing to challenge Claudio, the camera moves close to Benedick when Beatrice leaves, following her in **long shot** from his **subjective** viewpoint. From the moment near the film's beginning when the camera had forced us to sympathize with the feelings of Beatrice, we are now persuaded to identify our feelings with Benedick, the narrative control of the action switching to him. Although there are 'local' shifts of scene, mood and viewpoint still to take place in the last 35 minutes of film, in terms of inciting us to strong sympathy, little further change occurs, Benedick having the last word when he issues the instruction to 'Strike up, pipers.' Would that one could say that the comedy of Dogberry and Verges engages and entertains the movie audience; the reverse is rather the case. This is mainly owing to the exaggerated gestures, mugging and peculiarly 'Oirish' speaking voice adopted by Michael Keaton's Dogberry. His manner of expression is just too writhing and mangled to be comic. Dogberry's unintended malapropisms are capable of producing great humour, but Keaton's eccentric vocal delivery is too baffling to grasp. Branagh ensures all the other actors perform their lines clearly, knowing that the audience needs to be engaged by the vivacity of this play's verbal wit. A similar approach was needed for Dogberry. Antics and mugging may have worked with a stage audience, prepared as they must be to respond to stage farce. But for a film so dependent on words as *Much Ado* is, Keaton's mumming grotesquerie falls flat.

Branagh states in his screenplay introduction that he wanted 'to give a different kind of space to the Claudio/Hero plot' since 'Beatrice and Benedick are, after all, the subplot.' Claudio and Hero are given a different treatment in two ways, both aiming to provide animation and interest to characters originally written as conventional and colourless. Branagh tells us he and Thompson wanted to suggest Benedick and Beatrice were re-encountering each other as former lovers whose first romantic entanglement and break-up might have occurred ten years before, at the age of 20, about the age that the young lovers Claudio and Hero now are. Linking the lives of the two pairs of lovers in this way is perhaps meant to make them more significant and interesting, but it is questionable whether this is achieved. What *does* significantly affect how Claudio is 'read' by the screen audience is the sentimental way he is played by Robert Sean Leonard. For this actor had become for the crucially important teenage segment of the audience an emotional screen icon identified with the persecuted figure of Neal Perry in the movie *Dead Poets Society* (1989). For much of the film, Leonard tends to play Claudio as a vulnerable figure whose face registers immediately his internal emotional state, and this becomes no more apparent than when the camera captures in tight **close-up** his response to being shown (by Don John) Hero's supposed illicit coupling at her window. As Crowl so acutely observes, this response 'severely skews the audience's reaction'. As an experienced teacher of US undergraduates he is able to explain how this moment in the film

> rarely fails to elicit an audible flow of sympathy – particularly from the teenagers who became the prime market for the film – for Leonard's grief. After all, this was the same actor who, as many in the audience know, had already suffered and died for Shakespeare in his previous film, *Dead Poets Society*. (Crowl, 2003, 77)

Together with the sentimental religious music accompanying the night-time vigil procession to Hero's tomb where Claudio does solemn penance for her 'death', the cumulative effect of Leonard's playing is to manipulate us into sympathizing with him as a 'wounded lover', instead of the rather shallow and unthinking fellow of Shakespeare's play. The casting and playing of Claudio to convey these effects suggests Branagh's weakness for what Crowl calls a 'particularly American sentimentality about the precariousness of youthful innocence', a trait which has made deep inroads into the literature of the American high-school curriculum.

Despite this element of the film 'skewing' it in the direction of a more receptive reading of the play than the awkwardness provided by the original text, it does have the effect of making the final reconciliation of Claudio and Hero as fulfilling for the audience as that of Beatrice and Benedick. After the wedding of Claudio and Hero in the presence of the whole ensemble, we get a **long shot** of Benedick calling for Beatrice, followed by an **eyeline match** with her as part of the group. Thereafter, the **POV** moves from that of the group observing them as a couple in a series of **two-shot**s where they are finally 'united', to that of the remainder of the action, where the whole group is observed uniting in celebration. This warming conclusion begins to be captured as the song that began the film is struck up, and everything starts 'rising' to the joyous occasion, including the ubiquitous **Steadicam** operator, who, after following the group round the villa as they sing and dance, steps on to a ramp to be craned high up in a final and continuous two-and-a-half-minute **crane shot** that literally gives a soaring and uplifting overview of the scene. The full-throated voices of a choir provide an emotionally satisfying ending, very reminiscent of the climaxes of American light comedy musicals of the 1930s and 1940s. This is the most popularly successful adaptation of a Shakespearean comedy on film.

Adrian Noble's *A Midsummer Night's Dream* (UK, 1996)

Medium: Technicolor, 35mm, *c*.99 minutes

Main actors: Alex Jennings (Theseus/Oberon); Lindsay Duncan (Hippolyta/Titania); Desmond Barrit (Bottom); Finbar Lynch (Puck/Philostrate); Monica Dolan (Hermia); Kevin Doyle (Demetrius); Daniel Evans (Lysander); Emily Raymond (Helena); Osheen Jones (the Boy)

Director: Adrian Noble

Adaptation: Adrian Noble

Production and costume design: Anthony Ward

Producer: Paul Arnott

Photography: Ian Wilson

Music: Howard Blake

Adrian Noble's film of *A Midsummer Night's Dream* frequently draws on his highly successful 1994 RSC production of the play, which toured both England and the USA to great acclaim. Many RSC productions of this play have since 1970 been influenced to one degree or another by Peter Brook's groundbreaking 'abstract' version, in which the colourfully costumed actors frequently performed from a trapeze inside a three-sided 'white box' having doors through which they could enter and exit. Noble's film also uses (free-standing) doors, is brilliantly colourful and employs aerial techniques to suggest the sense of magical and fantastical transformation so essential for this Shakespeare comedy. Another element now considered essential for productions, besides the verbal and knockabout humour of the mechanicals (which even the most amateur of productions can get to work well, such is the efficacy of Shakespeare's actor-led dialogue), is the suggestion of darkly sensual eroticism and desire, particularly for the relationship between Titania and the 'translated' Bottom. This movie does generate such eroticism on occasion – overtly at times. But it is finally mediated through the device of an unusual optic, that of a young boy's dream.

Noble had already wanted the actors in the stage production to 'find the child-like in themselves', arguing that 'the logic of the *Dream* is experienced by the characters in an extraordinarily intense way'. When it came to finding 'an overall camera angle' that would open up the text for cinema audiences, he took the notion of utilizing 'the child-like' one radical step further:

> I thought we should look at literally making it a dream – a child's dream; someone through whom we could relive the story …[and allowing us] to quote in quite a saucy and playful way a wide range of childhood fictions. And that was joyful too as it seemed quite in keeping with the spirit of Shakespeare's text.   (Crowl, 2003, 176)

The result is a film which dramatically conveys the *Dream* as if it is being dreamed by a young boy (the Boy, Osheen Jones), who also takes part in the action. We approach the beginning of this action when the movie opens, the camera moving down through a cloudy night sky into the open window of the Boy's bedroom (reminding us a little of the way Olivier's *Henry V* starts). The music having shifted from a light, waltz-time romantic violin tune to a sombre, more mysterious repeated bassoon figure, the camera moves round the room showing us its contents – various dolls, puppets and teddy bears (one of which sits on a toy swan), a toy Victorian theatre, a cricket bat, and many other toy objects and figures: an aeroplane, cars, a rabbit, a harlequin doll, a rocking-horse, a radio. This is clearly an imaginative child deeply interested in 'play' and the pretend world of the theatre. A bedside clock tells us it is midnight, the 'witching hour'. The camera finally settles on the figure of the slumbering Boy, who has fallen asleep with the light on while reading the book at his elbow, an Edwardian edition of *A Midsummer Night's Dream* illustrated by Arthur Rackham (1908). A **close-up** of the Boy's face reveals flickering eyelid movements, suggesting he is dreaming, and since he has been reading *this* book, Rackham's illustrations are likely to be the stimulant for the pictures that fill the frame of his dreaming mind's eye. The Rackham edition is well chosen for this purpose, since many of its illustrations suggest a dark Otherness: the mysterious woodland world alive with semi-alien life-forms – snakes, toads, spiders, giant beetles – or images carrying a strongly erotic implication. For instance, 'Titania lying asleep', Rackham's first illustration, shows her draped on the ground asleep in the dark wood, the shapely contours of her 'open' limbs and body clearly visible beneath clinging, flimsy garb. And in the stylized line drawing adorning a margin of the text's first page, two scantily clad maidens (possibly representing Hermia and Helena) are shown slumbering on winding tree boughs, one figure revealing the nipple of a bared breast, while an observant Puck is imaged leering across at them from the neighbouring margin: a 'saucy' source for the Boy's dream indeed.

At the beginning of that dream, then, when we see him peeping goggle-eyed through the keyhole of a door while a receptive Hippolyta is slowly and erotically caressed by Theseus murmuring to her the first words of the play, it is no surprise to see the Boy's voyeuristic impulses so vividly aroused. For this is a situation plausibly linking a young lad's natural and dreamy curiosity about his parents' sex life (we assume this is what makes him seek out their bedroom door) to the semi-erotic illustrations of the Rackham *Dream* edition in which he has been so 'innocently' absorbed. Once the vexed Egeus bustles past, angrily interrupting the 'pre-nuptials' of the Duke and his betrothed by flinging Hermia into the room and arguing how Lysander has 'bewitched' her into rebellion, the film's story can begin in earnest. The way is clear for the Boy to find himself both observing at close quarters that story, and sometimes to become a close part of it. Inspired by a dreamer's impulsive curiosity to pursue Helena out of the room to the wood, we then see him careering down a whirling vortex into a stove pipe, ending up in the hut where the 'rude mechanicals' are arriving to rehearse *Pyramus and Thisbe*. His terrifying descent echoes elements of two more of Noble's 'childhood fictions': the descent of Alice down the rabbit hole in Lewis Carroll's *Alice's Adventures in Wonderland* (1865) and the account of the tornado in L. Frank Baum's *The Wonderful Wizard of Oz* (1900). In one of the best essays on this *Dream* movie, Mark Thornton Burnett identifies these and many other allusions to literary or film narratives used by it to evoke a child's perceptual world (Burnett, in Burnett and Wray, 2000, 92). Hence the airborne umbrellas facilitating the entrances and exits of the fairies recall P. L. Travers's *Mary Poppins* (1934). When Titania takes away the 'translated' Bottom in her deep-pink upturned umbrella across the wide water towards the giant moon, this is evocative (as Burnett says) of 'Edward Lear's sea-loving and moon-seeking animals, the owl and the pussycat'; while the silhouettes of Bottom riding his motorbike and Peter Quince his bicycle across the same moon directly reference the escape of 'ET' in Steven Spielberg's famous movie. In all these literary and film narratives a child or children typically displace the power of parental figures as key triggers of the action, previous popular films like the *Home Alone* series also cueing film or DVD audiences to embrace Noble's child-mediated design. In this movie, too, the Boy sometimes 'makes things happen', and most interestingly when his toy Victorian theatre is incorporated into the scene where, in imitation of Puck's bubble-blowing creation of an image of the Boy dressed as the 'changeling boy', the Boy himself blows bubbles into his toy theatre, whereupon he looks down (as do we) to behold Titania's fairies and finally Titania herself bursting forth from these bubbles to take up their stage roles. When we look up at the Boy's delighted reaction, it is we who are part of his spectacular creation, too, a dream-inflected spectacle that looks forward to the final frames of the movie.

The Boy's controlling hand is also seen at work later on. Following Puck's return with the 'little western flower', he and Oberon crouch as a two-fairy audience before the toy theatre, and *we* view them and the scene from the Boy's backstage **POV**, he initially being shown drawing aside a back **flat** depicting the wood, as if he has emerged from it. We watch the Boy push forward on to the stage a miniature figure of the 'sweet Athenian lady' (Helena) and Oberon instructs Puck to 'anoint' the eyes of the 'disdainful youth' (Demetrius) so that he may prove 'fond on her'. As Oberon and Puck grasp their 'Mary Poppins' umbrellas to depart, we cut to a shot showing the Boy manipulating their upward movement as if they are marionettes on strings. Both the **shot/ reverse shot**s that switch us back and forth between views of the Boy and Oberon and Puck, and this seemingly directorial control of the action by the Boy, are visually suggestive at a number of levels. They imply that in dreams *anything* can happen, 'agency' constantly shifting between controller and controlled; they foreground the notion that the theatre/performing space is a space of transformation; *and* they convey 'fairyland' where magical transformations take place. Sequences such as this are filmically effective, besides others where 'transformation' occurs, best of all perhaps the erotically charged scenes between Titania and Bottom, and those towards the end of the film.

Since the Boy's eyes once again threaten to pop out while gazing on the heaving bosom of a voluptuous Titania lying at rest in her deep-pink umbrella bower – especially since she seems to shoot an inviting glance at him – it is no surprise to discover that Titania's seduction of Bottom is sexually suggestive in the extreme – and very funny too. The playing of this sequence seems to illustrate both of Freud's observations that 'the word "No" does not seem to exist for a dream', and that dreams 'take the liberty of representing any element whatever by its desired opposite'. The shapely Titania refuses to take 'no' for an answer from an initially timid, pot-bellied Bottom whose tail she caresses suggestively before making him 'bray' by nuzzling her head into his private parts. Conforming to the dreamlike logic of his statement that 'reason and love keep little company together these days', Titania follows up her deluded response of 'thou art as wise as thou art beautiful' by rubbing Bottom's crotch with her toes, visibly arousing him. Upon his removal of her foot, offering him a glimpse of her genitalia, initial embarrassment is soon overcome by his further arousal, so that her command to 'go with me' (with the emphasis on *go*, in Shakespearean usage meaning to 'come' sexually) is only weakly resisted by Bottom, and later we see him energetically pumping into a Titania abandoned to sexual ecstasy. Although at this point onlooking Oberon seems to approve, telling Puck that 'this falls out better than I could devise', in fact his disapproval is shown by the smile draining from his face, an 'ironic insertion' by Noble at Oberon's expense, if ever there was one.

The screen audience is successfully engaged by erotic sequences like this, or by visually experimental ones that 'toy' with notions of what theatre might be, objectifying it, or by sequences where the playing of witty dialogue does the trick. Typically, these are ones in which Bottom and the 'rude mechanicals' play – even extending to their amusing antics when they 'double' as Titania's personal fairy entourage. But the attention of the screen audience will tend to wander or be lost in the forest sequences involving the trials and tribulations of the lovers. This is simply because Noble uses the same staging techniques for the film in these sequences as he used in the stage production. For the stage production's depiction of the forest scenes, a set of four free-standing doors in their frames were the means by which the lovers made repeated entrances and exits, their growing confusions and tempers producing farcical antics that made for truly comical effects. As Peter Holland has said of the stage production, 'The lovers became mechanical creatures in a farce which, like all good farces, depended on doorways' (Holland, 1997, 188). But while such antics can be an enticing delight for stage audiences, who accept and even relish the comic conventions being used as a matter of course, the use of such devices on film fall flat. Despite Noble's use of fast-cutting and many **close-up** shots of the lovers as they move in and out of their tangles and through the doorways, it is always very obvious to the viewer they are acting on a plain open wooden stage, with the result that the film (as *The Times* of London review in 1996 put it) is 'lacking in screen presence'. Douglas Lanier generously comments that most of 'the film's *mise-en-scène* actively flaunts its artificiality' (Lanier, in Burt and Boose, 2003, 160). But Noble's later comments make it clear that the dramatic shortcomings of the film's forest scenes were due to financial constraints: 'Everything in the forest was compromised by resources.' Had he known this earlier, he 'would have done everything differently', shooting the scenes outside in order 'to provide another dimension to the multiple layers of reality the text and film represent. All those elements like the lake I could develop more fully ... I'd create a strange world of forest and water' (Crowl, 2003, 178).

Despite the dramatic shortcomings of the fairy wood scenes, many elements of Noble's film do make an extraordinary impression, drawing us into its **metatheatrical** probing of the meanings and effects of 'dramatic representation' which this play, entertaining 'comedy' though it primarily is, is also concerned to engage us in. The last 20 minutes of the film are especially winning in this sense, partly because the mechanicals' performance of *Pyramus and Thisbe* before the 'onstage audience' of Athenian nobles (here seated as a conventional theatrical audience) allows the movie audience to be simultaneously entertained and metatheatrically challenged by this deployment of an 'inset' play by Shakespeare. Theseus himself provides a thoughtful comment when defending their attempts as novice actors: 'The best in this kind are but shadows, and the worst / Are no worse if imagination amend them', a point not wholly answered by Hippolyta's 'put-down' response of 'It must be your imagination, then, and not theirs' (5.1.208–10). His reference to shadows also has a double resonance these days because the movie characters we watch in the cinema are, quite literally, illusory shadows made visible on the screen only by an electric light shining through images on moving strips of celluloid or digitally projected from film files. But this last section of the film, following the resolution of the lovers' difficulties and chiefly devoted to the mechanicals' performance and Robin's Epilogue, engages us also because it begins and ends with the movie's imaginative device of the Boy, offering a resolution of sorts. But it does this in such a way that strange queries linger on about the relationships between dream and reality, theatre and performance, performers and audience. A hint as to what the key element in these relationships might be is given when the Boy flings open double doors to reveal a feasting court, this action causing a momentary quiet in the proceedings, and Theseus, Hippolyta and the lovers all turn round to greet the new arrivals – the camera, the Boy, us? – with glad smiles. This creates a strange and estranging moment of relationship between us and the film actors not paralleled in the theatre, an effect repeated in a slightly different way at the film's end, when the Boy's presence is embraced more fully into the action.

The Boy's fuller involvement in the 'theatricals' of the final section begins in earnest with another use of doors. A moment after Philostrate

takes the Boy's hand, they run like the wind through a red corridor
(recalling the Boy's original dreamy wandering from his bedroom),
and for a few seconds we see Philostrate metamorphosed into Puck
(Finbar Lynch playing both parts), suggesting that their crossing of the
threshold into theatre marks a transition from one kind of (real) world
into another (fairylike) world of dreams and magic. As he stands gazing around in wonder at the theatre space, we understand how the Boy
is feeling this to be a 'dream come true', his realization that he has
made the shift from toy theatre to real theatre, from childish pretence
to grown-up pretence, a translation galvanizing him into the stage-
hand activity of hauling on a rope to raise the curtain on the mechanicals' play. After the completion of what is a satisfyingly entertaining
and involving play for all concerned – players included, besides the
Athenian nobles and the Boy too – the bergomask dance performed
by Bottom and Flute is interrupted by midnight's tolling bell and all
stand stock-still, looking up, entranced. For midnight marks the transition into that entrancing dreamtime which had begun the film, here
punctuated by a series of rapidly **intercut slam-zoom** shots showing
the Boy watching alone from the theatre balcony, the hands of his bedroom clock at midnight. This is a repeat of his panic-stricken calling for
mummy from bed, Oberon roaring like a lion, a large risen moon with
howling wind heard behind, and the Boy's toy theatre stage with two
characters on it, one of them seeming to be a caricature of Shakespeare
himself. After Theseus's announcement that the 'iron tongue of midnight' signals fairytime and their need to retire, all disperse, and in a
kind of *hommage* to Branagh's *Henry V*, the theatre is closed down to
the sound of light switches being clunkily turned off.

Now, (as if) through the magic of cinema, the footlights of the theatre come on again, giving us at the witching hour of that darkness so
necessary for moviegoers to view their entertainment, a **long shot** of
Puck from the **POV** of the Boy up in the balcony (it is his dream we
are in, remember). Soon, Robin and the Boy are in a misty backstage
realm overhung by a firmament of yellow light bulbs, looking out
together towards Oberon, Titania and the fairy band advancing in a
group across the water on which Titania and Bottom had made love,
an enormous moon looming behind them. After Puck's closing speech,
he leads the Boy and the fairies back on to the stage to meet Bottom
and the other characters. The Boy now becomes their focus of attention as he is hoisted aloft and passed around the group, all holding out
hands lovingly towards him before he is finally set down at the front of
the colourful assembly, which closes up as if posing for a group

photograph, each member of the group gradually and self-consciously shifting their gaze up from the Boy towards us, we who are watching the Dream they have created. It is a memorable and strangely moving tableau, bearing witness both to the magic of theatre and to the peculiar cinematic magic that makes this kind of moment between performer and movie audience possible. If Noble's is not a uniformly successful adaptation, this is the best of many sections of a movie which points the way towards an imaginatively produced account of this play on film that could one day be more fully realized.

Michael Hoffman's *A Midsummer Night's Dream* (USA, 1999)

Medium: Technicolor, 35mm, *c*.115 minutes

Main actors: Rupert Everett (Oberon); Michelle Pfeiffer (Titania); David Strathairn (Theseus); Sophie Marceau (Hippolyta); Kevin Kline (Bottom); Stanley Tucci (Puck); Anna Friel (Hermia); Christian Bale (Demetrius); Dominic West (Lysander); Calista Flockhart (Helena); Roger Rees (Peter Quince); John Sessions (Philostrate); Bernard Hill (Egeus)

Director: Michael Hoffman

Adaptation: Michael Hoffman

Production design: Luciana Arrighi

Costume design: Gabriella Pescucci

Producers: Leslie Urdang, Michael Hoffman

Photography: Oliver Stapleton

Music: Simon Boswell, Robert Urdang

Michael Hoffman's *A Midsummer Night's Dream* did not emerge from a stage production. Rather, it was influenced in its concepts, design and casting by other films, in particular those of Hollywood, which lavishly funded the movie in pursuit of a popular audience. Much of the lavish funding is spent creating visual spectacle, particularly for Theseus's palace and the fairy-wood scenes, as well as for costuming, and in these respects the film echoes the glittering Hollywood Reinhardt/Dieterle *A Midsummer Night's Dream* of 1935, creating similar, but updated, effects. In terms of period, setting and casting Hoffman also attempts to follow Branagh's highly successful *Much Ado About Nothing* (1993). His chosen period is similarly late Victorian, so making the strict social codes of the play plausible – although Theseus's early pronouncement that Hermia should 'prepare to die / For disobedience to your father's will' (1.1.86–7) is here harshly *implausible*, even for the social rigidities of 1900 Italy. The lush and colourful Tuscan setting of fictitious hill town Monte Athena also follows *Much Ado*, offering a version of that film's summery golden glow. What Crowl calls an 'all-star Anglo-American cast' is an idea also borrowed from Branagh, leading Hollywood actors Michelle Pfeiffer (Titania) and Kevin Kline (Bottom) playing romantic leads, ensuring a strong box-office allure.

Without the experience of a stage production to help guide him, what shaped the director's dramatic vision? Hoffman explains in the Introduction to his screenplay what he felt were the key contrasts and elements of the play – 'love and dignity, conditioning and subversion, a rich world of images'. Yet for him, 'still the adaptation lacked a center in terms of character'. The 'character' he creates to give the film the 'emotional spine' he felt it needed is a more sophisticated Bottom, a character he regards as someone who 'clings to delusions of grandeur because he has no love in his life'. That Hoffman wants to turn the relatively two-dimensional characters of Shakespeare's comedy into realistic three-dimensional *people* who have 'emotional backstories' is confirmed by further character readings. Egeus (he tells us) has 'an obsessive attachment' to Hermia, who in turn 'is unable to empathize'; Puck has a 'fundamental love of chaos' (actually, it is mischief that truly animates him); and, following his discovery that it is 'Nick Bottom the dreamer, the actor, the pretender' who will become the 'emotional spine' of his movie, Hoffman had a revelation as to how Titania should be presented: 'I suddenly saw her as a woman who wanted to love simply, unconditionally, in a way the politics of her relationship with Oberon made impossible.' Therefore, for him 'Titania and Bottom's struggle with love and pride, and their simple, if brief, discovery of each other, felt like a gift.' I dwell on Hoffman's explanation of how he came to conceive of Shakespeare's *A Midsummer Night's Dream* for the big screen conveyed in the language of depth psychology, in the knowledge that the 'what's my motivation?' approach to dramatic adaptations may and perhaps even could help to make some Shakespearean comedies on film 'work'. But this play is not (for example) *Much Ado About Nothing*, where characters like Beatrice and Benedick provide sufficient textual complexity to justify the addition of little dramatic touches which the 'reality-demanding' Hollywood screen audience needs. But concentrating so much of his film's emotional intensity in the character of Bottom (Kline is on screen for almost a third of the movie), what makes for one of the film's major strengths – Bottom's Dream – also becomes its weakness. Skewing the adaptation towards a kind of character study in melancholia does not sit well with this Shakespearean comedy. Most of these comedies work best when played as ensemble pieces.

However, despite the film's tone and atmosphere creating a more 'dimensioned' Bottom than it requires, there are many impressive elements in the movie that work well to make it hugely enjoyable. For example, Hoffman makes intelligent, effective and entertaining use of music throughout his film, creating a musical correspondence for the various groups of characters. Like its 1935 Hollywood predecessor it opens with the incidental music from Mendelssohn's 'A Midsummer Night's Dream', possibly a tribute, but music which provides an appropriately majestic register for establishing the fact of Duke Theseus's imposing rule over Monte Athena. (After the muddle and mayhem of the woodland dream ends and order is restored, the 'Wedding March' from the same composition is fittingly used for the processional entry of the noble Athenian couples to the 'Pyramus and Thisbe' performance at the end.) Mendelssohn's high-pitched *presto* violin music fits perfectly the dancing of the Disneyesque fireflies (later identified as fairies) around the frame over the opening titles, until the use of **time-lapse** photography rapidly brings up a dawn, the film title breaking up into fluttering butterflies until the camera takes us into the environs of Theseus's palace. Here we are treated to a **montage** sequence where the mobile camera **cranes** and **pans** around showing the bustle of preparations for the Duke and Duchess's forthcoming marriage. A **Steadicam** noses through the palace to show mountains of colourful food being prepared amid Italian kitchen clatter and chatter; we also see two dwarf figures (who later turn out to be Titania's fairies) steal silver plate and a gramophone, the latter to figure significantly in the film's central scene between Bottom and Titania in her bower. Near the beginning we also see Hippolyta listening to a gramophone record playing, suggesting that the Mendelssohn we thought was only the film's soundtrack is actually part of the film's **diegetic** meaning.

Which is perhaps the appropriate point to say that if Mendelssohn works well to support the opening of the movie at its most serious and 'formal' moments, then the use made of operatic song to reinforce the 'emotional spine' of the film is an inspired one. The gramophone was new as Italy, the film's location, moved into the twentieth century, and just as the 'high culture' of Shakespeare was starting to be adapted for (silent) film in Europe and the USA, so was the 'high culture' of Italian grand opera music beginning to be circulated more widely through gramophone records. The phonograph stolen from Theseus's palace by Titania's fairies figures prominently at the film's emotional epicentre when a newly 'translated' Bottom, sitting under the entranced gaze of Titania in her bower, is offered fruit by Cobweb from a phonograph disc being used as a food tray. When Bottom clears this and places it on the turntable to play, the sound that emerges ravishes the ears of Titania and her fairy retinue. The beautiful cavatina 'Casta Diva' from Bellini's *Norma* so enthrals them, astonished at music emerging from thin air, that their cries of 'Hail mortal' convey utter conviction. But the stirring music also overcomes the evidently unprepared emotions of Bottom too, the song becoming the soundtrack to the 'falling-in-love' moment so treasured by popular movie audiences. Later, when he and Titania make high-spirited love in her bower, the music is heard again, this time played in **non-diegetic** instrumental form. In grand opera, the leading tenor frequently plays the heroic lover seeking his female counterpart, the soprano who will fulfil his dreams. Bottom, the (anti)-hero of this film, cannot sing, but in his moment of glory he becomes (in his dreams as it were) the heroic tenor finding his soprano in Titania. The song Norma sings, embodying an appeal to the chaste goddess of the moon to give her strength, does not really fit the case of Titania. But this is less important than the ravishing effects of the singing on the susceptible emotions of Bottom, Titania – and us. This outcome is very different from an earlier episode in the film when Bottom had his spirits and his suit dampened by practical jokers pouring Chianti over him. Then, he had retreated to the misery of what Hoffman calls 'a lousy marriage' and a 'dingy flat', his rejection and loneliness caught well by the non-diegetic use of the cavatina 'Una Furtiva Lagrima' from Donizetti's opera *L'Elisir d'Amore*, an effective aural underlining of Bottom's mood of dejection.

A quite different mood is captured at those points where the movie makes use of the brindisi (drinking song) from Verdi's *La Traviata* celebrating the pleasures of love and living life to the full. It is first heard when we are introduced to the bustling activity of Monte Athena and the spirited optimism of the mechanicals in their enthusiasm to put on a play for the Duke and Duchess. The song is amusingly reprised when the mechanicals enter the woods for their rehearsal singing it *a capella* as part of the **diegesis**. Much later, when Quince and the mechanicals are delighted by the reappearance of Bottom, their star turn, the breezy brindisi is again played, extra-diegetically, supporting the upbeat mood that leads into their performance of 'Pyramus and Thisbe'. However, because the 'emotional spine' of Hoffman's movie is provided by a Bottom whom even Kline dubs 'an artist at heart', when he returns home alone following the triumphant entertainment of the Athenian nobility, he again finds himself dejected, gazing out blankly from his window. Then, as he sighs, revolving in his fingers the miniature crown so resembling a ring that he vaguely identifies it with some lost happiness, Hoffman provides him with an image that momentarily lifts up his heart. Among a cloud of Disneyesque dancing fairies that hover outside his window, one brighter than the rest seems to be dancing for him alone, the Titania who had so completely caught his heart. Suddenly they vanish: Bottom must return to being the unhappy weaver. It is like a fairy tale, not only in the use of Disneyesque digital effects, but also in the deep swathes of sentimental melody conjured up by the film score's writer Simon Boswell, elaborating on music drawn from Mascagni's *Cavalleria Rusticana*.

Those aspects of the film so effectively carried along by music are unfortunately not matched in quality by some of its other key features. In particular, Hoffman's movie often puts spectacle and extravagance of detail ahead of ensuring that Shakespeare's text is communicated more effectively. The film's opening does have visual strength, but as soon as Theseus and Hippolyta begin speaking the gains are quickly lost, partly because Hippolyta's thick foreign accent makes her words hard to understand. Weakness also enters because the halting exchange between them excises Theseus's apologies in the text for wooing Hippolyta with his 'sword' and doing her 'injuries', promising to wed her 'in another key'. Presumably, since Hoffman had decided that 'everyone in the play wants to be loved', the implication that Theseus has conquered Hippolyta by raping her would disfigure the anodyne Hollywood romance he seems determined to create. As it is, we are left guessing the reason for the evident discord that lingers between them. An unaccountable textual omission is noticeable too when Theseus, responding to Hippolyta's wonderment at the 'strange' reports the lovers have been giving of their night in the woods, is prevented by Hoffman's script from speaking eleven of the most famous lines in the Shakespearean dramatic corpus (and *only* those eleven!). It is from his speech at the beginning of 5.1, starting: 'The lunatic, the lover, and the poet / Are of imagination all compact' and ending 'and gives to airy nothing / A local habitation and a name' (5.1.7–17). Perhaps Hoffman felt the lines might somehow prove distracting – if so, this would be odd since Theseus is credited with being a 'poet' and a 'lover' on page one of his own script.

Hoffman was clearly very taken with the idea of supplying his Tuscan setting with resonant images, but the fairyland wood scenes are often overloaded with elaborate 'Etruscan' scenery. Little and large monsters and set-piece tableaux bear no dramatic relation to the text, providing merely surface effects. Neither does his drawing on Moreau's 'The Muses Leaving Their Father Apollo' for Oberon's court setting, or on Waterhouse for images of the 'gentle innocent sensuality' of Titania's fairy band provide significant impact, rather conveying static insipidity. At the other extreme, creating a crowded grotto Fairy Bar (based on Jabba the Hut's bar in George Lucas's *Return of the Jedi*) out of which Puck and one of Titania's fairies stagger, rolling drunk, is a novel idea. But it hardly fits in with the sense of exorbitant magic that dreams should produce. One clever piece of magic that does 'work' is when Bottom, having gone 'to see a noise that he heard' instead finds a top hat and a walking stick (crowned with an ass's head) at a tree stump. Bottom responds to the unseen Puck's blowing on to him by slapping his neck (a bit of business copied from the 1935 *Dream*) and when Puck blows again, the tree stump (through **digital imaging**) changes into a shimmering, liquid gold mirror that the vain Bottom cannot resist gazing into. There is a commendable logic to making his vainglorious ambitions the cause of his 'translation' into an ass, and the movie would benefit from utilizing more such insightful devices.

If there is one scene embracing the best elements of the film it would have to be the three-minute one between Bottom and Titania in her bower, culminating in the 'Casta Diva' song from *Norma*. Just as Pfeiffer's Titania is stunned into admiration and love of Bottom for his seemingly magical creation of divine-sounding music, so does Kline's Bottom become quickly bewitched by her beauty and the romantic embrace of the moment. The dawning of some profound realization is registered so movingly on his face that we are thoroughly persuaded: without Kline's acting gifts, the film would undoubtedly not only lack an 'emotional spine', it would be hopelessly shallow.

2. Histories

INTRODUCTORY NOTE

It is important to remember that the plays listed under the genre heading of 'histories' in the first Folio are just that: 'plays'. To be sure, all their titles give the name of a monarch who had reigned in English history, and each play dramatizes the events of that reign, frequently ending with the monarch's death. That is the case with *The Life and Death of Richard the Third*. Yet the play title printed in the first Folio is *The Tragedy of King Richard the Third*. So is the play a history or a tragedy? The conventions of comedies dictate an ending concluding with marriage: The *Life of Henry the Fifth* ends in marriage, so does that make it a comedy? Clearly not, for it is most famous for its portrayal of the battle of Agincourt. Similarly, no one thinks of *Richard III* as a tragedy, as it too is famous for ending with the battle of Bosworth.

The 'histories' are not *history* in the sense we understand that term nowadays, that is to say, a discipline based on the sifting and careful evaluation of a wide range of written or other items of primary evidence to reach an impartial account of past events. Shakespeare drew on the limited historical sources at his disposal in the 1590s to give *dramatic shape* to those materials, so that he could produce plays of about two hours in length to entertain and engage an audience who then had a great interest in hearing about their English past. His purpose was to create a *performable* and *dramatic* representation of English history for the stage, not a 'documentary': history *plays*. If this meant omitting, inventing or altering historical figures to give dramatic shape or impact to the play, or indeed creating elements of comedy or tragedy to strengthen its entertainment and story values, then he did not scruple to do so.

What implications do the above observations have for creating film adaptations of the histories? First and foremost, although such plays differ from the tragedies by seeking to dramatize the activities of England's governing royal order, they do nevertheless tend to focus on the fortunes of a single character, their deliberations, anxieties and accomplishments. Where this focus on character is particularly well-developed and engaging, as it is in the plays of *Richard III* and *Henry V*, filmmakers are not slow to use the camera to scrutinize in **close-up** and **medium-shot** the behaviour and state of mind of central characters, just as they would do for key characters in the tragedies. Though Olivier in his *Henry V* tends to avoid the use of **close shot**s (his Henry is rarely troubled by doubts), in *Richard III* he does use the **close-up** more, and neither Loncraine nor Branagh in their movies waste any filming opportunities to explore character in this way.

Film's capacity for creating spectacle can obviously come into its own when filming histories, since the mobile camera can be used in exterior locations to capture all the clash and excitement of battle to great involving effect. Interestingly, each of the four films discussed here handles its scenes of battle in quite different ways. Little of the anguish, blood and violence of war is to be seen in Olivier's battle scenes; Branagh's Agincourt, by contrast, is more realistic, full of blood and mud. Loncraine's Bosworth field is set in the environs of London's old Bankside power station in the mid-1930s, aiming for a portrayal of more modern warfare on ground and in the air.

Laurence Olivier's *Henry V* (UK, 1944)

Medium: Technicolor, 35mm, 137 minutes

Main actors: Laurence Olivier (Henry V); Leslie Banks (Chorus); Felix Aylmer (Canterbury); Nicholas Hannen (Exeter); Robert Newton (Pistol); Renée Asherson (Princess Katharine)

Director: Laurence Olivier

Producer: Laurence Olivier

Photography: Robert Krasker

Music: William Walton

One kind of modern critical orthodoxy has been content to conclude that Laurence Olivier's *Henry V* was 'designed as propaganda, or escapist fantasy which glamorizes war and boosts morale' (Cartmell, 2000, 100). Judged solely in ideological terms, no doubt the film can be seen this way, but such an evaluation takes no account of those dimensions of the movie that make it a brilliantly innovative *filmic* adaptation of Shakespeare's play, as well as a movie of immense popularity. Instead of dismissing it as a kind of euphoric patriotic hymn, we need to comprehend the film in terms of its *cinematic* achievement, to appreciate why film theorist Andre Bazin should assert that 'there is more cinema, and great cinema at that, in *Henry V* alone than in 90% of original scripts' (quoted in Jorgens, 1991, 133).

Olivier in 1944 regarded his *Henry V* as part of the war effort, as the film's pre-titles statement makes clear: 'To the Commandos and Airborne Troops of Great Britain, the spirit of whose ancestors it has been humbly attempted to recapture in some ensuing scenes, This Film is Dedicated.' Olivier was a serving pilot in the Fleet Air Arm, and his patriotic motivations for making *Henry V* are also evident in his published account of the film's making. 'There we were,' says Olivier, 'a band of artists and technicians, humble in our souls because Hitler was killing our countrymen, imbued with a sense of history ... As I flew over the country in my Walrus [a sea plane] I kept seeing it as Shakespeare's sceptred isle.' (The 'sceptred isle' reference relates to part of John of Gaunt's apparently 'patriotic' speech in *Richard II* (2.1.40).) A kind of conservatism also colours Olivier's view of Shakespeare and his play: 'We were inspired by the warmth, humanity, wisdom and Britishness just beneath the surface of Shakespeare's brilliant jingoism' (Olivier, 1987, 171, 167–8). One-dimensional as this vision of *Henry V* might seem, it nevertheless supplied Olivier with the vital and clearly focused *vision* that all outstanding film adaptations of Shakespeare require, even if this vision may necessitate many textual cuts to realize it. Olivier was determined to project Henry as the kind of heroic figure wartime audiences would warm to and be inspired by, requiring scriptwriters Olivier and Alan Dent to remove 50 per cent of the play's lines. Much of the cutting turns a complex and sometimes equivocal play into a film where the English side is shown as heroic and resolute, led by the valiantly charismatic Henry, while the French are portrayed as vain and dissipated, their leaders concerned more with elegant living than with the gritty challenge of war.

In order for Henry to come across as a benign and goodly king whose reign is relatively trouble-free, many lines and passages are edited out. A few examples must suffice. When speaking to the French Ambassador, Henry boldly states, 'We are no tyrant, but a Christian king', omitting to speak the next lines: 'Unto whose grace our passion is as subject / As is our wretches fettered in our prisons' (1.2.241–3). The whole of the Cambridge, Scrope and Grey treason plot is also removed, even though at Southampton Olivier allows Scrope to remonstrate with Henry for pardoning a man who had 'railed against [the King's royal] person' (2.2.41). This excision was presumably made because the episode shows Henry cunningly toying with the courtiers' pretended loyalty to him, prior to the chilling moment when he hands them their death warrants as traitors. Displaying Henry in such a devious mode complicates the positive image of 'Britishness' Olivier wanted to convey for his king. Other cuts serve the same purpose of playing down Henry's violent side. The intimidating message he sends via Exeter to King Charles threatening a 'hungry war' that will consume French 'husbands, fathers, and betrothed lovers', leaving widows, orphans and maidens weeping (2.4.103–8), is excised. So is Henry's vicious (if rhetorical) speech before the gates of Harfleur in which he conjures up images of daughters defiled, the 'reverend' heads of old men 'dashed to the walls' and 'naked infants spitted on spikes' (3.3.112–15). Other troublesome parts of the text are also removed: Henry's decision to hang Bardolph for stealing; the part of his anguished pre-Agincourt prayer in which he conjures God not to 'think upon the fault / My father made in compassing the crown' (4.2.275–6) (Henry's father Bolingbroke usurped the throne from its rightful possessor, Richard II); and the strategic command to have all the French prisoners' throats cut (4.7.55–7). Finally, Olivier cancels those lines of Chorus's Epilogue telling the Elizabethan audience what many of them would know already from seeing *1 Henry VI* (presumably hardly any, in a popular film audience): how King Harry was to die all too soon after his triumph, his successor Henry VI leading a state in which 'so many had the managing / That they lost France and made his England bleed'. Such a climax would hardly be welcomed by a wartime film audience expecting victory without qualification. They did welcome it on release, turning it into an Academy Award winner.

How did the world's first significant Shakespeare film adaptation achieve this? How did one make a popular *Shakespeare* movie in English, when Shakespeare had for the most part been perceived as poison at the box office? Part of the answer is that the film followed a heavily cut text designed to satisfy the narrative expectations of a cinema audience whose encounter with the struggles of love and war occurred in the relatively uncomplicated screen worlds of Westerns and Romances. Olivier's own answer is that his was 'the first serious attempt to make a truly Shakespearean film' (Olivier, 1984). By 'truly Shakespearean' he seems to mean something as inventive in using the possibilities of cinematic technique as Shakespeare had been in exploring the theatrical possibilities of his own day, when theatre was new. By 1943 Olivier had learned much about the techniques of popular filmmaking, especially from William Wyler, in whose movie *Wuthering Heights* (1939) he had starred as Heathcliff. 'I was amazed', said Olivier, 'how easily I thought in the language of film: panorama shots, tracking shots, dolly shots, medium short, close-ups, and movement and prying of the camera.' (This 'movement and prying of the camera' was to become a lasting technical signature of his Shakespeare films.) Yet even with a sound grasp of film language, for him the problem remained of finding 'a style which Shakespearean actors could act and yet which would be acceptable to the audience of the time, used to little other than the most obvious propaganda' (Olivier, 1987, 168) (i.e. the 'reverential' approach to Shakespeare that had turned so many off).

His solution emerged from the text itself, when he noticed how in *Henry V* more than any other of his plays, 'Shakespeare moans about the confines of his Globe Theatre – "Or may we cram/ Within this wooden O the very casques / That did affright the air at Agincourt?"' Mulling over this key **metatheatrical** issue that Shakespeare has Chorus raise when speaking of the Globe Theatre's constraints for showing a battle, he realized that 'the goddamn play was telling me the style of the film':

> Dress the Chorus as an Elizabethan actor (which he was), get him – with broad gestures – to challenge the imaginations of the unruly audience in the

pit. Maybe that way the film audience would be challenged. Play the first few scenes on the Globe stage in a highly, absolutely deliberate, theatrical style; get the film audience used to the language, and let them laugh its excesses out of their systems before the story really begins. I was deter-mined to bring in the comics, Falstaff and his friends Nym, Bardolph and Pistol, for without them, it would have been two and a half hours of Henry, Henry, Henry: the film cried out for light relief! (Olivier, 1987, 169)

At one stroke Olivier had hit upon a brilliant device and structure for delivering *Henry V* on film and for making a movie that could be intriguingly accessible to a popular (wartime) audience. By using an Elizabethan performance of the play to frame the movie – a very Shakespearean 'play within a play' contrivance after all – Olivier over-came the common resistance to Shakespeare among cinema audiences so often repelled by reverential adaptations, by using Shakespeare's own secret weapon – *entertainment*. The artificial style of theatrical presentation he used to do this is completely evident from the outset, when from an overhead **crane shot**, as described in the opening lines of the screenplay:

> We see an aerial view of London, based on Visscher's engraving of 1600. Track back to show the City in long shot, then track in on the Bear Playhouse and then to the Globe Playhouse, where a flag is being hoisted.
> (Olivier, 1984)

In fact, what we see first of all is a handbill fluttering through the air to the accompaniment of a chortling flute, the handbill announcing a forthcoming performance of '"King Henry the Fift, with his battle fought at Agincourt in France" by Will Shakespeare at the Globe Playhouse'. The camera then cranes over a vast model of Elizabethan London, 'mistakenly' zooming in on the Bear Baiting theatre before swerving right to find its true goal, the Globe, where *Henry V* is about to start. (Olivier had evidently not been looking at Visscher's London panorama but that of Hollar, where the names on the Bear Baiting (dual purpose Hope) and Globe theatres were transposed in error.) The camera swerve is the film's first **metacinematic** shot, alerting us to the fact that what we see is facilitated by the movement of the record-ing camera and its lens. A second 'baring of the device' occurs when Leslie Banks's Chorus, having addressed the Globe audience, now strides **downstage** to look into the camera, inciting the film audience to 'on your imaginary forces work'. Curiously, it is as if we are being asked to prepare ourselves for the privilege that will be denied to the

diegetic audience – the privilege of not merely imagining, but of *seeing* the Agincourt battle. We will see it, of course, represented for the first time ever through the magic of location film shooting, making the imaginary cinematically real.

Before the performance does begin, the hustle and bustle of back-stage (**tiring-house**) preparations of the actors is shown – including a **close-up** of Olivier himself coughing nervously before his entrance as Henry. Then the colourful spectacle of a pseudo-Elizabethan per-formance commences. This includes the boisterous response of the Globe audience, whose noisy delight at the antics of Falstaff–surrogate Pistol helps to convey the kind of sturdy register of 'Britishness' that Olivier was aiming to establish. Casting the twinkle-eyed and loveable rough-diamond movie actor Robert Newton in the part of Pistol was a shrewdly effective way to code for popular cinematic success. Yet we never come to feel we are being *enjoined to believe* in what has been called the 'comedy of incompetence' going on between the actors playing churchmen Canterbury and Ely. In fact, this strategically comic opening enables Olivier to achieve just the kind of *distance* between film audience and Globe actors needed in order that his own confident, forceful playing of Henry as heroic king *will* be persuasive and believable. This is achieved by at least three aspects of Olivier's performance. When the French ambassa-dors have presented the Dauphin's twin insults – his message, 'you savour too much of your youth', and his 'tun of treasure', the tennis balls – Henry's cool, initially amused expression sours rapidly into one of deadly threat, the camera backing away from him as he stands up to deliver the Olivierean verbal dynamics. This technique – used again for the 'once more unto the breach' and St Crispin's day speeches – was introduced by Olivier to manage a Shakespearean vocal 'climax' on film that he noticed had always failed in previous films employing a **close-up** static camera shot. This climax sets up the terms of the coming war as much in the tone of a Western hero's menacing threat, as it does the warning offered by a monarch on behalf of his nation. The cowboy style is taken further when, 'relax-ing' after the departure of the ambassadors, Henry casually slings his crown on to the back of his throne chair, just as John Wayne might have done had he been playing the part. The Western style is adopted again much later when, after the triumphant St Crispin's day speech, Henry slips effortlessly into the saddle of his waiting horse, in slick contrast to the helplessly armoured French knights who need to be winched down on to their horses by block and tackle.

So far in the film, Olivier's device of the Elizabethan Globe performance has been achieved in a **metatheatrical** register. But when Chorus pulls across a stage curtain that changes to a kind of gauze through which a **medium-long shot** of Southampton comes into focus, we witness the mingling of filmic and theatrical transitions as one form of scenic artifice moves into another. The artifice of both mediums is thus revealed, compelling the film audience to feel a shift from **metatheatrical** to **metacinematic** forms of visual representation. Moving from the patently Victorian theatrical spectacle of Henry's ship and preparations for war with France at Southampton, Chorus, now speaking in the filmic register of **voice-over**, asks us to 'still be kind, and eke out our performance with your mind'. This firmly engages the film audience, Olivier now employing his 'prying camera' to take us through the upper window of the Boar's Head tavern into a room where Falstaff is dying. Walton's music – scored to brilliantly dramatic effect for many parts of this film – accompanies the camera in this interpolated scene at Falstaff's deathbed, creating a strong emotional effect by the use of a short repeated passage in the bass, upon which the main structure of the music is built. Complemented by Mistress Quickly's famous description of his death to Pistol *et al.* (2.3.9–23), the loss of this 'loveable rogue' of the English stage is feelingly conveyed in a nostalgically 'British' tone, prior to our encounter with the French court, Harfleur, Agincourt, and finally Henry's wooing and marriage to Princess Katharine, following British victory.

Conducted by our aerial courier Chorus to France through 'royal purple' mists created by conventional trick photography, we move above (a model of) the English armada ploughing through the Channel far below us – more film artifice. After the conquest of Harfleur, we are introduced to a ***mise-en-scène*** of the French court modelled after the medieval illustrations for the *Calendar of the Book of Hours* of the Duke of Berry, whom we are shown reading his own book, the visual source for the scene in which he is standing. Exeter presents Henry's ultimatum to King Charles in a heavily abridged version of 2.4, and the French king faints into the arms of an exasperated Dauphin. This and other satirical tableaux depict the French as over-refined and vain, utterly ill-prepared for war. Such 'distanced' portrayal of a feeble enemy contrasts strongly with the display of a brave Henry, cleverly depicted in the night scene before Agincourt in what Chorus calls 'a little touch of Henry in the night'. The full text expressing Williams's animus following Henry's 'I think the King is but a man, as I am' speech, is retained (4.1.130–42), as is his challenge to the disguised king after the ransom discussion. It is to Olivier's credit that the uncomfortable complaints of Williams and Bates are not cut. Much of the 'Upon the king' speech is included too, Henry reflecting quietly in the dark on the burdens shouldered by a monarch in wartime (though without the reference to Richard II). His ruminations upon the coming battle being coupled with an interpolated view of his commanders at prayer in their tent offer visual and aural registers that help produce the kind of sentimental mood of sympathetic **identification** Olivier clearly wished to establish with the screen audience at the movie's crucial centre-point.

In great contrast to this low-key prelude is the spectacular and colourful battle of Agincourt itself, arguably the film's most memorable sequence. It is a battle all audiences until now had only been able to imagine. It was re-created for the movie using location settings in Eire, hundreds of extras, and a mile-long set of tracks permitting the camera to travel with the speeding advance of the French cavalry upon the English. Olivier introduced the French cavalry charge to create 'pace, rhythm and conflict' (Oliver, 1987, 172), the long **tracking shot** following it from gentle horse-trot to thunderous gallop, and alternating this horizontal tracking by the camera of the galloping French cavalry with shots of the waiting English army. Lines of archers, bows raised to shoot, anxiously watch for Henry's poised sword to drop as the signal to release both arrows – and tension. As the cloud of hissing arrows sound in a quiet pause from Walton's stirring music it becomes clear that here we have a considerable actor-king (Henry) whose talent for manipulating events is matched by the multiple role-playing figure of Olivier himself: the leading actor, director and producer of a war film inspired by the needs of wartime.

Olivier said that ideally Agincourt should have been enacted on green velvet, in order to fit in with the 'picture-book' look of the film (Oliver, 1987, 173). Instead, he made a film which offers a balance of the artificially 'medieval' and the dynamically real. Much of this contrast is achieved on the one hand by aligning 'the artificial' with the slightly ridiculous French, who, along with the relatively anonymous military ranks of the English, we are never really allowed to know. On the other hand, we do come to sympathize with Olivier's heroic, Western-style Henry, who, among all the visual artifice, emerges as the likeable leader whose bluff, 'no-nonsense' and sexually attractive style is successfully adapted to appeal to the cinema audience of the time.

Kenneth Branagh's *Henry V* (UK, 1989)

Medium: Eastmancolor, 35mm, 132 minutes

Main actors: Kenneth Branagh (Henry V); Derek Jacobi (Chorus); Brian Blessed (Exeter); Ian Holm (Fluellen); Judi Dench (Mistress Quickly); Robert Stephens (Pistol); Richard Briers (Bardolph); Emma Thompson (Princess Katharine); Paul Scofield (French King)

Director: Kenneth Branagh

Producer: Stephen Evans

Photography: Kenneth MacMillan

Music: Pat Doyle

When Branagh adapted *Henry V* for the screen – setting off the great wave of Shakespeare movies of the 1990s – his aim was to 'make a truly popular film' (like Olivier), believing the play could be told as a story 'that would make you laugh, make you cry, and be utterly accessible to anyone of whatever age or background'. But instead of scripting a movie with a 'seeming[ly] nationalistic and militaristic emphasis' – the way he saw Olivier's version – he understood the play as 'a deeply questioning, ever-relevant and compassionate survey of people and war'. This inquiring approach would need quite a different style of acting and presentation, especially in the case of Henry himself. Noticing the play suggested 'an especially young Henry with more than a little of the Hamlet in him', Branagh wanted to convey the king as a more complex figure than Olivier's heroic monarch (Branagh, 1989, 10, 9, 12, 10). A daunting challenge, it was in some ways parallel to the test presented by his own youthful project to lead a new style Renaissance Theatre Company (RTC) to triumph in the realm of Shakespeare performance. In a post-Falklands and post-Vietnam era, part of the complexity would also be shown by presenting many (but not all) of the more negative and controversial aspects of Shakespeare's play that Olivier's film had left out, while at the same time bringing the film audience closer to the human experiences and dilemmas of the key characters.

Central to Branagh's modern approach and the film's success was his 'idea of abandoning large-theatre projection and allowing **close-ups** and low-level dialogue to draw the audience deep into the human side of this distant mediaeval world' (Branagh, 1989, 10). This is in marked contrast to Olivier's method, which is to maintain distance between the audience and his characters. Olivier's heroic Henry is aloof (even in the night-time sequence when Henry confides his thoughts in **voice-over**); the foppish French court and their bumbling king are a laughing stock; and most of the other main characters, including Henry's followers both high and low, tend to be portrayed as character 'types'. Olivier's use of an identification shot followed by framed **long** and very long **shot**s positioning Henry as actor-king surrounded by his soldier-cast each doing their bit towards the final English triumph creates this distancing effect. Branagh's key strategy of filming almost throughout using **mid-shot**s and **close-up**s is to draw the audience into the inner life of his characters: he wants us to identify with the feelings, emotions and anxieties, not only of Henry and his friends, but of the French too.

The **close-up** camerawork is apparent from the film's opening, when, offering a visual pun on his first line as Chorus, Derek Jacobi wishes for 'a muse of fire' while simultaneously illuminating his own face with the flare of a struck match. From here to the end of 1.1, the way light and shadow reveal or hide characters and settings within the frame of the screen provides a clever and teasing commentary on the opening of Olivier's film, while also offering a much more serious and dramatic introduction to the figure of a radically different Henry. Olivier had used the conventions and backstage setting of the Elizabethan theatre to intrigue and engage his film audience. Here, once Jacobi throws a massive light switch, the camera follows him through what we see is a film studio, with all the paraphernalia of movie-making littered about that will be used in making this film: camera, arc lights, scenery, **props**. We are clearly being told that the 'brightest heaven of invention' (Prologue, 2) these days comprises the full resources of the film studio. Jacobi flings open huge double doors on to black, and after light streams from the gap behind a cautiously opened door, in **close-up** we see a sinister Canterbury (Charles Kay) looking stealthily out as he whispers conspiratorially with Ely (Alec McCowen): the **metacine-matic** point has been made that we are entering the constructed world of – a film.

Henry's entrance, interrupting a series of **shot/reverse shot**s of Canterbury and Ely in secret conference, is spectacularly effective. From Henry's **POV**, we briefly see huge double doors again flung open, and then, accompanied by a fanfare of startled strings, a **long shot** from his courtiers' viewpoint reveals a small, becloaked figure in silhouette standing alone in the vast open doorway against blinding arc lights. For the Star Wars generation, it is something like a mysterious Darth Vader-like Henry we see. From Henry's advancing **POV** the camera shows us in **mid-shot** his courtiers bowing down as we move through this avenue of figures towards the throne, where the camera gives the briefest of glimpses of him as he turns to sit down. It is only now that the face and bareheaded figure of Henry is fully revealed, young, boyish and vulnerable on his large throne. The remainder of the scene is played in a very different acting register to that of Olivier's film. Instead of the knockabout humour between the clerics and Henry, there is a deadly seriousness about the young and inexperienced king that proves more than a match for the wiles of Canterbury and, in turn, for the insulting embassy sent by the Dauphin. Proceeding with a range of **close** and **mid-shot**s recording the responses of all protagonists, by the end of the scene Henry has united his own court and impressed the ambassador Mountjoy with a strength of character displaying the potential force of his rule – and his resolve to take France. This is despite the fact that the scene is *also* shot to convey something of the way the play arouses *doubts* about the legality of the planned war.

Branagh uses the **close** and **mid-shot** most carefully when revealing a Henry with doubts as well as certainties – his 'on the king' soliloquy at the end of the night-time sequence (in 4.1) will be the best example. Sequences of such shots are used nowhere more effectively to create emotional connections with the audience than when showing the male camaraderie Henry develops with his men as the prerequisite to military success. We see this very effectively at work in their response to his highly rhetorical 'once more unto the breach' speech at Harfleur. But Henry builds the 'male-bonding' process in earnest most effectively when responding to Warwick's anxious wish before Agincourt for 'But one ten thousand of those men in England / That do no work today.' 'What's he that wishes so?' calls out Branagh's Henry, and as he begins what will become the famous St Crispin's Day speech, his men trail after him towards the cart where he will finish it, the **tilted-up** camera planted among them capturing from their **POV** his charismatic delivery as he stands above. Doyle's stirring music gathering beneath his delivery, Henry articulates for them in a quiet voice full of emotion how they who are to fight together will 'be remembered, / We few, we happy few, we band of brothers. / For he today that sheds his blood with me / Shall be my brother' (4.3.59–62).

As Henry utters 'we band of brothers', there is a **reaction-shot** intercut (one of many during this and the Harfleur speeches) of a small group of his men photographed from above, their faces shining with devoted enthusiasm at their king's words. Not only does this Henry seem spontaneous, natural and convincing, in contrast to Olivier's more controlled and declamatory style, but his emotion is tinglingly persuasive. Branagh's determination to move his audience is conveyed nowhere better than in the muddy battle scenes with the French, in great contrast to Olivier's relatively 'clean' style of portraying battle. His appropriation of Vietnam War movie film codes is at the heart of his emotionalizing technique, the sequence in which Henry's cousin York dies being remarkable for its similarity to one in _Platoon_. This is when Oliver Stone's **slow-motion** camera in **medium-shot** captures the death of the stranded Sergeant Elias, whose upflung arms as Samuel Barber's 'Adagio for Strings' plays, are so suggestive of a Christ-like martyrdom. In the midst of Branagh's **slow-motion** battle sequence, also accompanied by a repeated musical figure using strings, York is shown holding his sword aloft ready to strike, when he is cut down by the French soldiers surrounding him, blood spurting from his mouth, his death becoming a kind of ritualized sacrificial offering for what will be Henry's final victory.

Despite also borrowing much from the grimly effective shooting techniques of Welles's battle sequence in _Chimes at Midnight_, the conclusion of Branagh's Agincourt battle scene is very much his own, an interesting combination of the sentimental and the serious. The sentimental strand begins when Fluellen discovers the French have killed all 'the poys [boys] and the luggage' (4.7.1) in the English camp. Branagh's script (and film) omits the fact that Henry orders his soldiers to cut the throats of all their prisoners as a strategic move in response to the military regrouping of the French (not obvious in Shakespeare's text but recoverable from Shakespeare's source, Holinshed). Instead, the action is carried forward by implying that Henry's statement, 'I was not angry since I came to France / Until this instant' (4.7.47–8) is a response to the killing of the English boys.

When it becomes clear the English have triumphed, in what Branagh calls the 'greatest **tracking shot** in the world' he has an exhausted Henry carry Falstaff's dead Boy (Christian Bale) the whole length of the corpse-littered battlefield, depositing him finally upon a cart already bearing youthful corpses. The serious point Branagh undoubtedly wants to make by offering this end-of-battle scene is conveyed by his hope that, in providing the sequence (together with Doyle's music producing a 'tremendous climax'), 'There would be no question about the statement this movie was making about war' (Branagh, 1991, 235, 236). Olivier had gone to much trouble to construct in Ireland a set of camera tracks that would ultimately capture an extended travelling shot of the French on horseback speeding along for their attack on the English, carrying the viewer *into* battle. Branagh exploits the emotions of the audience by thrusting forward the image of children killed in battle to deliver an anti-war message. Yet one must also observe that Branagh makes his serious point by using a long **tracking shot** to carry the viewer *out* of battle, and in a way that reveals the human price we pay for entering into it.

Laurence Olivier's *Richard III* (UK, 1955)

Medium: VistaVision-Technicolor, 35mm, *c*.150 minutes

Main actors: Laurence Olivier (Richard III); Ralph Richardson (Duke of Buckingham); John Gielgud (Duke of Clarence); Cedric Hardwicke (Edward IV); Alec Clunes (Lord Hastings); Laurence Naismith (Lord Stanley); Claire Bloom (Lady Anne); Andrew Cruickshank (Brackenbury); Norman Wooland (Catesby); Mary Kerridge (Queen Elizabeth); Pamela Brown (Jane Shore); Stanley Baker (Richmond)

Director: Laurence Olivier

Producers: Laurence Olivier, Alexander Korda

Script: Laurence Olivier, Alan Dent

Photography: Otto Heller

Design: Carmen Dillon, Roger Furse

Music: William Walton

Sound: Bert Rule

Laurence Olivier's third Shakespeare adaptation developed and took forward stylistic features of his earlier films *Henry V* and *Hamlet*. Indeed, an identifiably 'Olivieresque' Shakespearean cinematic style could be said to have emerged in these movies, combining four distinctive areas of approach. First, the structural design of each film carries what Anthony Davies has called a 'broad cyclical movement', the concluding frames of every film returning to and repeating those which opened it. Then there is the device introduced in *Henry V*, and developed significantly in *Hamlet*, where Olivier turns his camera into a kind of probing, actively 'showing' narrator. *Richard III* takes this narrative device one audacious step further when the eye of the camera (at least for the first half of the film) is put under the narrative authority and control of Richard himself. Thirdly, each movie evidences a balance consistently struck by Olivier between a theatricality of dramatic action and forms of cinematic expressiveness that are never less than ingeniously effective. A final yet significant feature inextricably bound up with Olivier's desire to showcase his own considerable acting talents is the fact that the principal characters he plays in each film are monarchs or princely leaders in conflict with the society around them. Henry V's goal is to prove himself to be heroically worthy of the crown to a sceptical English court and country; Hamlet has been cheated of the kingship and aims to retrieve it by avenging Old Hamlet's killer; the amoral Richard of Gloucester sweeps all before him as he plots, manipulates and ruthlessly murders his way to the English crown.

Olivier noted special difficulties in bringing *Richard III* to the screen, as he told Roger Manvell after filming completed in 1955:

> To start with it's a very long play. It's not until the little princes come on that the story forms that nice river sweep, going swiftly to its conclusion from about half way through the play. The first part up until that moment is an absolute delta of plot and presupposed foreknowledge of events. After all, *Richard III* forms the last part of a cycle of four plays, the other three being parts of *Henry VI* ... Yet it's always been a popular play – as Dr Johnson said, its popularity derives from the character of Richard.
>
> (Manvell, 1971, 48)

Olivier here identifies a key problem and a key solution in approaching his own adaptation: the 'absolute delta of plot', as he says, is the most formidable obstacle facing the understanding of a movie audience, yet it is by focusing on 'the character of Richard', so evil and yet so compelling, that the audience can be helped to engage with the world of the film. To provide a **backstory** for the beginning of *Richard III* Olivier opens with the final scene of *3 Henry VI*, which presents the coronation of Richard's eldest brother, Edward IV (5.7). Starting this way allows Olivier to introduce a range of visual elements to engage the audience's attention, chief of which is the actual image of the English crown. We have already read rolling titles informing us how the film's story begins as the 'White Rose of York was in its final flowering', that is, towards the end of that period of conflict known as the Wars of the Roses. As the ornate lettering cues us into the history, the swelling sonorities of Walton's regal score, so evocative of a grand historical English heritage, soothes our ears. That sense of stability is soon shaken, when we read, 'Here begins one of the most famous and at the same time most infamous of the legends that are attached to: The Crown of England.' As the frame proclaiming this **dissolves** to a **close-up** of a pendant golden crown, so does the stately music shift gear into high, rapidly bowed shrill notes on the strings, linking the crown anew with a sense of terror and danger. This crown image that starts the film proper with Edward IV's coronation will also end it prior to Richmond's being crowned first Tudor king of England as

Henry VII. Olivier's visual/acoustic rendering of an English crown connoting terror and danger is a precise **metonymic** for the character and the theme which thread unerringly through the play – Richard Gloucester, and his murderous schemes to become and to remain king.

With Technicolor stock conveying for Edward's coronation the kind of eye-catching pageantry that made Olivier's *Henry V* so visually attractive, one would not know from viewing the sequence that this ceremony occurs only because the Lancastrian Henry VI had been murdered by Yorkist Richard in the Tower. This was shortly after Richard, Edward and the middle brother Clarence had together stabbed to death Henry's son Prince Edward (*3 Henry VI*, 5.6, 5.5), thus removing the immediate Lancastrian occupier and inheritor of the English throne. All is not therefore what it seems, and Olivier's shooting of the scene offers hints that the crown is not secure on Edward's head, that intrigue and intrafamilial strife lurk under the surface of courtly gentility. An initial shot of the cardinal lowering the crown towards the new king's head is replaced by a shot over Richard's shoulder where the latter's placing of a crown on the long, luxuriantly thick curls of his own head significantly obscures the crowning of the king. At the third cry of 'Long live King Edward IV!' from the assembled court, Richard spins round to leer at the camera and (as we think) us – the cinema audience. But we are wrong. Although there will be many occasions to come when Richard does address us via the camera, we are this time tricked by Olivier: the following shot of Buckingham blinking attentively and a return to Richard's gaze reveals that the **shot/reverse shot** sequence actually consisted of Richard and *Buckingham* exchanging significant conspiratorial glances. The sequence of glances continues, in what amounts to Olivier's introduction of all the main characters. Buckingham glances towards brother Clarence, who in turn looks benignly on the scene while trumpet fanfares sound and Edward, after receiving blessings from the Cardinal, descends to be joined by Queen Elizabeth as they process through to the adjacent throne room of the Palace, where he addresses the court. On the way, he pauses to gently touch the arm of his mistress Jane Shore with the royal mace – to the Queen's obvious annoyance. Shore is a character only mentioned in Shakespeare's play, yet Olivier includes her as a frequently visible (non-speaking) figure, almost certainly to provide sexual interest, but also perhaps to make up for the film's excision of Queen Margaret, the forthright and martial-minded widow of Henry VI.

The coronation scene over and the crowds dispersed, we are made to encounter 'crookback' Richard, the camera nosing its way into the throne room of the palace where he hovers, a dark, hook-nosed, crow-like figure awaiting us, we whom Olivier implicates in Richard's scheming by forcing us to be party to it. The famous – but ironical – opening lines of *Richard III*: 'Now is the winter of our discontent / Made glorious summer by this son of York' provide the first of many occasions when Olivier has Richard audaciously break through the 'fourth wall' of the cinema screen to address us via the camera, affronting the normal cinematic conventions. Olivier has explained how he self-consciously performed the first seventeen lines of this celebrated soliloquy 'as though to each one of us personally' – 'you can do that on film', he observes (Olivier, 1987, 187), revealing his understanding of film technique. The direct address works here, as elsewhere in the film, because Olivier knows (from making his *Henry V*) that he can only rant when further away from the camera, and he also keeps the camera moving, as if it (i.e. our **POV**) is a character attentively listening to him (which we are). What we therefore see in the opening sequences and at other places in the movie are Olivier's skills in deploying a clever combination of theatrical and cinematic techniques both to dramatize Richard's perverted designs and to put us in touch with the mind behind the mask.

Richard's flirting with the cinema audience is shortly followed by his flirting seduction of Lady Anne (Claire Bloom). This scene of the play is difficult enough to carry off persuasively in the best of performances, Richard having assassinated both Anne's husband Prince Edward and his father Henry VI. Although Olivier reports that on stage his 'hideous wooing of Lady Anne' had worked brilliantly (false modesty was never his style), he perceptively realized that 'if it's too sudden on the screen the unaccustomed audience' will not be persuaded. He therefore slows down the length of the seduction by splitting the scene into two parts, rearranging the lines so that Richard gets 'two glorious climaxes': 'I'll have her, but I will not keep her long', and 'Was ever woman in this humour woo'd? / Was ever woman in this humour won?' (Olivier, 1987, 184) At the end of each sequence, Olivier introduces the dramatically effective visual device of shadows – a **motif** that will recur – conveying the evil lurking behind all of Richard's dark manoeuvres. The earliest deployment of this motif is at the conclusion of the first part of his seduction of Anne, when Richard performs more lines borrowed from *3 Henry VI*: 'Clarence, beware; thou kept'st me from the light – / But I will sort a pitchy day for thee. /

For I will buzz abroad such prophecies / That Edward shall be fearful of his life, / And then, to purge his fear, I'll be thy death' (5.6.85–9). These lines are spoken as if emerging from Richard's bulky, batlike shadow as it slopes off from Westminster Abbey, filling the frame on the word 'death'. The camera follows his shadow until we see it stooping to 'buzz' the ear of Edward's throne-seated shadow with the requisite lies, while monks are heard chanting, providing an ironically 'holy' counterpoint to Richard's 'pitchy' (dark) plotting. His evil message delivered, Richard kisses the royal hand, and as he moves away passes close to the camera, showing us in significant **close-up** the Gloucester heraldic badge pinned to his breast – a snarling boar. (A **close-up** in the closing frames of the film will have the camera lingering on the motto of the Order of the Garter emblazoned on the upper part of Richard's boot – his dead body slung across a horse – that reads: 'Honi soit qui mal y pense' – Shame to him who evil thinks.) The second key use of the shadow motif follows Richard's subduing of Anne, again triggered by a performance of his lines. This time, preening himself on his success, vanity prompts the comment: 'Shine out, fair sun, till I have bought a glass, / That I may see my shadow as I pass' (*Richard III*, 1.2.249–50). Richard kicks open the door of Lady Anne's apartment, and his long, vampire-like shadow is shown engulfing the white dress-clad form of Anne who, standing near her bed, turns towards him. The implication of impending sexual conquest is inescapable, confirmed (though indirectly) by the next shot where, to the accompaniment of a chirpy flute tune, we cut to a Richard merrily pulling on his gloves in a significant **close-up** revealing them decorated with his personal emblem – the snarling boar.

Walton's musical score frequently provides an appropriate heightening of the film's various dramatic moods. In emphasizing Richard's terrifying control over events and our viewpoint, this heightening occurs powerfully in the sequence when Clarence relates his bad dreams to Brackenbury in the Tower, music and clever camerawork subtly combining to create chilling effects. From gentle monks chanting and the closing up of their missal, we suddenly cut to the green-tinged, stony gothic arches of the Tower's subterranean vaults, a dissonant clash of brass, woodwind and percussion simultaneously sounding every bit as frightening as the horror-genre scores that will come to characterize the music of Hammer films starting to appear in the mid-1950s. The dissonant fanfare succeeds to a sinister chugging and pounding rhythm in the low register of woodwind and strings as we are shown Clarence moaning in his 'ghastly dreams' of drowning, until the music spirals into a crash of cymbals when he wakes in terror. He now recounts his horrific dream to Brackenbury in a mixture of (mostly) **two-shot**s filmed from inside the cell. But after Clarence sinks down to rest, the camera cuts to a perspective of him from the high barred window. More surging dissonant brass and woodwind now quickly segue into a sinister flurry of strings while the camera pulls back to reveal the ominous shadow of Richard's hat and long hair framing our view of his doomed brother through the cell window. The music suddenly halts as Buckingham's cheery greeting breaks the spell of our concentration: 'Good time of day unto your royal grace!' Richard spins round, alarmed, and we cut to a **mid-shot** of him responding with relief to the man he elsewhere describes as his 'other self'. Until this moment, there was no clue that the events we had been witnessing were being seen from Richard's narrative **POV**, this brilliantly contrived sequence exemplifying Olivier's cinematic skill in enforcing our complicity with Richard's outlook and manipulative methods.

There are further chilling moments created by Olivier that deploy frenzied Hammer-like musical scoring, and more examples, too, of his capacity to blend cinematic inventiveness and theatricality. The terrifying music accompanying the stuffing of Clarence's body into the malmsey butt (wine barrel) is not only of the Hammer variety, but his murderers are played by two actors who would appear repeatedly as villains in future Hammer horror films, Michael Gough and Michael Ripper, as would Patrick Troughton, playing Tyrell, murderer of the young princes. The **deep-focus** shooting Olivier used so extensively in *Hamlet* is used to good effect again in *Richard III*, the VistaVision camera giving solidity of image in **wide shot**s and detailed expression in **close-up**s. When Richard and Buckingham are shown quietly plotting at the window of the throne room, the young Prince Edward standing in the background, the power of the former over the latter is amply visualized through their relative size differences in the film frame. In this scene, too, there is the visual device of the vertical window bar ironically prefiguring the estrangement to come between the currently amicable pair, a near-repeat of the image where they conspire at the foot of King Edward's deathbed. There, the vertical line of a narrow wall-column between them suggests inevitable division. The part played by Charles Laughton in *The Hunchback of Notre Dame* (1939) seems to have provided Olivier with an irresistibly relevant image to apply to the crippled Richard when, following the latter's 'reluctant' agreement to accept the crown, he slithers down a bell rope to join the conspirators. He compels them to bow down before his twisted body, the bell clanging manically to signal that the crown is now his.

Richard having attained his goal, there is little remaining in the movie to rival the compelling interest generated by his manipulative rise to power. The theatricality of action so expertly managed throughout (helped in great part by a studio set where Abbey, Palace and Tower locations are made immediately contiguous) in some ways comes to the fore in the film's late scenes, where Richard's strangely attractive combination of the demonic and the witty reappear. There is a kind of comic vitality in the throne-room scene (end of 4.4.) where Richard is assailed by numerous messengers bringing him news of hostile forces up in arms from all corners of the kingdom. His death on Bosworth Field has a certain grotesque and desperate comedy about it, too. In the play, Richmond kills Richard in single combat, but Olivier has Richard mobbed and assaulted by Richmond's men. After his throat has been cut, they draw back, and we all watch him twitching violently about on the ground. His jerky movements are punctuated – somewhat comically – by the stabbing sound of trumpet notes stepping upward in pitch while he vainly jabs the air with his sword. He eventually thrusts the blade aloft as if – performer to the end – proclaiming his essential calling, that of the soldier and military tactician.

Richard Loncraine's *Richard III* (UK, 1995)

Medium: Eastman colour, 35mm, *c*.100 minutes

Main actors: Ian McKellen (Richard III); Jim Broadbent (Duke of Buckingham); Nigel Hawthorne (Duke of Clarence); John Wood (Edward IV); Annette Bening (Queen Elizabeth); Maggie Smith (Duchess of York); Robert Downey, Jr (Rivers); Jim Carter (Lord Hastings); Edward Hardwicke (Lord Stanley); Kristin Scott Thomas (Lady Anne); Donald Sumpter (Brackenbury); Tim McInnerny (Catesby); Adrian Dunbar (Tyrell); Bill Patterson (Ratcliffe); Dominic West (Richmond)

Director: Richard Loncraine

Producers: Lisa Katselas Paré, Stephen Bayly

Screenplay: Ian McKellen, Richard Loncraine

Photography: Peter Biziou

Design: Tony Burrough

Music: Trevor Jones

Sound: David Stephenson

The key strategy of the Loncraine/McKellen *Richard III* adaptation is to relocate what Ian McKellen calls this 'family drama of power-politics, more tragic than melodramatic' (McKellen, 1996, 24) to a 1930s Britain where Richard's rise to power is made to resemble the deadly contemporary dictatorships of Germany, Italy, Spain and the USSR. The rigid, aristocratic haughtiness of McKellen's army commander-in-chief Richard Gloucester specifically echoes that of baronet-politician Sir Oswald Mosley, who broke away from 1930s consensus politics to lead the Blackshirt-garbed British Union of Fascists. The film was therefore set in the most recent period when a dictatorship like Richard III's might credibly have assumed power in the UK. This design originated in Richard Eyre's successful London stage production of *Richard III*, which McKellen was enthusiastic to extend to a wider audience through popular film, an aim accomplished by a unique combination of two essential inputs. The first was the deep knowledge of Shakespeare, enabling McKellen to produce a draft screenplay cutting the text by over 70 per cent, while retaining enough dramatic excitement to capture the filmic imagination of a moviemaker able to translate his screenplay into popular cinema. McKellen was fortunate to secure this second essential input in the form of prominent com-mercial and feature filmmaker Richard Loncraine and his longtime cinematographic collaborator, Peter Biziou.

In much of what follows I will trace and comment on examples of what James Loehlin calls the movie's pattern of 'interwoven and over-lapping visual codes derived from historical and film iconography' (in Burt and Boose, 2003, 175). These visual codes are Loncraine's cine-matic means for bringing the invented historical setting and design to dramatic life, such that this complex play of intertwined characters becomes accessible to a regular film audience (Loncraine's radical cin-ematic approach to this challenge is also discussed in the Introduction and in Part III). First, I want to identify some of the ways in which this 1995 adaptation differs from Olivier's 1955 medieval-costumed film. McKellen has said that the 'crucial advantage of a modern setting is clarity of storytelling', and for those who are unfamiliar with *Richard III* (let alone the *Henry VI* plays) a clear storyline is vital. The characters are therefore dressed in costumes visibly reflecting their status and profession in the social order, instead of forcing the audi-ence to distinguish one medieval-dressed figure from another. Of course, the audience will have no problem identifying Olivier in his 'star vehicle' approach of foregrounding the grotesque, insinuating, 'witch-like' characterization (Olivier's description) of a Richard so very reminiscent of the cajoling 'Vice' figure of medieval religious drama. McKellen's Gloucester, by contrast, is played as a military tyrant whose grim obsession to rule gains coherence and a plausible chilling interest by making the dynastic political 'family' conflicts of the play reflect the realities of a weakly led and old-fashioned mid-1930s British state potentially ripe for totalitarian takeover.

The film's casting of American actors Annette Bening as Queen Elizabeth and Robert Downey, Jr as her brother Lord Rivers gives the new 'interloping' Woodvilles a social identity so distinctively different from the traditional British aristocratic York family we are shown, that the audience will immediately discern the cultural contrast from their accents and performances. Of equal importance, with the film set in 1936 Britain, the historical resonances of Edward VIII's abdication that year to marry American divorcée Mrs Wallis Simpson, leaving the British throne in some disarray, are all too apt and suggestive (as is the fact of Edward's pro-German sympathies). A further and astute form of the film's economizing narrative method (all of a piece with a gen-eral reliance on short, clear sequences) is the way some of the charac-ters are omitted, while others are 'blended' together. Neither film includes the hate-filled figure of Queen Margaret, resentful widow of the Lancastrian Henry VI. But while the female characters of Olivier's film are portrayed as either relatively quiescent – as in the case of the Duchess of York and Queen Elizabeth – or are only there to arouse sexual intrigue – as with the (silent) figure of Jane Shore – in Loncraine's movie the deep animus of Margaret is felt through the forthright characters of Maggie Smith's Duchess of York (who is given some of Margaret's lines) and Annette Bening's Queen Elizabeth. And while Olivier included both of Elizabeth's sons Dorset and Grey to no great filmic effect, Loncraine omits these characters and instead makes the identity (and loss) of the male Woodville line felt more strongly by embodying it in the single figure of Elizabeth's brother Rivers, brilliantly played by Robert Downey, Jr. A final 'user-friendly' method that Loncraine deploys throughout to communicate the story to his audience is by introducing elements from a whole variety of film genres. Downey had himself been a star icon from light comedy (*Chaplin*, 1992) whose destiny is to be horrifically murdered in a manner derived from the slasher movie. Action films, science fiction, the Western, musicals, the British Heritage film (if in parodic form here, it gives Shakespeare-naïve audiences a 'key' into some of the film's characters via familiar heritage film icons Maggie Smith *et al.*), and above all, the traditional American gangster film genre. I will conclude with a discussion of the way this genre is cleverly used to shape the film as a whole.

Loncraine's visual storytelling method is exemplified by the series of connected sequences in the first nine minutes or so before Richard begins his famous opening speech, though the initial three-minute sequence actually starts not with images but (partly echoing Olivier's opening) with a seven-line written explanation orientating the viewer to 'the story so far':

> Civil war divides the nation. The King is under attack from the rebel York family, who are fighting to place their eldest son, Edward, on the throne. Edward's army advances, led by his youngest brother [5-second pause for dramatic effect until the final line is added] – Richard of Gloucester.

While this statement in blood-red appears – a signal of the carnage to come – in the background we hear a clacking tickertape machine working, then heard more loudly as it reveals in **close-up** grim news for King Henry and his son Prince Edward at their battlefield HQ in a country mansion: 'Richard Gloucester at hand. He holds his course toward Tewkesbury.' Looking every inch the well-groomed British

senior officer, Edward settles at his desk to a traditional English sup-
per with wine, his faithful black Labrador gnawing a bone before the
open fire – a quiet, homely scene, although the bone-chewing is an
early sign of the animalistic appetites to be released by Richard's evil
later on. The comfortable tableau is suddenly shattered by the long
snout of a tank's gun bursting through the fireplace wall, and a gas-
masked soldier emerging to shoot Edward stone-dead with a bullet
between the eyes. His hoarse breathing now scarily dominating the
soundtrack, this masked figure seeks out King Henry and shoots him
in the back of the head as he prays, the shot triggering a blood-red 'R'
on the screen. As Henry's executioner wrenches off his mask, the
'snout' of which has made him resemble (for those who know the play)
the boar's head of Richard Gloucester's personal crest, further away
gunshots seem to blast more red letters on to the screen, ricocheting
bullet sounds and a title leaving us in no doubt who this bloody
killer is: RICHARD III. Not only has 95 per cent of this three minutes
of **backstory**-infilling been achieved visually, but the effects used
draw on a range of popular film-genre codes, Richard's icy power
being conveyed through his hoarse, Darth Vader-like sounds behind
the gas mask – a horrifying aural variant on the shadowy visual echo
of Darth Vader used to evoke regal power near the opening of
Branagh's *Henry V*.

   The first sequence moves into the second with a **sound bridge** of
ricocheting gunshots segueing into the smooth saxophone rhythms of
a Thirties' swing dance band as we join a pensive and anxiously smoking Richard being swept along in his military staff car to the Yorkist
victory party at the royal palace. The following two minutes use short
scenes to introduce triumphant royal family members preparing for
the party, the sequence ending with Clarence (a keen amateur photographer trying to capture on camera a world he cannot fathom) dashing
up a staircase for the York family photo, his camera on timer-release.
As the shutter's click freezes the colour film frame into photographic
black and white, a **metacinematic** hint of how alert this movie is to the
transformative shifts taking place in 1930s media technologies is neatly
made. A cut takes us into the third sequence of three and a quarter
minutes and the York victory ball proper. Here, all are entertained by
glamorous chanteuse Stacey Kent crooning lines from Marlowe's
poem *The Passionate Shepherd to His Love* set to a catchy 1930s style
tune, while she and the Glenn Miller lookalike bandleader make eyes
at one another. (Shakespeare's initials decorate the music stands.)
Dialogue is still absent as more principal characters and relationships

are revealed by 'showing' their interactions with each another. King Edward's already ailing condition is confirmed by his cutting short a dance with the vivacious queen, who comes alive with the arrival of her brother Rivers. His offhand treatment of the royal platform and spontaneous embrace of Elizabeth on the dance floor produce visible disapproval of the American arrivistes among royals and courtiers, the beginnings of a potential social division that Richard Gloucester will ruthlessly exploit, widening it for his own ends.

A key alliance in Richard's manoeuvrings is suggested when the camera, showing both he and Buckingham observing the Queen's daughter Elizabeth and Richmond getting up to dance, then discovers them laughing and shaking hands heartily together, as if the crook-back plotter and the oily yes-man had instinctively discovered common conspiratorial cause in what they have seen. Firmer evidence of Richard's plotting comes when the camera, following his gaze as he takes pause during uneasy efforts to be sociable, shows him watching a whispered exchange between Catesby and King Edward before it **pans** across to reveal his brother Clarence being arrested and led away by Brackenbury and two (tuxedoed) soldiers. 'Plots have I laid ... To set my brothers, Clarence and the King, / In deadly hate, the one against the other', Richard will be telling us soon. Evidently satisfied by his scheming efforts, he grimly stubs out his cigarette, coolly making his way to the bandstand to begin his 'Now is the winter of our discontent' speech. Squeals from the loudspeakers and his tentative tapping of the microphone draw our attention again to the new Thirties' sound technology, and as Richard starts to speak at the mike we are given a foretaste of how he will look when, as British dictator, he comes to address a mass rally of Blackshirt followers.

That moment is as yet some way off, but within a minute's screen time we see Richard shifting in style from the clever public rhetoric Buckingham finds so entertaining, to what we are to suppose is a repetition of these words sneeringly spoken in the privacy of the Palace's spacious male urinal – though within our hearing. This transition from calculated public oratory to resentful private complaint is cleverly managed on a cut at the end of, 'And now – instead of mounting bar-bèd steeds / To fright the souls of fearful adversaries –, / He' – words hissed out through gnashing teeth that in ultra-**close-up** are shown in all of their nicotine-stained griminess. Richard completes the ironic lines – 'capers nimbly in a lady's chamber / To the lascivious pleasing of a lute' while hobbling towards the urinal, the deep sigh he exhales while peeing not only seeming natural to the moment, but an action entirely suited to the words of bitter regret shortly following. These words concern the physical limitations preventing him from performing 'sportive tricks' or courting 'an amorous looking-glass' – his being 'deformed, unfinished, sent before my time / Into this breathing world, / Scarce half made up'. Although seeming to make light of his bodily deformity, Richard's psyche is deeply troubled by it. This vulnerability never showed in the stage version, where his only weakness appeared in the 'nightmare of despair' sequence, his conscience for multiple murders temporarily getting the better of him.

Yet for the most part, McKellen plays Richard as the ultimate narcissist whose feelings of rejection persuade him that the only way to gain power and control is to murder those who stand in his way. The strategy of utter self-reliance which in the play leads him to utter the extraordinarily bleak and Samuel Beckett-like declaration, 'Richard loves Richard; that is, I am I', emerges in the clever use of mirrors in the men's-room scene. The moment he turns round after peeing, adjusting his clothing with military briskness, he advances towards and actually begins to 'court' the men's-room mirror, gazing with close confidence into his own reflection, determining to 'smile, and murder while I smile', to wet his cheeks with 'artificial tears', and to frame his face 'to all occasions' (*3 Henry VI*, 3.2.182, 185). Even though while speaking these confidences to his entranced mirror image he catches sight of us/the camera watching him, he is by no means fazed, but turns round and boastfully confesses his resolve 'to prove a villain / And hate the pleasures of these days,' then beckoning us to look and see his brother Clarence being taken away across the river to the Tower. Of far more forbidding aspect than the medieval Tower of London, the vast anonymous edifice of the Bankside Power Station (now the Tate Modern art gallery) fittingly resembles for this periodizing film the kind of 1930s state prison of terrifying reputation that someone of Richard's fearsome and murderous methods would control (e.g. Stalin's notorious Lubyanka prison in Moscow).

From the film's mid-point, when the Duchess of York snubs Richard following the deaths of Clarence and Edward, and Buckingham for the first time addresses him as 'my Lord Protector', the pace of the movie quickens. This is signalled by light martial music being played as Richard and Buckingham sweep into Richard's gigantic new headquarters as Lord Protector in a limousine very similar to the large black sedans favoured by mobster leaders of the 1930s. (Scenes in the Lord Protector's HQ were filmed in the grand marbled interior of London University's Senate House building, built in 1936 and occupied in the Second World War by the Ministry of Information; George Orwell had this modernist building in mind when creating the headquarters of the 'Ministry of Truth' in his novel *1984*.) The assassinations that remove all obstacles to Richard's rule soon follow: Rivers; Hastings (after which the black fascist uniform of Richard's private army are introduced); the young princes. There is also what we assume must be the drug-induced death of Lady Anne, indicated in the horrific shot of a spider crawling across her immobile face, a visual **metonymic** cleverly recalling Elizabeth's hissed description of Richard as 'bottled spider'. Richard's last assassination – the garrotting of Buckingham – is one that removes his chief henchman at court. This leaves him without senior support ('He has no friends', says Stanley) to battle it out with Richmond's army and Stanley's RAF near the Tower.

I started by mentioning McKellen's description of *Richard III* as a 'family drama of power-politics, more tragic than melodramatic', his reflection on how later twentieth-century productions (including his own) had eschewed the 'one-man-show' approach in favour of giving the supporting characters more prominence. The traditional melodramatic style from Colley Cibber to Olivier had functioned largely as 'star vehicles' for the main player, while the 'tragic' style emphasizes the intractable *circumstances* driving a central character to behave in ways that eventually destroy them. In this film, the cursing outburst against Richard by the Duchess of York his mother (4.4.167ff, 186ff) exemplifies (in McKellen's words) 'the verbal and emotional abuse which from infancy has formed her youngest son's character and behaviour' (McKellen, 1996, 22). For once, we here see Richard at a loss, his visible dismay in response to her attack startlingly exposing the vulnerability of a man supposedly impervious to normal human feelings. This susceptibility to the mother's influence and rejection is treated as part of the 'circumstances' which make Richard a tragic figure in the film. Nowhere apparent in Eyre's stage version, this dramatic inflection seems a key element in the psychological structure introduced by Loncraine so that Richard's rise and fall in the play will adapt closely to the story contour of the classic Hollywood gangster genre, familiar to cinema audiences since the 1930s.

The final confrontation between Richard and Richmond on the smoking girders of the Tower elaborates and confirms the use of the gangster genre by Loncraine in a very specific way. Simultaneously echoing the genre styles of Western showdown, gangster movie cop and villain shoot-out, as well as the pursuit-and-kill climax of political thrillers, Loncraine also explicitly alludes to the final scene of the classic gangster movie *White Heat* (1949), where James Cagney as the deserted mother-obsessed mobster shoots into gas tanks and immolates himself by leaping into the flames while defiantly shouting 'Made it Ma, top of the world!' As with the many gangster movies in which a fleeing villain seeks escape by climbing a building only to topple to his death, McKellen's Richard climbs the burning Tower pursued by the ruggedly handsome and clean-cut Richmond until, with nowhere to go, he holds out a hand to his rival offering the mock invitation: 'Let us to't pell-mell – / If not to heaven, then hand in hand to hell' (5.6.43–3). This is originally spoken in the play by Richard to his troops before battle, but his ironical delivery here, grinning insanely at the camera while leaning back to plunge into a blazing inferno, is not the only element suggesting disturbed mental fixations are at work in this denouement. While the style of suicidal exit and the soundtrack of Al Jolson singing 'I'm Sitting on Top of the World' (from the first sound film ever made, *The Jazz Singer* (1929)) code Richard as an asocial maniacal criminal, there is also our final view of the supposedly 'heroic' Richmond to reckon with. For as Richard tumbles, Richmond fires two revolver shots into him, a superfluous gesture since the man is already plunging to his death. This gesture is then compounded by the knowing smirk Richmond offers the camera, leaving us with the chilling thought that perhaps life is as cheap to him as it was to Richard, the man who was also fond of sharing his viciously evil outlook with us. In these last highly filmic 30 seconds of the movie, as the fall of Richard III gives way to the rise of Henry VII, we seem to be left with the kind of question around which Jan Kott's cynical reading of the Shakespearean histories revolve: has one tyrant been defeated only to be succeeded by another?

3. Tragedies

INTRODUCTORY NOTE

Of all the dramatic genres in which Shakespeare wrote plays, it is his tragedies which have proved most attractive for directors to adapt to film. It is not difficult to see why this should be. There are inherent problems in successfully accommodating the stage conventions of comedy to those of the screen (see Introductory Note to Comedies), while Shakespeare's history plays tend to have a limited interest for modern screen audiences. By contrast, Shakespeare's tragedies have maintained a consistent appeal for both film directors and their movie audiences, new adaptations of particular plays being made repeatedly over the years.

The tragedies to have been filmed most often are *Hamlet, Macbeth, Romeo and Juliet, King Lear* and *Othello*, their main attraction probably centring on the compelling creation of powerful conflicts between powerful characters whose strong passions we like to identify with, these conflicts being so intractable that only the death of the principals caught up in them seems to offer a resolution to the problems experienced. Ultimately, our experience of being carried along on the emotional 'roller-coaster ride' that **identification** with the clashing characters portrayed offers is likely to be linked to the 'purging' effects on our roused passions that Aristotle argued in his *Poetics* over two millennia ago to be the real value of watching tragic dramas. Furthermore, since each of these plays offers a superbly structured story with plot and dramatic development providing the kinds of twists, turns, tensions and releases that appeal to the most demanding moviegoer, it is not surprising that so many film versions of them do continue to appear.

The full range of cinematographic techniques for conveying these emotionally demanding plays on film tends to be used, though style and approach over the years have varied. One indispensable camera technique used for most of these films is the **close shot**, since it is obviously important to convey to the audience with some precision a character's emotional feelings or state of mind. There can be enormous emotional or intellectual pressures bearing on the central characters of these dramas, access to their often conflicting thoughts and feelings being what we want most of all – as in a novel – so that we can become involved in and hopefully be entertained by the effort of making some sense of what is going on. From the 1940s of the twentieth century onwards, Freudian theory, psychoanalysis and a massive interest in depth psychology made their impact felt in films perhaps more than in any other medium of artistic expression.

The brooding figures of Welles's *Macbeth* and Olivier's *Hamlet* in their 1948 films communicated even more broodingly to audiences because of the gloomy, shadowy sets in which their dramas were acted out, access to Hamlet's mind often being afforded particularly well by use of the **voice-over** technique. Polanski's later use of the same technique for his *Macbeth* – the most extensive of any Shakespeare adaptation – gives us even more privileged access to the innermost thoughts and desires of the thane and his wife. The approaches of Branagh and Almereyda in their *Hamlet* films are quite different. The former broadens his out to present an epic, maximal-text version expressing all the play's themes and characters in the context of a precarious nineteenth-century political state. Almereyda's low-budget movie focuses on the way media technology shapes and cramps communication and the creative integrity of youthful aspiration in the ruthless, high-powered corporate setting of modern Manhattan. The two extremely popular versions of *Romeo and Juliet* by Zeffirelli and Luhrmann discussed here concern themselves more with techniques of presenting colourful, exciting imagery and using the power of music to sway emotions in the audience, than finding ways of exploring complex states of mind. Exploring complex states of mind is not a priority in popular cinema at the time of writing.

Franco Zeffirelli's *Romeo and Juliet* (UK/Italy, 1968)

Director: Franco Zeffirelli

Producers: Anthony Havelock-Allan, John Brabourne

Script: Franco Brusati, Masolino D'Amico, Franco Zeffirelli

Medium: Technicolor, 35mm, widescreen, 132 minutes

Main actors: Leonard Whiting (Romeo); Olivia Hussey (Juliet); Milo O'Shea (Friar Laurence); John McEnery (Mercutio); Michael York (Tybalt); Pat Heywood (Nurse); Natasha Parry (Lady Capulet); Paul Hardwick (Capulet); Robert Stephens (Prince Escalus); Bruce Robinson (Benvolio); Antonio Pierfederici (Montague); Esmerelda Ruspoli (Lady Montague); Keith Skinner (Balthazar)

Photography: Pasquale De Santis

Costume design: Danilo Donati

Music: Nino Rota

As with so many other high-achieving Shakespeare film adaptations, Franco Zeffirelli's *Romeo and Juliet* was preceded by a stage production, and in this case one that was not only hugely successful in 1960 at London's Old Vic theatre (world famous for its Shakespeare productions) but equally so in 1961 at the City Centre in New York. The essential reason for its stage success was the same as the movie version's triumph later in 1968: they both connected with the emotions and understanding of contemporary youth. Since the teenage cinema audience would be all-important for moviemakers in the decades to come (including Shakespeare moviemakers, of course), it is well worth considering first of all what ingredients Zeffirelli brought to his Old Vic production that made it so appealing to these new consumers of Shakespeare.

Old Vic general manager Michael Benthall had seen Zeffirelli's sunny production of the Italian opera *Cavalleria Rusticana* in the winter of 1959 at London's Royal Opera House. So impressed was he that he asked the opera director and designer to inject the same bright magic into a new *Romeo and Juliet*, to bring to the production (according to Zeffirelli's own report) 'the feel of Italy, not the Victorian interpretation that still dominated the English stage but something truly Mediterranean ... sunlight on a fountain, wine and olives and garlic, new, different, real, young' (Zeffirelli, 1986, 157 – all further page references relate to this source). Fresh from a 1960 summer during which he experienced the Olympic Games in a 'joyful, colourful, sunny Rome awash with bright, healthy young people from all over the world', he returned to England feeling that 'even at the very beginning of the 1960s ... young people were about to give everyone a very pleasant jolt, and it was this that I wanted to bring to the London stage' (160, 167). Years of training as assistant to neo-realist Italian filmmaker Luchino Visconti had given Zeffirelli the imaginative credentials to create such a theatrical jolt, his strategy including a determination to 'demolish' the 'Norma Shearer/Leslie Howard approach' of George Cukor, replacing it with 'a real story in a plausible mediaeval city at the opening of the Renaissance'. Instead of the usual set-piece balcony scene tastefully positioned amid 'Italianate verandas and artificial flowers', Zeffirelli had Juliet (a young Judi Dench) step out on to the more realistic battlement of 'a Capulet fortress built to keep foes out and treasures in' (163), forcing Romeo (John Stride) to climb a cypress tree to get to her. In this erotic production it was powerful 'young love, impetuous, unstoppable' that transformed them into 'amorous young animals who had been kept apart' (164). Such passion, played by youthful actors whom Zeffirelli insisted could not use wigs but had to grow their hair long (both boys and girls) for a natural Renaissance look, was a long way from the bleak 'kitchen-sink' dramas then playing on London stages.

Despite a predictably savage response from the London drama critics, who saw Shakespeare being destroyed by an irreverent Italian opera director ignorant of Shakespeare and verse speaking, the day was saved when leading critic and future dramaturge of the National Theatre, Kenneth Tynan, saw fit to praise Zeffirelli, calling his *Romeo and Juliet* 'a revelation, perhaps a revolution ... a masterly production ... a glorious evening' (164). Thereafter, the theatre was packed out night after night, often by young people who, by the end of the play's extended run, were also wearing the long hair soon to be made fashionable by the Beatles. Even the Shakespearean theatre's senior player John Gielgud, who had sat in the audience 'surrounded by laughing, crying kids', had to admit afterwards that 'I've never had the luck to have an audience like that' (165). By the time it was clear that Zeffirelli's first Shakespeare movie *The Taming of the Shrew* (1966) would be a worldwide hit, he and its stars Elizabeth Taylor and Richard Burton all agreed that his next project must be a movie of his theatre hit *Romeo and Juliet*: 'that youthful production at the Old Vic had somehow to be translated on to film for the vast international audience we felt sure would flock to see it' (223). Luckily Paramount's head of productions in Europe, Bud Ornstein, had seen the original stage production, declaring that 'If this man can put one-tenth of the energy from that stage play on screen then we ought to do it' (224). Unfortunately Paramount in the USA were less confident, willing only to back a movie that could recover from **arthouse** audiences and television sales the $800,000 offered, an amount described as 'derisory' by Zeffirelli (225). For them Shakespeare was still bad box office, despite the evidence of *Shrew*, the success of which was seen as entirely due to the bankable international movie stardom of Burton and Taylor. As in the 1960 theatrical performances, the two leads for the *Romeo and Juliet* film would be unknowns: an essential and necessary risk for Zeffirelli, who refused to cast older actors.

The film began shooting in Italy during the hot 'summer of love' of 1967, exterior locations being found at Tuscania, Pienza and Gubbio, while interior sets were built at the Cinecittà studios near Rome. Whether filming interiors or exteriors, Zeffirelli's twin skills of designing sets and settings for opera and of assisting Visconti in the design and making of his meticulously visualized neo-realist Italian films now came to the fore. With the same realistic, energetic and colorful style of approach used to film *The Taming of the Shrew*, he applied his experience to produce the right 'look' for *Romeo and Juliet*. As a native Florentine passionate about his city's art, architecture and culture, the 'look' produced by Zeffirelli is primarily concerned with seducing the eye with rich colours and textures, gracefully reconstructed Renaissance interiors and costumes recalling old-master paintings (the film won best costume design and cinematography Academy Awards), images being typically bathed in that special soft, golden light for which Italy is so famous. The impact of light is made apparent from the seemingly quiet opening frames of the film. We are shown a panoramic view of Verona shrouded in pale morning mist, soon to be dispersed by the hot sun, while the voice of Laurence Olivier announces the grim tidings of the Prologue over one of the simple but compelling tunes that Nino Rota provides for the movie. In fact, this opening (the aerial **pan** being a tribute to the beginning of Olivier's *Henry V* that inspired Zeffirelli towards theatre and film in 1945) offers in condensed cinematic form the contrasts of cold, tragic death (the white veil of mist) and the passions of love and hate (the circle of burning sun) of which the Prologue speaks, appropriately distanced from the life of Verona below to suit its sombre register.

Such distancing does not last long, for as the camera takes us down to ground level and into the colourful bustle of the Verona market, we encounter in the violent clash of the Capulets and Montagues three key aspects of Zeffirelli's cinematic style: his use of **close-up**s, rapid **cutting** and **pan shot**s, and a distinct preference for action over dia-logue. Of course, when a fight is at hand, that is what the audience (especially a youthful one) wants to see, and the fast-cutting, **zooms** and blurred pan shots all effectively convey the excitement and chaos of the violent mayhem. Nevertheless, the sparse nature of the dialogue spoken in the film could be seen as an issue, Zeffirelli retaining only 30 per cent of Shakespeare's lines. But to Zeffirelli himself the beauty of the original poetic language of Shakespeare 'is not what makes it inter-nationally unbetterable, with no peers'; he feels instead that 'to the author, youth was more important than enunciation' (162) in this play. Clearly it is the heartbreakingly sentimental *story* of *Romeo and Juliet* which appeals so much to this filmmaker, and one commentator has gone so far as to say that the film is a 'version of the Romeo and Juliet narrative more like Shakespeare's sources'. To some extent this may be true, since Zeffirelli has said that in one of the source tales Juliet is danc-ing with two men at a masked ball, one having a cold. clammy hand, and the other, Romeo, having a warm, gentle one. Zeffirelli comments: 'So by the touch of the two hands she knows their characters' (162). This not only points to Shakespeare's own emphasis on hands in the 'shared son-net' voiced by Romeo and Juliet when they meet at the Capulet ball, but also explains the extent to which 'hands' are factored in as a key visual **motif** of meaning throughout this movie.

   In fact, it is by deploying a whole range of *non-verbal* devices in the film that Zeffirelli succeeds so well in conveying his interpretation of the Romeo and Juliet story to us. I have already mentioned his prefer-ence for showing the dramatic actions and reactions of characters over and above verbal telling, as well as providing the eye-pleasing con-trasts of vivid and subtle colours all bathed in the golden Italian light. Just as important for this director are the use of gesture, of looking, of touching, and of using music and the choreography of bodily move-ment – especially the dance at the Capulet ball and the open-air sword fights – to communicate the dramatic story. In addition to their touch-ing of hands and lips, it is when they visit their clinging gazes upon one another at the Capulet ball that Romeo and Juliet fall in love. The Moresca dance and the cleverly inserted sentimental song 'What is a Youth?' trigger the remaining emotional effects on them and us, the susceptible screen audience. For the young of the film, words are an inadequate means for communicating the powerful impulses of lust, love and hate in the world they are forced to live by their elders, and instinctively distrust the language that governs it. Tybalt needs no words but only one *look* at the entranced Romeo to discover what his enemy is up to at the Capulet ball; Juliet asks 'What's in a name?'; Mercutio in the sweltering Verona square impatiently responds to Benvolio's repetition of the Prince's cautions with his dismissive 'blah, blah, blah'; a Romeo hot to couple with Juliet impatiently completes the sentences of hackneyed sayings Friar Laurence counsels him with prior to their marriage. No more outstanding example of Zeffirelli's drive to replace text with **shot** can be noticed than when he has the young men of the feud signify their masculinist sexuality by ceaselessly brandishing and thrusting forth their weapons; the references to the male member pervading the play text are repeatedly 'spoken' by the bodily gestures and rapier jabs of Mercutio and his like.

Despite the bright colours, busy action and rich visual detail that in many ways are appropriate for the more 'comedic' first half of the film, the darker and bleaker episodes of the movie, which occur after the deaths of Mercutio and Tybalt, are sometimes foreshadowed by visual moments that erupt in and interrupt this first half. For example, we see Mercutio bellowing about 'nothing' and 'the frozen bosom of the north' (1.4.96,101) into the empty square bathed in an ominous blue light (a colour sometimes associated with death) at the end of his Queen Mab speech. There is the strange 'betwixt and between' moment when Juliet pauses in the shadowy Capulet courtyard by the statue after the ball, listening to different voices calling in the night for her and for Romeo. And we see Romeo being pursued along the narrow, claustrophobic streets of Verona. For the second half of the film, it is important to note how Zeffirelli fittingly alters the film's visual style, suspending the hectic activity and fast-cutting, and emptying the screen of its vivid colour to reflect the darkening shift of tone that Shakespeare gives to this part of the play. What we see now is a range of more subdued images and sometimes longer takes: there are the white tones of Juliet's room; the gloominess of Friar Laurence's cell and his blowing out of the candle after giving Juliet the potion, an action even he catches himself noticing as dangerously symbolic. Then there is the darkness of the Capulet house; the gloominess of Juliet's 'funeral'; the dim interior of exiled Romeo's Mantuan room; the grimness of the Capulet tomb; and finally, when all of those we have been made to care about are dead, there is the desolate wind-blown square filled with mourners in black, the 'scourge laid upon their heads' being the price to be paid for the reconciliation between opposing households that we observe taking place as the former enemies file into church side by side.

However, important as all these cinematic meanings and effects are, none of them would matter unless the actors playing Romeo and Juliet were believable and attractive lovers, attractive and believable in the way that those previously playing the roles in Cukor's and Castellani's films were not. Fortunately, trained in the Italian school of Visconti's cinematic neo-realism where acting skills were frowned upon in favour of a beautiful 'look', Zeffirelli, by choosing Olivia Hussey and Leonard Whiting as his two principals, was immensely lucky. As the director himself so truly says, 'the cinema with its huge **close-up**s exaggerates everything', so his Romeo and Juliet would need be 'extra beautiful and exceptionally talented' for the film to be successful. At 15 the voluptuous Hussey had a 'magnificent bone structure', possessed 'wide expressive eyes', and altogether presented a 'gawky colt of a girl waiting for life to begin' (226). Zeffirelli felt that 17-year-old Whiting was 'the most exquisitely beautiful male adolescent' (228) he had ever met. In fact, he makes sure we are able to gaze longer on the naked body of this male than that of Hussey, in the scene after Romeo and Juliet's night of love. When Richard Burton was shown early rushes of the film, he broached the perennial problem of inexperienced actors being cast for the parts of Romeo and Juliet: 'You've got problems with the verse.' However, as if realizing as quickly as he had said it that for *this film*, being shown at *this time* – in the middle of the very first 'decade of youth' – perhaps the conventional objections of the seasoned Shakespearean on correct verse-speaking did not apply: 'But perhaps it doesn't matter – you're probably right. It certainly looks great', said Burton (228). It is true that neither teenage actor performs Shakespeare's verse very skilfully. But then neither does the rest of the cast, except perhaps for John McEnery's Mercutio, whose Queen Mab speech is so expertly 'physicalized' into meaning for us. For the most part, the actors were all encouraged to speak and act as naturalistically as possible. Nevertheless, without the emotional energy and physical spontaneity that Hussey and Whiting bring to their playing, the film could never have succeeded. As it is, that energy was powerfully present, especially in the case of initiative-taking Hussey, whose beguiling glances and attractively spontaneous energy provide immense sympathy and appeal for the viewing audience.

The year 1968 was before the days of the **test screening**s now used by film companies to gauge audience reaction to a movie, taking action where necessary to avoid a failure. In the case of *Romeo and Juliet*, when Zeffirelli ran out of funds half-way through filming, the response of one teenager who saw the rushes was decisive both in ensuring

further funds would be released to complete the movie, and in illustrating that it was the response of *youth* which would matter most to
the success of this film. Charlie Bluhdorn, as head of Gulf and Western
– the oil company that owned Paramount – was the only one able to
authorize the money to finish the film. Yet he was utterly bewildered
by the scenes he was shown – until his teenage son Paul interrupted
proceedings in tears to say that he liked what he'd seen. The baffled
father had to confess: 'He understands, well can ya beat that! An' I
thought we were gonna haf to dub it' (229).

Baz Luhrmann's *William Shakespeare's Romeo + Juliet* (USA, 1996)

Director: Baz Luhrmann

Producers: Gabriella Martinelli, Baz Luhrmann

Script: Craig Pearce and Baz Luhrmann

Medium: Color De Luxe, 35mm, 115 minutes

Main actors: Leonardo DiCaprio (Romeo); Claire Danes (Juliet); Pete Postlethwaite (Friar Laurence); Harold Perrineau (Mercutio); John Leguizamo (Tybalt); Miriam Margolyes (Nurse); Diane Venora (Gloria Capulet); Paul Sorvino (Fulgencio Capulet); Vondie Curtis-Hall (Captain Prince); Dash Minok (Benvolio); Brian Dennery (Ted Montague); Christina Pickles (Caroline Montague); Jesse Bradford (Balthazar)

Photography: Donald McAlpine

Costume design: Kym Barrett

Production designer: Catherine Martin

Editor: Jill Bilcock

Music: Nellee Hooper; original score composed by Craig Armstrong, Marius de Vries, Nellee Hooper

As with Zeffirelli throughout his career, Luhrmann has worked in the theatre and opera house besides making popular films, and the benefit of these professional experiences can be seen in *William Shakespeare's Romeo + Juliet* (hereafter cited as *Romeo + Juliet*). A significant 'theatrical' site in the movie is the ruined proscenium theatre arch at the beachside Sycamore Grove, one of the film's three key locations (the others being Verona Beach and the Capulet mansion), important because it was 'the originating image of Luhrmann's design, imagined and built as a model two full years before shooting began in Mexico City'. I will return to this aspect of Sycamore Grove, where 'real performance' in what is effectively a post-theatrical and post-cinematic space may be seen to provide a challenge to the image-saturated televisual and corporate power 'values' that ironically pervade the film. Yet almost the first area to explore is the movie's notoriously dense deployment of the kinds of images and sounds already discussed to an extent in Part III concerning the 'intertextuality' in film, that is, the way (especially post-) modern movies frequently refer to 'other works, genres and styles, whether as homage, parody, simple imitation, or even unconscious duplication' (Hayward, 1996, 259–72).

I say almost the first area, because prior to everything else is the fact that the whole substance and story of this film is 'contained' by its status as (a decidedly long, admittedly) 'item' on a TV news programme, delivered from the screen of a 1970s-style television set appearing centre frame at the very opening of the movie. An audible clicking of the dial tells us that (click) 'Twentieth Century Fox presents' (click) 'A Bazmark Production', a final click bringing up an African-American newscaster who speaks the play's Prologue with the predictable blandness of modern TV reportage. The same TV screen appears again centre frame at the end of the film when the reporter returns to relate the play's gloomy Epilogue in the selfsame bland tones. This highly self-conscious 'containing' filmic device not only suggests that what we see between Prologue and Epilogue is little more than another news 'story' rather than 'Shakespeare', but also that communications through screen and image in consumer culture are so pervasive that there is little difference between our experience of reality and its media representations. This suggestion becomes more assertive in the opening sequence when a slow **zoom** enlarges the TV image to reveal over the newsreader's shoulder a projected headline icon, 'Star-Cross'd Lovers'. Next to this is an image of Romeo and Juliet's broken wedding ring, and as the newsreader speaks the line 'two hours' traffic of our stage' (*Prologue*, 12) studio coverage 'goes live'. We are now catapulted *through* the TV screen into a film **montage** of **slam-zoom** images of urban violence too fast-changing to register clearly, while an ostentatious choral piece parodying Carl Orff's 'O Fortuna' assaults our ears. We are being shown what passes for **establishing shot**s of the cityscape of Verona Beach, which the film's production website describes as 'a violent otherworld, neither future nor past, ruled by two families, the Montagues and the Capulets', but which the bold letters of a title card (twice) ironically proclaims is 'Fair Verona'. It would be nearer the mark to say that Verona Beach and Sycamore Grove bear a similar relationship to each other, as do Los Angeles and Venice Beach. Sycamore Grove is so named because Benvolio soon tells the concerned mother of Romeo how 'underneath the grove of sycamore / ... So early walking did I see your son' (1.1.114, 116) – such trees were once associated with melancholy lovers who were 'sick-amour'.

Aerial shots of Captain Prince's police helicopters striving to control outbreaks of urban violence below are now **intercut** with images
of giant statues of Christ and of the Madonna, flanked and dwarfed –
significantly so, we will come to realize – by the skyscraping towers of
Montague and Capulet business corporations. The frame then cuts
from video footage to a slow **zoom**-out of newsprint imaging Christ's
monumental head surrounded by members of the feuding families,
and we hear the Prologue spoken again, this time voiced with nervous
deliberation by Pete Postlethwaite, the British Shakespearean actor
who will play Friar Laurence. Illustrating his speech are various shots
intercutting images of the Montague and Capulet parents and news-
magazine photo versions of Jesus and Mary, with snatches of the
Prologue shown in newsprint. In the white gothic lettering on black
that becomes the film's trademark print style we finally read that 'a
pair of star-cross'd lovers take their life', the 't' in 'take' formed into a
crucifix, the first of many to appear in this movie.

We are now introduced to the story's main protagonists in **freeze-
frame** shots that use titling evocative of the opening of *The Good, the
Bad and the Ugly* (a style repeated to introduce the Capulet and
Montague 'boys' later) – except that we are only given a tiny glimpse
of Romeo (unnamed) in the briefest of proleptic shots as he opens a
church door to reveal the cross-blazoned aisle leading to Juliet's 'death
bier' towards the end of the film. Juliet herself is neither shown nor
named, but we do get further proleptic glimpses of future events in an
amazing 7-second **montage** of 26 shots spliced together in such rapid
succession that they can only be subliminally registered – just one of
the devices used by Luhrmann to engage the young MTV audience.
The last of these subliminal images is of a Montague gang member
being gunned down, followed by a **match cut** to the falling body that
forms a cruciform shape briefly in space before being replaced by a
fiery red gothic cross with a tiny ampersand at its centre, this finally
shrinking to the '+' of the white block lettering of the film's titling
frames, 'William Shakespeare's Romeo + Juliet'. (The ampersand is
clearly imaged in the packaging publicity for the DVD, though the
screenplay book cover prints 'William Shakespeare's Romeo and
Juliet', suggesting that the cross/ampersand conjunction was a late
addition to the production.)

Following a **wipe** that removes the titles, we are taken into a densely
packed six-minute sequence using a variety of cleverly inspired
camera techniques to introduce us to members of the Montague and
Capulet gangs in violent but witty confrontation. It does this by

imitating or parodying previous film styles, principally the fast-cutting and speeded-up action-movie approach of John Woo as the gangs shoot it out. Luhrmann also quotes from the tough-guy acting styles and gestures of Clint Eastwood in *A Fistful of Dollars* and Charles Bronson in *Once Upon a Time in the West*, while the twanging guitar and haunting whistles that punctuate the entry of the dapperly sinister Tybalt echo the trademark scores of Ennio Morricone in both Sergio Leone films. Despite its fast-cutting, **slo-mo**s, **whip-pan**s, **slam-zoom**s and ultra **close-up**s, the excitement of this narrative sequence is almost wholly conveyed by very short **shot/reverse shot**s no more than a few seconds long at most, filmed tight on the gang members' faces as they act and react hysterically to each other. Among the punning references to Shakespeare and visual jokes in the sequence ('hubble bubble toil and trouble', 'add more fuel to your fire'), the cross **motif** is highly visible: crucifixes that hang around the necks of a convent college girl, and opposing gang members, and which dangles from Benvolio's gun; a cross shaved on the head of Petruchio Capulet; the crosshairs of the telescopic sight on Tybalt's gun; the flaming cross formed on the gas-station forecourt when gasoline is ignited by Tybalt's discarded cheroot. The Christian iconography is most noticeable when Tybalt declares, 'Turn thee Benvolio, look upon thy death', and opens his jacket not only to reveal two holstered pistols, but also on his bullet-proof vest an image of Christ displaying the Sacred Heart. This depiction at least could argue for a more complicating account of what otherwise becomes a repetitious crowding of the film with signs of the Christian 'brand' among other noticeable 'brand names', including those drawing on the play so that modern weapons could be included: Sword, Longsword, Dagger, and so on. The effect of juxtaposing such holy signs with deadly weapons or the various scenes of violence – including the violence visited on his daughter in her crucifix-festooned bedroom by Fulgencio Capulet – is to suggest that the Christianity proclaimed in Verona Beach is always likely to be shaped by the needs of ruthlessly violent corporate rivalry, or the ritual blood sacrifices associated with the feud ('fuel') helping feed it.

In this movie, there is a strong sense that one man at least – albeit a possibly drug-addicted priest – has the faith to believe that such a feud might be ended. This sense emerges in the cinematically inventive sequence of Friar Laurence's 'vision', where a succession of converging images – including a white dove of peace entering the Sacred Heart of Christ – inspires him to attempt a resolution of the feud by marrying

Romeo and Juliet. His vision is supported by the weak but sincere efforts of a Romeo whose impulse to create peace and harmony comes only after his confused 'doting' on Rosaline is replaced by his love for Juliet. There is some justification, then, for Luhrmann's view that Romeo is 'a young rebel in love with the idea of love itself', although his true rebellion will be in abandoning the Montague boys' gang for a female – Juliet. This is a desertion registered most acutely in the hurt response of Mercutio, whose homoerotic feelings for Romeo are made clearer in this film than in any previous adaptation. Despite the astute casting of teen heart-throb de Caprio to code the film for success with its target audience, in many ways it is the anti-macho impact – 'wimp-ishness' even – conveyed by his performance that tends to win out over his heterosexual appeal.

Luhrmann's use of a water **motif** emblematizing the love-bond of Romeo and Juliet is probably a response to two of their statements in the play (unvoiced in the film): Romeo's response to Juliet's problem over his name being to tell her to 'call me but love, and I'll be new baptized' (2.1.93) (he 'new baptizes' both of them, of course, when they first plunge into the Capulet pool); while she declares later that 'My bounty is as boundless as the sea, / My love as deep' (2.175–6). Water is repeatedly associated with the lovers at different points in the film, linking them together in romantic and peaceful escape from their discontented lives. We first encounter Juliet dreamily submerged in a bathtub, unable to hear her mother and Nurse calling her. And after we see him plunging his head in a bowl of water to shake off the effects of Mercutio's drug at the Capulet party, Romeo and Juliet glimpse each other for the first time through the glass of an aquarium of blue and yellow tropical fish, colours which are associated with the Madonna, but which are increasingly identified with Romeo and Juliet as the film progresses. Such identification culminates in their final scene together at Juliet's 'death bier' when he swallows the yellow poi-son (sold to him by the apothecary/Globe Pool Hall owner who pulled it from its hiding place inside a Madonna lamp), both of them being bathed in the glow of golden yellow candlelight and surrounded by a virtual 'sea' of illuminated blue crosses. A reprised **freeze-frame** shot of them kissing in the underwater retreat of the blue-lit Capulet pool is our parting view of Romeo and Juliet.

For some, this last drawn-out scene in which Romeo and Juliet are left to themselves and their 'tragic' destiny, may be the most moving and memorable of the film, as it is no doubt meant to be, the gentle, closing strains of Wagner's *Liebestod* providing a fittingly romantic and sad conclusion. Such a conclusion is made possible not only because Luhrmann alters the death scene in the same way that Thomas Otway had done for his Restoration version of the play in the late seventeenth century, cutting and manipulating the dialogue so that Juliet wakes before Romeo dies, allowing for a reunion. Other changes are made, too, shots included in the published screenplay involving Friar Laurence and Captain Prince's police rushing into the Madonna chapel being excised, permitting the lovers to be uninterrupted in their last moments together. Yet it is also possible to see this ending as rather contrived and sentimental, and to point to other parts of the film as providing more interesting and genuinely 'performative' as well as more tragic moments. In terms of theatricality, there are of course the early Capulet mansion scenes where a narcissistic, pill-popping and neurotic Gloria prances down the staircase, half-dressed as Cleopatra. In fact, Diane Venora's Lady Capulet provides more interest as Tybalt's would-be lover, a situation registering the intensely dysfunctional nature of the play's families – although her 'speeded-up' antics do offer a prelude of sorts to Mercutio's more exhibitionist and campy descent in silver-sequinned mini-skirt and top later, miming to Kym Mazelle's 'Young Hearts Run Free'.

The sentimental 'set-piece' ending gives us the beautiful and almost identical 'Anglo' faces of Romeo and Juliet looking their last on each other before the TV newswoman and the Seventies TV set reduce what we have seen to transient 'news media history'. But it is worth recalling how Luhrmann's first design for the film had been the ruined proscenium theatre arch at the beachside Sycamore Grove. It is here that his cinematic achievement is greatest, assembling the most interesting visual commentary on what it means to film Shakespeare in a post-theatrical, post-cinematic and postmodern period, when mass culture is so dominated by screen-mediated versions of reality that it is hard for the performative of 'real life' to find a location to express itself. Luhrmann claims that the film's 'created world' comprising twentieth-century icons and images 'are there to clarify what's being said' in the Shakespeare text. Yet we are forced to conclude that it is really the icons and images of the film, and Luhrmann's cinematic flair in delivering them, which dominate, turning much of the Shakespearean dialogue, which for 'the most part, the actors speak with toneless naturalism' (Loehlin, in Burnett and Wray, 2000, 123), into the film's subtext. In wanting to 'make it easier for the audience to receive this heightened language', Luhrmann seems to fall into the trap of treating the Shakespearean text with kid gloves. Thankfully, it is the inspired cinematic language he uses to convey his concept of how to deliver *Romeo and Juliet* to a worldwide youth audience in 1996 that becomes 'heightened', leaving the Shakespearean text to survive as best it may in the American and Latino voices he so rightly wanted to bring forward in his production.

This cinematic language is nowhere better employed than in the scenes at Sycamore Grove where Mercutio meets his death. There is always the danger in any production of *Romeo and Juliet* that this half-way point of the play can seem like its climax, since most of the engaging 'action' occurs in the early acts and in the aftermath of Mercutio's death when Romeo kills Tybalt. Yet the scenes around Mercutio's death are probably the most dramatically powerful and cinematically insightful of the whole movie. The culturally decayed stretch of beach and the amusement park at Sycamore Grove, inhabited by drunks, whores, hustlers, the poor and marginalized, is a horizontal open space where the feud-entrapped Montague and Capulet boys can express their real dissatisfactions without interference. It is a liminal space ideally suited for them to 'play out' their own frustrated destiny, literally so on the ruined **proscenium-arch** stage where the only audience is themselves. Following the well-paced sequence of fast-cut **shot/reverse shot**s tracking the 'fight' between vengeful Tybalt and peace-loving Romeo, Mercutio is stabbed by Tybalt using a shard of glass from a shattered window of the old theatre. Mortally wounded – though no one knows this – he climbs on to the stage, and announces with an Olivier-like theatrical flourish that he has 'a scratch' (3.1.89), a parodic gesture shown in **wide shot** giving him the massive scope as solo stage performer that he so relishes. It is only then that he reveals his fatal wound, shouting 'a plague on both your houses' at Romeo and Tybalt, chief members of his audience, and it is a shout that Luhrmann has echo around the whole location, implicating us all. Meanwhile, **matted-in shot**s of storm clouds are seen through and behind the open stage, accompanied by the rumbling thunder of the gathering storm that actually hit on the day of shooting.

This is building to an effective virtual climax during the saddest moments of the film. Tybalt's anguished gazing on the death scene from the stage reinforces the feeling of tragedy which the soaring voices of the **non-diegetic** choir now express with such power and finality. After we are shown the faces of the comprehending and uncomprehending alike who happen to be around watching, we are left with a **wide shot** of the now deserted stage and beach; waves beating on the shore can be seen through the jagged opening of the **proscenium arch**; night is shown falling through **time-lapse photography**. In a film so often dominated by hi-tech flashiness, it is a sequence encouraging us to reflect on how the tragedies of life might best be represented.

Laurence Olivier's *Hamlet* (UK, 1948)

Director: Laurence Olivier

Producers: Laurence Olivier, Reginald Beck

Script: Laurence Olivier, Alan Dent

Medium: Black and white, 35mm, 152 minutes

Main actors: Laurence Olivier (Hamlet); Eileen Herlie (Gertrude); Basil Sydney (Claudius); Jean Simmons (Ophelia); Felix Aylmer (Polonius); Norman Wooland (Horatio); Terence Morgan (Laertes)

Photography: Desmond Dickenson

Music: William Walton

Although Olivier's *Hamlet* may now look rather dated, in conception and execution the film is even more of a dramatic success than *Henry V*. This is because Olivier is able to make a cinematic version of Shakespeare's most complex play accessible to all by drawing on contemporary Freudian theory, and especially cinematic codes and techniques already used successfully in German Expressionist film and in American **film noir**. A musical score again specially written by William Walton was also key to this screen dramatization. The main filmic qualities that make this *Hamlet* such a cinematic *tour de force* are embodied in three powerful elements meshing together with great dramatic effect: the 'Oedipal' conception of Hamlet's character; the film's imaginative design and setting; and its innovative use of the camera. These interwoven elements come into play from the outset, and are observable working very effectively in the first ten minutes of the movie, where all its main themes are introduced.

Olivier's *Henry V* had begun with a bird's-eye view of Elizabethan London, and *Hamlet al*so starts with a **high-angle** camera, but this time moving in on the ramparts of Elsinore from above while Olivier's **voice-over** solemnly recites from Hamlet's 'vicious mole of nature' speech, also provided on screen for us to read. Filling our eyes and ears with the famous Prince's words tells us how we are to think of this Hamlet – as a damaged melancholic. Giving words from the play text also suggests to a general audience that this view of Hamlet is underpinned by 'Bardic authority'. In fact the speech is torn from its original context (in Q2, not in F) where Hamlet explains to Horatio the predilection of Danes to drunkenness (on the occasion of Claudius's rowdy 'wassail' to celebrate his marriage to Gertrude) as they wait for the ghost of Hamlet's father to appear on the ramparts (1.4.18.7–20). The view we are to accept is that it is 'the stamp of one defect ... breaking down the forts and pales of reason' which results in 'a tragedy of a man who could not make up his mind' (these last being Olivier's words, not Shakespeare's) – the tragedy of Hamlet. As Olivier voices his own psychological explanation for the 'destiny' of the Prince of Denmark, we are shown a sombre night-time tableau in which the dead Hamlet is held ceremoniously aloft by pall-bearers on a castle tower.

Just as Olivier created a fairly straightforward 'heroic' character for his Henry V by much textual excision, he fashions by the same method a Hamlet whose 'problems' are reckoned to be the outcome of an aberrant mind. The 'external' political dimensions of the play are cut out by removing Fortinbras and all mention of Norway, and also by removing Rosencrantz and Guildenstern, who work for Claudius as spies on Hamlet. This allows Olivier to deliver a *Hamlet* focusing on its more 'internal' psychological dimensions, with signals that the mysteries of the mind are to be key for the film's approach occurring as early as the first scene, set amid the swirling mists on Elsinore's battlements. (This is one visual **metonymic** indicating both ghostliness *and* an unfocused mind, just as a later metonymic of mental instability is imaged as a swirling sea inside Hamlet's troubled brain before he makes the 'To be or not to be' speech again on Elsinore's battlements.) Grateful to be relieved of his watch by Barnardo on the castle ramparts, Francisco states that 'It is bitter cold', but then pauses before saying, with puzzlement on his face, '– and I am sick at heart', as if some strange (possibly mental) distemper is afflicting him. Then, as Barnardo explains what 'we two nights have seen' to Marcellus and Horatio, a pounding heartbeat is heard on the soundtrack, signalling anxiety. The camera moves in and out of focus to the pulsing heartbeat before closing in on the face of a Marcellus whose perceptions have been disturbed by the presence of Old Hamlet's ghost, and who now observes: 'Peace. Break thee off', before screaming, 'Look where it comes again.' Finally, that there is a distemper afflicting the inmates of Elsinore is strongly indicated by Marcellus proclaiming his line from 1.4.67 somewhat ahead of time – 'Something is rotten in the state of Denmark.' At which point he and Horatio turn as one, and gaze expectantly at the camera lens as if the onus is now on us to explore these grim matters for ourselves. The camera therefore becomes our **POV**, moving to the right as if bidden to search out the cause of the 'rottenness', then nosing its way down a stone staircase, past two empty thrones in a dark hall, pausing to view an archway while an oboe theme soon to become associated with Ophelia plays pleasantly on the soundtrack. A disturbing theme from the strings now enters, the search proceeding rapidly into Gertrude's bedchamber, the thematic heart of Olivier's film. As if satisfied it has found its goal, the camera zooms in, lingering on the 'enseamed bed' of Denmark, before the image **dissolves** to a **close-up** of Claudius drinking greedily from a goblet in the Great Hall, with courtiers laughing around him while he drunkenly celebrates the acquisition of Old Hamlet's throne and wife Gertrude, Hamlet's mother. The logic of the camera's quest and discovery is clear: if something is rotten in the state of Denmark, this has been brought about by Gertrude's incestuous marriage with Claudius, this amply preparing us to meet a young Hamlet tormented by an 'Oedipal conflict'.

As the Great Hall scene develops, both this conflict and the isolation of a troubled Hamlet are conveyed visibly by Olivier's deployment of the camera. Olivier has stated that for the most part the film 'realized the drama through Hamlet's eyes', and 'when he's not present, through his imagination – his paranoia'. A great deal of the cinematic shape and logic of the film falls into place when we are told this, such as the camera's probing of Elsinore in search of 'rottenness': the 'character' that Marcellus and Horatio had turned to for an explanation being the paranoiac mind's-eye of Hamlet, provided by the camera's eye. However, for Olivier, the 'core of Hamlet is his loneliness and desolation after the death of his father, and his feeling of alienation from the new court' (Olivier, 1987, 178). This is conveyed very effectively by Olivier's use of **deep-focus** photography, evident in much of the film, and beginning with the Great Hall scene. Black-and-white film stock not only facilitated this technique, which, by keeping everything in the frame in focus, allows Olivier to show Hamlet as visually connected with those around him *at the same time* as he is at a physical, social and emotional distance from them. Black and white was also used because the 'tangerine and apricot faces' of Technicolor were not the faces Olivier wanted to haunt his 'melancholy Hamlet'. In this Great Hall scene, after a **shot/reverse shot** sequence featuring the faces of Claudius, Polonius and Laertes, there is a six-second deep-focus **long shot** from the perspective of Hamlet (whom we have yet to see). This is followed by a **medium-shot** of Polonius rising, succeeded by another **deep-focus long shot** tableau of the whole court with the blond-haired Hamlet in the left foreground. (Olivier wanted his Hamlet to stand out from those around him, so giving him blond hair made him 'conspicuous in long and middle shots', but also helped to 'get well away from the glamorous brunette of a mediaeval king' – his look in *Henry V.*) This **deep-focus** shot enables Olivier to present simultaneously both Hamlet's perspective of what is going on around him, but also to establish his estrangement from an environment in which he is virtually a prisoner. The 'Oedipal' disclosure enters when, after Claudius remonstrates with Hamlet for the 'unmanly grief' he shows in mourning his father's death, Eileen Herlie as Gertrude bends close towards the seated Hamlet. To her plea that he 'Go not to Wittenberg', Hamlet replies, 'I shall in all my best obey you, madam', gazing deeply into his mother's lowered cleavage as he does so. Her response is to plant passionate, lingering kisses on his mouth before an irritated Claudius is forced to break up the lover-like exchange: 'Madam, come' (1.2.119–22). Such an exchange will be repeated between them at the end of the closet scene (3.4) on Gertrude's bed.

The court's departure from the Great Hall, leaving Hamlet alone, is shot from a **high angle**, emphasizing his isolation and powerlessness, expressed vocally by the 'O that this too too solid flesh would melt' soliloquy. This is mainly spoken by Olivier in 'interiorized' **voice-over** as he paces around empty regal thrones and chairs, a visual **motif** repeated throughout the film to signal the absence of Old Hamlet. Instead of next having Horatio, Marcellus and Barnardo enter to report their sighting of the Ghost, Olivier introduces 'light' as a contrast with Hamlet's darkness by moving away from an enclosed space towards a series of arches opening out on to the light of day and the white-gowned figure of Ophelia. She is saying goodbye to her brother Laertes, who chides her for receiving the attentions of Hamlet, a chiding soon repeated by Polonius after we have been given a **deep-focus** shot of Hamlet from her **POV**, he turning to gaze at her from far away at the other end of an arched corridor. The shot is then reversed and we see Ophelia in **deep focus** from over the shoulder of a seated Hamlet, a moment described by Olivier as when

> Hamlet sees Ophelia, in her innocent Victorian dress, an eternity away down the long corridor (150 feet away, actually), sitting in a solid wooden chair – in focus – with love clearly in her eyes. (Olivier, 1987, 179)

Deep-focus photography not only enables Olivier to suggest both connection and alienation between characters. By a refusal to focus exclusively on individuals, the technique also has the effect of depriving these human beings of significance.

Illustration 3 **Laurence Olivier's Hamlet (1948).** This shot of Olivier as Hamlet and Jean Simmons as Ophelia exchanging looks at a distance is a fine example of the film's frequent use of deep-focus cinematography. This technique, by keeping both foreground and background in focus, has the effect of suggesting how characters may be both simultaneously connected to, *and* alienated from, one another.

As well as describing Olivier's *Hamlet* as a 'film about insanity', script co-author Alan Dent also wrote a review of the film comparing its cinematic style to that of Robert Wiene's Expressionist masterpiece *The Cabinet of Dr Caligari* (1920). Expressionist films like *Caligari* or *Nosferatu* (1922, Friedrich Murnau's version of Bram Stoker's *Dracula*) offer what Guntner calls a 'dramaturgy of light and shadows' to convey mood, emotion and an atmosphere expressive of anxiety, uncertainty and mental instability. Such **chiaroscuro** lighting and cavernous sets are also used by Olivier to communicate the dark, brooding and oppressively mysterious atmosphere of a claustrophobic Elsinore, all provided as a visual analogue of the insecure and angst-ridden interior worlds of the movie's characters, in particular, of course, the alienated inner world of Hamlet. Shadows particularly tend to signal impending doom, and in conjunction with staircases, the doom of the person ascending or descending. Examples abound in *Hamlet*, such as when Hamlet is led up the tower stairs by the Ghost, or is followed by his own shadow going up to Gertrude's bedchamber. Estrangement is conveyed using stairs when Olivier objectifies an Ophelia abandoned, isolated and left helpless by Hamlet in the 'nunnery scene', the camera viewing her from a rising **crane shot** as it spirals up and up a winding staircase that Hamlet climbs to the battlements to make his 'To be or not to be' speech. (This is relocated from its textual position *before* the nunnery scene, which has the effect of suggesting that the agonized debate on suicide is caused by his troubled relationship with Ophelia, excluding the wider range of (political) pressures upon him.) As Lawrence Guntner observes, in both the Expressionist film and **film noir**, stairways serve frequently 'as a bridge between appearance and reality, bourgeois normalcy and the unexplored depths of the human soul, the conscious and the subconscious' (Guntner, in Klein and Daphinoff, eds, 1997, 139).

The film-noir tradition largely established by German émigré directors like Fritz Lang, Otto Preminger and Billy Wilder in the 1940s are typically films in which an alienated hero struggles single-handedly to solve a crime (usually murder) in 'a strange, dark and threatening world in which the real and the unreal are very close to each other'. By 1948, Hollywood film audiences were so familiar with *noir* thrillers and detective movies infused with a bleak, claustrophobic fatalism, that Olivier's *Hamlet* would seem to be addressing familiar psychological territory, albeit in the language of a Shakespearean tragedy.

Kenneth Branagh's *Hamlet* (UK, 1996)

Director: Kenneth Branagh

Producer: David Barron

Script: Kenneth Branagh

Medium: Colour, 70mm, 242 minutes

Main actors: Kenneth Branagh (Hamlet); Julie Christie (Gertrude); Derek Jacobi (Claudius); Kate Winslet (Ophelia); Richard Briers (Polonius); Nicholas Farrell (Horatio); Michael Maloney (Laertes); Brian Blessed (Ghost)

Photography: Alex Thomson

Music: Patrick Doyle

If Olivier was obliged to cut the lines of *Hamlet* by half to make a film that cinema audiences accustomed to watching two-hour entertainment movies would find acceptable, Branagh was enabled to realize his vision of a 'full-text' *Hamlet* extending to over double that length, making it the longest Shakespeare movie adaptation ever made. He had been trying to finance such a film for years, but (as ever) 'the perpetual reluctance of film companies to finance Shakespeare had frustrated each attempt.' Yet the man who had more or less single-handedly relaunched the Shakespeare-on-film genre with *Henry V* (1989) and *Much Ado About Nothing* (1993) now took the astute move of making *Mary Shelley's Frankenstein* (1994). The $22 million that this movie snatched in its seven–week cinematic release must have persuaded its financiers Castle Rock Entertainment to back Branagh's dream of making an epic-length film of Shakespeare's most famous play.

Basing his screenplay on a conflation of Folio and Q2 texts, Branagh wanted to present a *Hamlet* 'both personal, with enormous attention to the intimate relations between the characters, and at the same time epic, with a sense of the country at large and of a dynasty in decay' (Branagh, 1996, xiv–xv). Quibbles there may be about the degree to which the film achieves these aims. But by delivering the maximum amount of text possible, and finding effective cinematic means to keep us watching the 'eternity version' of *Hamlet* for 242 minutes, Branagh managed to convey all the themes of the play. The epic (political) dimensions of the story excised by the two major film versions of Olivier and Zeffirelli are restored here, being given visual emphasis in various ways. Hamlet's personal dilemmas and struggles are set in the context of military struggles between Denmark and Norway, the 'Fortinbras plot' being fully realized at the beginning, middle and end of the film, containing the epic dimensions of the story in a coherent dramatic framework. In turn, Branagh developed the political dimensions of the play more than any previous film version, reminding us in the process that the situation of a thwarted son's struggle for self-assertion is not confined to the Danish royal family.

The movie's nineteenth-century setting in a war-alert military state with most male characters in military uniform (Claudius and Polonius ostentatiously so) and martial training frequently going on in the background emphasizes how imperialistic ambitions are at stake here. This perspective is made emphatic by using Blenheim Palace for the Elsinore exteriors, Blenheim being the home of the Dukes of Marlborough since 1704, and where their descendant Sir Winston Churchill was born and grew up. Claudius is described in the screenplay as speaking 'with a great Churchillian flourish' when, after dragging a reluctant Hamlet on to the dais he declares how the world should take note that his nephew is the 'most immediate to our throne' (1.2.108–9).

The aspects of political intrigue so integral to *Hamlet*'s dramatic edge are in this version brought out clearly by giving prominence to characters and parts of the play text usually cut. The first half of 2.1 where Polonius instructs his 'agent' Reynaldo in the techniques of spying on his son Laertes in France is invariably removed. Its inclusion here reveals how Polonius is as much a deviously hard-headed schemer as he is a bumbling senior state official (the way he is frequently played). Rosencrantz and Guildenstern – absent from the Olivier version – are shown here treacherously complicit with the usurping king against Hamlet, and their underhand willingness to comply with Claudius's deadly plan to have their old schoolfriend assassinated in England clearly shows that 'they did make love to this employment', as Hamlet later reports to Horatio (5.2.58). Playing the full version of the scene in which Claudius skilfully manipulates Laertes into a plot to kill Hamlet in revenge for the death of his father Polonius (4.7), as Branagh himself says, helps to 'flesh out a richer portrait' of Claudius, instead of making Old Hamlet's murderer the 'conventional stage villain'.

Beyond the fuller account that all these textual restorations give to *Hamlet*'s scope as a political play, two other areas which benefit from the process concern the Ghost, and Hamlet's interactions with the visiting Players. The beginning of the film does all it can to suggest the uncanny atmosphere and anxiety implied by the play's opening words, Barnardo's inquiry, 'Who's there?' Without cast list or indeed any credits whatever, the first image seen in epic 70mm film gauge is what Branagh (in the screenplay) calls 'the screen-filling legend carved deep in the stone, HAMLET', the word turning out to be carved on the stone plinth of the tomb upon which a statue of the (murdered) Old Hamlet stands. The director achieves several weighty effects simultaneously with this unmediated portentous articulation: a signal, of course, that we are about to see the 'legendary' Shakespeare play which has attained this status partly because of its worldwide fame and reputation as an impenetrable work of art. But it is portentous also in *exhibiting* a name that in one gesture symbolically displays the whole text on the screen at the same time as its location on a tombstone suggests that what follows may be associated with destiny and death. A few frames later, having shown us the icy grandeur of Elsinore's exterior and Barnardo's terror, the camera pulls back to focus on the hand of the statue shockingly wrenching the sword from its scabbard: we are being prepared for the chilling event of a Ghost's appearance. For the first time in any *Hamlet* film adaptation of this scene, the camera now assumes the **POV** of the (advancing) Ghost, swooping 'down on the retreating figures racing across the snow' who just in time 'fling themselves behind a pillar'. Branagh here seems to have taken a lesson from horror films that implicate the audience in the visceral atmospherics of terror by having us pursue the victims from '**POV** the monster'.

'Point of view' is important for the way that Branagh shoots this movie. The delivery of a full text and no less than 45 (silent) visual interpolations to 'illustrate' various elements of the story mean that Hamlet's point of view in the drama is no longer distinctly privileged over the viewpoints of other key characters (as it is in Olivier's version, for instance). Such postmodern 'decentring' is accentuated by Branagh's use of international stars to play some of the minor roles: for example, Gerard Depardieu as Reynaldo, Billy Crystal as First Gravedigger and Robin Williams as Osric. I shall return shortly to this key area of **POV**, in relation to spying, and **identification**. The film gives a brilliantly played version of the scene where Hamlet, having in fantasy killed Claudius while he is at prayer in a confessional (a murder we see in a subliminal flash), then finds himself unable to carry this out. He realizes that by killing Claudius at prayer he will 'send to heaven' the selfsame 'villain' who had denied such a passage to Old

Hamlet by assassinating his brother 'with all his crimes broad blown' (3.3.74–96). This spiritually motivated refusal, together with the uncut, highly dramatic delivery of the Ghost's speeches in this *Hamlet*, convey how complex Christian belief had become in a newly Protestant England where Catholic convictions were very much alive among many. Towards the end of his second soliloquy, Hamlet worries that the Ghost he has seen may 'be the devil, and the devil hath power / T'assume a pleasing shape', an idea concerning ghostly visitations still common in Shakespeare's era. A surprisingly potent *religious* context is thus provided in this version for Hamlet's dilemmas about life, death and the afterlife in the play, a context entirely missing (for example) in Zeffirelli's 'action' *Hamlet*, where the Ghost is virtually excised. This religious context in turn signals the importance of Hamlet's words to Horatio after he has been discoursing with the Ghost: 'There are more things in heaven and earth, Horatio, / Than are dreamt of in our philosophy' (1.5.168–9). The deficient 'philosophy' he refers to here is the Lutheran-based creed they have imbibed at their *alma mater*, Wittenberg (where the anti-Catholic Martin Luther had taught philosophy).

It has been said that *Hamlet* is 'a meditation on the multiple uses of theatrical conventions', that the theatre is the 'mode, the subject, the driving force and the central metaphor of the play'. If this is so, then Branagh, with an equal facility for playing Shakespeare in the theatre and on film, here points up analogies between stage and screen, and in drawing our attention to the conventions of both filmic and theatrical representation, makes **metatheatrical** and **metacinematic** statements. Two illustrations must suffice. In the play-within-the-play, the stage and audience spaces are distinguished by using a flat horizontal stage for 'theatrical' space, and an almost vertically raked stack of bleachers for the auditorium in front. On the one hand, Branagh as Hamlet moves between stage and audience, blurring the line between the two spheres, yet by doing so also signals his role as player and director *within* the play, providing additional **metacinematic** comment on his role as filmmaker. A further, more variable code is introduced in this scene by making the gazes of different characters determine where the actual performance or stage space *is*, for the spectacle keeps shifting, depending on *who* is being watched by *whom*. For example, Horatio's spying gaze through his opera glasses is focused on how Claudius, Gertrude and Ophelia are 'acting' when Hamlet taunts them during the progress of the play; meanwhile a shocked and fascinated court audience turns in alarm towards the king and queen to gauge their response when Hamlet publically blurts out his various scandalizing comments (3.2.85–138, 209–48).

A second, brilliant conjunction of devices for exploring and exposing how theatrical and filmic conventions may convey meaning is when Branagh performs Hamlet's third soliloquy while advancing menacingly upon his own image in a mirrored door. This occurs after the cleverly shot sequence in which Branagh's camera circles round and round the figures of Claudius, Rosencrantz, Guildenstern, Gertrude, Ophelia and Polonius as they debate the causes of Hamlet's 'crafty madness'. The instability of the situation is here reproduced by the camera's refusal to settle for any single **POV** adjudged reliable, the viewpoints of all being tainted in one way or another by ignorance or deception. Polonius and Claudius hide behind the two-way mirrored door, for the purpose of spying on the actions of Hamlet, to whom Polonius has 'loosed' his daughter Ophelia, and they jump in terror when he suddenly whips out a dagger at the lines, 'When he himself might his quietus make / With a bare bodkin' (3.1.77–8). As the camera continues to close towards the mirror with Hamlet, we come to see his self-threatening reflection almost from *his* **POV**, forcing us to reflect, along with him perhaps – 'who's there?' The effects of using the mirror in this way are multiple. We unfold ourselves along with Hamlet and become him as, with dagger drawn, he confronts both himself and his enemies Claudius and Polonius behind the mirror. Not only are we here offered a visual expression of the processes of **identification** at work in the soliloquy: the reflective mechanism used shows how Shakespeare's own definition of the function of drama – 'to hold, as 'twere, the mirror up to nature' (3.2.20) – can work for film as well as for theatre.

Running at four hours as it does, Branagh's *Hamlet* may not always manage to sustain the tautness of dramatic effect that more economically cinematic translations of Shakespeare's play might accomplish, such as Zeffirelli's film. And errors there were in casting, such as Jack Lemmon's Marcellus, whose articulation is embarrassingly wooden. Or in design, where the ground splintering under the feet of Hamlet as he pursues his father's ghost is a brilliant attempt to reproduce the terror of the underworld that Elizabethan audiences would have felt, but which is realized here in ways that verge on the clunky. Yet this is a *Hamlet* whose blemishes are minor. It features much fine acting (especially Branagh's), making the full text utterly accessible and providing a dramatic delivery in settings that uniquely reveal a coherent wide-arcing plot at the same time as multiple thematic resonances are repeatedly exposed. The movie also breaks new ground, not only by melding and toying with theatrical and cinematic conventions already noted, but also by creating a new cinematic device. These are the silent flashbacks and inset sequences introduced by Branagh to visualize elements in the **backstory** of the play, or to offer visual extrapolations implied by various reported situations in it (e.g. the preparations for war, or the 'invented' love sequence between Ophelia and Hamlet shown as Polonius reads Hamlet's letter to Claudius and Gertrude). These are often far more than unsophisticated visual illustrations of the text, which they may seem to be at first glance. At their best, they not only offer an imaginative method of enabling the director to blend together elements of film and theatre. They can also be seen as the cinematic equivalent of Shakespeare's own dramatic insets, films-with-in-the-film in dumb show which inform and entertain at the same time as a homage of the silent screen to the silent stage is presented.

Michael Almereyda's *Hamlet* (USA, 2000)

Director: Michael Almereyda

Producer: Amy Hobby and Andrew Fierberg

Script: Michael Almereyda

Medium: Colour, 35mm (enlarged from 16mm), 106 minutes

Main actors: Ethan Hawke (Hamlet); Diane Venora (Gertrude); Kyle MacLachlan (Claudius); Julia Stiles (Ophelia); Bill Murray (Polonius); Karl Geary (Horatio); Liev Schreiber (Laertes); Sam Shepard (Ghost)

Photography: John de Borman

Original Music: Carter Burwell

Forced by tight funding to shoot his *Hamlet* 'fast and cheap' on 16mm stock, Michael Almereyda was nevertheless sufficiently assured by the example of what Welles called his 'rough charcoal sketch' – *Macbeth* (1948) – to believe that 'you don't need lavish production values to make a Shakespeare movie that's accessible and alive. Shakespeare's language, after all, is lavish enough' (Almereyda, vii). In other words, if a director can offer imaginative visual translations of Shakespeare's verbal text to communicate its meaning well enough, there may be less of a need for this text to be spoken in full: a little of Shakespeare's rich poetic language may go a long way on screen. A viewing of Almereyda's film confirms this, for despite utilizing only about 40 per cent of the play's lines and running at a mere 106 minutes – well over two hours shorter than Branagh's 'unexpurgated, all-star treatment' (as Almereyda calls it) – it is a pleasant surprise to discover that this very American adaptation captures much of the dramatic essence of Shakespeare's *Hamlet*. Shifting the royal court of Elsinore into an 'omnipresent Denmark Corp' that rules supreme in 2000 Manhattan's glossy but cut-throat business world, Almereyda's Shakespeare update with its soundtrack mix of modern music and hip-youth lead actors would seem to be following in the footsteps of Luhrmann's *Romeo + Juliet*. But the film is targeted at an **arthouse** rather than MTV audience, and uses film technique, codes and language with a subtlety and power seriously different from the brilliant but ultimately flashy and sentimental effects achieved by Luhrmann.

Crucial to this cinematic re-visioning of *Hamlet* was Almereyda's determination to maintain

> a parallel visual language that might hold a candle to Shakespeare's poetry. There was no wish to illustrate the text, but to focus it, building a visual structure to accommodate Shakespeare's imagery and ideas. (Almereyda, x)

The skilful weaving of cinematic language and **editing** to realize this aesthetic mode produces many brilliant shots and sequences, some examples of which are discussed below. But perhaps the principal device used to invest the movie with the essential dramatic energies and meanings of Shakespeare's play is that of presenting two radically contrasting visual worlds and viewpoints. One world, represented and shot in colour from some notionally 'objective' **POV** using the 'master' Super 16mm camera, provides the dominant visual and narrative structure of the film, displaying the glitzy but controlling modern terrains of Claudius's Manhattan business empire. The other world is Hamlet's, a radically intimate perspective frequently presented through the lens of his work as amateur filmmaker (Ophelia is a young photographer). Hamlet's **POV** and world is often shown to us in the grainy black-and-white images of his own pixelvision camera's video diary, or in *The Mousetrap: A tragedy by Hamlet, Prince of Denmark*, since here the 'play within the play' becomes a 'video within the film', Hamlet's successful device for inciting Claudius to 'unkennel' his 'occulted guilt' (3.2.74, 73). We are admitted to Hamlet's painful consciousness so effectively, compared with the world of scheming corporate power led by Claudius, that the understated, fragmented approach used creates a strongly sympathetic alternative reality for the viewer. For this postmodern Hamlet with a conscience, Manhattan is a prison-house of ruthless commercialism – and it's personal.

One reason Almereyda's *Hamlet* turns into what he calls 'the most condensed straight film adaptation in English' is that a lot of the footage shot to reproduce scenes from the play was discarded, many of the 'best and worst ideas' being 'sacrificed for the sake of clarity and momentum' (Almereyda, xii). An excellent example of how such cutting becomes necessary to satisfy the needs of the screen audience comes at the beginning of the film, where the original opening playing a version of 1.1 in the lobby of the Hotel Elsinore was found at a **test screening** by Miramax to have yielded the second worst scores in the company's history. As Almereyda says, not only was the Elizabethan language exchanged by Bernardo, Horatio and Marcella (a female version of Marcellus, recast as Horatio's girlfriend) too confusingly dense and fast for the audience to follow, but 'it was troublingly clear that Hamlet's first appearance in the film came too late and felt flat' (Almereyda, 135). Realizing that 'a more urgent start' was required, a new introduction now not only brought in Ethan Hawke's Hamlet more quickly, but it demonstrated how a little of Shakespeare's rich poetic language can indeed go a long way on screen, dramatically speaking. The first 13 minutes embodying five sequences take us up to the moment that the Ghost (Sam Shepard), refusing Horatio's appeal to speak to him, **dissolves** into this film's version of purgatory, a Pepsi drinks machine, offering a sequence of events whose meaning and drama are conveyed with superb filmic economy.

The two-minute sequence inserted prior to the white-on-red title of HAMLET appearing on screen offers a brilliant collage of images and words setting the Manhattan scene and introducing the figure and character of Hamlet himself. From the rear window of Claudius's stretch limo advancing towards Times Square at night we see the bright colours of neon-lit buildings looming high and flashing by while on screen appears a series of pithy statements giving 'the story so far':

- New York City, 2000
- The King and CEO of Denmark Corporation is dead
- The King's widow has hastily remarried his younger brother
- The King's son, Hamlet, returns from school, suspecting foul play ...

When the limo stops, Hamlet, in Nepalese beanie hat, slouches across the street towards the Hotel Elsinore with shoulder bag full of camera gear, moving out of frame right to leave Almereyda's lens lingering long and close on the Hamlet Corporation logo fixed high up on a giant plasma screen bearing the equally large legend, 'Panasonic'. The message that visual representation and communication are to be compelling themes here is confirmed when, backed 'by a cross-mix of Morcheeba and orchestral music by Niels Gade', we are shown the face of 'poet/filmmaker/perpetual grad student' Hamlet in close-up grainy black-and-white pixelvision pictures, confiding to his own camera some of his character's most heartfelt lines from the play. These short, fragmented takes of Hamlet on himself are cut together to give dramatic emphasis to his performer/film editor's cynically tortured outlook on a world pervaded by man's inhumanity to man:

> I have of late – but wherefore I know not – lost all my mirth.

> What a piece of work is a man! How noble in reason, how infinite in faculties, in form and moving how express and admirable, in action how like an angel, in apprehension how like a god –

A ringing phone forces Hamlet to interrupt his 'take', the video diary resuming with cut-in images that include TV shots of a Stealth Bomber creating explosive devastation, while his flat-solemn **voice-over** offers a verbal statement on man in severe ironic contradiction:

> – the beauty of the world, the paragon of animals

As the soundtrack brings in Morcheeba again, he mutters his bleak, questioning conclusion:

> And yet to me, what is this quintessence of dust?

We now pull back to see Hamlet in the 16mm 'real-time' colour film/ master narrative where, at his editing desk, he cuts together further shots of his own attempt 'to be' Hamlet. These are the first of many **metacinematic** statements of the film; the camera 'invading' his clamshell **editing** screen that first turns to snow before dissolving to the white-on-red HAMLET title beginning the film proper: what kind of status and value will the succeeding edited-together visual representations have for us?

This two-minute sequence of visual fragments that now 'kickstarts the movie' not only gives 'the Prince a series of intimate close-ups and a private (pixelated) language', as Almereyda says. This engaging opening **montage** also offers both a concentrated slice of the film's overall approach to representing and involving us in the mind of its main character, as well as demonstrating the typical way its cool style of 'focusing' the Shakespeare text will deliver that very 'visual structure' the director wanted in order 'to accommodate Shakespeare's imagery and ideas'. The glossily explicit colour master-narrative of the enclosing 'frame' film starts and continues to convey the Manhattan spaces and surfaces among which it is shot as hard and impersonal, creating the feeling of an excluding and insensitive prison – a 'hot' medium in the jargon of Sixties' mass-media guru Marshall McLuhan. By contrast, Hamlet's grainy, cynical and agonized black-and-white movie of himself and the cruel world around him is conveyed inclusively and sensitively, supplying a 'cool' and involving account of 'the Hamlet dilemma', if ever there was one.

When we follow Hamlet into the Hotel Elsinore press conference where Claudius is announcing his takeover of Denmark Corp and his marriage to Gertrude – a 'first lady' who stands supportively at his side – it is once again apparent that this film is to be all about competing visual representations of the world in which Hamlet finds himself. Pixel camera and clamshell monitor in his hands, he moves about conspicuously filming the event hordes of press photographers are also recording. Out on the sidewalk, Almereyda uses Wellesian **low-angle** shooting to convey a powerful family in crisis as the mystified Gertrude and a dapper, irritated Claudius (his ever-present bodyguard in tow) quiz Hamlet on his melancholy condition while they walk along. Hamlet's halting on the sidewalk to tell the queen that he has 'that within which passes show; / These but the trappings and the suits of woe' is a rare moment when Hamlet's power 'to be' is asserted over the 'seeming' of Gertrude and Claudius. Shortly after, the tense power relation of mother, son and uncle is conveyed in one of the most effective filmic images of the movie. This is when Gertrude, now sitting in the limousine, winds her window halfway down, and takes off her sunglasses to plead with Hamlet not to return to Wittenberg. While she speaks, we also see Hamlet and his deadly enemy Claudius reflected in the car window, standing side by side against the Manhattan skyscrapers so emblematic of the power of this usurper.

Hawke's filmmaking Hamlet uses his pixelcamera and **editing** machine to reflect on and to become the character/persona of the Shakespeare text, going so far as to shoot himself about to shoot himself (gun to head) before the master-camera gets to secure the 'objectifying' setting for his 'To be or not to be' soliloquy. This is performed by Hawke in **voice-over** as he paces irritably up and down the 'Action' aisles of a Blockbuster video store, ironically showing us the thwarted man of action surrounded by numerous video films counterfeiting 'Action'. Reflections and refractions suggesting the devious, sinister, evasive and oblique nature of much of the reality of the Manhattan Hamlet world are also communicated on and through glass and other surfaces in the movie, occurring almost as pervasively as the facilitating yet entrapping items of electronic communication gadgetry that find their way into nearly every scene. Ophelia is frequently seen and sees herself reflected in water: that of Claudius's penthouse pool, and especially in the Guggenheim Museum water feature where she will

drown. We see Rosencrantz asking Hamlet where Polonius's dead
body is, their images reflected in the round glass door of a Laundromat
washing machine as the prince gazes at his bloodstained clothes going
round and round. We see Hamlet completing his 'How all occasions do
inform against me' soliloquy while gazing at himself in a toilet mirror
on the plane in which Rosencrantz and Guildenstern are taking him to
England. One of the film's most resonant reflections occurs just before
Kyle MacLachlan's sleek but rattled Claudius confides his plot to kill
Hamlet to Laertes. Here we see the king gazing into the wardrobe mirror shattered and splintered by the bullet from Hamlet's gun that had
killed Polonius. 'Where th'offence is, let the great axe fall', he mutters,
unaware that the mirror he abstractedly looks into as a reminder of
Hamlet as killer offers to *us* a fractured image **metonymically** conveying *him* as a murderer whose diabolical scheming sets him apart as the
guilty instigator of a commercial dynasty suffering collapse.

Illustration 4   **Michael Almereyda's *Hamlet* (2000)**. Ethan Hawke as Hamlet
roams the 'Action' aisles of a Blockbuster video store while performing the 'to
be or not to be' soliloquy (3.1.58–90). Visual ironies abound as Hamlet, surrounded by numerous videos counterfeiting and arresting 'action' on tape,
reflects on how his own 'native hue of resolution / Is sicklied o'er with the pale
cast of thought', causing the currents of his own avenging impulses to 'lose the
name of action'.

As I said at the beginning, this is a film which gains much of its power from using two counterpointed visual discourses. The fine actors playing the parts of the 'older-generation' characters, MacLachlan's Claudius, Diane Venora's Gertrude, Bill Murray's Polonius and above all Sam Shepard's chillingly naturalistic Ghost, all are given space and time to speak their lines often in continuous takes, conveyed by the colour master-camera. But it is the contrasting, more visually and verbally cross-cut and uneven discourse conveying the emotional plight of young Hamlet and his friends – especially Julia Stiles's so-young and victimized Ophelia and Karl Geary's laid-back but movingly loyal Horatio – that is brought forward to impress and convince us. Furthermore, the film undoubtedly gains much of its power from the surly anguish with which Hawke invests his Hamlet, a power drawing on American cinema history to make itself felt. This is revealed when, without the impassioned acting of the Player King for him to respond to, TV images of James Dean 'suffering beautifully in *East of Eden*' (as Almereyda states in the screenplay) are used to incite Hamlet to his 'O what a rogue and peasant slave am I' soliloquy. In coming to reconstruct *Hamlet* for an **arthouse** film audience, Almereyda says he kept remembering the 'adolescence-primed impact and meaning' that this play had always held for him, and the 'rampant parallels between the melancholy Dane' and his 'many doomed and damaged heroes', among them James Dean and Holden Caulfield ('anti-hero' of *The Catcher in the Rye*).

Ethan Hawke's complementary reading of the play is made plain when he states that the reason Hamlet for him had always come off 'so annoying, infantile, and self-indulgent is that the guy playing him is 10 to 20 years too old for the part':

> He is a bright young man struggling deeply with his identity, his moral code, his relationship to his parents and with his entire surrounding community. Hamlet was always much more like Kurt Cobain or Holden Caulfield than Sir Laurence Olivier. (Almereyda, xiv)

These readings of Hamlet by the film's director and leading actor partly explain why this skilfully cut-down but cleverly shot movie delivers such a rich visual and aural translation of Shakespeare's language for a modern film audience. Never before had there been a *Hamlet* movie in which the Prince was played by an actor in his twenties: even Branagh was 35 when he shot his *Hamlet*. At 27, Hawke was not only the right age for the Hamlet of the play, but by consistently

presenting the Prince as a smoulderingly melancholic James Dean figure done down by a power-obsessed corporate culture, a fine American
Shakespeare film has been made. It is a movie that speaks 'with most
miraculous organ' to the youthful audience who are the prime target
for Shakespeare movie-makers of the new millennium.

Orson Welles's *Macbeth* (USA, 1948)

Director: Orson Welles

Producers: Charles K. Feldman, Orson Welles

Script: Orson Welles

Medium: Black and white, 35mm, 107 minutes

Main actors: Orson Welles (Macbeth); Jeanette Nolan (Lady Macbeth); Edgar Barrier (Banquo); Dan O'Herlihy (Macduff); Peggy Webber (Lady Macduff); Erskine Sanford (Duncan); Roddy McDowall (Malcolm); Alan Napier (a holy father); John Dierkes (Ross); Keene Curtis (Lennox)

Photography: John L. Russell

Music: Jacques Ibert

Coming from the maker of *Citizen Kane* (USA, 1941), the virtuoso experiment in cinematic style and technique which many still regard as one of the greatest twentieth-century movies, one might expect Orson Welles's film adaptation of *Macbeth* to display similar filmic sophistication. It does do that in many ways, despite such restrictions as Welles having to work with the facilities of low-budget Hollywood 'B'- movie-studio Republic Pictures, and a tight 23-day shooting schedule. The film bears some comparison with Olivier's *Hamlet* of the same year (1948), since both black-and-white movies use Expressionist techniques of **chiaroscuro** lighting to create claustrophobic sets conveying the psychological oppressiveness and anxiety which inhabits both plays. Despite the technical brilliance of Olivier's movie, Welles's approach to Shakespearean adaptation here involves a more self-consciously cinematic reworking. The endeavours of Welles in his various drama projects were always best focused when making films as works of art, a process in which he drew as inventively as possible on the grammar of film – sometimes even extending its language somewhat – in order to achieve the dramatic effects he wanted.

The dramatic effects established from the outset in *Macbeth* are ones that focus on its potential as a mysterious drama of supernatural malevolence; these are apparent from the first sixty seconds of film prior to opening titles and credits. Against a background of ever-moving clouds and mist, the figures of the three witches are seen in silhouette bending over a steaming, bubbling cauldron, cackling their incantatory chorus from 4.1: 'Double, double, toil and trouble, / Fire burn, and cauldron bubble.' As Welles has them continuing to mutter more lines of magical formulae from the play, we see **close-up**s of the fiercely bubbling and fiery 'hell-broth' being concocted, until out of it they draw a figure hand-fashioned from the clayey mixture, hold it aloft and utter the name 'Macbeth!' – the title now appearing on screen. The arched brows of this clay doll's visage give it a remarkable resemblance to Welles as Macbeth. At the outset the assumption is therefore established that by magically fashioning his likeness, the witches are able to exert an evil power over the thane similar to the way voodoo witch doctors of Haiti are able to over their victims. Welles had produced an all-black 'voodoo' *Macbeth* for the stage ten years before in Harlem, New York, now drawing on this earlier production, together with other 'pagan' elements. However, the key point to note in this movie opening is the pictorial method Welles uses to convey chilling meanings and effects that prefigure his approach to the whole adaptation. For example, everything glimpsed among the swirling clouds, mists and hideous broth of the cauldron, except for the doll's visage, is indistinct and murkily anonymous. This indistinctness applies to the figures and faces of the witches, only ever visible in **backlit**-created silhouettes, but it is also paralleled by camera shots that continually **dissolve** one into another, reproducing cinematically the very fluidity of magical transformation performed by the witches.

Welles omits 1.2, where Duncan greets the bleeding Captain and hears his report of the battle. This is perhaps because he wants to foreground not a specifically historical, social, political or military setting for the play, but provide instead a blurred, decontextualized state of affairs in which the evil manipulations of the witches over Macbeth are the most powerful forces present. This creates a space of dreamlike psychological terror for the dramatic events to unfold in, rather than one of realistic, everyday surfaces. The resulting impenetrable and swirling mist becomes a kind of external simulacrum of Macbeth's disturbed and metamorphosing thoughts as the witches' spells activate his susceptible ambitions. The mixture of 'fair and foul' elements in what we see is a kind of preparation for the mental torments that will later afflict Macbeth. These obscure and terrific effects established by the witches in the mist develop when we see Macbeth and Banquo riding through it towards them. For after we hear on the soundtrack the second witch's incantation from 4.1, 'By the pricking of my thumbs, / Something wicked this way comes', Macbeth voices his innocent comment to Banquo of how 'so fair and foul a day' he has not seen, ominously announcing the fortune that is shortly to be visited on him. 'Hailing' him as Thane of Cawdor, the witches in their catlike screeching reveal that Macbeth 'shall be king hereafter', the Cawdor regalia being hung around the voodoo doll's neck and a miniature crown set on its head. These are the very head and crown that will be lopped off at the end of the film, a clever device to avoid having to depict Macbeth's decapitation, yet which will signal the end of his bloody reign. The Gothic atmosphere now intensifies as 'a holy father' arrives brandishing a large Celtic cross, the hissing witches being forced to back off like vampires confronted by a crucifix. The genre conventions and style of 1930s black-and-white horror films like *Dracula* and *Frankenstein* appear not to have been very far away from Welles's mind in his design of the ***mise-en-scène*** for this film. The 'holy father' character wholly invented by Welles is introduced to provide the film with a 'good versus evil' structure, a design evident from the original spoken Prologue by Welles, dropped for the DVD/video releases. This statement had described the setting as an 'ancient Scotland, savage', where 'the cross itself is newly arrived' and where,

> Plotting against Christian law and order are the agents of chaos, priests of hell and magic; sorcerers and witches. Their tools are ambitious men.
>
> Men like Macbeth.

When Macbeth and his entourage ride off following the announcement of the witches' prophecy, we are left with a stunning image of the three witches on top of their rock chorusing 'Hail!' while each grips (in a play tinctured throughout with the equivocations of evil) a forked stave in the shape of the letter Y. This cleverly suggests the sinister question 'Why?' as a counterpoint to the 'newly arrived' but evidently feeble powers of the Christian cross (what Anthony Davies calls a 'semiotic dichotomy'). That the Christian light is very limited in its powers to thwart evil is revealed in the remaining scenes of the film, where the forces of a primitive malevolence are shown to hold sway. As the holy father writes out the letter dictated by Macbeth to Lady Macbeth, we see that the metallic blisters on Macbeth's tunic echo the muddy, bubbling appearance of the witches' hell-broth, identifying him with their evil powers and purposes. This **metonymic**ally menacing connection is followed by another effective linking transition when, towards the end of dictating his letter, Macbeth's voice segues into that of Jeanette Nolan's Lady Macbeth, this 'verbal dissolve' coinciding with a visual **dissolve** to his 'dearest partner of greatness' as she reads it lying on the bed in their castle. Their collusion visually and aurally established, her candle is ominously blown out by the wind, leaving her in a fittingly 'thick night' to conjure up the evil spirits she requires to help 'stop up th'access and passage to remorse', an emotion inimical to her planned murder of Duncan, which will facilitate the fulfilment of the witches' prophecy of Macbeth becoming king. She begins this speech of darkness while sensuously stroking an animal fur on the bed, suggesting bestial impulses that are echoed soon after when Cawdor is led to the scaffold accompanied by the ritualistic pounding of primitive drums. Eroticism and violence are evidently in play when we see Macbeth and Lady Macbeth embrace while the axe slices through Cawdor's head. And even though this execution is meant as a Christian rite, together with the collective ceremony overseen by the holy father as a prophylactic against Satan, when the 'amen' is spoken, all present blow out their lighted candles, strangely suggesting a pagan *denial* of the 'Christian light', rather than its affirmation.

Camera movement is rare in *Macbeth*, but the camera skilfully conveys meanings produced by Shakespeare's text, primarily those associated with Macbeth's disturbed subjective state, or projecting the troubled identity he battles with on to other characters. There are two instances where **subjective camera shot**s are used to convey Macbeth's troubled interior state. The first occurs in the long **film-noir**ish prelude to Duncan's murder, following Macbeth's emergence from the shadows where he wished Banquo 'good repose'. After we hear him speak (in **voice-over**) of 'withered murder' moving 'like a ghost' from his second soliloquy (2.1.52, 56), the camera **dissolves** from his image using blurred focus into a **close-up** of the head of the Macbeth voodoo doll being 'penetrated' by a dagger blade superimposed over it. This image then blurs back into that of Macbeth advancing slowly towards the dagger-as-camera, failing in his attempt to grab it: 'Is this a dagger which I see before me, / The handle toward my hand?' (2.1.33–4). After more camera-blur **dissolve**s into and out of images that include for him the feared entrance to Duncan's room, he sees that this and the 'dagger of the mind' are indeed 'false' creations 'proceeding from the heat-oppressèd brain' (2.1.38–9). The second example occurs at the banquet, when an anxious, sweating Macbeth, now king, raises a toast to the absent Banquo. But his face becomes fearful, and as in a trance he lowers his goblet, the camera shows from his **POV** the diners imitating him, his stricken gaze transfixed in terror by something he has seen. The shadow created by the lowering of his arm now functions as a kind of **wipe** moving his focus from the actuality of the banquet and its attendees, to the 'shadow realm' of his guilty mind, creator of the ghost of Banquo that he now sees. Gripped by this apparition, he asks, staring, 'Behold, look, lo – how say you?' (3.4.68), the camera following the movement of an elongated shadow of his pointing finger along the rough-hewn walls of the chamber towards the figure of Banquo's ghost, sitting alone at the end of the table, and seen, as it must be, from Macbeth's **POV**, for it is invisible to anyone else's perceptions, as other camera shots reveal. It is a brilliant visual transition, soon matched by another in which Macbeth advances angrily towards his hallucination, muttering, 'Well, what care I?', the camera now cutting to the **POV** of Banquo's ghost that focuses on the man who ordered his murder. It is a remarkable shot, for in this **subjective camera**work the camera is recording Macbeth's reaction to the consequences of his own actions, viewed from the POV of those grim consequences.

Welles's economic use of **montage** to create narrative energy and pace in the early part of the movie switches at certain points into a more theatrical mode, sometimes employing long unbroken takes, as with the ten-minute sequence featuring Macbeth and Lady Macbeth before and after the ('offstage') murder of Duncan. In this notable sequence (unaccountably cut by Republic in the film's original release), we see examples of camera use that are classically Wellesian, and the visual outcome of which captures some of the 'equivocating' elements so essential to the meanings of this play. It has been said of Welles's films that from being shown the spatial disposition and angles between characters, it should be possible without the aid of one word of dialogue to understand the relationships between them. Throughout this sequence, the power-relationship between Macbeth and Lady Macbeth tends to be defined by the vertical relation of one to the other – the character looming above suggesting dominance over the lower character. This meaning-effect can also be enhanced by the position of the camera: a powerful figure conjured by looking down at the camera, and a weaker one by looking up at it. For much of the early part of the sequence, before Macbeth goes to murder Duncan, we see an uneasy Macbeth – this is not long after the 'dagger of the mind' episode – being berated and sexually taunted for his equivocation by a Lady Macbeth standing above him. With some reluctance, Macbeth now mounts the stairs to undertake the murder, thereby showing activity and some dominance. After killing Duncan, he descends the staircase, pausing on it above Lady Macbeth to say, 'I have done the deed' (2.2.14), and so maintaining a dominant power relation. But once he walks on down past her, he stays below, until, refusing to put the bloody daggers back next to Duncan's drugged grooms, he is chastised by Lady Macbeth, this time for being 'Infirm of purpose!' (2.2.50). On her return from replacing the daggers, she pauses to stand above him on the staircase, maintaining her dominance as he stands lost in a daze, only disappearing from view for a time while he complies with Lady Macbeth's order to don his nightgown. The **cutaway** that ends this ten-minute 'theatrical' **take** shows Macduff running along the castle ramparts from Duncan's apartment, and in the following five minutes there could not be more of a contrast in pace and style of shooting. No fewer than 45 camera shots of varying closeness and angle are swiftly cut together in these minutes to convey the confusion and agitation while numerous characters speak, move and interact in their various responses to the murder's discovery.

At the end of the movie, isolated by his tyrannical and murderous efforts to maintain power, Macbeth is slaughtered by the avenging Macduff, with rapid-cutting multiple **zoom**-out **shot**s of cheering troops holding blazing torches and crosses aloft seeming to confirm Macduff's proclamation that now 'The time is free' (5.11.21). Yet the final frames of the movie belong to the witches, bringing us back full circle to the film's unease-making use of visual and aural **dissolves**. From brass fanfares and the zoom-out shots of torchbearing troops conveying dynamic victory, the camera **dissolve**s to a crown-like image of Macbeth's castle continuing the slow zoom-out, a movement soon revealing the three witches and their 'questioning' Y staves at the bottom of the frame. The music has metamorphosed from a mood of boisterous triumphalism to that of quiet and sinister mystery, several more visual **dissolve**s taking us through the mists of the film's opening to a **close-up** of the 'weird sisters', one of whom is given the film's last words: 'Peace: the charm's wound up' (1.3.35). Through its fluidity of images and sounds, this film undoubtedly not only suggests the unease and ambiguity of the evil world Macbeth is drawn into and creates; through the fluxions of film technique that he commands so well, Welles also manages to convey the vulnerable mutability of the human mind, its desires and emotions, phenomena dramatized so pervasively in Shakespeare's tragic plays.

Roman Polanski's *Macbeth* (UK, 1971)

Director: Roman Polanski

Producer: Andrew Braunsburg

Script: Roman Polanski, Kenneth Tynan

Medium: Colour, Todd A-O 35mm, 134 minutes

Main actors: Jon Finch (Macbeth); Francesca Annis (Lady Macbeth); Martin Shaw (Banquo); Terence Bayler (Macduff); Diane Fletcher (Lady Macduff); Nicholas Selby (Duncan); Stephen Chase (Malcolm); John Stride (Ross); Paul Shelley (Donalbain)

Photography: Gilbert Taylor

Music: The Third Ear Band

The opening of Polanski's *Macbeth* resembles that of Welles's film in two respects: it begins with the witches, and there is mist. But there the similarity ends. Much of the power of Welles's black-and-white movie comes from his use of Expressionist and **film noir** conventions on a studio set of high artifice to convey a drama of mysteriously super-natural evil overcoming Christian good. Evil pervades Polanski's film too, but this is shown as emerging more realistically from the 'natural' psychological motivations of the characters, rather than through the 'supernatural' magic of the witches, not semi-ethereal beings here but 'practising' flesh and blood witches, living in a female community of their own. They, Macbeth, Banquo and the others are filmed realisti-cally amid the bleak, rain-swept hilly landscape of North Wales, a nat-ural exterior location assisting the projection of an eleventh-century Scottish society of quasi-tribal clans led by a king who rules by the warrior codes of courage and loyalty. It is a setting in which Polanski's understanding of *Macbeth* as a play exploring 'the violence at the heart of usurpation' (Kliman, 1992, 119) can be developed and exposed with some power. An apt location of this sort was important for providing the film with the appropriate tone of social rivalry Polanski wanted to establish in realistic characters inhabiting a raw, godless world of self-serving evil and violence. Yet this setting is only one of the many ele-ments that make the film among the most enduring – because so artistically effective – Shakespeare adaptations ever made. Casting choices, *mise-en-scène,* **montage**, use of colour, visual and sound **motifs**, careful textual **editing**, and chillingly effective 'period' music by The Third Ear Band – all these factors are creatively exploited to make a coherent and engaging dramatic mix by Polanski, and I will explore some of these in what follows.

It is useful at the outset to notice a good example of how Polanski manipulates both cinematic space and Shakespeare's text to make psychology predominate in character motivation. After Macbeth and Banquo have heard the witches' prophecies early on in the film, an intensely curious Macbeth dismounts from his horse to follow the weird sisters, who have retreated out of sight to the door of their underground lair, slamming it shut on him. Unable to see this, Banquo asks, 'Whither are they vanished?' Macbeth replies with the lines the play gives him, but his report is a lie: 'Into the air, and what seemed corporal / Melted as breath into the wind' (1.3.78–80). Quickly seduced by the promise of a high destiny ('All Hail Macbeth, that shall be king hereafter'), Macbeth craftily keeps the location of the witches' lair to himself: later he will return to consult them and their oracular powers in pursuit of his own power-obsessed interests.

With a reputation for an interest and involvement in the macabre at the time of making *Macbeth* – especially through his 1968 Hitchcockian gothic melodrama *Rosemary's Baby* and the shockingly bloody murder of his wife Sharon Tate by the Manson gang in 1969 – Polanski said in an interview at the time that he was 'more interested in the behaviour of people under stress'. Certainly, from the moment that Macbeth hears the witches' prophesy that he will 'be king hereafter', he is a character under stress, a mind divided. This is in the play, revealed by his early conflicting reflections on the prophecy: 'My thought, whose murder yet is but fantastical, / Shakes so my single state of man that function / Is smothered in surmise, and nothing is / But what is not' (1.3.138–41). This reflection is spoken in **voice-over** interior monologue, a device that enables Polanski to emphasize the 'split state of man' motivating the mind of Macbeth, and which is sustained to such an extent that it is used more in this study of psychological obsession and its outcomes than in any previous Shakespeare adaptation. In a wider sense, Polanski also juxtaposes the everyday with the disturbed for much of the time, pursuing his typical filmic goal of presenting 'a realistic situation where things don't quite fit in' – the domesticity of Macbeth's castle coexisting alongside the bloody horror of Duncan's murder, for instance.

Apart from producing the first *Macbeth* to graphically depict several of the acts of violence always previously played 'offstage' in both theatrical and cinematic productions – mainly the murders of Duncan and Banquo, and the decapitating of Macbeth – Polanski also broke new 'realistic' ground by casting young actors to play Lady Macbeth and Macbeth. But instead of repeating what he saw as a clichéd depiction of them as 'a couple of crowing gangsters', he wanted to make the Macbeths at the outset a youthfully attractive loving couple, sexually active and emotionally involved. 'She has to be a woman for him, and not another witch', he has said, and their affectionate relationship is noticeable in the many **two-shot**s in **close-up** of young actors Jon Finch and Francesca Annis in the first third of the film. Making the Macbeths young, good-looking and innocent on the outside, but hatching evil plans within, also helps to convey the play's pervasive ambiguity theme exemplified by the witches' expression, 'fair is foul'. At the same time, together with a tendency for the impact of the Shakespearean verse to be reduced by the actors' speaking it prosaically and the frequent use of 'internalized' **voice-over**, their attractiveness could be thought to reduce their stature as tragic figures. This is especially so for Lady Macbeth, who does not speak the lines concerning her plucking the nipple from her babe and dashing out its brains, nor is she described as a 'fiend-like queen' by Malcolm at the end. Instead, what we see in their 'squabbling couple' exchanges at the first banquet is a Lady Macbeth shedding genuine tears of frustration at Macbeth's initial refusal to kill Duncan, revealing her naïve grasp of their plotting, seen as a kind of exciting game. She may glide beautifully along the corridors of the castle like Kurosawa's equivalent of Lady Macbeth, Asaji, but she does not possess her menace. Fainting at the sight of the severed heads of the guards whom Macbeth kills, slowly sinking into madness after Banquo's murder while Macbeth neglects her for the witches, murdering with increased obsessiveness to secure the throne, she comes across as pathetic, rather than tragic.

It is true that Lady Macbeth's reproaches about his lost 'beast' at the first banquet turn into a cajoling and coaxing full of sexual appeal that in many ways restores Macbeth's sense of masculine purpose. Yet there is something even more masculinist motivating this crucial sequence of the film, for prior to her winning him over comes a moment of taunting perhaps more decisive in restoring Macbeth's motivation to kill Duncan. This is when Malcolm gestures for Macbeth to fill up his goblet with wine for him, then offering in effect a jeer instead of a cheer with his 'Hail, Thane of Cawdor' – the toast functioning as a taunting reminder of the witches' crucial supplement to their: 'All Hail Macbeth, that shall be king hereafter.'

But even if this is a sexy, naïve Lady Macbeth who lacks tragic stature, the 'beast' which she accuses Macbeth of having abandoned is nevertheless in evidence throughout the film, not only through numerous references to animals and animality, but by the use of cleverly deployed visual and aural **motifs**. We know this is a play where, from the moment that King Duncan asks, 'What bloody man is that?' (1.2.1) to the chopping off of Macbeth's head by Macduff in their hand-to-hand combat, hardly a scene goes by without blood being spilt or an act of violence being committed. Polanski's film signals even earlier than this that blood and violence will be major themes. The opening frame shows a red dawn sky bathing the sandy ridges of a seashore in the same hue, and this is only the first of many blood-red dawns and sunsets that will create memorable visual motifs to energize the movie's dark yet vividly unrelenting interpretation. The first view of Macbeth's castle is against a blood-red evening sky. It is dawn when Duncan's murder is discovered, the faces of all in Macbeth's castle yard being tinted with red. The evening that his plot to kill Banquo is carried out Macbeth's gaze is on a deep-red sunset. The speech where he admits that he is 'in blood so far' is made against a blood-red dawn. And he stands again in the glow of a red sunset on his castle ramparts when spotting the approach of Malcolm's rebel thanes with the English army, noting with grim appropriateness in his isolation how he begins 'to be aweary of the sun'.

The soundtrack over the opening frames delivers eerie sounds, sourced from a **diegetic** and **non-diegetic** mix, before **time-lapse** photography speeds our view of the same scene forward into the flat light of day. These sounds continue, until, with the cry of a gull – and what sounds like the distant bellow of an elephant! – a cough is heard, and a witch's crooked stick punctures the frame from screen right, a mild enough action in itself, but which functions as and feels like a violation, the first of many much more cruel and brutal violations to come. The murderous nature of what some of these will be are signalled by objects ritually buried in the sand by the three witches: a hangman's noose (the hanging of Duncan's enemies, including the execution of Cawdor) and a dagger placed in the hand of a severed forearm (Macbeth's stabbing of Duncan, and the final severing of his own head). The emptying of a vial of blood over the burial place by the eyeless witch while all chant the ambiguous magical formula 'foul is fair and fair is foul' (their own appearance could be said to be a mixture of 'foul and fair') marks the first spilling of blood in the film. Indeed, as the witches walk off into the fog now filling the screen while the titles come up, the sounds of the battle mentioned by them is heard: horses galloping and neighing, metal on metal clashing, the murderous and desperate cries of those who kill or who are being killed. These sounds are not just more effective for being only heard, but bring the impact of the one act of violence we do see committed – a half-dead soldier 'finished off' by a spiked iron ball repeatedly and bloodily thudded into his back (Banquo will later be axed to death in a similar way) – sickeningly home.

By bathing everyone and everything in the *mise-en-scène* in the colour of blood Polanski vividly reminds us of the hideous human cost that societies pay for maintaining ruthless tyrannies. But he also deepens the violence theme here by stressing in various ways the animality underlying the struggle for existence in this semi-tribal medieval society. Our first encounter with Lady Macbeth is in the bustle of a castle courtyard full of animals, and as she reads his 'partner of greatness' speech, two enormous dogs lick her hands. In preparation for the banquet in Duncan's honour, we see a squealing pig being caught for the feast. A grim reminder of this comes when Macbeth later plunges his dagger into Duncan's throat, producing what sounds like the grunt of a stuck pig. Bears figure large both in the play and in this film. (We should remember that in the public entertainment stakes, Shakespeare's Globe vied with the nearby Bear Baiting for business.) Prior to the banquet that celebrates his own accession to the crown, Macbeth gazes amusedly at a caged bear, declaring, 'Here's our chief guest' – an ironic comment in many ways, given that an animal struggle for existence will henceforth prevail under his kingship. This fact reveals its greatest personal relevance and force for Macbeth by the time all have deserted him, when he states, glancing at the iron ring in the wall to which the bear had originally been tethered: 'I cannot fly, / But bear-like I must fight' (5.7.1–2).

A fascinating if grim pattern established through character plotting in this *Macbeth* by Polanski concerns the figure of Ross, made emblematic here of the screenplay authors' cynicism regarding the way power structures can attract self-seeking political opportunists. Ross, aptly described by Rothwell as a 'smirking sociopath', is a character offering a variation on the theme of 'foul and fair'. He is fair-haired, draws little attention to himself, but is in fact an amoral opportunist who without scruple attaches himself by turns to whoever has power and wealth and will serve his interests. He appears first as the deliverer of treacherous Cawdor to Duncan, bringing the chain of office to Macbeth as the new thane, and obsequiously helping him on to his horse. He stares suspiciously when Macbeth declares that he has killed Duncan's grooms, and is one of the small circle of thanes who lift Macbeth on his coronation shield, remaining mute along with his neighbour Banquo when the 'Hail Macbeth! King of Scotland' is called, yet looking with a strange kind of glee at Macbeth's old friend, who remains emotionless. Gone over completely to Macbeth's side, he becomes the baffling third murderer, only failing to kill Fleance because Banquo downs his horse with an arrow. When the other two murderers are led into the castle dungeons, it is Ross who oversees their deaths, snatching the forked stick that serves as a crutch for the younger one (and as a homage to Welles's witches) to push him cruelly down a well himself. Ross invites Macbeth to the place where Banquo's ghost sits at the second banquet, and who organizes the massacre of Macduff's family, while giving bland assurances to Lady Macduff and blessing in his arms the Macduff son who is shortly to be slaughtered by his accomplices. When he is casually passed over for advancement by Macbeth, he deserts to Malcolm's side, and with concerned looks breaks the news of the massacre and rape that he has stage-managed to Macduff. However, not only does Ross not suffer for his crimes in the end, but he joins Malcolm's triumphant regime, wiping the blood from the crown he takes from Macbeth's severed head, and placing it as he offers the cry of 'Hail Malcolm King of Scotland!' on to the head of his new master.

The magic circle drawn in the sand in the movie's opening frames by the sightless witch is but the first example of a key visual **motif** deployed by Polanski throughout. It recurs in the hangman's noose buried by the witches, and with the noose-like well-bucket hook seen swinging ominously back and forth in the long-held shot in Macbeth's castle yard after Duncan's murder. We see it in the golden crown which falls spinning to the ground from Duncan's head as Macbeth butchers the king, and in the golden goblet that not only also falls spinning to the ground when Macbeth hallucinates Banquo's ghost, but from which Macbeth drinks the witches' potion, after which he sees the various visions by gazing into their circular cauldron. We see the circle motif in the giant shield upon which Macbeth is raised at his coronation, and we see it in the iron collars around the necks of Cawdor and the bear, as well as in the chains of office slung around the necks of all those caught in Macbeth's lethal web. When Macduff destroys this web by slicing off Macbeth's head, the most macabre use of the circle motif is created not only by seeing the head whirled about on a pole to the delight of Malcolm's soldiers, but also by **subjective camera shot**s giving us glimpses of their jeering faces from its wildly spinning **POV**.

The use of sound to stimulate the fearful capacities of what Shakespeare famously calls the 'mind's eye' is also exploited in the kind of music we hear at many points in the film. The Third Ear Band's often harshly sour music on period instruments is very effective in suggesting a feeling of sinister threat, most pointedly with the drearily unpleasant droning bagpipe tune played whenever we are shown the witches' lair. A remarkable use of this music accompanies Duncan's approach to Macbeth's castle. It begins light and pleasant, but gradually falters and slows as Duncan and his entourage's procession snake their way along the serpentine road, descending lower and lower in pitch, until, in deep, drab discords, it finishes with a dull, twisting twang – the finality of death lies here, it seems to say.

Music is important at the end of the film, too, with the addition of a scene not in the play, but which makes for a feeling of awful enclosure and inescapable repetition. Macbeth has been killed, and Malcolm crowned. But the camera then cuts to the exact same spot where Macbeth and Banquo had at the beginning encountered the witches, and the familiar sour bagpipe **motif** linked to this place enters once again, as we see the figure of Malcolm's younger brother Donalbain riding across the heath in driving rain, just as his predecessors had. Lured to dismount by the sound of the witches' chanting, he disappears out of sight into their underground lair, closing credits coming up as a primitive five-note phrase is plucked repeatedly over thin, harsh, sounds of wind instruments. The camera pulls back to objectify the moment, making the emphatic point: as one usurper of the crown drawn into his wild obsession by 'fair and foul' prophecy is vanquished, so is another victim seen being drawn into the same process. The pessimistic implication in this final 'circle' is that the lure to possess absolute power will go on in an endless cycle of temptation, desire, deceit and death.

Part V

Shakespeare on the Small Screen

Shakespeare on the Small Screen

1

Film, TV and Small-screen Shakespeare

Whether we watch dramas in the cinema, on TV, a **DVD** or **Blu-ray Disc** player, a laptop computer, a tablet, or even a smart phone, the visual images we see are mediated by screens. So why not use the term 'Shakespeare on screen' to embrace all these media? It is convenient to do so in a broad sense, particularly as the quality of images has improved so significantly on small screens with twenty-first-century developments in digital technology. Yet even with the **HD** (High Definition) digital revolution, where picture clarity for theatrical and smaller 'domestic' screens share the same high quality, there are some differences to be pointed out, primarily in the differing *contexts* of audience locations for watching Shakespearean drama. Having begun to explore the practices of communicating Shakespeare on stage and film in Part I, I begin this concluding part with a discussion of how TV Shakespeare contrasts with 'film' Shakespeare.

Film, VHS and DVD

Until recently, the distinguishing feature of cinematic film since its beginnings in the late nineteenth century had been that it was *photographic*. A large number of very highly defined and textured images were chemically 'fixed' on to long rolls of celluloid strip 35mm wide (the industry standard), a filmmaker having exposed the moving film to light through the lens of a 35mm movie camera. After editing and processing, these successive picture frames were projected on to a large screen providing detailed visual information usually of the story-telling kind to a large audience who sat together watching in the dark semi-public space of a movie theatre. This situation is as true for 2015 as it was in 1915. People leaving home to see a movie at the cinema, whether a single screen, **miniplex** or **megaplex**, will be paying to sit in the dark, mostly with strangers, in order to be entertained by moving pictures on a screen that is, however small, bigger than the one at home. Often, customers want to see the latest movie, and to do that, you have to go the cinema, an excursion that can promise a feeling of magic. Nowadays, since the revolution in digital cinematic projection of 2010–12, most mainstream movie theatres have replaced their 35mm projectors with **2K** and **4K** digital-imaging projectors. But the experience for watching audiences has changed little.

The moving images are just as sharp and clear as they ever were, and the sound quality – vital for drama films where verbal exchanges are integral to the meaning of the screen dynamic – is the best it's ever been. It is true that serious film fans can become nostalgic (perhaps with some justification) for the crisp, photochemical texture of celluloid film. Unlike 'digital capture' this texture can have to it a characteristic 'shimmer, the sense that even static objects have a little bit of life to them ... Watch fluffy clouds or a distant forest in a digital display, and you'll see them hang there, dead as a postcard vista. In a film, clouds and trees pulsate and shift a little' (Bordwell, 2012, 199–200). However, the centre of attention for a Shakespeare film viewer will typically be the drama being played out on screen, rather than other more distant cinematic details.

As I pointed out at the end of Part I, this 'centre of interest' for the viewer of screen Shakespeare was picked up on by filmmakers interested in extending the market for their films into domestic living rooms, when from the late Sixties onwards, the domestic TV screen started to displace cinemagoing. By the 1980s the TV viewer began to benefit from the fact that many directors and producers of movies were shooting films with the needs of the domestic viewer in mind, anticipating a significant **VHS** home-video market for their films. Happily, this chimed in with the revival of Shakespeare on film that started with Branagh's 1989 *Henry V*, its 'post-theatrical' life commencing on VHS before moving to DVD. The **DVD** format was replacing VHS by the turn of the millennium, the trend of filmmaking with the domestic viewer in mind developing even further, particularly in relation to the techniques associated with **intensified continuity**.

This process can be seen at work in Ralph Fiennes's film of *Coriolanus* (2012), where many of the sequences are in **close, medium** or **medium-close shot**, with a continuing aim to capture the significant glances of characters as they look at and interact with each other. Using **Blu-ray** levels of High Definition, the clarity of image in these shots is as good for domestic consumption as it is on the big screen for a larger audience. In addition, with the higher quality of sound and sound design used for digitally shot movies, the expressive force of the drama conveyed on the movie-theatre screen now makes the experience of 'home cinema' a plausible reality. Directors of Shakespeare film adaptations with an eye to the follow-up DVD/Blu-ray market clearly *do* shoot their films with the needs of the domestic-screen viewer in mind. As has been observed, 'The video market sustains most commercial filmmaking in the long run' (Bordwell & Thompson, 42). Even when a Shakespeare film is shot mainly on location (as with *Coriolanus*), decisions taken about (for instance) the organization of a film set, or the **depth of focus** of shots, or the duration of shot sequences, will be informed by the needs of an **intensified continuity** approach that is required for all audiences, whether experiencing the film in the cinema, at home, or on a moveable tablet or smart phone. However, there is a kind of exclusive *grandeur* associated with the movie-theatre experience, whereby, ultimately, the needs of the movie audience are defined by a desire-led expectation of gazing at characters acting out a story in a realistic space in compellingly detailed pin-sharp big-screen images in a special context: the magically unique darkened cinema space. Here, the moviegoer gains voyeuristic pleasure from gazing on an image 'marked by present absence', a situation afforded by the 'sense of cinema's consent to the act of being watched' (Ellis, 1992, 138).

Television

The situation experienced by someone watching TV is different, since broadcast TV typically constructs an image for a viewing regime marked by (as John Ellis notes) 'co-presence of image and viewer'. In the crisp and subtly articulated world of the big film image, we are usually presented with a fluidly dynamic modelling of characters interacting in a whole variety of pictorially realistic settings, where what is *said* by those characters can often be of secondary importance to the way that their gestures, behaviour, world and 'look' are visually conveyed and received. Ralph Fiennes expresses this succinctly by describing how with film 'the interior life' of a character can so well be 'transmitted in the landscape of a close-up' (Logan, 2011, v). By contrast, it is what the characters have to *say* in the world of the traditional TV screen that usually takes precedence over the setting in which they are *seen*, for TV does not usually provide an array of finely detailed images articulated within an extensive **depth of field**.

What TV *can* provide very effectively is a sense of 'liveness' and immediacy, creating a situation in which the figures or characters on screen seem to be *speaking* to us personally in our living rooms. John Ellis has explored the distinctions between film and TV media in some depth:

> The image is the central reference in cinema. But for TV, sound has a more centrally defining role ... This is a tendency towards a different sound/image balance than in cinema, rather than a marked and consistent difference. Broadcast TV has areas which tend towards the cinematic, especially the areas of serious drama or of various kinds of TV film. But many of TV's characteristic broadcast forms rely upon sound as the major carrier of information and the major means of ensuring continuity of attention. ... Sound tends to anchor meaning on TV, where the image tends to anchor it with cinema.   (Ellis, 1992, 129)

Consequently, persuading a TV audience to *listen* will be crucial where the aim is to capture and hold the attention of viewers of a Shakespeare play, since the *verbal text* is such a vital dimension of his work. (Especially so in the case of the 37 Shakespeare plays that BBC-TV produced, since the policy of the series was to perform each play either complete or only sparingly cut.) The task of engaging the TV viewer's attention is therefore perhaps not so very different from stage actors involving their audience: in both cases the audience needs to *listen* for communication to take place. Of course, a major difficulty in TV communication compared to that of the stage – and this is not so very different from the situation with film – is that TV actors cannot *directly* interact with or respond to their audience, but must perform with and for each other – and for the director controlling the cameras. So how *have* producers of TV screen Shakespeare handled this challenge?

The BBC's *An Age of Kings* (1960)

BBC TV had been broadcasting productions of Shakespeare every year (excluding the war years) since 1937, focusing on the better known comedies or tragedies. Apart from *Richard II* in 1950, *King John* in 1952, and *Henry V* in 1951 and 1953, no other English history plays were broadcast. Then, as the Sixties dawned, a startlingly innovative approach appeared. Encouraged by the success in 1957 of a fresh production of *Henry V* by new BBC producer Peter Dews, the BBC permitted him to assemble a regular company of over twenty actors for the first ever TV dramatization of the eight history plays of Shakespeare sometimes called the major tetralogy or Henriad (*Richard II*, *1* and *2 Henry IV*, *Henry V*) and the minor tetralogy (*1*, *2* and *3 Henry VI*, *Richard III*). Organized chronologically by reign, these were broadcast from April to November 1960 in 15 live episodes allocating two 60–75-minute slots to each play, except *1 Henry VI*, squeezed into one episode (with unfortunate results). Each episode of *An Age of Kings* was screened fortnightly on Thursday evenings. Unseen in Britain for over fifty years, the series reappeared in 2013 for purchase on DVD, revealing to a new audience why *Guardian* TV critic Mary Crozier could describe it in 1960 as 'exciting...a striking example of the creative use of television'.

If we make allowances for the 405-line monochrome screen images and cramped studio sets, this televisual creativity is plentifully evident in the inventive direction and camerawork of Michael Hayes, and many fine performances, including those of Eileen Atkins, Robert Hardy, Sean Connery and Judi Dench. (Dench in that same year also played Juliet in Zeffirelli's groundbreaking *Romeo and Juliet* London stage production.) The vibrant edginess of the live performances also no doubt owes something to the tight production schedule limiting rehearsal time and which put producer, director and designer on their mettle to make inventive choices. Certainly, Shakespeare's text is brought to life with flair and both verbal and visual clarity. By collecting the succession of plays into a 'serial' format where no episode indicates the title of the Shakespeare play being broadcast at any point, Peter Dews was perhaps thinking of broadening TV audience appeal at a time when popular culture was expanding rapidly. Instead, each episode had a thematically descriptive title, the first two that screened *Richard II* being entitled 'The Hollow Crown' and 'The Deposing of a King'. In many ways, by emphasizing the developing roles of characters and political issues from episode to episode, such links give viewers the feeling of watching a kind of epic TV serial.

The productions used a limited but serviceable number of smallish unit sets which led to a camerawork regime invariably capturing performances in tight, controlled **close-up**s, in **two-** and **three-shot**s or larger-ensemble clusters. These tend to enhance rather than diminish the impact of the many scenes of conflict played between characters, or where deep emotion occurs. In the same way some **developing single shot**s capture a flow of great dramatic invention, rather than interruptedly cutting between cameras. From the many impactful sequences played in the series, I discuss a few of these below.

An excellent example of how well a mix of **close**, ensemble and **two-** and **three-shot**s can convey intensely developing drama on the limited space of the TV screen occurs when, early on in 'The Hollow Crown', after Edgar Wreford's impassioned delivery of John of Gaunt's renowned 'this sceptred isle' speech is caught in **close shot**, Richard II (David William) enters with his queen and 'flattering' courtly entourage. The emotional temperature surges when Gaunt's verbal attack on the proud young king's financial profligacy merely triggers a scorn in Richard that spirals into angry exchanges caught beautifully in **shot/reverse**, **close** and **two-shot**s, until, near collapse, Gaunt is carried out – to die (2.1.69–139). Honourable York remonstrates with the callously indifferent Richard, the king departing with his courtiers. A dark debate soon ensues between Northumberland, Willoughby and Ross. These conspiring exchanges are recorded in a tense three-minute **three-shot**, involving us in the beginnings of their plan to join the banished Bolingbroke, newly returned with an army to challenge Richard's misgovernance of England (2.1.225–303). The TV stage is set, thriller-like, for the many struggles for the English crown that are to come.

A number of remarkably effective **developing single shot**s are played in the series, including one towards the end of the second episode where Richard's musings on his imprisoned life at Pomfret, and then his murder, are captured by a sequence containing virtuoso performance and imaginative camerawork. We see him through the bars of his cell, used to frame him and the scene in constantly changing ways, for a shot lasting nearly ten minutes. This ends with a **close-up** of him, stabbed, gazing at us in agony, hoarsely speaking his last while futilely clinging to and sliding down, Christ-like, the prison bars (5.5.1–112). A very different use of the same technique occurs with Sean Connery, who as Hotspur in *1 Henry IV* mostly plays Harry Percy with fiery physical energy, especially when confronting King Henry and ranting high-spiritedly in the company of his father Northumberland and Worcester (1.3). By contrast, the scene he later plays with his wife Kate, prior to his secret departure to meet fellow challengers to Henry IV's new supremacy, is tender, intimate and playful. Initially reticent and distant, having leapt on to their bed to join Kate, he becomes more teasing and affectionate, as she now does. The camera follows their physical play and bantering love talk, their loving caresses challenging the mobile camera to track the frolicking in **medium** and **close two-shot**s. It is a delight to watch (2.4.30–108).

One very interesting feature of the series occurs at the end of *2 Henry IV* ('The New Conspiracy') and the beginning of *Henry V* ('Signs of War'). As Prince John hints to the Lord Chief Justice the new king could plan to invade France, the series music by Sir Arthur Bliss strikes up to close the action of *2 Henry IV* and they exit, walking out of shot. A **cutaway** then takes us to a new view of them walking towards us as if they are removing to the **tiring-house** of an old Shakespearean playhouse, the credits start rolling and they join the other actors disrobing and taking off their make-up. The last actor to disrobe is William Squire (Shallow) who, following the end of the credits, performs the final words of the play's Epilogue. Then, at the opening of *Henry V*, Squire reappears to pick up (as it were) from where he left off at the end of *2 Henry IV*, but now performing Prologue's speech, launching into 'O for a muse of fire!' from among the tiring-room **props**. As he speaks to us, the camera follows him moving on to the TV studio stage, where we join the actors, and he invites us to 'kindly judge our play'. The use of this unexpected but enlivening **metatheatrical** device of creating a kind of theatrical continuity between the two plays was possibly inspired by the pre-stage performance **tiring-house** preparations scene inserted by Olivier into his film version of *Henry V*.

A brilliantly structured and played **developing single shot** occurs in 1.3 of *Richard III*, by clever use of a ***mise-en-scène*** in which eight clustering actors are blocked such that the **depth of field** of their skilfully choreographed movements can be caught dramatically by the camera. The three-and-a-half-minute sequence starts with Queen Margaret entering, her presence initially captured in **cutaway** shots as she mutters asides, and then most effectively when she steps forward into the verbal brawl Richard is having with Queen Elizabeth and her 'commoner' family at 'Hear me, you wrangling pirates, that fall out / In sharing that which you have pilled [pillaged] from me' (1.3.158–9). As Richard, Rivers, Dorset and Buckingham step forward to denounce her in turn for killing Richard's brother Rutland, she is driven forward towards the camera, which, having registered her humiliation, now pulls back to record her own threatening recoil on *them*. Margaret, a strongly persistent force of female nature played by Mary Morris, makes her forceful presence felt in all four of these minor tetralogy dramas. Here, she puts her scary witchlike spell on to Elizabeth, Richard, Hastings and the Queen's relations, her pointing finger singling them out in turn, with chilling effects visibly registered in each face (3.1.158–300). In the play, Hastings responds with, 'My hair doth stand on end to hear her curses' – so may ours.

Yet that comment by Hastings and much else in the sequence is cut, just as judicious paring is applied to many series episodes. If Dews was aiming to attract a popular audience – or indeed *any* small-screen audience looking to be entertained by Shakespearean performance so early in BBC TV's post-war broadcasting history – then, as with Shakespeare for the big screen, the focus on driving the *story* forward to retain audience interest always takes precedence over full-text dramatization. Only in the instance of *1 Henry VI*, made into a single episode of 58 minutes, 'The Red Rose and the White', does this halving of the regular allotted time seriously maim the production. This is because *1 Henry VI* is structured by two lines of conflict, that foregrounded in the struggle between English and French forces in France, and the feuding going on at home among the English nobility. This internal squabbling of the English leadership at home keeps them from giving proper support to their soldiers in the field, resulting in the slaughter of Talbot's forces by those of Charles and Joan before the walls of Bordeaux. Having the action of 1.4, where Gloucester's and Winchester's men clash at the Tower, immediately precede 2.4, the (invented) scene Shakespeare wrote to formalize an origin for the later 'Wars of the Roses' dynastic struggles, certainly gives a shape to the headline title 'The Red Rose and the White'. But excising all of the intervening scenes, and others that dramatize Lord Talbot's many struggles and triumphs over the French Dauphin's army – amounting to nearly half the play – deprives it of the historical dimension and texture that bring to it the integrity and coherence a viewing audience requires.

At the same time, it would be churlish not to admit that for 1960, the creative approaches to Shakespearean production undertaken in this TV series were a remarkable small-screen breakthrough. In many ways, it has yet to be matched.

2

The BBC-TV Series: Shooting the Complete Canon

I want now to explore the BBC Shakespeare adaptations that were taped and broadcast between 1978 and 1985 on BBC-TV, and in the USA between 1979 and 1985 in the PBS *Great Performances* slot. Uniquely, the series comprises the 36 'canonical' Shakespeare's plays plus *Pericles*, all initially available on **VHS** for educational use, then available commercially from 2006 on DVD. Therefore, at least one small-screen version of each Shakespeare play with its full or sparingly cut text is accessible to any viewer able to pay for it. The adaptations were produced by three different producers over a six-and-a-half year period, with sixteen different directors bringing a range of often quite different perspectives, interests and skills to bear on these productions. Such diversity of interpretative style and dramatic approach draws on a significant range of methods for shooting Shakespeare on TV.

As Susan Willis has noted (following André Bazin), the core of the stylistic debate about presenting Shakespeare on TV revolves around whether drama should aspire to film or to the theatre, one aiming for a strong *representation*, or realism of place, and the other a *suggestivity* of place or space, a strategy often employed in open-staging productions (Willis, 1991, 87). In terms of TV camera deployment, the choice is between using the cinematic technique of **montage** (cutting back and forth between different shots or short sequences) and the more theatrical practice of *mise-en-scène*, composing and manipulating what is to be seen into the totality of a single shot and its **depth of field**. BBC directors responded to the challenge in different ways from play to play, but their responses resulted in strategies that can be categorized under the three broad headings of approach suggested by Michèle Willems: the *naturalistic*, the *pictorial* and the *stylized* (Willems, 1999, 74).

The realistic/naturalistic approach

It was inevitable that many of the BBC directors would opt for a 'realistic' solution to the design of a production, given the series requirement to create settings that would convey the period implied by the world of each play's story. At the beginning of the series, much effort was put into constructing an 'authentic' representation of the world of each play, resulting in a 'preoccupation that badges, banners, and weapons should look genuine', publicity proudly proclaiming (for example) the 'authentic recreation of Caesar's Rome' for *Julius Caesar*, and the filming of *As You Like It* in a 'real forest' (Willems, 1999, 75). The rationale for this approach stemmed from the idea that the viewing habits and perceptions of TV viewers unfamiliar with Shakespeare's plays, people whom the BBC wanted to attract and educate, were shaped by news programmes and documentaries. The view of Alvin Rakoff, director of the first play to be broadcast, *Romeo and Juliet*, was that in 'order to grab the audience's attention you've got to do it as realistically as possible' (Willis, 91). More often than not, doing it 'realistically' means creating a large representational set designed to model historically accurate constructions for a play's interior and exterior settings.

Where such representationalism supports the dramatic forwarding of text and plot, this can be involving for the TV audience, especially when interior settings suggest an atmosphere relevant to the text being dramatized. Interior settings support the text well in Desmond Davis's award-winning *Measure for Measure*. These move from the Duke's elegant and formal audience hall with the gripping interviews between Angelo and Isabella being captured by imaginative **shot/reverse shot**s and **two-shot**s, to the rowdy clamour of the brothel styled like a Western saloon. In turn, the prison set suggests the 'torch-lit, scream-filled grotesquerie of a horror film' that the director wished to emulate. However, although Davis's staging of the last scene on a platform is an apt elevation for the Duke's revelations and pronouncements, while also providing an allusion to the Globe, this exterior scene 'nonetheless suffers the same limits of stylized realism as the first season's other studio exteriors' (Willis, 199). Exteriors suffer most when the realistic approach is followed, for however elaborate or detailed a design is, the TV camera exposes any scenic artifice as a 'clunky' distraction from the all-important dialogue. This is the case even for an adaptation broadcast four years into the series, David Jones's *The Merry Wives of Windsor*. It may have won a design award for its painstaking reconstruction of Tudor Windsor, but not even outstanding actors like Ben Kingsley, Alan Bennett or Prunella Scales can rescue it from the deadliness of an exterior looking so studio-bound that the importance given to it 'is probably just as detrimental to the comic effect as the absence of a live public' (Willems, 1999, 77). Swapping the studio for the real outdoors may seem a solution, but Basil Coleman's *As You Like It* shot on location in a 'real forest' shows that it is not, the forest setting tending to distract us from the performance. As Susan Willis comments, 'it is not ultimately a play about trees' (Willis, 211). By contrast, when the (only) other play to be taped on location was shot, the less well-known *Henry VIII*, Kevin Billington was enabled to use the solid, stone walls and ceilinged rooms of Penshurst Place and Hever and Leeds castles to advantage, bringing the political intrigues and atmosphere of the Tudor court to life, and in the process producing an unexpected early success for the series.

Alvin Rakoff's *Romeo and Juliet* exemplifies the limitations of realistic and naturalistic approaches. With famous Shakespearean Sir John Gielgud as Chorus, a role he had already played in Castellani's 1954 film of the play, the opening seems promising. But Rakoff's attempt to mimic the market-place setting of Castellani and Zeffirelli films feels deadly, the constructed piazza where Capulet and Montague youths brawl looking so obviously like a TV set rather than any kind of real place that the action and performance fail to convince, the same problem occurring with the arbour's painted drop, the balcony, the Capulets' ballroom and the tomb. Realism of representation is also tested out and found wanting in the casting of 14-year-old Rebecca Saire as Juliet, especially noticeable when her small girlish voice and undemonstrative acting encounter the fruity baritone of Patrick Ryecart's manly Romeo: when man and girl interact, little happens to interest us.

The pictorial approach

When BBC internal politics forced series architect Cedric Messina to stand down after two years, Jonathan Miller entered as series producer, and saw the series 'house style' as an opportunity to bring a Renaissance manner and look to the productions. He also brought in three new directors, Elijah Moshinsky, Jack Gold and Jane Howell, ensuring that nearly half of the remaining adaptations would be delivered with what Susan Willis calls a 'conscious aestheticism' of attitude, though each director would also develop their own lines of approach. Both Miller and Moshinsky use the TV screen in their productions like a canvas, creating *mises-en-scène* that reproduce the styles of specific artists and their paintings from the Renaissance and later: Dutch interiors out of Vermeer in particular, but also Veronese, Watteau and others.

For *The Taming of the Shrew*, Miller uses Dutch and Italian paintings to design the Paduan street and Baptista's interiors, all aspects of Vermeer's *The Music Lesson* being exactly reproduced for the scene where Petruccio (John Cleese) woos Katherine. Although he saturates most of his adaptations with ideas and images drawn from Renaissance paintings, for the Cyprus interior scenes of *Othello*, Miller provides a set 'carefully based on period architecture, a palace in Urbino, and the dark street in Cyprus based on a real street'. Surfaces and spaces are fashioned to help convey the play he thinks of as a 'closet tragedy', even rooms of 'airy spacious confinement' finally coming to feel like 'an awful prison' (Willis, 216, 123).

Miller's *Shrew* convinced Moshinsky of the value of following Vermeer's use of period space, as can be seen in the Roussillon and Widow's house sets in his *All's Well That Ends Well*. Another example of his artistic quoting occurs in *A Midsummer Night's Dream*, where the image of Titania reclining in her forest bower beautifully resembles Rembrandt's *Danae's Bower*, a delight for the eye, whether one knows the allusion or not. Moshinsky uses art-related effects so much he confesses that his *Love's Labour's Lost* is not merely set in the eighteenth century, it is 'set in Watteau' (Willis, 160). His goal of ravishing the viewer's eye is often achieved by using the techniques of old-master paintings that include **chiaroscuro** lighting effects derived from Georges de la Tour. But he also draws on a skilful deployment of camera and **blocking** to frame numerous kinds of shot – **establishing, close, high-angle, crane**, **subjective**. In addition he uses **voice-over**s, music, the **sound bridge** (a fine example opens *Cymbeline*), precision **montage** for effective **continuity editing** – and much more. His preoccupation with using highly studied and creatively lit camera shots for aesthetic effect, together with **cutting** techniques that prioritize story continuity over capturing **two-shot** dialogue exchanges, can make Moshinsky seem like a frustrated big-screen film director, rather than an adapter for the small screen.

The stylized approach

Michèle Willems poses the key question about the use of a pictorial approach for engaging viewers in TV Shakespeare: 'Is there not a danger in this profusion of visual signs that the picture will interfere with the reception of the words?' (Willems, 1999, 79). In fact, the BBC directors who deploy a stylized approach do so because they want viewers to connect with and to understand the performance of a text *without* such distraction. It is unsurprising to find six of the ten tragedies are delivered as stylized productions. For one thing, the often substantial amount of dialogue that reveals the agitated inner lives of the primary characters is so important in these plays that the approach can be vital. The frequency with which Rodney Bennett has Derek Jacobi confide Hamlet's innermost thoughts to the viewer in to-camera **close-ups** for his *Hamlet* production is one obvious example. A number of directors use the stylized approach, but I shall concentrate here on the work of Jack Gold and Jane Howell, since both use it exclusively and offer valuable comments on its value and efficacy.

What soon becomes apparent from viewing the plays directed by Gold and Howell is their use of techniques that create theatre-like playing conditions in the TV studio. Given the intimate kind of contact which can be set up between actor and viewer with this domestic medium, it is no surprise to hear Jane Howell saying that 'what TV can give you is the excitement of an actor's performance' (Willems ed., 1987, 80). Since performing the text is at the heart of an actor's Shakespeare performance, and given the series requirement to present minimally cut plays means the audience must listen to a *lot* of performed text, how can viewers be encouraged to listen in the way Shakespeare's audience might also have done? Of course, as Jack Gold observes, Shakespearean dialogue 'is not our own. You have to concentrate.' And he asserts that the only way to encourage this kind of viewer-concentration is 'to get rid of everything on the screen that does not actually make clear what is being said' (Willems ed., 1987, 47).

Gold's stylized productions of *Macbeth* and *The Merchant of Venice* demonstrate how this approach works in practice. The theatrical playing conventions he deploys use minimal **props** and abstract set designs to *suggest* rather than to *realize* the kind of space conjured up by Shakespeare's dialogue. In the Scottish play, Gold therefore has Macbeth and Banquo hear the news of Macbeth's elevation to Thane of Cawdor on what he calls a 'not-quite-real-heath'. With an acute observation on how using several cameras to cut between shots makes 'most TV productions ... very static', he argues for retaining dramatic complexity and flow by employing long **take**s with a single camera. This approach differs from Miller, whom he thinks 'does not compose enough' or 'use the camera's mobility and actors' mobility enough'

(Willems ed., 1987, 47). A good example of this technique is seen during the first banquet, from when the camera **pan**s along the banqueting table to a passageway where Macbeth mutters his soliloquy starting 'If it were done when 'tis done, then 'twere well / It were done quickly' (1.7). Lady Macbeth soon arrives to upbraid him for his cowardice, hatching her assassination plan, convincing him that they will succeed. Gold ends the scene with the camera following their return hand-in-hand to the banquet, and **zoom**ing in slowly for an ironic **close shot** of Duncan's smiling face as they part hands. He explains the reason for this six-minute **take**: 'I thought it would lose the tension, the mood, if I did it on more than one camera. So I made *them* more mobile and the *camera* mobile. It took a lot of rehearsing' (Willems ed., 1987, 44).

Gold's style of working is very similar to that of Jane Howell, an experienced theatrical director whose first adaptation *The Winter's Tale* contains a 48-minute sequence played and taped without a break, the country scene in Bohemia (4.4). Her approach to the direction and design of any play initially requires 'a spark', an idea – 'I don't like concepts', she says. The idea she had for this production concerns 'the sense of rebirth ... the returning of spring [being] obviously fundamental to the play'. The shifts in season are registered visually by changes in the colour and texture of the set, sparingly composed of two large wedges (between which the actors enter and leave) and a tree in the left foreground. Both tree and wedges change colour with the seasons, from Sicilia's wintry white to the stony grey of Bohemia's coasts, then to the gold of Bohemia's fields, with spring green appearing for the concluding scenes in Sicilia. Such a setting of seasonal rebirth also supports her idea of this play as one where 'everyone can have a second chance' (Willems ed., 1987, 84). Howell's commitment to melding the theatrical with the televisual is even more apparent in her four productions of the minor tetralogy, the three parts of *Henry VI* and *Richard III*, all broadcast in sequence over succeeding Sunday evenings in 1983. The unit set for these adaptations is simple but effective, comprising a wooden adventure-playground structure like a stockade with an upper level, swing-doors at either side being used by the actors for their entries and exits. This provides a structure and a space fortuitously equivalent to the platform stage of the Globe Theatre, and very adaptable to the playing of outdoor or indoor scenes. Most importantly, it is a design allowing Howell to offer an underlying visual reminder of an interpretation of these four Wars of the Roses histories in which the action starts with a kind of boyish playground brawling game, but then shifts into political manoeuvring and violence, powermongering struggles and battles that result in piles of corpses darkly punctuating the end of each adaptation. 'It struck me', says Howell, 'that the behaviour of the lords of England was a lot like children – prep school children' (Willis, 167). This view of the nobles' behaviour is shown in 1.3 of *1 Henry VI* where Gloucester and Winchester confront each other on hobbyhorses as their men scrap, while soon after 1.4 begins, three French boys squabble over a toy longbow. (The use of young Lucius as a 'witness' to the nightmarish violence in her *Titus Andronicus* – borrowed by Taymor for her film *Titus* – is a related idea.)

Howell's decision to dramatize all four plays as a continuous story informs a key aspect of her 'theatrical' approach: her directorial relationship with and use of the actors. Using what is in effect a large-scale repertory company of about fifty actors, her casting of some of them in two or even three different roles throughout the sequence is done purposely to attract the audience's attention: after seeing their faces in various guises throughout the three plays (she says), '*Richard III* should be like a nightmare' (Willis, 170). Despite the seriousness of the material, Howell manages to get her large, talented and versatile company to bring out the inherent theatricalism of these histories such that the performance is **metatheatrical**ly celebrated *as performance*. For instance, near the beginning of *1* and *2 Henry VI*, the play titles are announced on banners over the door, in *3 Henry VI* the title is proclaimed on a shroud covering the pile of corpses, while Ron Cook as Richard chalks up the title on a board at the beginning of *Richard III*. Furthermore, with the numerous opportunities for ensemble playing in front of the camera that these plays afford, Howell not only demonstrates a sure grasp of how to place her actors in the playing space to gain maximum effect, but when they do perform, addressing and confiding in the camera far more in these productions than happens in other series adaptations, she conjures performances that make what are often thought of as difficult and dense plays, very clear for the TV viewer to follow. To say so is not mere assertion, for after the tetralogy was broadcast, Howell reports receiving 140 letters, 'all from families, not from critics or theatre-going people, families who said: "we happened to watch the first one, we became interested, what are we going to do now they've stopped?"' (Willems ed., 1987, 89).

3

The Stage–Screen Hybrid: Shakespeare on TV/DVD/Blu-ray

All of the BBC-TV Shakespeare adaptations cast actors with experience of performing the plays on stage, yet none emerged directly from
actual stage productions. In what follows, I discuss only five 'made-
for-TV' Shakespeare adaptations without a stage precursor, Michael
Elliott's 1983 *King Lear*, and the four Shakespeare English history adaptations made for the year of the 2012 British Olympics, *The Hollow
Crown*. The other eleven productions discussed that were broadcast
between 1972 and 2012 all emerged from celebrated stage performances, reworked for the small screen. Many would agree that the primary motivation for creating such small-screen versions has been to
make a permanent record of productions that enjoyed popular and critical success on the stage, and to provide confirmation of the undoubted
truth expressed in Kenneth Rothwell's statement that 'acting remains
the one crucial variable determining success on stage or [small] screen'
(2000, 110). The chance for many more people via the small screen to
enjoy what a comparatively tiny number of people have enjoyed in the
theatre is also a major reason for creating such productions (in the USA
often to be seen in the PBS Masterpiece Theatre series). In Part III I
observed how, although Tony Richardson's film of his London
Roundhouse *Hamlet* with Nicol Williamson was shot on celluloid, the
intimate camerawork of the production makes it very suitable for
domestic consumption on the small screen, and many more people have
no doubt viewed it on VHS or DVD than ever saw the limited big-
screen theatrical release.

Trevor Nunn: 'Shooting the text'

The same statement surely applies to the small-screen adaptations of Shakespeare stage productions directed by Trevor Nunn, his first being a reworking of the *Antony and Cleopatra* staged as part of the 'Roman season' of plays put on by the RSC at Stratford in 1972. The **1974 ATV** network broadcast of this adaptation won a BAFTA in London as best single TV play for 1975. Part of the reason for this is interestingly conveyed by Patrick Stewart (the production's Enobarbus), who commends Nunn's approach to Michèle Willems in an interview conducted on the occasion of his playing Claudius in the BBC *Hamlet*:

> I still think the style he adopted for that *Antony and Cleopatra* was so successful that many of the BBC directors should have observed it themselves. Rather than trying to build architecture for the play, sets and so on, he used light and smoke and gauzes only.

Jonathan Miller tried for a minimalist set of 'drapes and boards' with his *Antony and Cleopatra*, but the contrasting atmospheric settings created for Rome and Egypt and the inspired acting of a cast thoroughly attuned to their parts in Nunn's earlier production elevate the latter far above the BBC version. The contrast between Cleopatra's exotically sensuous Egyptian court and the martial exactitudes of a Rome that Antony has all but forsaken are conveyed from the outset, with Egyptian scenes and costumes played in a soft, warm, golden glow further softened by a screen image often blurred at the edges; while the Roman scenes are monochromatic, the white and black costumes of Octavius's men providing a harder uncompromising sharpness. Neither are we left in any doubt of the power that the cunning allure of Janet Suzman's 'tawny fronted' Cleopatra has over Richard Johnson's shrewd yet vulnerable Antony, revealed as this is by Nunn's camera consistently focusing (as Stewart notes) on 'the actors' faces and the text' (Willems ed., 1987, 94).

Nunn himself characterizes the difference between film and TV Shakespeare production as between 'shooting the action' and 'shooting the text' (Willems, 2000, 40). Among the stage-to-TV-screen productions he has masterminded, there is none that exemplifies his approach to 'shooting the text' better than the *Macbeth* transposed from an award-winning RSC production at Stratford's The Other Place in 1976 to the **Thames TV** dramatization, broadcast in **1979**. The 'live' stage origins of this fine production are not only signalled by its title,

'A Performance of *Macbeth* by William Shakespeare', but the whole
enterprise is designed to re-create for home-viewers the kind of chilling performance effects experienced by small audiences crammed into
the intimate studio confines of The Other Place. The play is acted out
within a ritualistic magic circle where a saintly looking white-bearded
Duncan, dressed more like a high churchman than a king, falls prey to
a Macbeth (Ian McKellen) murderously infected with the malevolent
designs of the sensuous Lady Macbeth (Judi Dench), who infatuates
him. McKellen reports how in the theatre the effects were 'properly
alarming', as shown by the fact that a 'priest queued for a returned
ticket again and again, so that he could sit at our feet, discreetly holding out his crucifix to protect us from the evil summoned up in the
stifling air'. With the whole production conveyed through **mid-shot**s or
close-ups in a frequently smoky atmosphere minimally lit for maximum spookiness, the effect of actors playing close to the camera is so
captivating that McKellen is surely right to assert that the small screen
is able to communicate 'an intimate horror that is still thrilling'
(McKellen, 1996, 9). This kind of impact is felt particularly with
McKellen's Macbeth, which Patrick Stewart regards as 'so marvellous
on the screen because he thinks so brilliantly, so brightly and quickly,
and the camera observes the thought, and it's the thought that's full of
impact' (Willems ed., 1987, 95). McKellen achieves this kind of performing brilliance throughout, but an especially unnerving moment
occurs in the soliloquy beginning, 'Is this a dagger which I see before
me'. Muttering as if under compulsion how 'withered murder .../ With
Tarquin's ravishing strides, towards his design / Moves like a ghost'
(2.1.52, 55–6) – when he moves towards the camera and a shadow
passes across his face, for a moment we really feel as if this entranced
being closing in on us *is* 'like a ghost'.

Ten years later, in **1990**, Nunn transferred his successful RSC production of ***Othello*** (again at The Other Place) to TV, and since this
play is, like *Macbeth*, a drama of claustrophobic themes ideally suited
for a studio space, the translation to the domestic screen was again flu-
ently achieved, although Ian McKellen, who won honours for his performance of Iago, did not feel this *Othello* surpassed Nunn's *Macbeth*.
Ten years on, **2001** saw Nunn creating a transposition to TV of his
award-winning RNT production of ***The Merchant of Venice***, the stagelike sets and costumes this time periodized for a late 1920s Europe
that worked most effectively for this so-called 'comedy'. The setting
was chosen, says Nunn, because 'it was that very period when anti-
Semitic thought and anti-Semitic behaviour was becoming current

and even – it's ghastly to think it – voguish and the subject of wit and amusement'. Such an approach allows Nunn to dramatize unflinchingly the sufferings visited upon and invited by Shylock (Henry Goodman), his daughter Jessica (Gabrielle Jordan) and Antonio (David Bamber). Shot and cut very like a film, Nunn's camera observes the actors' performances in a variety of **two**-, **three**- and ensemble **shot**s, with the **shot/reverse shot** being put to efficient use for a drama of often hostile exchanges, climaxing in a courtroom confrontation. At times carrying some genuinely funny sequences, the adaptation nevertheless tends to bring us back to a sombreness seeming to deny the possibility of social reconciliation. Nevertheless, it concludes with two elements of hopefulness in Belmont: learning of Shylock's humiliation, Jessica separates herself from the others in tears to sing a Hebrew song she and her father had earlier sung together, an assertion of her Jewish identity that is positive and which gains a kind of faint support from Portia's closing announcement that 'It is almost morning.' It is Henry Goodman's deeply impressive (and award-winning) performance as the proud and sensitive Shylock which gives the adaptation its dramatic weight, his urgent portrayal of a committed orthodox Jew with strong Yiddish accent, yarmulke and tallit bringing an intense authenticity of feeling and drama to the part.

Three TV adaptations of the 1980s and 1990s

Six months after Jonathan Miller's BBC *Lear* was broadcast, Granada TV produced its own *King Lear* **(1983)**, directed by Michael Elliott and starring 75-year-old Laurence Olivier, with a host of famous actors in the other parts, including Dorothy Tutin, Colin Blakely, Diana Rigg, Leo McKern and John Hurt. The $2 million production certainly showcased the acting talents of its star-studded cast, but as a dramatization of an important Shakespeare play it is conventional in design, shooting and interpretation, failing to draw us into the horrors and anxieties of the drama in any deeply imaginative way. However, the presumed aim of providing the elder statesman of British Shakespearean theatre and film with a vehicle for a fine farewell performance is certainly met by the production, a nice moment occurring early on in the Stonehenge setting when Olivier's Lear imperiously surveys with evident satisfaction each member of the court bowing low before him. This is an image that cannot fail to suggest how the long reign of the elderly fictional king has its counterpart in Olivier's sovereign position as the world's leading Shakespearean actor. The performance design tends to feed the image of an ailing king wronged by his ungrateful daughters and owed a justified sympathy, this valuation assisted (for instance) by the omission of Edgar's 'But who comes here?' (4.6.80) and related asides, persuading us to view Lear as a kind of 'unaccommodated man of nature' in what becomes almost a new scene of the old man joyfully fending for himself in the wild – not at all what the allusion to 'nature' means at this stage of the play.

The stage-to-TV-screen BBC2/WGBH Boston **2004** adaptation of **Richard Eyre's** award-winning 1998 RNT production of *King Lear*, by contrast, is not only a revelation of the great acting talents of Ian Holm, but a wrenchingly insightful exposure of the play's profound and diverse human themes. Observing that 'Every family is a state in miniature', Eyre achieves this exposure by presenting the play as a drama of failing family relationships. In Lear's family such critical dysfunction is occasioned by the tyrannical behaviour of a father seemingly driven by uncontrollable parental rages for most of his life. Notwithstanding his compact physical stature (indeed perhaps because of it), Holm drives the production along with acting of great emotional intensity, captured in **close** and **medium-close** camera shots. In contrast to Elliott's production, this adaptation does not endorse Lear's claim that he is 'a man / More sinned against than sinning' (3.2.57–8), the close-observing camera also capturing on many occasions (before malice enters their hearts) the shocked distress of Goneril and Regan as daughters who have long suffered the pressures of an overbearing father. Expressions of desperate hurt and unhappiness caused by Lear's vicious cursing tongue are especially noticeable on the face of Goneril. The clever use of lighting on a relatively bare set supports strong performances from a strong cast, with camerawork revealing many moments of insight and feeling in the second half of the play. The camera **close-up**s allow us to witness an almost unbearably moving reconciliation scene between Cordelia and her father, one that would be more difficult for a theatre audience to observe. Despite 'shooting a text' that is heavily cut in places, Eyre's riveting TV adaptation of *King Lear* is a revelation.

It was in **1988** that **Kenneth Branagh's** Renaissance Theatre Company first properly gained notice, the *Twelfth Night* he directed at London's Riverside Studios becoming a great theatrical hit following a Royal Gala Preview attended by the RTC's new patron, Prince Charles. Soon after, the production was adapted for the small screen and broadcast by **Thames Television** just before Christmas. Branagh designed the production to be set in winter, 'with snow covering a mysterious Victorian garden [to] bring out the brooding melancholy of the play'. The spare unit set, although unadventurous, offers a sound frame for delivering the bitter-sweet aspects of the play while also supporting both the boisterous scenes with Sir Toby we all enjoy, and the pivotal scene of Malvolio's gulling. The strong cast includes Anton Lesser as Feste and the versatile Richard Briers as Malvolio, his outstanding performance probably justifying the claim that 'a great comic actor can be a great tragic actor' (Branagh, 1989, 198). Unfortunately, however good the comic performances are, the problem of getting such Shakespeare comedies to work effectively on TV will remain so long as 'one important participant is missing: the reacting audience' (Wells, 1982, 272).

Small-screen Shakespeare in the twenty-first century

A new century brought along some interesting excursions in TV Shakespeare adaptation. The stage-to-screen reworking of **Gregory Doran's** acclaimed 1999 **RSC** *Macbeth* production originally staged at the Swan Theatre, Stratford, was filmed in 2000 for the RSC by the London-based *Illuminations* company, in association with British **Channel Four**, who broadcast the film in **2001**. Following sell-out seasons at the Swan, the stage production went to Japan and New York, where *The New York Times* applauded Doran's version of the Scottish play as a 'harrowing and disturbingly funny parable for the dawn of the 21st century'. Shot for the wide screen, the TV film was directed by Doran, who worked with the original cast to reproduce as closely as possible on film the dynamics of the stage production which had impressed its audiences so much. According to *Illuminations* producer John Wyver, this was achieved by following two key decisions: (1) to work with a single camera, 'which allowed a level of precision and control of the images that is hard if not impossible to achieve recording as-live in a theatre with multiple cameras', and (2) to use 'London's Roundhouse as a single location for the filming. Greg Doran wanted to film the play in an environment where the drama's events could unfold and, as it were, be captured by a documentary camera.' For this he and production designer Stephen Brimson Lewis sought a location to film in that was not a theatre, and which offered what Doran described as 'a vivid neutrality' (the *Appendix* comprises an interview with John Wyver about filming Shakespeare for the small screen).

Whereas Tony Richardson's 1969 *Hamlet* at this same location was filmed in **close-up** and **medium-shot** in the enormous open arena of the venue, Doran used every available space in the cavernous Roundhouse to deliver his *Macbeth*. These included dripping subterranean passages and the circling upper gallery, each space being lit to convey a variety of tense, forbidding and sometimes alarming effects. Many of the heightened effects are achieved by scenes being shot in confined passages or on stairways. For example, the frantic exchange which takes place on a narrow staircase between Macbeth (Antony Sher) and Lady Macbeth (Harriet Walter) after Duncan's murder provides a singularly appropriate liminal location for the brilliant playing out of their terrifyingly agitated states. Agitation and instability are also frequently conveyed by the skilful deployment of edgy **hand-held** camera sequences by outstanding **DoP** Ernie Vincze, and although conventionally steady camerawork of **close-, medium-** and sometimes **long shot**s are used too, there are also surprises – as with the startling 'upside-down' head and shoulders **close-up** we are given of a naked Lady Macbeth eerily submerged in a bathtub while her chilling 'Come, you spirits' soliloquy is heard in **voice-over**. This is a punchy postmodern presentation which does not flinch from making contemporary political allusions either, the extraordinary Porter's speech that emphasizes 'equivocation' so much featuring an uncannily accurate impersonation of the then British Prime Minister, Tony Blair.

Trevor Nunn's *King Lear* (2008, jointly directed with **Chris Hunt** of **Iambic Productions)** comes thirty -four years after his first Shakespeare stage-to-small-screen adaptation *Antony and Cleopatra*. The result shows that Nunn's already innovative flair for 'shooting the text' was still vividly apparent. Shot at London's Pinewood Studios using the same strongly cast RSC playing company that toured the stage production of *King Lear* around the Anglophone world to great acclaim in 2007, this co-production (first shown on British TV at Christmas 2008) boasts an extraordinarily powerful performance of the king by Ian McKellen. It has been tellingly remarked that 'when you are old enough to play King Lear, you are too old to play King Lear'. Drawing on the superlatively honed acting talents of a long stage and film career, the performance of Olivier in the 1983 Granada TV *King Lear* had not always succeeded in plumbing the depths of Shakespeare's capaciously mercurial character. At 68, McKellen inhabits and discovers to an almost disturbing degree the hugely variegated dimensions of this character, which Shakespeare creates by having the man of power who has shed his position of power confront with increasing pain a shifting myriad of situations, impulses and awkward emotions in his declining years. McKellen somehow finds the appropriate energies to enable the character to move from imperiousness, through gradations of anger, rage and distraught defiance, into a playfully inventive lunacy mimicking some of dementia's clinical features; then through episodes displaying lucid political and psychological insights, before his over-tried energies visibly relax into a profound serenity on being reunited with Cordelia. Her tragic loss has him sobbing his way into a distracted defeat, death finally releasing him from life's torments.

As with all of the most engaging, persuasive and therefore impactful ensemble productions of Shakespeare, McKellen's artistic achievement is realized in the context of a cast whose fine playing frequently stimulates and incites him into making the best creative responses the text allows. His performance in turn provides them with similar opportunities, under the direction of Nunn and Hunt. Examples abound. Early on, Lear's momentously unwise question to his daughters as to 'Which of you shall we say doth love us most?' triggers deeply unsettled looks in **medium-close shot** of Goneril (Frances Barber) and Regan (Monica Dolan), followed by what Cordelia (Romola Garai) later informs her father are her sisters' 'glib and oily professions' of love. Her own plain speaking soon causes the self-regarding old king to disown her, to banish the protesting Kent who tells him he is mad, does evil and needs to 'see better', and to inform Burgundy that Cordelia's 'price is fallen'; whereupon she is 'given away' dowerless to an incredulous and delighted France. The **three-shot** of Lear coming between Cordelia and France as if to crown his youngest daughter but then, instead, raising this golden zero to peer through it as he snarls spitefully at her 'Nothing! I have sworn' – this is a ghastly, but utterly inspired dramatic gesture (1.1.49, 222, 105, 156, 195, 243).

Lear's unchallengeable and stubborn intransigence at this stage of the play is all of a piece with how Trevor Nunn presents the nature of this man's power. Initially, 'Lear is a conduit of the gods and he has total autocratic authority', says Nunn, who set the play 'in a seemingly nineteenth-century environment with resonances of the tsarist order in Russia' in order to stress Lear's supremacy, deriving 'from the god with whom he communicates' (Bate and Rasmussen, 2009, 184). This sense of personal power is strikingly conveyed at the film's opening, where Lear enters richly clad in religious robes to the sound of mighty organ chords, his court bowing submissively before him. But by the end of the audacious soliloquy in 1.2 by Gloucester's bastard son Edmund, who invokes the gods only to laughingly dismiss them, demanding that they 'Stand up for bastards', we are being presented with motivations and appetites wholly opposite to those embedded in the deferential traditional order. Edmund's direct address to camera in **close-up** chillingly conveys how the 'outcast' bastard status, which his father mocks so easily but dangerously in his presence, has incited him to exchange the beliefs of the 'legitimate' ruling elite and their gods for a this-worldly creed that he addresses thus: 'Thou, nature, art my goddess: to thy law / My services are bound' (1.2.1–2). It is this creed, following a self-seeking 'nature', that Edmund proceeds to utilize in his plan to usurp the 'legitimate' position of his older brother Edgar. Once Goneril and Regan conspire under the leadership of Cornwall to overturn Lear's rule, and Edmund joins in, all of them motivated by the self-same 'nature' to serve their own ruthless ends, the scene is set for a battle in which, as in all battles, only one side can win.

Many versions of this play have been produced on stage and film over the years, differing elements being stressed. Traditionally, it had often followed Lear's self-evaluation as 'a man more sinned against than sinning', then became a drama of resentment and family dysfunction (as in Richard Eyre's production), and, since Peter Brook's earlier ground-breaking approach of practically exonerating Lear's daughters and making of Lear a figure whose behaviour is often unacceptable (particularly in his macabre curse on Goneril's womb), becoming a play of existential bleakness. Forty years after first directing it in 1968, Trevor Nunn in 2008 characterizes *King Lear* as Shakespeare's 'investigation of the extremes of human behaviour, into the nature of man the species'. Nunn's whole production exposes us to Shakespeare's mode of investigating these behavioral extremes with both sensitivity and force, this being achieved most tellingly after the mid-point of the play, when Lear has removed from Gloucester's castle in disgust at his inhospitable treatment by Goneril, Cornwall and Regan. It is after the scene when Gloucester is blinded, where (as Bate and Rasmussen rightly observe) Regan 'behaves with sadistic glee that's also a kind of fear', that Shakespeare progressively 'shows us more people praying for the intervention of the gods, to no avail' (Bate and Rasmussen, 2009, 195).

From the storm scene and Lear's mock trial of Goneril, through to the arrival of 'Poor Tom'/Edgar with his blind father at the end of their trek to Dover, where they encounter Lear, all that we see has become drained of colour, cool grey-blue tints suggesting that what Lear calls the 'hard hearts' are now in the ascendant. Indeed, when the opposing forces finally clash in battle and Gloucester is urged by Edgar to 'Pray that the right may thrive', as Nunn notes, 'He does. They don't.' After a death sentence has been passed on Lear and Cordelia, Albany leads all present in a final prayer while soldiers run to the prison – '"The gods defend her!" The first word of the next line is "Howl". Cordelia is dead. No intervention. The gods aren't mentioned again' (Bate and Rasmussen, 2009, 195). Bleak and empty as the denouement of Shakespeare's *King Lear* seems to leave us, when a performance and production of such quality conveys so presently and vividly the best and worst of human capacities, it really does seem (as Aristotle originally argued) that the experience of tragic drama can neverthless have a purging effect on our emotions and intellect, such that we are forced to think and feel deeply about what we like to call our 'humanity'.

Gregory Doran's *Hamlet* **(2009)** came eight years after *Illuminations* adapted the RSC *Macbeth* to film, now embarking on another RSC collaboration working with the same director, the outcome being a BBC TV broadcast and wider distribution. Like *Macbeth* (2000), *Hamlet*, also in modern dress, demonstrates the benefits of adapting from a successful long-run stage production with original cast and director. Furthermore, the superlative ensemble cast (including Patrick Stewart as Claudius, Penny Downie as Gertrude and Oliver Ford Davies as Polonius) was led by a brilliant newcomer to Shakespeare, David Tennant, whose performance earned him the prestigious Critics' Circle Theatre Award for best Shakespearean Performance for 2009. The star of the show for American audiences was Patrick Stewart (Claudius), whose impact in *Star Trek: The Next Generation* as Captain Jean-Luc Picard had made him a screen icon. Tennant's impressive acting virtuosity somehow brings a new kind of energy to the playing of the mercurial Prince, politically and psychologically entrapped as he is by the 'prison' that is King Claudius's Denmark.

The filming location at St Joseph's College, Mill Hill, an ex-Catholic seminary in north London, is in many ways an ideal setting for Shakespeare's *Hamlet*. With a deconsecrated chapel at its heart, structurally sound but dilapidated, the late Victorian college unobtrusively offers a range of spaces suitable for mediating *Hamlet*, which has at *its* heart issues of political and moral corruption, social and religious unease in a palatial complex. The opening frames show Francisco patrolling the Elsinore battlements (the old college cloisters), captured on a black-and-white CCTV security camera, and suggesting an environment where everyone is under surveillance. When Francisco raises his rifle to challenge Barnardo with 'Who's there?' we move to the natural colour of the film's regular 'narrative camera', a switching manoeuvre repeated throughout the movie at key points, reminding us how the action is taking place in a kind of police state. When Horatio and Marcellus arrive and debate with Marcellus the appearance of the Ghost over recent nights, and are suddenly interrupted by its visitation again, we see this via the ground-level narrative camera, but not on the CCTV. From that camera, we see them stagger backwards in terror from what they behold – an eerie blank. Since the Ghost also advances on them from the **POV** of the narrative camera (as in the Branagh movie), there is a suggestion that the perception of a ghostly presence may be an effect of subjectivity. Similarly, when the Ghost appears to Hamlet (and us) in the closet scene, Gertrude is unable to see it either. Why not? Who's there?

What is very definitely there in this production is a meticulous directorial attention ensuring that we understand clearly the play's rich complex of relationships, particularly that between Hamlet and Claudius, as established in the court scene of 1.2. While Claudius is smugly holding forth to the court in **wide shot**, Prince Hamlet visible on the sidelines, the new king is triumphant in having 'taken to wife' Gertrude, his dead brother's widow. But the radiant smile of Pennie Downie (Gertrude), captured in **medium-close shot**, quickly drains away when she glances across towards Prince Hamlet for approval, the **reaction shot** as he stands immobile on the edge of things clearly revealing his disapproval of and misery at the marriage. A few moments later Claudius's own wariness and hostility towards Hamlet is then clearly revealed by some cleverly choreographed performance manoeuvres. After ambassadors Voltemand and Cornelius have been dismissed by Claudius, he, Gertrude and the whole court turn to look at Prince Hamlet, whom we all expect to be addressed next, even Hamlet himself, who is glanced at by the camera showing his expectation. However, after declaring 'And now ...' towards Hamlet, Claudius suddenly turns away from him and says '... Laertes, what's the news with you?' much to the consternation and even shock of Gertrude, as well as Laertes himself, nonplussed at being addressed ahead of the Prince. The snub is a brilliant *coup de théâtre* that makes Claudius's negative attitude towards Hamlet crystal clear from the beginning.

The five and a half minutes of dramatic exchanges in **one-** and **two-shot**s between Tennant's Hamlet and Stewart's Ghost are utterly convincing. Stewart, his body seeming to give off smoke in the eerie grey-blue light as if returned from the fires of hell, conveys the story of his murder with such unearthly, gravel-voiced conviction that

Tennant is mesmerized and terrorized, his horrified looks at the Ghost's revelations feeling viscerally real. As the Ghost departs, bidding Hamlet 'Adieu, remember me', Hamlet's receding figure is viewed from its/the camera's **POV**, the son's outstretched appealing arms and anguished expression as his father's spirit disappears offering a vision of human loss that is truly heart-rending. Although some of the techniques used for this difficult scene are similar to those used in Branagh's production, the acting and production skills employed here are thoroughly persuasive. There is more. After the Ghost's departure, Tennant, with the gruesome account of his father's spirit fresh in his mind, embarks on a brilliant physicalizing of the text by a self-inflicted mauling and beating of his own brains: 'Remember thee? Aye, thou poor ghost, while memory holds a seat / In this distracted globe.' His 'globe' dwelling on Claudius as the 'smiling damnéd villain', we now watch Tennant's Hamlet enjoying the revelatory thought that 'one may smile, and smile, and be a villain' – until a clever **jump cut** takes him safely away from that dangerous insight to the more sombre and pragmatic thought – 'at least, I'm sure it may be so in Denmark' (1.5.95–7, 106, 110).

An important element of this production's stage and screen success probably lies in Doran's having shaped it by following the plot structure of Shakespeare's first edition of the published play (Q1, 1603). One key feature of the Q1 *Hamlet* is the earlier placing of the 'To be or not to be' soliloquy, and the associated 'nunnery' encounter between Hamlet and Ophelia. Although including the bulk of the Q2 and Folio edition texts (the film running 3 hours) instead of the much sparser Q1 text, Doran uses the latter edition to bring forward 'To be or not to be' to a position only two scenes after Hamlet's harrowing encounter with the Ghost. This allows the audience to enjoy a coherent and plausible train of events that is 'gripping and affecting' and which prioritizes 'theatre, not literature' (Thompson and Taylor, 2006, Q1:7.115–37, Introduction: 29, 30).

With this plot structure, the language of Hamlet's soliloquy clearly reveals a state of mind sorely troubled by the searing memory of his encounter with his father's Ghost. It also voices the profoundly challenging questions of life, death, dream, the afterlife, and of the courage needed to comply with the dictates of his conscience. In turn, the playing of this 'To be' speech by Tennant, the most intimate of the movie for the most intimate soliloquy, is stunningly filmed and performed. He enters the film frame from the right, and rests his weary head against the wall in such a way that although most of it is in black silhouette, the left profile of his face is lit so that 'the skull beneath the skin' becomes shockingly yet beautifully visible, a **close shot** that relates all too tangibly to the existential questionings he now voices. A different kind of shock then occurs when, on a cut from this left profile of Tennant at his 'To die, to sleep – /', to a **close-up** in which, with eyes closed, his right profile enters scarily from frame left, sliding into its black body while he murmurs, 'No more'. It is scary because, if only momentarily, we witness here fraught reflections that we might prefer to avoid, but which most of us will confront at some time in our lives. This **close-up** sequence, combining the imaginative work of Doran, director of photography Chris Seager, and Tennant's revelatory playing, has captured Hamlet's most famous soliloquy in a way that feels dramatically unique on film.

Mirrors and reflective surfaces pervade the film, triggering reflections and refractions similar to those conveying Almereyda's *Hamlet*, and which suggest the 'devious, sinister, and oblique nature' of Denmark under Claudius's rule (p. 223). Hamlet's accidental shooting of Polonius results here in a similarly shattered wardrobe mirror, and in the closet scene it also figures as the 'portal' through which old Hamlet's ghost appears and finally passes out of the room. From this moment on, the splintered mirror of death remains as a disturbing presence in the film, suggesting the dislocating agitation visited on various key characters, not only Hamlet, but most prominently Gertrude and Ophelia at the opening of 4.5, and Laertes and Claudius for the remainder of the scene. It also figures prominently at the end of the cleverly devised **sound bridge** connecting the close of Ophelia's funeral and Hamlet's words to Horatio: 'There's a divinity shapes our ends, / Rough-hew them how we will ...' (5.2.10–11). The ill-reflecting mirror thereafter functions as a kind of background visual **metonymic** in the remaining hall scenes, telling witness of the disintegration of Denmark's court, right up to the final moments of duelling and death.

The film's climax is gripping and emotional. The final **wide shot** of the court, with Laertes, Gertrude and Claudius lying dead and Hamlet soon to join them, is taken from the former position of the hall CCTV camera, now perhaps abandoned by Claudius's security men. It shows in **close-up** Hamlet's final moving moments with Horatio, and gives the 'true' narrative ending, a closure revealing graphically what deadly rewards await the perpetrators of treachery and their victims. Horatio remains to tell the true story, surrounded by the dead on the reflecting polished floor where trainee Catholic priests had been wont to gather in the heyday of St Joseph's seminary around 1900, 300 years after *Hamlet* was first performed.

Rupert Goold's *Macbeth* (2010) was the second version of this play to be filmed by *Illuminations*, and in many ways embodies the excellent production values and approaches to filming stage-to-film productions previously deployed for the RSC *Macbeth* and *Hamlet*. Starting out modestly at the Chichester Festival Theatre, the production had transferred to London's West End, and thereafter via Brooklyn to Broadway, gaining immense success and sell-out runs on the way. Screen icon and seasoned Shakespearean Patrick Stewart was deservedly the draw for this. But, as before, *Illuminations* were able to work with a fine original cast and director, Rupert Goold making his screen debut in shooting film, completed in eighteen days on location in the strange below-ground rooms, corridors and tunnels of Nottinghamshire's Welbeck Abbey, originally a monastery. This location enabled Goold to reproduce one of the key features of his stage production, the elevator in which the Macbeths and the Witches could ascend to and descend from the stage action, mainly set in the kitchen of Macbeth's 'castle'. According to Goold, these ascents and descents were meant to suggest a drama occurring in different levels of Hell.

The kind of Hell Goold had in mind for a play that is, however complexly wrought and poetically conveyed by Shakespeare, a drama of blood and insane ambition, is one that had already been politically enacted in Stalinist Russia. Although reproducing the look of a generic military regime rather than resembling any particular Soviet bloc country, the allusion to Russia is there from the start, the opening title *Macbeth* being in Cyrillic-style lettering. A crash of cymbals is soon heard, succeeded by pounding, brass-dominated martial music, and we are given a **montage** of rapidly intercut shots of the guns, planes, bombings and explosions of modern warfare, including mid-twentieth-century newsreel footage. Interleaved into the montage are shots of this production's Macbeth and Banquo, trudging back from battle to their military HQ, and we soon realise it is there, where the wounded are brought to a makeshift hospital, which the grim opening shot of the movie relates to. This first shot kick-starts the **montage** sequence, and is a **close-up** of a prone wounded soldier's heavily bloodied arm and desperately groping hand, hanging over the edge of a hospital trolley as he is wheeled hurriedly along a corridor: this is the brave and 'bloody' Captain that King Duncan speaks to in 1.2. In this adaptation, so far from having surgeons treat his wounds as Duncan requests, the three nurses into whose hands he falls turn out to be the Witches, the

First proceeding to kill him by lethal injection before the Third plunges her hand into his chest and pulls out his heart, holding it triumphantly aloft as these characters march down the corridor together chanting, 'Fair is foul, and foul is fair. / Hover through the fog and filthy air' (1.1.10–11). Whence comes this deployment of a graphically gory 'body horror' killing enacted by malevolently murderous nurse-sisters of weirdness?

These are only the first of many images and scenes in which blood (a word much repeated in this play) is viscerally foregrounded by the film, and partly explained by Rupert Goold's penchant for 1970s and contemporary 'slasher horror' films, especially the 'Saw' horror franchise. Using horror film **DoP** Sam McCurdy, Goold certainly succeeds in making a movie that he wanted 'to be really, really scary' (DVD interview). Yet, for all its elements of graphic horror (especially the glamorous/repulsive witch-nurses), the movie is primarily distinguished by fine ensemble acting (Michael Feast as Macduff and Scott Handy as Malcolm both give moving character studies), with standout lead performances by Patrick Stewart as Macbeth and Kate Fleetwood as Lady Macbeth. Honed from playing experience gathered in numerous performances at different venues, this adaptation takes an idiosyncratically designed stage piece and translates it into a form that works well in front of the camera, the creative deployment of which Goold evidently relishes. Luckily, the camera loves both Patrick Stewart and Kate Fleetwood, and with their combination of exceptional performance in cleverly lit and shot sequences, these two become utterly persuasive as Macbeth and Lady Macbeth. Stewart insisted on having a young actress play Lady Macbeth to his more senior soldierly character, and since Kate Fleetwood was also relatively unknown compared to Stewart, as Goold observes, this generational disparity 'made her presence creepier and more powerful on Macbeth as a figure'.

Fleetwood also brings an extraordinarily physical beauty to the part of this Lady Macbeth, her pale Slavic features, long black hair, piercing eyes, bright red lips and slim build all assisting to project a character embodying what Stewart helpfully calls 'brittleness'. As well as showing itself in her last appearance in the sleepwalking scene, this characteristic comes across consistently in the first two acts up to Duncan's murder and its aftermath. When Stewart, returning from the murder, confronts Fleetwood in the dark, creepy and wide expanse of dank space at the sink, and refuses to take the daggers back, Lady Macbeth angrily retorts, 'Infirm of purpose!' (2.2.50). When reappearing from planting the knives in the hands of Duncan's grooms, she totters mincingly in high heels to the sink (as Goold describes), 'mad with blood lust', her hands, chest and face all smothered in blood. Shortly after, in a **two-shot close-up** with Fleetwood in focus at left foreground, while Stewart stands back right, out of focus, but clearly still in shock in his unblemished white shirt, she reveals the brittleness of which Stewart speaks while busying herself at the sink, muttering psychotically, 'A little water clears us of this deed. / How easy is it then! Your constancy / Hath left you unattended' (2.2.65–7). The image would not be out of place in any Hammer horror film. They both ascend in the elevator, holding hands, still unwashed.

The power of Stewart's 50-year experience as a leading actor of stage and screen begins to reveal itself fully in the final three acts of this production. 'To know my deed 'twere best not know myself', his character states with bleak insight at the end of Act 2. This could provide the text for almost all of Macbeth's subsequent actions, his ambitious plan to become – and to remain – king, only achievable by replacing the normal dictates of his conscience with a cruel and murderously paranoiac sense of purpose. The fluency and imaginative power of Stewart's playing can be illustrated by looking briefly at two scenes. The stage production had been played almost exclusively in the Macbeths' kitchen, where, in a scene that became the most talked about, Macbeth makes a sandwich, some of which he gives to each murderer as he addresses them, following the departure of Banquo and Fleance for their ride. For Goold, the kitchen provides a metaphor for both the domestic (where Lady Macbeth had shamed, cajoled and seduced Macbeth into becoming a regicide), and where food is prepared – with knives (the witch-nurses and their knives were evident earlier). Any 'man of power' – as Macbeth now is – who openly prepares food for others, feels menacing and scary. Stewart, playing Macbeth the battle-scarred warrior, and himself the proud son of a professional army man, here takes command by skilfully wielding and flourishing his knife in the kitchen as he talks and prepares a sandwich. He shares this with the quivering murderers he has taken on to kill Banquo and Fleance, continuing his fluent delivery of around fifty lines of speech that gains its cajoling, deadly emphasis through the physicality of his actions: they are made to obey, and we are only glad it is not us.

At 5.10, in the final scenes of the film, although Macbeth sees his end is in sight, he remains cockily defiant, ostentatiously swigging wine in front of the avenging blade of Macduff. Stewart here demonstrates his superlative acting skills when, through the camera's **close** and

Illustration 5 **Rupert Goold's *Macbeth* (2010).** 'My hands are of your colour, but I shame / To wear a heart so white' (2.2.62–3), says Lady Macbeth
(Kate Fleetwood), while Macbeth (Patrick Stewart) stands back, petrified by
the physical reminder of his brutal slaughter of King Duncan. This gore-dripping exposure of Lady Macbeth's grim attempt to cover up the murder is but
one example of the 'body horror' imagery Goold uses to frighten us, underlining with forbidding emphasis the fearful path of bloody terror the
Macbeths have embarked upon.

mid-shots of him, he puts the unseen screen audience under his control, and continues to do so by inventively reintroducing lines for the film not performed on the stage. At his own lines 'Before my body / I throw my warlike shield', with a manic laugh he sluices the remaining contents of his wine bottle over his own head, crazily convinced that he is somehow shielded from harm by the booze, and then whipping out his dagger to launch the warrior-like taunt, 'Lay on Macduff, / And damned be him that first cries "Hold, enough!"' (5.10.33–5).

As Stewart explains, 'With the camera lens, it is possible – and necessary – for the actor to put a circle of concentration around yourself. This makes the world of the film *real* and *tangible* – not make-believe – since in such a situation the actor suspends his disbelief, and it's *real*' (DVD interview). As is the effect of the movie's final 'body horror' shot, where Goold's obsession with film horror and Stewart's charismatic 'look' come together. Having beaten Macbeth in hand-to-hand combat, weary Macduff brings his adversary's severed head to the nervously triumphant Malcolm, who, holding the gore-dripping object in his hands and speechifying as a new monarch with increasing confidence to his incredulous followers, thrusts it aloft for all to see – especially us. The likeness to Patrick Stewart is remarkable!

The year **2012** was the one in which Britain hosted the Olympic Games, and as its contribution to the so-called World Shakespeare Festival, **BBC TV** commissioned adaptations of Shakespeare's second tetralogy of history plays for broadcast in **HD**, *Richard II*, *1* and *2 Henry IV* and *Henry V*, presented under the title *The Hollow Crown*. Given that 'Britain' and 'history' are for many people the same thing, it was inevitable that an appropriation of the national poet Shakespeare for big-budget prime-time period drama productions, in this year of years, would be heavily tinged with a 'heritage' look and feel. All four adaptations are elegantly designed and ravishingly shot in 'authentic' spaces and landscapes, with actors in medieval period costume: perhaps a lavish bid to realize more effectively the period accuracy attempted for the prestigious complete canon BBC Shakespeare of the 1970s and 1980s. But although the heritage context of production for the films means that we should not look for innovation in dramatic design or interpretative purpose, these beautiful productions are also highly accessible TV movies led by some excellent acting and expert direction. Rupert Goold's *Richard II* explores filmic possibilities the most inventively, but, no doubt having to conform to a series format and look, without the bravado shown for his *Macbeth*. Rendered with political conservatism in each case, what the films do is to treat these

history plays as what Peter Kirwan has called 'mood pieces'. So in
Richard II Ben Wishaw expertly captures the full range of Richard's
youthfully perfidious character, Goold's decision to develop the
deposed king's self-dramatizing Christ figure being nicely caught in
his riding to his final arraignment on a small pony. Rory Kinnear provides a robust but uneasily precise Bolingbroke, while Patrick Stewart
is unerringly brilliant as Gaunt. Richard Eyre brings *1 Henry IV* and
2 Henry IV to the screen very capably indeed, the first borrowing the
look and settings of Welles's *Chimes at Midnight* to great distinctive
effect, especially in the energetic presentation of the Eastcheap scenes
and for the haunting spaces, framings and lighting in which Jeremy
Irons's Henry IV is shown. Tom Hiddleston as Hal heads up a mostly
exceptional cast, his 'easy charm' and 'handsome cool' (Kirwan) setting him in contrast to Irons's stunning portrayal of Henry IV and
Simon Russell Beale's amazingly accomplished Falstaff. Unfortunately,
sentimentality afflicts this film (as it does the others), most egregiously
when Falstaff's brilliant soliloquy on 'honour' (5.1.129–39) is down-
graded into a melancholy **voice-over** while he rambles around the battlefield. *2 Henry IV* is indeed capable, but a somewhat low-key affair.
Even though Welles described his *Chimes at Midnight* as a 'lament for
Merrie England', buoyant energies and humour animated his adaptation, whereas an anticipatory seriousness can create inertia in what
might otherwise be a very engaging film. In the final Eastcheap scenes
between Beale's Falstaff and Maxine Peake's Doll Tearsheet, there is
'no banter, no engagement, nothing to come down from – it is as if
Falstaff's rejection had already occurred'. For some reason, Richard
Eyre's refusal to find (as Peter Kirwan notes) 'variety and humour in
the film, works to its detriment'. Its high point, fortuitously, is Jeremy
Irons's moody midnight stroll around the castle, ending at the throne
room with his declaration to the empty space, 'Uneasy lies the head
that wears a crown' (3.1.31).

The effect of prolepsis is reinforced by the decision of director **Thea
Sharrock** to open her *Henry V* film with a sombre funeral for the king,
a scene utterly at variance with the stirring 'O for a muse of fire' speech
by Chorus (John Hurt) rendered in **voice-over**. Presumably such an
opening seemed to offer an opportunity to display 'historic grandeur'
to the viewing audience, just as the sight of Henry's majestic ship
ploughing through the English Channel waves to France with
Hiddleston's grim-faced Harry aboard makes for swashbuckling visual
excitement. Rightly, as Kirwan states, 'Hiddleston is a fine Henry V,
troubled throughout by the pain of his soldiers and keen to engage

with them.' But, if he is right that this film goes about its work to demonstrate 'that War is bad through the earnestly agonized faces and
pathos-laden deaths of name characters', then Branagh's 1989 *Henry V*
does a more convincing job of it.

Gregory Doran's *Julius Caesar* (2012) is at the time of writing the
latest RSC production to have been adapted from the Stratford stage
to the small screen by *Illuminations*. It was broadcast on 24 June 2012
by BBC4 TV, while the production was still playing in Stratford, before
later touring the UK and moving on to Moscow, New York and Ohio.
As with previous Illuminations/RSC collaborations, the film version of
the stage play used the same cast and director, Greg Doran by now
having become Artistic Director of the RSC. It was Doran's conception to set *Julius Caesar* in post-independence Africa and to employ an
all-black cast. This innovative move was inspired by Doran's having
discovered how Nelson Mandela and other African National Congress
members had had access to the complete works of Shakespeare when
imprisoned on Robben Island by the South African white apartheid
regime in the 1970s. As the volume passed among the black revolu-
tionaries, *Julius Caesar* became the play most heavily annotated by
readers. Mandela underlined Caesar's statement, 'Cowards die many
times before their deaths; / The valiant never taste of death but once'
(2.2.32–3), signing his name against it in December 1977. Doran realized that the play not only 'spoke' to black South African freedom
fighters, but also to post-colonial 'new' African nations where black
leaders had frequently been swept to power on a wave of popularity,
only to see their exploitative one-party states challenged and over-
thrown by 'revolutionary' military coups in which that leader is assassinated, the outcome often being confusion and ruinous civil conflict.
This common cycle of events broadly outlines the plot of Shakespeare's
Julius Caesar.

Yet Doran's concern was not to say, 'look, this play applies to Africa'
so much as to help audiences 'get beyond the togas and sandals' of this
Roman play, to discern the relevance of the political processes it dramatizes to the real political dramas of many modern states ('The Making
of *Julius Caesar*', DVD). At the same time, though the African setting
is not made to resemble any particular nation or to use a particular
African regional accent, a consensus that the mixture of West Indian
and West African actors would adopt an East African English speech
pattern for the production was a happy one. For not only is this diction
crystal clear to the ear, but it fits extremely well with the iambic speech
pattern used by the major characters in Shakespeare's text. We begin

to appreciate this from the play's opening scenes. The very first **close-ups** are of a gyrating white-painted dancer (later, the Soothsayer) ominously miming a repeated stabbing motion. The camera then pulls back to film a range of **wide** and rapidly changing **close** and **medium-close** action **shot**s that capture well this carnival-like celebration in the RSC theatre. It is here where the Roman common people – as the Cobbler tells the tribune Murellus – 'make holiday to see Caesar, and / to rejoice in his triumph' (1.1.29–30). But when the tribunes Flavius and Murellus enter (after 90 seconds of delightfully filmic carnival), it is to subdue the crowd. They succeed only after the Cobbler has bantered jokingly with Murellus, but return to dancing and singing after their departure, uninterested in the serious 'political fact' that they are celebrating Caesar's defeat of the sons of Pompey, *not* the fruits of a foreign triumph.

It is only *after* we are briefly introduced to most of the main characters with their entry at 1.2 into the theatre arena following Caesar (Jeffery Kissoon), who hears the Soothsayer's warning to 'Beware the ides of March' only to dismiss it, that we really experience at close quarters how brilliantly the production's African-English diction works. This experience becomes possible only through a further innovation, whereby the 'public' scenes are shot in the RSC theatre itself, that is to say, the opening, the forum speeches by Brutus and Antony, and the end – confusingly, since all of Act 5 takes place on the battlefield near Philippi, not in Rome. The rest of the play's text is regarded as constituting 'private' scenes that are shot on location in north London. The location was an abandoned shopping mall providing a variety of large open spaces, corridors and rooms that are cleverly exploited to help deliver dramatic atmosphere to the various scenes, especially a moving staircase which, its motion arrested, affords an apt liminal place to play the assassination of Julius Caesar. The first transition from theatre to location is so seamless as to be masterful. This comes on a cut from a shot of the Soothsayer to a dynamic shot of a double door being pushed open by Brutus, who proceeds to walk along a corridor followed by Cassius, the camera retreating before but capturing them both, as if they have left the theatre arena into an adjacent space. In fact, this is a corridor at the location, and it is here where we first experience a stunning combination of fine, **close-up** cinematography and emotionally precise acting that cannot but draw us into Shakespeare's tense but exquisitely developed plot, as it emerges through the text that Doran and **DoP** Steve Lawes shoot.

Certain it is that both Paterson Joseph as Brutus and Cyril Nri as Cassius deliver their characters so expressively that the passions and hesitations of their devoted friendship under pressure can invariably be read in their faces, frequently enhanced by subtle camera set-ups and movement that use lighting to telling emotional effect. Before the filming, Joseph had been anxious to learn how the actors could express themselves as successfully on camera in small playing locations as they had done in the large RSC theatre. 'But actually,' he says, 'what was brilliant was that we could actually *talk* to each other! Shakespeare is great roared, but Shakespeare is *sublime* when it's just spoken.' Adjoa Andoh (Portia) agrees: 'Working in film, there's a freedom you discover in the intimacy the camera allows you. I am surprised at how fantastically useful the stage rehearsal has been for the filming, and how the filming performance will be for putting it back on the stage. It's been a really great process' ('The Making of *Julius Caesar*', DVD).

After Caesar has been assassinated, Brutus, then Antony, perform as orators to the Roman crowd, so it is entirely appropriate that the filmed action moves back from location to the RSC arena theatre space, where each performer can raise or subdue his voice at will, according to the effect each aims at to win across the populace, whose reactions are skilfully recorded. Typically, an angry crowd responds best to simple emotional injunctions. Joseph as Brutus therefore gets his best response from the crowd when he says that, just as he slew Caesar 'for the good of Rome', he has the same dagger for himself 'when it shall please my country to need my death', drawing from the plebeians' shouts of 'Live, Brutus, live, live!' (3.2.41–4). Ray Fearon's Mark Antony shows himself to be the superior orator because he is able to convey superbly well to the crowd his feelings of personal loss as Caesar's best friend, something they can truly identify with. Whereas Brutus's passion is limited to his 'abstract' appeal for the people to see Caesar's murder as allowing them 'to live all free men', Antony's aim is to stir up the crowd into mutiny and vengeance for Caesar's death. As Ray Fearon explains, Antony 'appeals to the people emotionally, and wins them over' ('The Making of *Julius Caesar*', DVD). Successfully portraying rhetorical competition in these scenes is vital, so the decision to film the political persuaders and their hearers, the Roman populace, together in the large playing space that serves as the play's Forum, is beautifully judged. The same may be said about the supremely imaginative and skilful ways in which this movie communicates for a twenty-first-century film audience so clearly the questions posed by one of Shakespeare's most political plays, questions that, sadly, apply more than ever to states in political crisis around the world.

From the survey of Shakespeare adaptations explored here, the inescapable conclusion has to be that those nurtured into successful dramatic life in a prominent stage context have been the most impressive to appear on small screens. The BBC's 2012 *The Hollow Crown* series is splendid in many ways and an excellent educational resource. But in recent years, it is the films adapted from widely admired stage productions by *Illuminations* that have been best able to deliver high-quality Shakespearean drama for small-screen formats. Wyver's approach of having the original directors and casts of the successful stage productions work with a **DoP** using a single camera in a suitable single location has made this achievement possible. Significantly, the dramatically precise single-camera approach has been the standard mode of production in cinema since the earliest days of Hollywood. Since the **intensified continuity** system is also now always incorporated into such filmic versions of Shakespearean drama, they are not only highly suitable for the home TV screen, but are also 'well adapted to being watched on laptop computers, tablets, and smartphones' (Bordwell and Thompson, 249). High-quality digital cameras and sound-recording techniques now enable directors and producers committed to 'shooting the text' of Shakespeare's plays to attain a precision and impact hitherto unattainable for the small screen. This improved hybrid form of presenting Shakespeare on film to those who want to watch it around our global village is an extremely welcome development.

Appendix: Filming Shakespeare for the Small Screen – An Interview with John Wyver, *Illuminations* filmmaker and producer

John Wyver has produced five film adaptations of outstanding Shakespeare stage productions for the small screen with his London company Illuminations, *four of them broadcast by BBC TV:* Richard II *(Dir. Deborah Warner, 1998);* Macbeth *(Dir. Gregory Doran, 2000 [Channel 4]);* Hamlet *(Dir. Gregory Doran, 2009);* Macbeth *(Dir. Rupert Goold, 2010);* Julius Caesar *(Dir. Gregory Doran, 2012). The last four films are discussed in Part V of this book. In the interview that follows, Maurice Hindle (MH) explores with John Wyver (JW) the processes whereby acclaimed stage productions of Shakespeare have been brought to the small screen with equal success.*

MH   John, what requirements did the BBC have for the co-funded production of the RSC *Hamlet* you made for TV broadcast at Christmas 2009?

JW   It was very important to the BBC to be able to say to the audience, the press, and to their stakeholders that they were bringing the RSC's *Hamlet* with David Tennant to television, and to a wider audience. They wanted to preserve the values, the prestige and the qualities of that Stratford production, to stay close to the *Hamlet* stage version. They didn't want some other cultural artefact.

MH   The BBC Head of Vision apparently didn't want a 'movie' of *Hamlet* made. What did he mean by that?

JW   I think he feared that if we adapted it for the screen in too imaginative or interventionist a way, it would not be seen as the RSC *Hamlet* with David Tennant. I don't think he was talking about 'film' in stylistic terms, what we would see on the screen, but that in translating the stage production to television it needed to be *grounded* in this particular theatre piece. The RSC also wanted a screen version of that production, but not something that would take it somewhere completely different. The RSC stage director Gregory Doran and I, and the others who talked about it, all felt the same. We didn't want to make a radically different screen adaptation of it. But, we *did* want to find a visual language – a screen language – which would make it accessible and engaging for a contemporary television audience.

MH   How did you achieve that?

JW   The way that seemed to offer the best possible expressive achievement was to shoot it with a single camera, rather than with multiple cameras. With very few exceptions – the Trevor Nunn *Macbeth* unquestionably being a key one – the traditional multiple camera shooting of theatre productions either in the theatre or in a TV studio, although cost- and time-effective, didn't seem to give you the kind of expressive potential of the screen that this process *ought* to be able to achieve. It didn't give you sufficient *control* of what you put on the screen. The lighting from shot to shot would always be compromised, for example, and it felt like you were laying some kind of dead hand of form over the theatre production. We thought the way to break with that was to go with this single-camera approach. Of course, that then throws up various questions, as to what this single camera is going to do.

MH   How did you use the single-camera approach for the first *Macbeth* that *Illuminations* did in 2000?

JW   For the first *Macbeth*, we thought the single camera should work in an observational way, like a *vérité* documentary approach, where the camera operator isn't in control of the events taking place. They respond as best they can to capturing those events. That approach carries with it all sorts of tropes, like not using a tripod, rapid **pan**s, and not always being on the action, things like that. We built that approach into the production process also partly because we had to shoot it very quickly. We hired a supreme documentary cameraman, Ernie Vincze, and often he didn't really know what the scene was going to be. We didn't, as in the normal way of drama, break the scene down, rehearse it, shoot a wide **master shot**, and then do detailed shots. Greg Doran would say something like, 'So the scene is, Macbeth comes down those stairs, Lady Macbeth enters over there, they argue about the daggers, and then they rush out. That's what happened on the stage, and this is roughly equivalent to that, but in a real-world location. OK, that's what's going to happen, Ernie – shoot it.' So, it was like these events were happening in some real world, in some castle, a war zone or whatever, with Ernie trying to respond and capture it. This approach is what I think gives that *Macbeth* its particular filmic quality, its energy and excitement. It still carries across today.

MH   I agree, it really grabs the attention of the viewer. Did you approach *Hamlet* in a similar way?

JW   *Hamlet* had different qualities. We created a much more elegant, composed and controlled world – until that world starts to fall apart at the end. The style of camerawork we wanted to achieve was different. It was much more precise and controlled, and that's why we worked with a different director of photography. In our approach to translating Shakespeare stage productions to the small screen, the budget dictates that we have to shoot between eight and twelve minutes of finished film per shooting day. That's how you measure a schedule, by the number of minutes of cut film you achieve in a day. A big commercial movie is lucky if it shoots two and a half or three minutes a day. Conventional TV drama, *Poirot*, or whatever, probably aims to get six minutes of finished film a day. We're looking to get ten minutes a day because, crudely, that is all the money we have. Every day, you're paying for a film crew, a location, food, etc. – every shooting day is expensive. We've done each of our Shakespeare productions in exactly the number of days we budgeted for.

MH   So is this typical of the *Illuminations* way of shooting Shakespeare?

JW   Within *that* kind of framework, I'm not sure that there *is* a typical *Illuminations* shooting approach. The observational documentary approach is *one* way of getting ten minutes a day, the elegant and controlled form of filming that **DoP** Chris Seager achieved on *Hamlet* is *another* way. Chris was able to do it, in part, because many of the scenes were shot in the same space, in the hall of the ex-seminary college at Mill Hill. I should think that two-thirds of *Hamlet* was in that one big space. What we did was to almost turn that hall into a TV studio. We hung a scaffolding grid of lamps up in the ceiling, so Chris could then light scenes on the floor, bringing those lamps up and down in intensity. So he didn't have to move a lot of lamps around on the floor. One of the things slowing you down when you're trying to shoot a lot of drama is having to re-light every individual shot – moving lamps around and adjusting them is time-consuming. So, being in one location without having to do all that meant we could be rigorous, tight and precise, shooting fairly speedily. But I don't think having to shoot at that kind of speed entails a particular style of filming. It entails a production *process*. There are always different ways of responding to the box you're in, when you have to get ten minutes of cut film a day. *Hamlet* and the first *Macbeth* demonstrate these differences, I think.

MH   I will return to your preferred 'single-location' approach, but first want to ask about the 'director function'. Is it essential that the director of an original stage production should take the creative lead on your film productions, and if so, why?

JW   It is essential, because they understand the production and what the actors can bring to it in a way that no one else can. They have an understanding of every line, nuance, and facial expression that the actors brought to it, so they are the people to take that across to film. And I don't believe that they have to have made films before. Deborah [Warner] had had very limited experience of filmmaking before [*Richard II*], the same with Greg Doran, and Rupert [Goold], although he was steeped in cinema, hadn't made a film before. What you do is to give them a team of people immensely practised in making film: a director of photography, editor, first assistant director, a producer. You surround them with that team, and although the team doesn't make the film, this ensures that the film is made with the director being able to draw out all of the subtlety and richness that was in the original stage production. In the past people have worked with a television director to take something on to the screen. I simply don't think that's necessary: I think it's a wrong way of approaching it. For me, as long as the stage director is interested in doing this work – which they always have been – I think it's an inviolable principle.

MH   That's quite a conviction – thank you! Moving on to the '**DoP** function', I believe you regard the key relationship in creating these adaptations is between the director and the director of photography. What's important about that relationship?

JW   Well, it's because the director of photography is making the images to express the director's vision, essentially. The **DoP** has to find a style which brings out the ideas and concerns that the director has in the best way possible. In a sense, they are at the service of the director. But at its best it's a very close partnership, where together they are finding the right image for every moment of the play. The director by and large won't be able to say, 'I think it should be a **medium close-shot**, with an out-of-focus foreground, and a **dolly** shot on this line to the right.' You know? That isn't how most theatre directors work. But the stage director may say, 'At this point, Hamlet is bemused, lost, trying to think through what his life is about, and then he has an idea, and at that point everything changes.' The DoP might respond, 'Well, why don't we do it with this kind of shot and this kind of camera movement? That'll underscore what's in the performance and the text at this point.' So the production process is full of those little collaborative discussions.

MH   This suggests you need a DoP who's willing and able to respond to the needs of the director in quite a particular way.

JW   I think you haven't become a good DoP if you're not able to do that. You may not have shot any Shakespeare before, but you've got to be able to do the same thing whether you're shooting – I don't know – *The Life of Brian*, or *Prometheus*, or whatever. That's what being a DoP working with a director is. You're just in a slightly different Shakespeare context. But it's only a script, and it's only a bunch of actors you're working with.

MH   How does the director and DoP collaborative arrangement impact upon the work of the film editor?

JW   A good director of photography will shoot something so that the form is there in its rough shape. There won't be only one way to edit it, but there will be an *expected* and *preferred* way to edit it. The editor will take the shot film and refine and hone it. Sometimes, the editor will think what the DoP has come up with is completely useless, and they'll have to find another way through it. But ideally the DoP is creating something that the editor can respond to, and take it to another level, as it were. I would say the director/DoP relationship is the primary one, and DoP/editor relationship is secondary, but not very secondary. Because, say you've got a conversation being shot between two people very straightforwardly, once with the camera looking *this* way, and another time with the camera looking *that* way. Even though you are clearly going to cut between those two people, there are a thousand different variants on *how* you cut between them talking. You can *primarily* be looking at the person who's listening...

MH   ...the **reaction shot**...

JW   ...Right. So what the editor is doing is making those very fine judgements about when the viewer should be looking at the person who is talking, and when they should be looking at the person who's listening. Every one of those judgements about *when* you cut, and how long the camera stays on somebody, and what kind of rhythm you put into it all – all those judgements impact on the *meaning* of the work we come to see. That's what good editors do, and the director is *part* of that process. They check and refine and change what the editor has done, but all the heavy lifting of that process is done by the editor.

MH   Can I extend this tack of discussion a little by asking what you see as the parallels or differences between making feature films and your kind of adaptation?

JW   I don't think the large-/small-screen difference is necessarily the key one. I think the way we work is very similar to a lot of lower-budget feature films, whether made in the UK or in the US. I think it's very different though from a *big* budget feature film, where there will probably *not* be the same kind of personal collaboration between the director and DoP determining how the film is shot – at least during the shoot. I haven't *made* a big-budget feature film, but there's no question that if you make a hundred-million-dollar film, and you set up a day to film a particular scene, you are going to shoot a lot more material than *we* would shoot. There would be lots more choices created – more **cutaways** say, maybe a **close-up**, a **mid-shot**, and a **long shot** of the actor saying the same words. We'd already have made those decisions: 'it's going to be a **close-up**, and we're not going to shoot the other two, just so someone *might* want it later on'. But the 'just in case someone might want it later on' with a *big*-budget film is there because there are lots of other people in the movie production process, including audiences giving feedback on **test screening**s. Such an audience is not going to say, 'we wanted to see Batman in **long shot** at that point'. But it *is* going to say, 'we didn't see *enough* of Batman', or something, you know? So, the big movie will always want to keep lots of options open. *We* don't have the time or money to do that. But neither do lots of independent feature filmmakers and mainstream television drama producers either. So, I think *that's* the difference.

MH   Is part of the issue having to satisfy a larger popular audience for a big-budget film?

JW   Well, potentially. Basically you've got a lot more money at stake, and lots more people in the production process who think they can protect that money, so as to make lots more money. But ultimately, for me, it's not about making money. It's about making a really good product for television. I'm not even sure it's about that for the medium – it's ultimately about creating *prestige* for television.

MH   Can you say something about the role of the *Illuminations* producer in making one of these stage-to-small-screen adaptations?

JW   Well, it's like producing many other things. You try and formulate with other people a creative project. You try and find the money for that. If you've found some money, you try then to put a framework around it concerning rights and responsibilities, so that the money will deliver to those providing it what they want, both in quality terms but in rights terms as well. You then spend that money wisely by finding the right team, creating a production schedule, and finding the right location. Obviously, you do all this with lots of other people, but ultimately it's your responsibility. You provide a context for the creative teams to work in, and hopefully feed people and keep them happy while they're doing it; or at least vaguely happy, you know? And then you ensure that it's delivered at the end, and with a bit of luck, it'll be OK!

MH   So, it's like being a producer!

JW   It's like being a producer – that's it!

MH   Can we now turn to your preferred use of a single location to shoot these adaptations – say with the first *Macbeth* you made in 2000?

JW   Part of this attempt to keep something that felt vivid and alive from the theatre production was our wanting to move outside a studio, and exploit the qualities of the real world, you know? If you haven't got much money, it's very difficult to come up with a varied, convincing world by painting **flats** and putting rocks in a studio, or whatever. It's much easier to do that in the real world – it gives it a kind of – the word is very complicated – but it gives it a *reality*.

MH   And is cheaper too, if you can find the right place?

JW   Well, if you can find the right place, it's potentially cheaper, though you've got to bring lots of resources and facilities into it. So the secret for us was finding the one place which had a variety of different environments on the same site, because we didn't want to move the film unit. We wanted to put the unit in one place and shoot everything there. If you can bring the caravans in for changing rooms and toilets and a camera car at the beginning of a fortnight and take them out at the end of that time, then that's a really effective way of spending your money, rather than moving from place to place every other day. That's part of it. The other part is to be on one site, but to have a range of different environments. So, for the first *Macbeth* we looked at a lot of different places, but when we went to the Roundhouse [Camden Town, London] we immediately felt that could give us the qualities we wanted, both in the main space, which is big and airy, and then in all sorts of corners around it: staircases, the tunnels and caves underneath it, for example. So we could get lots of variety out of being on the one site. And that's what we've managed to do with each of the Shakespeare productions *Illuminations* has done.

MH   Greg Doran has used the phrase 'vivid neutrality' to describe the kind of space one is looking for to shoot these adaptations. That's an oxymoron, isn't it?

JW   I think that's the point of using it. What he's always looking for is something that is not too literal as a particular place. He wants a kind of generic environment which isn't abstract or stylized, a place which has a kind of immediacy and all the kind of qualities you associate with a real-world environment. So with the RSC *Hamlet* we did, you don't quite know when it's set, other than some time in the late twentieth century. Greg likes that ambiguity. He doesn't want it to be in Ceaușescu's palace, say, six weeks before the revolution.

MH   Can you say how this kind of immediacy shows itself in the *Hamlet* film?

JW   One of my best examples of this kind of vividness which the real world gives you and which a studio never can, is when Laertes is leaving the palace and saying goodbye to Ophelia in Act 1 ...

MH   ... oh, I know, at the bottom of the staircase ...

JW   ... yes, that's right, at the bottom of the staircase. Laertes gets up, turns around and is just about to walk away. And there is a brief shot, about two seconds or whatever, all the way down the corridor – it's a shot you haven't seen before. At the end of the corridor there is an open window with green trees beyond blowing slightly in the wind. You'd never build that corridor if you were in a studio, because it's only on screen for two seconds. You'd *certainly* never build it with a window looking out on to greenery beyond. But, for me, this shot in a way 'grounds' that scene, giving a sense of significance to Laertes's leaving in an incredible way. It probably just passes people by immediately, but that is a *really* good example of what, for me, shooting in a location can give you. So it's luck in a way that a good location will throw up lots of things like that.

MH   ...a bit like 'found art' ...

JW   Yes, yes, absolutely. And if you can bring that out with lighting or camera movement or whatever, it can be really wonderful.

MH   Let's now turn to how the audience has responded to your work. Following the BBC Two broadcast of *Hamlet* on 26 December 2010 a *Guardian* newspaper blog post by one Jude Burke stated that he 'really liked the way it was filmed. By keeping elements of the stage production it showed that it is, first and foremost, a play and not a film.' How do you react to that?

JW   Well, I think that *is* what we are trying to do. It goes back to 'not making a movie'. It's a hybrid form, somewhere between a theatre piece and a film, and that's why I find it interesting to do. It has been taken from the stage, placed in another world, and interpreted by the camera in a way that retains the essence of the original, but hopefully works distinctively in the new medium. Yet it has *not* been turned into a movie. If you had seen the stage production and then saw the film, you would recognize hundreds and hundreds of continuities and similarities between the two. It's not just about preserving a stage production, it's about using what's been created and developed over the process of making a stage production, and allowing that to enrich and inform what is on the TV or small screen. You know, the fact that the RSC *Macbeth* had been played around the world before it came to television is a real advantage. It gives a depth and sophistication and a subtlety to those performances and relationships which you would never achieve if it was, 'OK, let's make a *Macbeth* for television with Tony Sher and Harriet Walter – great! Well, we can give you two weeks' rehearsal ... .' You are *never* going to get what you really need, that way. What you *are* getting here is all of that richness that's been developed across a year's touring, and hopefully you find a responsible and appropriate way of achieving that on the screen.

MH   Turning towards some final thoughts about future projects. Are you content with your current approach to filming stage Shakespeare for TV? Or are there other variants you may want to try?

JW   What I and colleagues have always said is that we don't want this to become a formula. Each of these films has similarities, but each of them tries to tackle things in a different way. By mixing stuff shot in the theatre and stuff shot on location, our *Julius Caesar* takes it in another direction. Of *course* you are never satisfied with what you do. You never think, 'Now I can make another twenty of these' – that would be ridiculous! Also, each of these is very hard work to make ... [laughs] ... you know, you've got to be *really* interested to do it. You don't make a huge amount of money, and you work incredibly hard...

MH   ... I know, I've seen you doing it!

JW   It's pretty stressful. But what keeps you going is the interest of the process, right? I feel very privileged to be able to do that.

MH   Do you have anything innovatory in the works?

JW   You always want to try and do something different, so Greg and I have talked about trying to do one on a bigger scale, maybe in a different kind of location. I'm also really interested in whether you can do this kind of thing on a lower budget. Can you make something more guerrilla-like, edgier, rougher – and cheaper? Because they're expensive things, these films, and it's very hard to get those budgets.

Also, as you know, we'll be doing a live stage-to-cinema piece with the RSC in autumn 2013 [*Richard II*], which is going *back* to a multi-camera approach *in* a theatre, but hopefully trying to find a distinctive and interesting way of working with that. [See *Live Stage Productions of Shakespeare on Film in the Twenty-first Century*, The Theatrical Mode, Part III.]

MH   A final question. You wrote in 2011 of the *Illuminations Hamlet* that 'Doubtless it will in years to come be seen on many types of screen for audiences of all kinds.' What kinds of screen format for stage-to-screen Shakespeare productions will there be in the future?

JW   Well, I don't know ... it seems to me there are *already* all kinds of different opportunities. You can see this on broadcast, on DVD, or online. There are things like the Digital Theatre operation, there's live-to-cinema, and people can watch on their mobile phones or tablets. I don't know where it'll go in the future. But it seems incredibly healthy to me that there are so many opportunities of this kind. It's fantastic and really rich – particularly when, ten years ago TV was the only medium able to produce or disseminate it. For a healthy, broad-based culture, you need many ways of these things working, of being made, getting out into the world. It's great that these other possibilities have come along at a time when television seems to be retreating from its responsibility to do these kinds of things.

MH   Do you think the BBC ought to facilitate more of these productions?

JW   Yes, of course I do, unquestionably.

MH   Do you think it will?

JW   Who knows? I mean, will it change because Tony Hall [new BBC Director-General in 2013] has gone there? Maybe, he's got more interest in this than others. But even the BBC is a very commercially focused entity now, despite being publicly funded. Let's see.

References

Almereyda, Michael, 2000, *William Shakespeare's Hamlet: A Screenplay Adaptation* (London: Faber & Faber).

Ball, Robert Hamilton, 1968, *Shakespeare on Silent Film: A Strange Eventful History* (London: George Allen & Unwin).

Barber, C.L., 1972, *Shakespeare's Festive Comedy* (Princeton, NJ: Princeton University Press).

Bate, Jonathan, and Rasmussen, Eric (eds), 2009, *King Lear* (Basingstoke: Palgrave Macmillan).

Bordwell, David, 2012, *Pandora's Box: Films, Files, and the Future of Movies* (Madison, WI: Irvington Way Institute Press).

Bordwell, David and Thompson, Kristin, 2013, *Film Art: An Introduction* (New York: McGraw-Hill).

Branagh, Kenneth, 1989, *Henry V: A Screen Adaptation* (London: Chatto & Windus).

——, 1991, *Beginning* (New York: St. Martin's Press).

——, 1993, *Much Ado About Nothing: Screenplay, Introduction, and Notes on the Making of the Movie* (New York and London: W.W. Norton).

——, 1996, *Hamlet: Screenplay and Introduction* (New York and London: W.W.Norton).

Brook, Peter, 1987, *The Shifting Point: Forty Years of Theatrical Exploration 1946–1987* (London: Methuen).

Buchanan, Judith, 2000, 'Virgin and Ape, Venetian and Infidel: Labellings of Otherness in Oliver Parker's *Othello*', in Mark Thornton Burnett and Ramona Wray (eds), *Shakespeare, Film, Fin de Siècle* (Basingstoke: Palgrave Macmillan), 179–202.

Buhler, Stephen M., 2002, *Shakespeare in the Cinema: Ocular Proof* (Albany: State University of New York Press).

——, 2008, Review of *New Wave Shakespeare on Screen*, *Shakespeare Quarterly*, 59(2), 230–2.

Burch, Noel, 1979, *To the Distant Observer: Form and Meaning in the Japanese Cinema* (London: Scolar Press).

Burnett, Mark Thornton, 2000, 'Impressions of Fantasy: Adrian Noble's *A Midsummer Night's Dream*', in Mark Thornton Burnett and Ramona Wray (eds), *Shakespeare, Film, Fin de Siècle* (Basingstoke: Palgrave Macmillan), 89–101.

Cartmell, Deborah, 2000, *Interpreting Shakespeare on Screen* (Basingstoke: Palgrave Macmillan).

Corner, John, 1999, *Critical Ideas in Television Studies* (Oxford: Clarendon Press).

Crowl, Samuel, 2003, *Shakespeare at the Cineplex: The Kenneth Branagh Era* (Athens: Ohio University Press).

Davies, Anthony, 1988, *Filming Shakespeare's Plays: The Adaptations of Laurence Olivier, Orson Welles, Peter Brook and Akira Kurosawa* (Cambridge: Cambridge University Press).

——, 1996, 'The Film Versions of *Romeo and Juliet*', *Shakespeare Survey*, 49, 153–62.

Dent, Alan (ed.), 1948, *Hamlet: The Film and the Play* (London: World Film Publications).

Donaldson, Peter S., 1990, *Shakespearean Films/Shakespearean Directors* (Boston: Unwin Hyman).

Ellis, John, 1992, *Visible Fictions: Cinema: Television: Video* (London and Boston: Routledge & Kegan Paul).

Falk, Quentin, 2006, 'Going Japanese: Kenneth Branagh Finds Far Eastern Inspiration for His New, All-Star Film Version of *As You Like It*', *Exposure*: FujiFilm Magazine, 22.

Freedman, Barbara, 2000, 'Critical Junctures in Shakespeare Screen History: The Case of *Richard III*', in Russell Jackson (ed.), *The Cambridge Companion to Shakespeare on Film* (Cambridge: Cambridge University Press), 47–71.

Greenblatt, Stephen (ed.), 1997, *The Norton Shakespeare: Based on the Oxford Edition* (New York and London: W.W. Norton).

Guntner, Lawrence, 1995, 'Recycled Film Codes and "The Great Tradition of Shakespeare on Film"', in P. Drexler and L. Guntner (eds), *Negotiations with Hal: Multi-Media Perceptions of (Shakespeare's) Henry the Fifth* (Braunschweig: Technische Universität Braunschweig), 51–61.

——, 1997, 'A Microcosm of Art: Olivier's Expressionist *Hamlet* (1948)', in Holger Klein and Dimiter Daphinoff (eds), *Hamlet on Screen* (Lampeter: Edwin Mellen Press).

Hattaway, Michael, 2000, 'The Comedies on Film', in Russell Jackson (ed.), *The Cambridge Companion to Shakespeare on Film* (Cambridge: Cambridge University Press), 85–98.

Hayward, Susan, 1996, *Key Concepts in Cinema Studies* (London: Routledge).

Hoffman, Michael, 1999, *William Shakespeare's* A Midsummer Night's Dream, *Adapted for the Screen* (New York: HarperCollins).

Holland, Peter, 1996, 'Hand in Hand to Hell', *Times Literary Supplement*, 10 May.

——, 1997, *English Shakespeares: Shakespeare on the English Stage in the 1990s* (Cambridge: Cambridge University Press).

——, 1999, 'Two-Dimensional Shakespeare: "King Lear" on Film', in A. Davies and S. Wells (eds.), *Shakespeare and the Moving Image* (Cambridge: Cambridge University Press), 50–68.

Howard, Jean E., 1997, 'As You Like It', in *The Norton Shakespeare* (New York and London: W.W. Norton), 1591–5.

Jackson, Russell, 2000, 'Introduction: Shakespeare, Films and the Marketplace', in Russell Jackson (ed.), *The Cambridge Companion to Shakespeare on Film* (Cambridge: Cambridge University Press), 1–14.

Jorgens, Jack J., 1983, 'Kurosawa's *Throne of Blood*: Washizu and Miki Meet the Forest Spirit', *Literature/Film Quarterly*, 11(3), 167–73.

——, 1991, *Shakespeare on Film* (Lanham, MD and London: University Press of America).

Kael, Pauline, 1992, *Movie Love: Complete Reviews 1988–91* (London: Marion Boyars).

Kliman, Bernice, 1992, *Macbeth* (Manchester and New York: Manchester University Press).

Kott, Jan, 1974, *Shakespeare Our Contemporary*, trans. Boleslaw Taborski (New York and London: W.W. Norton).

Kozintsev, Grigori, 1967, *Shakespeare: Time and Conscience*, trans. Joyce Vining (London: Dennis Dobson).

——, 1972, '"Hamlet" and "King Lear": Stage and Film', in *Shakespeare 1971: Proceedings of the World Shakespeare Congress Vancouver, August 1971* (Toronto and Buffalo: University of Toronto Press).

Lanier, Douglas, 2003, 'Nostalgia and Theatricality: The Fate of the Shakespearean Stage in the *Midsummer Night's Dreams* of Hoffman, Noble, and Edzard', in Richard Burt and Lynda E. Boose (eds), *Shakespeare, The Movie II: Popularizing the Plays on Film, TV, Video, and DVD* (New York and London: Routledge), 154–72.

Loehlin, James N., 2000, '"These Violent Delights Have Violent Ends": Baz Luhrmann's Millennial Shakespeare', in Mark Thornton Burnett and Ramona Wray (eds), *Shakespeare, Film, Fin de Siècle* (London: Macmillan), 121–36.

——, 2003, '"Top of the World, Ma": *Richard III* and Cinematic Convention', in R. Burt and Lynda E. Boose (eds), *Shakespeare, The Movie II: Popularizing the Plays on Film, TV, Video, and DVD* (London and New York: Routledge), 173–85.

Logan, John, 2011, *Coriolanus: The Shooting Script* (New York: Newmarket Press).

McKellen, Ian, 1996, *William Shakespeare's Richard III: A Screenplay Written by Ian McKellen & Richard Loncraine, Annotated & Introduced by Ian McKellen* (Woodstock, NY: Overlook Press).

——, 1998, 'Shakespeare Is Up to Date: An Interview with Sir Ian McKellen', by Gary Crowdus, *Cineaste*, 24(1), 46–7.

McKernan, Luke and Terris, Olwen (eds), 1994, *Walking Shadows: Shakespeare in the National Film and Television Archive* (London: British Film Institute).

MacLiammóir, Micheál, 1994, *Put Money in Thy Purse: The Filming of Orson Welles's* Othello (London: Virgin Books).

McLuhan, Marshall, 1964, *Understanding Media: The Extensions of Man* (London: Routledge & Kegan Paul).

Magnus, Laury, 2010, 'The Tempest and Julie Taymor's Talkback at BAM for TFANA's Gala', *Shakespeare Newsletter*, 22 September.

Manvell, Roger, 1971, *Shakespeare and the Film* (New York and Washington, DC: Praeger).

——, 1979, *Theatre and Film: A Comparative Study of the Two Forms of Dramatic Art, and of the Problems of Adaptation of Stage Plays into Films* (Cranbury, NJ and London: Associated University Presses).

Mayer, Sophie, 2013, 'Preview: Joss Whedon's *Much Ado About Nothing*', *Sight & Sound*, July.

Metz, Christian, 1974, *Film Language: A Semiotics of the Cinema*, trans. Michael Taylor (New York: Oxford University Press).

Olivier, Laurence, 1984 [1945], *Henry V, Produced and Directed by Laurence Olivier* (London: Lorrimer).

——, 1987, *On Acting* (London: Sceptre).

Quarmby, Kevin A., 2011, 'Behind the Scenes: Penn & Teller, Taymor and the *Tempest* Divide Shakespeare's Globe, London', *Shakespeare Bulletin*, 29(3), 383–97.

Richie, Donald, 1970, *The Films of Akira Kurosawa* (Berkeley: University of California Press).

Rothwell, Kenneth S., 2000, *A History of Shakespeare on Screen: A Century of Film and Television* (Cambridge: Cambridge University Press).

Sullivan, Erin, 2014, Review of *Richard II*, RSC, Stratford-upon-Avon, *Shakespeare Bulletin*, 32(2), 272–5.

Thompson, Ann and Taylor, Neil (eds), 2006, *Hamlet: The Texts of 1603 and 1623* (London: Arden Shakespeare).

Wells, Stanley, 1982, 'Television Shakespeare', *Shakespeare Quarterly*, 33(3), 261–77.

Willems, Michèle (ed.), 1987, *Shakespeare à la television* (Rouen: Publications de l'Université de Rouen).

——, 1999, 'Verbal-Visual, Verbal-Pictorial or Textual-Televisual? Reflections on the BBC Shakespeare Series', in Anthony Davies and Stanley Wells (eds), *Shakespeare and the Moving Image* (Cambridge: Cambridge University Press), 69–85.

——, 2000, 'Video and Its Paradoxes', in Russell Jackson (ed.), *The Cambridge Companion to Shakespeare on Film* (Cambridge: Cambridge University Press), 35–46.

Willis, Susan, 1991, *The BBC Shakespeare Plays: Making the Televised Canon* (Chapel Hill and London: University of North Carolina Press).

Zeffirelli, Franco, 1986, *Zeffirelli: The Autobiography of Franco Zeffirelli* (New York: Weidenfeld & Nicholson).

Suggested Further Reading

Shakespeare on film

Anderegg, Michael, *Orson Welles: Shakespeare and Popular Culture* (New York: Columbia University Press, 1999).

Boose, Lynda E. and Richard Burt (eds), *Shakespeare, The Movie: Popularizing the Plays on Film, TV, and Video* (London and New York: Routledge, 1997).

Buhler, Stephen M., *Shakespeare in the Cinema: Ocular Proof* (Albany: State University of New York Press, 2002).

Bulman, J.C. and Coursen, H.R. (eds), *Shakespeare on Television: An Anthology of Essays and Reviews* (Hanover and London: University Press of New England, 1988).

Burnett, Mark Thornton, *Shakespeare and World Cinema* (Cambridge: Cambridge University Press, 2013).

Burnett, Mark Thornton and Ramona Wray (eds), *Shakespeare, Film, Fin de Siècle* (Basingstoke: Palgrave Macmillan, 2000).

Burt, Richard (ed.), *Shakespeare after Mass Media* (New York and Basingstoke: Palgrave, 2002).

Burt, Richard and Lynda E. Boose (eds), *Shakespeare, The Movie II: Popularizing the Plays on Film, TV, Video, and DVD* (New York and London: Routledge, 2003).

Cineaste Editors, 'Shakespeare in the Cinema: A Film Directors' Symposium, with Peter Brook, Sir Peter Hall, Richard Loncraine, Baz Luhrmann, Oliver Parker, Roman Polanski and Franco Zeffirelli', *Cineaste* 24(1), 1998, 48–55.

Davies, Anthony and Stanley Wells, *Shakespeare and the Moving Image: The Plays on Film and Television* (Cambridge: Cambridge University Press, 1994, repr. 1999).

Greenhalgh, Susanne (ed.), 'Live Cinema Relays of Shakespearean Performance', *Shakespeare Bulletin*, 32(2), Summer 2014, 255–78.

Jackson, Russell (ed.), *The Cambridge Companion to Shakespeare on Film* (Cambridge: Cambridge University Press, 2007).

——, *Shakespeare and the English-speaking Cinema* (Oxford: Oxford University Press, 2014).

Jorgens, Jack J., *Shakespeare on Film* (Lanham, MD and London: University Press of America, 1991).

Manvell, Roger, *Shakespeare and the Film* (New York and Washington, DC: Praeger, 1971).

McKernan, Luke, Eve Oesterlen and Olwen Terris (eds), *Shakespeare on Film, Television and Radio: The Researcher's Guide* (London: BUFC, 2009).

Starks, Lisa S. and Courtney Lehmann (eds), *The Reel Shakespeare: Alternative Cinema and Theory* (London: Associated University Presses, 2002).

Naremore, James, 'The Walking Shadow: Welles's Expressionist *Macbeth*', *Literature/Film Quarterly*, 1, 1973, 360–6.

Rothwell, Kenneth S., *A History of Shakespeare on Screen: A Century of Film and Television* (Cambridge: Cambridge University Press, 2012).

Film

Bordwell, David, *The Way Hollywood Tells It: Story and Style in Modern Movies* (Berkeley, Los Angeles and London: University of California Press, 2006).

——, *Pandora's Box: Films, Files, and the Future of Movies* (Madison, WI: Irvington Way Institute Press, 2012).

Bordwell, David and Kristin Thompson, *Film Art: An Introduction*, 10th edn (New York: McGraw-Hill, 2013).

Hollows, Joanne, Peter Hutchings and Mark Jancovich (eds), *The Film Studies Reader* (London: Arnold, 2000).

Monaco, James, *How to Read a Film: The World of Movies, Media, and Multimedia: Language, History, Theory*, 3rd edn (Oxford and New York: Oxford University Press, 2009).

Reference

Rothwell, Kenneth S. and Annabelle Henkin Melzer, *Shakespeare on Screen: An International Filmography and Videography* (New York and London: Neal-Schuman, 1990).

Select Shakespeare Filmography

Title	Director	Country	Date
As You Like It	Paul Czinner	USA	1936
As You Like It	Christine Edzard	UK	1992
As You Like It	Kenneth Branagh	UK/USA	2006
The Children's Midsummer Night's Dream	Christine Edzard	UK	2001
Chimes at Midnight (aka Falstaff)	Orson Welles	Spain/Switzerland	1965
Coriolanus	Ralph Fiennes	UK/Serbia/USA	2011
Cymbeline	Michael Almereyda	USA	2015
Hamlet, The Drama of Vengeance	Svend Gade	Germany	1920

(*Continued*)

Title	Director	Country	Date
Hamlet	Laurence Olivier	UK	1948
Hamlet	Grigori Kozintsev	Russia	1964
Hamlet	Tony Richardson	UK	1969
Hamlet	Franco Zeffirelli	USA/UK/France	1990
Hamlet	Kenneth Branagh	UK/USA	1996
Hamlet	Michael Almereyda	USA	2000
Henry V	Laurence Olivier	UK	1944
Henry V	Kenneth Branagh	UK	1989
Julius Caesar	Joseph Mankiewicz	USA	1953
King John	William Dickson	UK	1899
King Lear	Grigori Kozintsev	Russia	1971
King Lear	Peter Brook	UK	1971
King Lear	Edwin Sherin	USA	1974
Kumonosu-Jô	Akira Kurosawa	Japan	1957
Love's Labour's Lost	Kenneth Branagh	UK//France/USA	2000
Macbeth	–	USA	1908
Macbeth	Orson Welles	USA	1948
Macbeth	Roman Polanski	UK	1971
Macbeth	Justin Kurzel	USA	2015
A Midsummer Night's Dream	Charles Kent	USA	1909
A Midsummer Night's Dream	Max Reinhardt and William Dieterle	USA	1935
A Midsummer Night's Dream	Peter Hall	UK	1968
A Midsummer Night's Dream	Adrian Noble	UK	1996
A Midsummer Night's Dream	Michael Hoffman	USA/Italy/UK	1999
Much Ado About Nothing	Kenneth Branagh	UK	1993
Much Ado About Nothing	Joss Whedon	USA	2012
The Merchant of Venice	Michael Radford	UK/Luxembourg Italy/USA	2004
Othello	Orson Welles	Morocco/Italy/France	1952
Othello	Sergei Yutkevich	Russia	1955
Othello	Stuart Burge	UK	1965
Othello	Oliver Parker	UK	1995
Richard III	James Keane	USA	1912
Richard III	Laurence Olivier	UK	1955
Richard III	Richard Loncraine	UK	1995
Romeo & Juliet	George Cukor	USA	1936
Romeo & Juliet	Renato Castellani	Italy/UK	1954
Romeo & Juliet	Franco Zeffirelli	Italy/UK	1968
Romeo + Juliet	Baz Luhrmann	USA	1996
The Taming of the Shrew	Sam Taylor	USA	1929
The Taming of the Shrew	Franco Zeffirelli	Italy/USA	1966
The Tempest	Percy Stow	UK	1908
The Tempest	Julie Taymor	USA	2010
Titus	Julie Taymor	USA/Italy	1999
Twelfth Night	Trevor Nunn	UK	1996

Some useful websites

http://blogs.notting-
ham.ac.uk/bardathon/

The Bardathon. Shakespeare review blog set up by Peter Kirwan in 2006 at Warwick University reviewing and providing critical commentaries on stage and film productions of Shakespeare and other early modern dramatic productions until 30 July 2012. Kirwan's critical reviews/commentaries of BBC TV's *The Hollow Crown* adaptations of Shakespeare's second history tetralogy, *Richard II*, *1 Henry IV*, *2 Henry IV* and *Henry V* are highly recommended.

http://blogs.warwick.
ac.uk/pkirwan

The Bardathon. Peter Kirwan's Shakespeare review blog continued, now hosted at Nottingham University. It 'chronicles new productions of early modern plays around the UK, as well as related films, documentaries, books and events'. It also provides links with many Shakespeare-related sites, e.g. the RSC, Shakespeare's Globe, National Theatre, BBC, etc.

www.imdb.com

International Movie Database. Comprehensive historical source of information about all films generally released, including cast and crew, reviews, awards and nominations, company credits, release dates, business data, etc.

www.boxofficeguru.
com

Box-office data on motion pictures released since 1989. Note that 'domestic box office' relates to earnings at American movie theatres (in US dollars); 'foreign' relates to earnings in non-US countries.

www.bufvc.ac.uk/
Shakespeare

International database of Shakespeare on film, television and radio: ongoing project by the British Universities Film & Video Council aiming to compile information on every traceable film, television programme and radio broadcast, including selective video stage recordings, sound recordings, and 'the full range of audiovisual Shakespeare, including plot borrowings, significant quotations, and appearances by WS himself'.

www.mauricehindle.
com

Author website: for discussion, forum, and my own projects around Shakespeare and Shakespeare on film. Plus information on publications in other literary genres, work in progress and downloads.

http://www.illumina-tionsmedia.co.uk/	**Illuminations** has produced a number of Shakespeare adaptations for TV, and its website provides discussion of Shakespeare on film and TV as well as links to other sources for and samples of Shakespeare on screen.
http://www.pbs.org/wnet/gperf/	**Great Performances** website gives free access to some of the best small-screen Shakespeare productions for Region 1 (US) viewers.
https://globeplayer.tv/	**Globe Player**, from Shakespeare's Globe, London, makes Globe on Screen productions available for rental or purchase. There is also access to free content, such as the Sonnet Project NYC, celebrity interviews with actors and directors, and much more.
http://onscreen.rsc.org.uk/	**Royal Shakespeare** Company, Stratford-upon-Avon, gives information on live RSC performances to cinemas around the world.

Searching the internet for Shakespeare on Film

It is not possible here to offer any definitive guidance for gaining access to Shakespeare on film adaptations via the internet, either in full or in clips. My suggestion would be for you to use your internet browser (e.g. Google) to try and seek these out, entering the appropriate film title being sought, and/or doing the same when searching YouTube. Good luck!

Glossary of Terms

2K – Digital film format yielding 3.2 megapixels. 2K is the baseline standard for commercial theatrical projection.

4K – Digital film format yielding 12.6 megapixels. Many claim that 4K images are equal in visual quality to those of 35mm.

ADR (automated dialogue replacement) – When actors re-record their dialogue in synchronization (sync) with their lip movement in post-production. Becomes necessary (for example) when the speech recorded on set has been distorted by background interference.

Apparent motion – A quirk of human seeing whereby our eyes can be deceived into seeing movement if a visual display is changed rapidly enough. Besides applying to moving pictures, the illusory phenomenon occurs in flashing neon signs created by static lights flashing off and on at a specific rate.

Arthouse – Movies the aesthetic style and/or intellectual content of which appeal to a limited audience whose tastes are geared to these elements; as opposed to the (usually) less demanding 'Hollywood' films that rely on more 'formulaic' construction and casting.

Backlighting/backlit – Where a person or object is thrown into shadow by being lit from behind, often producing a ghostly effect.

Backstory – Narrative elements added to give more information and motivation to the original story, which does not include these elements.

Blocking – Positioning of actors within the *mise-en-scène*.

Blu-ray Disc (BD) – A High Definition digital optical storage disc for home video, similar to **DVD** but with higher storage capacity and a higher-resolution image, i.e. of 720p or 1080p ('p' indicating progressive scan).

CGI (Computer Generated Imagery) – See *Digital imaging*.

Chiaroscuro – Strong contrast of light and shadow in the *mise-en-scène*.

Close-up/close shot – Face or head and shoulders, used to reveal inner or emotional state of character.

Continuity editing – Cutting the film to sustain continuous and clear story action, relying on matching screen direction, position and temporal relations from shot to shot.

Coverage – The collection of shots taken for each particular sequence, conventionally including everything from **wide shot**s to matching **close-up**s.

Crane/overhead shot – Moving around at a significant height above ground level.

Critical flicker vision – Phenomenon whereby the 24 still frames per second (fps) at which films are shot and projected is the speed at which the film appears to produce moving images without 'flicker'.

Cross-cutting – **Editing** that alternates shots of two or more lines of action occurring in different places, usually simultaneously.

Cutaway – Used to bridge shots that do not cut together, and to allow for **editing**/shortening of the action in a continuous shot.

Deep focus – Use of camera lens and lighting to keep both close and distant planes being shot in focus.

Depth of field/focus – Distance between planes in front of the camera where everything remains in focus.

Developing single shot – Extended shot without **cutaway** enabling the camera to follow and capture the dramatically shifting actions of performing actors in an unbroken fashion.

Diegesis – The world of the film's story, including events presumed to have occurred and actions and spaces not shown on screen.

Diegetic sound – Any voice, music or sound presented as part of the screen world we are watching.

Digital imaging/compositing – Techniques of **editing** or altering images in filmmaking that use computer technology and software.

Dissolve/mix – Gradual merging of the end of one shot into the beginning of the next.

Dolly – Wheeled truck or trolley on which the camera and cameraperson are mounted; used for **tracking shot**s.

DoP – Director of photography. The person responsible for recording a scene on camera and who frequently works closely with movie directors to capture for the screen what they as interpreters of the screenplay envision in their heads.

Downstage – Front of a theatrical stage, nearest the audience.

DVD – Digital Video Disc (aka Digital Versatile Disc), an optical storage disc in a format that displaced tape-based **VHS** from around 2000, and having much higher picture-definition quality, i.e. of 480p ('p' indicating progressive scan).

Editing/Cutting – To assemble a film from its various component shots and sound tracks.

Establishing shot – Usually a **long shot** involving distant framing to show spatial relations among important characters, objects and setting in a scene, before moving to closer shots.

Exposition – The early scenes in a film conveying the foundations of situation and character in the plot.

Eyeline match – A cut in which the first shot shows a character looking off in one direction, and the next contains what they see.

Film noir – 'Dark film': term usually applied to detective or thriller genres using low-key lighting frequently generating **chiaroscuro** lighting effects designed to create moods of anxiety and unease.

Flat – Part of a painted scene mounted on a wooden frame, pushed horizontally or lowered on to a theatrical stage.

Focalizer/focalization – Character with whom we are made to sympathize/the process of bringing about such sympathy.

Freeze-frame – For celluloid film recording, the repeated printing of a single frame for a predetermined number of times; for digital film, holding the still digital image for the duration required, both creating an effect of 'freezing' the action for a set time duration.

Groundling – Spectator or audience member who stood in the open yard to watch a theatrical performance at one of the Shakespearean outdoor theatres of London in the period 1576–1642, when all playhouses were closed by Parliament as civil war loomed. A spectator or audience member similarly positioned at Shakespeare's Globe, London, from 1997, when the new theatre opened.

Hand-held shot – Moving about bumpily at eye level.

HD (camera) – High Definition video. Formats commonly at resolutions of 480p, 720p and 1080p ('p' indicating progressive scan).

High angle – Shot taken from above; can convey a sense of power over the objects shown.

Identification – Process whereby we are drawn to closely align our feelings and thoughts with a character on screen.

Image system – Repeated **motifs** of shape, colour or sound to sustain a theme, or to link together characters or stages of a narrative.

Intensified continuity – under the influence of television, where close-ups, fast cutting and considerable camera movement became common by the 1970s, this is an intensification of the correctly matched cutting of classical **continuity editing**.

Intercut – Editing by juxtaposition of elements that are related by time, place or action, or where the establishing of such a relationship depends on such juxtaposition.

Internal diegetic sound – Sound represented as coming from the mind of a character, which we and they hear, though we assume other characters cannot.

Jump cut – Effect obtained by removing a section from the middle of a **shot**, and joining the head and tail of the shot, thus provoking a jump in the action.

Leitmotif – Musical sound or phrase recurring as a kind of theme tune, often linked to the appearance of specific characters.

Long shot – Framing in which the scale of an object is relatively small; a standing human figure fills the screen.

Low angle – Shot taken from below. It can convey a sense of threat or danger.

Master shot – The shot covering a whole scene, both in terms of duration and in containing all relevant action. It is conventionally shot first so that all **coverage** (the collection of shots taken for each particular sequence) can be subsequently filmed to match.

Match-cut/match on action – Continuity cut placing two different framings of the same action together at the same moment in the gesture.

Matte shot – Where a painted backdrop is photographically/digitally incorporated into a shot to suggest a particular setting.

Medium- or mid-shot – Scale of object shown of moderate size, e.g. a human figure from waist up filling the screen.

Medium-close shot – Scale of object shown quite large, e.g. a human figure from chest up filling the screen.

Medium-long shot – Making an object about four to five feet high fill the screen, e.g. a human figure from shins up.

Megaplex – Cinema or movie theatre housing sixteen or more screens.

Metacinematic – Film using visual devices to expose the constructed nature of the visions the film provides.

Metadrama/metatheatre/metatheatrical – Theatrical process employing devices to expose the 'constructed' nature of the drama shown.

Metonymy/metonymic – A kind of cinematic shorthand in which details, objects, gestures, colour, etc., visually convey meanings or ideas, e.g. at the opening of Olivier's *Richard III*, the crown shown is a shorthand for kingship, the monarchy and its associated powers.

Miniplex – Cinema or movie theatre housing between two and seven screens.

Mise-en-scène – Everything we see in the frame, literally the visual elements 'put into the scene' and theatrically arranged before shooting starts. Such elements typically include setting, **props**, positioning, behaviour, facial expressions, body language, costume, hair and make-up of characters and their setting within the frame, as well as lighting and colour.

Montage – A 'dialectical' process in which meanings are built up or information is provided over a succession of shots; often contrasted with the *mise-en-scène* approach of creating meaning and information in a single frame.

Motif – Image, theme or element frequently repeated throughout a film. The use of the colour red to denote blood and bloody violence is a good example in Polanski's *Macbeth*.

Narrative film – A film in which a story is developed from beginning to end, made up of a chain of events in a cause–effect relationship occurring in time and space.

Non-diegetic sound – Any sound not coming from a source within the screen world, such as **voice-over**, background music or any sound effects added in post-production.

Open wide/narrow – Film shown at large/small number of theatrical outlets on its first opening.

Pan/panning shot – Shot moving from side to side from a fixed axis, producing a mobile framing on the screen that scans the space horizontally; an aerial pan makes the same movement high up in the air.

POV – Point of view.

Projection – (1) The process of transferring one's own hidden desires and impulses on to a screen character or situation; (2) the process of a theatre or film actor externalizing or conveying with emphasis the personality of the character they are playing; (3) the mechanical process of throwing up a film image on to a screen.

Props – Short for 'properties': any moveable object in a scene of stage, film or TV drama.

Proscenium arch – A 'picture-frame' opening that separates the stage/acting space from the auditorium/audience in many theatres.

Reaction shot – Showing the reaction of a character to something said or done.

Scenography – On the theatrical stage, the often sophisticated manipulation of scenery, lighting and sound to enhance the dramatic presentation of a play. Such dramatic staging practices have been deeply influenced by film techniques.

Shot – In shooting, one continuous run of the camera exposing a series of frames (also called a *take*) in the completed film, or one continuous image with a single static or mobile framing.

Shot/reverse shot – Two or more shots edited together in which the camera moves back and forth on two characters, usually in a conversation situation.

Slam-zoom – Extremely rapid enlargement of the image using a zoom lens.

Slow-motion/Slo-mo – An effect often used to emphasize spectacle or high drama, created by shooting at a higher frames per second (fps) rate than the regular 24; when projected at the normal rate, the action appears slower.

Sound bridge – At the end of a scene, the sound from the next is heard briefly before the new scene begins; at the beginning of a scene, the sound from the previous scene is heard briefly before the sound from the new scene begins.

Steadicam – Gimbal-balanced camera mount enabling a camera operator to produce mobile shots of great smoothness while tracking uneven movements of actors.

Stop-motion shooting – Crude trick photographic technique often used in silent films, splicing together separate shots to make them appear continuous.

Streaming – Process whereby films can be transferred online either live or on demand (**VOD**) to the computer or device of a recipient. 'On-demand streaming' by 'progressive download' saves the film to a hard disk, which is then played from that location.

Subjective camera/shot – Showing exactly what the character sees from their point of view. Rarely used without an **establishing shot** to orientate the viewer.

Take – During filmmaking, shot produced by one continuous run of the camera; a shot in the completed movie may be chosen from among several takes of the same action.

Test screening – Preview screening of a film in order to gauge audience reaction. A cross-section of viewers are asked to provide feedback on a new movie before its general release.

Thrust stage – Open stage projecting out into the theatre auditorium, permitting an audience to see and hear the performance on three sides.

Tilted-up/down-tilted/tilt shot – Shot using vertical movement of the camera without changing the horizontal level of the camera body.

Time-lapse cinematography – Accelerated motion cinematography that secures a moving picture of a slow process by exposing the film frame by frame over a considerable time interval (such as the passage from night into dawn at the opening of Polanski's *Macbeth*).

Tiring-house – A room where actors changed, lying behind the rear stage façade of sixteenth- and seventeenth-century Shakespearean theatre stages. The term alludes to the 'attire' or costumes worn by players.

Tracking shot – A mobile framing that travels through space forward, backward or laterally, the camera often being mounted on a **dolly** moving along specially laid tracks.

Two-shot/three-shot – Close shot of two or three persons with the camera as near as possible while keeping each group in shot.

Upstage – Rear of a theatrical stage, furthest away from the audience.

VHS (Video Home System) – consumer-level analogue recording videotape-based cassette standard developed in Japan, in domestic use globally from the 1970s until around 2000, when it was displaced by the digital **DVD** optical recording system.

VOD – Video on Demand, commercial service enabling viewers to watch movies rented or bought over a digital network, such as the World Wide Web.

Voice-over – When a screen character's voice or the voice of an unseen narrator is heard over the image on screen.

Whip (or zip) pan – Extremely fast movement of the camera blurring the image between two points in a **pan**.

Wide shot – Distant shot containing multiple elements in the frame (as in a landscape-like **establishing shot**), or emphasizing a horizontal composition. E.g. in Branagh's *Hamlet*, Hamlet's soliloquy beginning 'How all occasions do inform against me' begins with a **medium-close shot** on him, the camera moving back until the **wide shot** shows him as a tiny figure in the snowy landscape.

Wipe – Form of transition from one shot to another in which a margin moves across the screen to eliminate the first shot and reveal the second.

Zoom shot – Act of enlarging or reducing the image in the frame using zoom lens. See also **slam-zoom**.

Index